# Guide to RTA Liability

# Guide to RTA Liability

**General Editor**

Andrew Ritchie QC
*9 Gough Square, London*

## Contributors

Christopher Wilson

Andrew Ritchie QC

Mark Whalan

Aileen Downey

Laura Begley

Christopher Stevenson

Rajeev Shetty

Laura Elfield

Jeremy Ford

Tara Vindis

Giles Mooney

Shahram Sharghy

Linda Nelson

Adam Dawson

Robert McAllister

Oliver Millington

Esther Pounder

Emily Verity

Edward Lamb

*all of 9 Gough Square, London*

JORDANS

Published by
Jordan Publishing Limited
21 St Thomas Street
Bristol BS1 6JS

**British Library Cataloguing-in-Publication Data**

A catalogue record for this book is available from the British Library.

ISBN 978 1 84661 164 3

Typeset by Letterpart Ltd, Reigate, Surrey

Printed in Great Britain by CPI Antony Rowe, Chippenham and Eastbourne

# FOREWORD

I expected this book to be good but I already had a few personal favourites on this particular subject. I very quickly discovered upon reading it, that it is an absolute gem and this will now be my book of first choice when I need to check any of the finer points of road traffic liability law. It is presented in a very clear, user friendly format with practical step-by-step tips where the subject matter requires. Difficult subject areas are explored in straightforward terms without in any way trivialising the law.

I particularly like the breadth and depth of the subject matter presented. It is unusual in my experience to include detailed examination of pavements for slip and trip cases in a Road Traffic Act book but of course they are all incidents on the highway. The text explores a full range of legal options for presenting cases. I wonder, for example, how many people have thought of making a claim under the Occupiers' Liability Act for damage caused through disrepair of a vehicle? There are some witty one line observations which help make the reader feel grounded when exploring some of the finer points of law. The observation 'the wording is far too obscure for plain English or plain Englishmen to understand' is one such illustration.

Indications of future developments in the law are sufficiently succinct to be interesting and make sure one keeps an eye open for them without drifting into the realms of lengthy speculation.

I also like the distinction made in several places between pure accidents and negligence which is of course a recurring theme throughout APIL educational campaigns in the wider community.

In short, I consider that this will be useful text for all levels of practitioner and I commend it to you warmly. If you have the budget to buy just one more text on motor claims this year then make sure you buy this one. If you do not, it is worth the small outlay for a private copy! The editor and authors are to be congratulated on a job well done.

Amanda Stevens
APIL President
*February 2009*

# PREFACE

Road traffic accident cases are not all easy. Some throw up the most difficult challenges tort law can face:

- Should a child of 10 be found to have been negligent for failing to wear a bike helmet?
- Can a low velocity rear end shunt result in permanent neck pain?
- Should a police driver be held liable for racing through a red traffic light when he had his blues and twos on?

The landscape for RTA work has changed dramatically over the past 20 years. Successive governments have made significant changes to the regulation and funding of the legal system in which RTA cases are conducted. Many of these changes were demanded by the insurance industry which used its considerable resource to lobby governments. The impact of all these changes has been to:

- allow unregulated advertising to capture cases;
- abolish legal aid for personal injury cases;
- introduce CFAs moving risk to claimant solicitors and counsel, leaving success fees open to attack from insurers for technical breaches of the regulations set up not to protect the insurers, but the lay client;
- allow fixed fees in fast track cases irrespective of the work needed to adequately prove the case;
- allow worthless referral fees to be paid to claims farmers and insurance companies for capturing cases before they get to lawyers and for selling them on;
- increase the fast track limit to cover the vast majority of RTA claims (up to £25,000 in value);
- cause or allow an unimpressively slow assessment process;
- introduce court fees which are a barrier to access to justice;
- underfund civil courts so that administrative inefficiency is not uncommon and judges often have only out-of-date legal reference materials available to them at trial.

All of this assault on the solicitors and barristers working within the system might, some would say, have put off the best lawyers from practising in the field. But the opposite is true. Those involved in this work remain committed to providing a service to the injured and the tortfeasors which is high quality and impressive. The majority of cases are settled sensibly and those where an issue needs to be fought are brought to trial in the main in good temper and professionally with care and focus. The judges who try them are hard working and enormously committed to fairness and justice.

The editors of this text aim to assist all lawyers practising in the RTA claims field to determine liability without trial. However, if the case must go to trial we aim to provide the framework of the law fleshed out with the classic and the up-to-date cases to assist the parties and the judge.

The text sets out the law as at 31 January 2009.

If you have any comment or suggestions please send them to me at 9 Gough Square, London EC4A 3DG.

We hope you find this new text helpful. Any errors in the text are purely my responsibility.

Andrew Ritchie
9 Gough Square, London, EC4A 3DG
aritchie@9goughsquare.co.uk
*February 2009*

# ASSOCIATION OF PERSONAL INJURY LAWYERS

APIL is the UK's leading association of claimant personal injury lawyers, dedicated to protecting the rights of injured people.

Formed in 1990, APIL now represents over 5,000 solicitors, barristers, academics and students in the UK, Republic of Ireland and overseas.

APIL's objectives are:

- To promote full and just compensation for all types of personal injury;
- To promote and develop expertise in the practice of personal injury law;
- To promote wider redress for personal injury in the legal system;
- To campaign for improvements in personal injury law;
- To promote safety and alert the public to hazards;
- To provide a communication network for members.

APIL is a growing and influential forum pushing for law reform, and improvements, which will benefit victims of personal injury.

APIL has been running CPD training events, accredited by the Solicitors Regulation Authority and Bar Standards Board, for well over fifteen years and has a wealth of experience in developing the most practical up-to-date courses, delivered by eminent leading speakers, either publicly or in-house.

APIL training now runs almost 200 personal injury training events nationally each year, plus up to a further 100 meetings of our regional and special interest groups. Topics cover a wide range of subjects and are geared towards giving personal injury lawyers a thorough grounding in the core areas of personal injury law, whilst keeping lawyers thoroughly up-to-date in all subjects.

APIL is also an authoritative information source for personal injury lawyers, providing up-to-the minute PI bulletins, regular newsletters and publications, information databases and online services.

For further information contact:

APIL
11 Castle Quay
Nottingham
NG7 1FW

DX 716208 Nottingham 42

Tel: 0115 9580585
Email: mail@apil.org.uk
Website: www.apil.org.uk

# CONTENTS

# TABLE OF CASES

References are to paragraph numbers.

# TABLE OF STATUTES

References are to paragraph numbers.

# TABLE OF STATUTORY INSTRUMENTS

References are to paragraph numbers.

# TABLE OF EUROPEAN MATERIALS

References are to paragraph numbers.

# CHAPTER 1

## THE INCIDENCE OF ROAD TRAFFIC ACCIDENTS IN GREAT BRITAIN

*Andrew Ritchie*

### 1.1 HOW MANY ACCIDENTS PER YEAR DO WE SUFFER?

In 2001 there were 204,839 road traffic accidents in England, and 9,499 in Wales.

The number of road traffic accidents suffered each year from 1992 to 2002 is set out in the table on pp 2–5 below.

### 1.2 FATALITIES

The average number of road traffic accidents which cause fatalities each year in England and Wales is as follows:

- England 30,276 (2001); and

- Wales 1,352 (2001).

The figures for the 4 previous years are roughly equivalent.

### 1.3 FATALITIES DURING THE WEEK

A total of 27,800 people were killed or seriously injured on Great Britain's roads on weekdays during 2002, or an average of 107 people each day.

**Road accident casualties : by road user type and severity**

**Great Britain**

| Year | | 1992 | 1993 | 1994 | 1995 | 1996 | 1997 | 1998 | 1999 | 2000 | 2001 | 2002 |
|---|---|---|---|---|---|---|---|---|---|---|---|---|
| **Child pedestrians:** | | | | | | | | | | | | |
| Killed | ZCDH | 180 | 165 | 160 | 132 | 131 | 138 | 103 | 107 | 107 | 107 | 79 |
| Killed or seriously injured | KIJS | 4,901 | 4,231 | 4,610 | 4,400 | 4,132 | 3,954 | 3,737 | 3,457 | 3,226 | 3,144 | 2,828 |
| All severities | ZCDI | 20,124 | 18,250 | 19,263 | 18,590 | 18,510 | 18,407 | 17,971 | 16,876 | 16,184 | 15,819 | 14,231 |
| **Adult pedestrians:** | | | | | | | | | | | | |
| Killed | ZCDJ | 1,163 | 1,072 | 953 | 897 | 858 | 835 | 803 | 760 | 750 | 719 | 696 |
| Killed or seriously injured | KIJT | 9,125 | 8,260 | 8,114 | 7,716 | 7,300 | 6,925 | 6,592 | 6,221 | 6,112 | 5,920 | 5,803 |
| All severities | ZCDK | 30,354 | 28,750 | 28,129 | 27,178 | 26,827 | 26,223 | 25,827 | 24,806 | 24,481 | 24,758 | 24,553 |
| **Child pedal cyclists:** | | | | | | | | | | | | |
| Killed | ZCDL | 48 | 37 | 42 | 48 | 54 | 33 | 32 | 36 | 27 | 25 | 22 |
| Killed or seriously injured | KIJU | 1,195 | 1,146 | 1,234 | 1,249 | 1,231 | 1,016 | 915 | 950 | 758 | 674 | 594 |

**Road accident casualties : by road user type and severity**

**Great Britain**

| Year | | 1992 | 1993 | 1994 | 1995 | 1996 | 1997 | 1998 | 1999 | 2000 | 2001 | 2002 |
|---|---|---|---|---|---|---|---|---|---|---|---|---|
| All severities | ZCDM | 7,725 | 7,386 | 8,075 | 8,133 | 8,217 | 7,899 | 6,930 | 7,920 | 6,260 | 5,451 | 4,809 |
| **Adult pedal cyclists:** | | | | | | | | | | | | |
| Killed | ZCDN | 156 | 148 | 129 | 164 | 148 | 150 | 126 | 135 | 98 | 113 | 108 |
| Killed or seriously injured | KIJV | 2,752 | 2,598 | 2,710 | 2,673 | 2,517 | 2,542 | 2,345 | 2,172 | 1,954 | 2,004 | 1,856 |
| All severities | ZCDO | 16,488 | 16,115 | 16,097 | 16,140 | 15,778 | 16,181 | 15,326 | 14,834 | 13,630 | 13,663 | 12,298 |
| **Motorcyclists and passengers:** | | | | | | | | | | | | |
| Killed | ZCDP | 469 | 427 | 444 | 445 | 440 | 509 | 498 | 547 | 605 | 569 | 609 |
| Killed or seriously injured | ZCDQ | 7,338 | 6,882 | 6,666 | 6,615 | 6,208 | 6,446 | 6,442 | 6,908 | 7,374 | 6,595 | 7,500 |
| All severities | BMDH | 26,891 | 25,094 | 24,354 | 23,524 | 23,133 | 24,492 | 24,610 | 26,192 | 28,212 | 24,164 | 28,353 |
| **Car drivers and passengers:** | | | | | | | | | | | | |
| Killed | ZCDS | 1,978 | 1,760 | 1,764 | 1,749 | 1,806 | 1,795 | 1,696 | 1,687 | 1,665 | 1,749 | 1,747 |
| Killed or seriously injured | ZCDT | 25,124 | 22,833 | 23,892 | 23,461 | 24,048 | 23,191 | 21,676 | 20,368 | 19,719 | 19,424 | 18,728 |

**Road accident casualties : by road user type and severity**

**Great Britain**

| Year | | 1992 | 1993 | 1994 | 1995 | 1996 | 1997 | 1998 | 1999 | 2000 | 2001 | 2002 |
|---|---|---|---|---|---|---|---|---|---|---|---|---|
| All severities | ZCDU | 185,662 | 187,479 | 195,154 | 194,027 | 205,336 | 211,448 | 210,474 | 205,735 | 206,799 | 202,802 | 197,425 |
| **Bus/coach drivers and passengers:** | | | | | | | | | | | | |
| Killed | ZCDV | 19 | 35 | 21 | 35 | 11 | 14 | 18 | 11 | 15 | 14 | 19 |
| Killed or seriously injured | KCUZ | 655 | 725 | 815 | 836 | 695 | 601 | 631 | 611 | 578 | 562 | 551 |
| All severities | ZCDW | 9,103 | 9,307 | 10,090 | 9,278 | 9,345 | 9,439 | 9,839 | 10,252 | 10,088 | 9,884 | 9,005 |
| **LGV drivers and passengers:** | | | | | | | | | | | | |
| Killed | ZCDX | 117 | 91 | 64 | 69 | 61 | 64 | 67 | 65 | 66 | 64 | 70 |
| Killed or seriously injured | ZCDY | 1,308 | 1,082 | 1,101 | 1,106 | 989 | 928 | 949 | 867 | 813 | 811 | 780 |
| All severities | ZCDZ | 8,129 | 7,420 | 7,558 | 7,200 | 7,215 | 7,476 | 7,672 | 7,124 | 7,007 | 7,304 | 7,007 |
| **HGV drivers and passengers:** | | | | | | | | | | | | |
| Killed | ZCEA | 70 | 59 | 41 | 57 | 63 | 45 | 60 | 52 | 55 | 54 | 63 |
| Killed or seriously injured | ZCEB | 659 | 635 | 571 | 635 | 555 | 573 | 560 | 540 | 571 | 500 | 524 |

**Road accident casualties : by road user type and severity**

**Great Britain**

| Year | | 1992 | 1993 | 1994 | 1995 | 1996 | 1997 | 1998 | 1999 | 2000 | 2001 | 2002 |
|---|---|---|---|---|---|---|---|---|---|---|---|---|
| All severities | ZCEC | 3,326 | 3,333 | 3,370 | 3,331 | 3,245 | 3,302 | 3,444 | 3,484 | 3,597 | 3,388 | 3,178 |
| **All road users:** | | | | | | | | | | | | |
| Killed | BMDC | 4,229 | 3,814 | 3,650 | 3,621 | 3,598 | 3,599 | 3,421 | 3,423 | 3,409 | 3,450 | 3,431 |
| Killed or seriously injured | ZCEE | 53,485 | 48,834 | 50,190 | 49,154 | 48,097 | 46,583 | 44,255 | 42,545 | 41,564 | 40,560 | 39,407 |
| All severities | BMDA | 310,753 | 306,135 | 315,359 | 310,687 | 320,578 | 327,803 | 325,212 | 320,310 | 320,283 | 313,309 | 302,605 |

*Source: Department for Transport 020 7944 3078*

## 1.4   WHAT TIME OF DAY DO ACCIDENTS OCCUR?

The incidence of people being killed or seriously injured in road accidents is not uniform throughout the day. Among pedestrians and car users most casualties occur during in the morning and evening 'rush hours', with the highest number coming during the extended evening period.

The first peak occurs during the hour beginning at 08:00 am. 719 car users and 362 pedestrians were killed or seriously injured during this hour in 2002.

The number of pedestrians killed or seriously injured is highest during the hour starting at 15:00 hours (during which hour many schools finish for the day). There were 718 casualties during this hour in 2002.

The number of car users killed or seriously injured reaches its highest in the hour starting at 17:00 (876 people in 2002), over three a day on average.

## 1.5   DRINK AND DRUGS

Two of the major contributors to road accidents in Great Britain are excessive speed and alcohol or banned drugs. Over the years there have been many campaigns to discourage drink-driving and the numbers of casualties from road accidents involving illegal alcohol levels have fallen. However in 1999, 12% of people dying in road accidents in Great Britain tested positive for illegal levels of alcohol.

## 1.6   RECENT STATISTICS FOR 2007

Figures for 2007 have been revised slightly since the publication of 'Road Casualties in Great Britain: 2007'. The number of fatalities was 2,946 and the number of seriously injured casualties was 27,774.

The main results show that:

- The number of people killed in road accidents fell by 7% from 3,172 in 2006 to 2,946 in 2007.

- 30,720 people were killed or seriously injured in 2007, 4% fewer than in 2006.

- There were 247,780 road casualties in Great Britain in 2007, 4% less than in 2006.

- There were 182,115 road accidents involving personal injury in 2007, 4% fewer than in 2006. Of these, 27,036 accidents involved death or serious injury, 3% fewer than in 2006 (27,872).

- The number of deaths among car users in 2007 was 1,432, 11% less than in the previous year. The number seriously injured fell by 9% to 11,535. Total casualties among car users were 161,433, 6% lower than 2006. Provisional traffic estimates indicate a 1% fall in car and taxi traffic over the period.

- Child casualties fell by 7%. The number of children killed or seriously injured in 2007 was 3,090 (down 6% on 2006). Of those, 1,899 were pedestrians, 6% down on 2006. 121 children died on the roads, 28% fewer than in 2006, this is the lowest ever recorded figure.

- There were 646 pedestrian deaths, 4% less than in 2006. Killed or seriously injured casualties fell by 2% to 6,924. The all pedestrian casualty figure fell to 30,191 in 2007, 3% lower than 2006.

- The number of pedal cyclists killed fell by 7% from 146 in 2006 to 136 in 2007. The number of seriously injured rose by 6% to 2,428. The total casualties among pedal cyclists remained at the same level as 2006.

- There were 588 motorcycle user fatalities in 2007, 2% lower than during 2006. The number of killed or seriously injured rose compared to 2006 (up 4% from 6,484 in 2006 to 6,737 in 2007). The all motorcycle user casualties figure for 2007 of 23,459 is 1% higher than in 2006.

# CHAPTER 2

# RTA LIABILITY – GENERAL PRINCIPLES

*Mark Whalan*

## 2.1 INTRODUCTION

As far back as 1832 the courts recognised that pedestrians and vehicle drivers owed each other a duty to exercise due care and attention:

> 'All persons, paralytic as well as others, have a right to walk on the road and are entitled to the exercise of reasonable care on the part of persons driving carriages upon it.' *Boss v Litton* (1832) 5 C & P 407.

Whilst the 'carriages' may now be anything from electric cars to multi-tonne juggernauts, the same principle remains.

Determining liability in a road traffic case can be amongst the most difficult exercises in the range of legal challenges. Rear end shunts may be easy, or may not, for instance where low velocity impact whiplash is involved. Often the drivers both assert that the other was to blame. Sometimes accident reconstruction evidence is the only clue to the cause, because one driver is dead and the other has brain damage and hence no recollection. In multiple car impacts the witnesses to the impacts will often have only partial recollections of parts of the pre-accident movements of the vehicles involved and they rarely match.

The Courts and the Lord Chancellors Department appear to regard RTA work as less worthy of public finance through court time than commercial cases, family or criminal law cases and utterly unworthy of legal aid. Yet the same men, women and children who may be involved in commerce, crime or family law are all involved in RTA cases. All may suffer injuries which interfere with their commercial, family or criminal activity and their lives. Some will suffer death. Tax will be lost and State benefits claims will arise.

It is a strange quirk of the late 20th century that Governments have looked down on RTA work and sought to sideline it despite the massive and terrible impact which road traffic accidents have on those involved. In this text we examine the principles developed over the last 100 years in Great Britain which determine liability for road traffic accidents.

## 2.2   LIABILITY GENERALLY IN RTA CLAIMS

There may be no tortious liability for a road traffic accident. But if all of the drivers and pedestrians involved were careful then why did the accident occur? In the majority of cases one or other party has lapsed into carelessness. Most cases involve a failure to keep a proper look out, a failure to concentrate or a failure to follow the highway code.

In general the duty of a driver or motor bike rider or cyclist or indeed a pedestrian when using the highway is similar to the duty owed in all other areas of life – to take such care as is reasonable in the circumstances to ensure that he does not injure his neighbour. In *Bourhill v Young*,[1] a case where a motorcycle collided with a tram, Lord Macmillan summarised the duty owed by motorists to other road users, pedestrians and persons occupying property adjacent to the highway:

> 'The duty to take care is the duty to avoid doing or omitting to do anything which may have as its reasonable and probable consequence the injury to others and the duty is owed to those to whom injury may reasonably and probably be anticipated if the duty is not observed.'

The standard of care is that of the ordinary, skilful, average motorist, described in *Nettleship v Weston*[2] as the standard to be expected of a competent and experienced driver.

Yet negligence in RTA cases is still as slippery to tie down as an 'eel in grease'. For instance in *Sam v Atkins*,[3] the Court of Appeal made some important observations as to the nature of negligence in the context of a road traffic accident claim, specifically a vehicle-pedestrian collision. In this case the defendant motorist overtook a row of stationary vehicles at 20mph. The traffic had stopped to allow pedestrians, including the claimant, to cross the road. At a point where the defendant drew level with a stationary transit van, which the motorist could not see through, the claimant emerged into the immediate path of the vehicle. The trial judge, finding that both the pedestrian and motorist were negligent, apportioned liability between the claimant and defendant. The Court of Appeal acknowledged that 20mph was too fast for the road and traffic conditions, but declined to make a finding against the motorist, as the accident could not have been avoided unless the defendant had been driving at 1–2mph, which the court considered to be 'an unreasonable counsel of perfection'. May LJ stated (at paragraph 14) that:

> 'It is common place to analyse a course of action in negligence compartmentally, examining duty of care, breach of the duty, causation and

---

[1]   1943] AC 92.
[2]   [1971] 2 QB 691.
[3]   [2005] EWCA Civ 1452.

damage. That is convenient, but technically wrong. Negligence is a composite concept necessarily combining all the elements I have mentioned.'

It is not enough, in other words, for a litigant to demonstrate that a motorist was at fault. The culpability will not amount to 'negligence' unless all three elements to the cause of action (duty, breach and causation) are satisfied.

## 2.3 FACTORS WHEN ASSESSING LIABILITY

### 2.3.1 The Highway Code

In most cases judges place weight on breaches of the highway code when determining whether a driver has been negligent. Section 38(7) of the Road Traffic Act 1988 states:

'A failure on the part of a person to observe a provision of the Highway Code shall not of itself render that person liable to criminal proceedings of any kind, but any such failure may in any proceedings (whether civil or criminal) be relied upon by any party to the proceedings as tending to establish or to negative any liability which is in question in those proceedings.'

The most recent edition of the Highway Code was published in 2007. Supplementary guidance can be found in two DSO publications, 'The Official Guide to Driving' and 'The Official Guide to Riding'.

In *Croston v Vaughan*[4] it was held that:

'The Highway Code is not binding as a statutory regulation; it is only something which may be regarded as information and advice to drivers. It does not follow that, if they fail to carry out any provisions of the Highway Code, they are necessarily negligent. The Road Traffic Act provides that a failure to provide any provision of the Code may in any proceedings be relied upon as tending to establish or rebut any liability which is in question in those proceedings. Nor is it sufficient as an excuse for any person to say, in answer to a claim of negligence, that he carried out every provision of the Code.'

This guidance was followed in *Wakeling v McDonagh & MIB*[5] where Mackie J stated (at paragraph 24) that:

'Any breach of the Highway Code is relevant but not determinative.'

In that case the claimant, a pedal cyclist, could not give evidence but had been run over by a van driver high on cocaine and drink. Considering a

---

[4]   [1938] 1 KB 540 at 551–552.
[5]   [2007] EWHC 1201 (QB).

breach of the highway code by the claimant Mackie J stated that the test for contributory negligence was set out in the Law Reform (Contributory Negligence) Act 1945, s 1(1). The defendant had to establish on the balance of probabilities that the claimant was at fault, that the fault was causative of the injury and that it would be just and equitable for the damages to be reduced. The judge accepted the evidence of the eye witness of the incident who said that the claimant had looked down the road at some point prior to crossing on his bike. Expert evidence suggested that the claimant had not looked again before moving out from behind the van and had he done so, he would have seen the defendant's oncoming vehicle. The judge held that a breach of the Highway Code did not create a presumption of negligence but was merely a factor to be taken into account when considering the issue (*Powell v Phillips*[6]) and on the evidence available, the claimant probably took adequate steps to look out before crossing the road but was deceived by the speed of the oncoming vehicle so that the defendant was unable to discharge the burden of establishing contributory fault.

In *Morris v Luton Corporation*[7] it was noted (at 115) that:

'There is sometimes a temptation for judges in dealing with these traffic cases to decide questions of fact in language which appears to lay down some rule which users of the road must observe. This is a habit into which one perhaps sometime slips unconsciously – and I have done it myself no doubt but it is much to be deprecated, because there are questions of fact dependent on the circumstances of each case.'

Reported cases can accordingly yield a useful source of guidance and general interpretation, although few purport to lay down binding or even persuasive authority.

### 2.3.2   Criminal convictions

If one driver has been charged with careless driving and convicted then the civil courts will take that into account.

Section 11 of the Civil Evidence Act 1968 provides that proof of a criminal conviction can be adduced as evidence of a motorist's negligence.

A conviction will usually, but not invariably, settle the issue of primary liability.

Section 11(2) allows a motorist to challenge the conviction if he has good reason to do so and can satisfy the onus of proof to a civil standard. It was held in *McCauley v Hope*[8] that where, with the support of an expert

---
[6]   [1972] 3 All ER 864, CA (Civ Div).
[7]   [1946] KB 114.
[8]   (1998) *The Independent*, December 21.

report, a motorist wishes to maintain such a challenge, it is not appropriate for the court to entertain an application for summary judgment under CPR, r 24.7.

### 2.3.3 The usual failings

In most cases the usual failings of the drivers and pedestrians involved are:

(1)   failing to keep a proper look out; and/or

(2)   driving too fast.

These really are the BIG TWO failings in road traffic cases.

All of the other failings feed off these two, so turning into or out of a side road when it is not safe to do so is really part of the first failing – to keep a proper look out. Likewise failing to brake in time or at all is part of the first failing – to keep a proper look out and overtaking when it is not safe to do so contains part of the first failing and the second – speed. The same principles apply in motorway driving where changing lanes at an unsafe time is really just part of the first failing. So if there is one guiding principle when determining liability in road traffic cases, it is to determine whether each party involved kept a proper look out for the other.

## 2.4   CAUSATION

For the claimant in a road traffic case to succeed he must prove that the defendant's negligent driving caused the accident *and* the injuries or damage. Usually this is not an issue in road traffic cases.

However, in speed negligence cases involving pedestrians causation issues do arise which are quite interesting, particularly where the defence is raised that an impact would have occurred in any event even at a lower speed.

So in *Osborne v Campbell*[9] the trial judge held that a driver who ran down a pedestrian crossing through stationery traffic caused the claimant's closed head injury. The claimant should not have crossed in front of the car and the driver was travelling at less than the 30 mph speed limit, but the driver was held to have been going too fast for the circumstances and also to have failed to keep a proper look out. Dealing with the defence that the accident would have occurred anyway even at a lower speed, the trial judge accepted evidence from an accident reconstruction expert that at lower speeds (under 15 mph) there was less likelihood of brain damage from a pedestrian impact.

---

[9]   (Unreported) (1989) HCT Nottingham DR, O 3415.

In *Sparrow v Mark*[10] Owen J ruled that the driver was going too fast and should have been going no faster than 20 mph. He then went on to consider whether (1) the impact would have been avoided or (2) the pedestrian's injuries would have been less severe at that speed. On the facts the impact could not have been avoided, so he considered whether the injuries would have been less severe at the lower speed. No evidence had been called by the claimant that the injuries would have been less severe so the claimant lost the causation issue.

Finally, in the recent case of *Shakian v McDonnell*[11] Foster QC sitting as a High Court Judge ruled that the defendant was negligent for driving too fast (although within the speed limit) and on expert evidence, that the excess speed did cause an increase in the extent and severity of the injuries. The claimant was 50% to blame as well for failing to look as she crossed the road. Causation was therefore established.

See also *Russell v Smith*[12] in which the driver who ran down a child in a residential street was found to be driving too fast despite going at less than the speed limit (27.5 in a 30 mile limit) and on expert evidence was held to have caused 50% of the child's damage. The child was also 50% to blame.

## 2.5 DEFENCES

Once liability has been established then the lawyer involved must consider whether a defence will defeat the claim. In this section we consider a number of potential defences that may be applicable in a road traffic accident claim.

### 2.5.1 Contributory negligence

In any case where the driver is primarily liable he may plead that the other party was guilty of contributory negligence. The Law Reform (Contributory Negligence) Act 1945, s 1(1) states:

> 'Where any person suffers damage as a result partly of his own fault and partly of the fault of any other person or persons, a claim in respect of that damage shall not be defeated by reason of the fault of the persons suffering the damage, but the damages recoverable in respect thereof shall be reduced to such an extent as the court thinks just and equitable having regard to the claimant's share of the responsibility for the damage.'

In *Davies v Swan Motor Co*[13] Denning LJ (at 326) gave guidance on contributory negligence in relation to road traffic accident claims:

---

[10]   [2002] EWHC 23 (QB).
[11]   [2007] EWHC 3242 (QB).
[12]   [2003] EWHC 2060 (QB).
[13]   [1949] 2 KB 291.

'Speaking generally, therefore, the questions in road accidents are simply these: What faults were there which caused the damage? What are the proportions in which the damages should be apportioned having regard to the respective responsibilities of those in fault?'

For a discussion of the principles applicable to apportionment of liability between drivers, passengers and pedestrians, reference should be made to the relevant chapters later in this book.

Children present a particular issue in relation to responsibility for road traffic accidents. In general children under 9 or 10 years of age do not bear responsibility in tort. So in *Gough v Thorne*,[14] Lord Denning MR held that a 'very young child' cannot be guilty of contributory negligence. But what is meant by 'very young child'? This is not wholly clear. For instance in *Jones v Lawrence*,[15] no finding of contributory negligence was made against a pedestrian aged 7, as his behaviour 'was such as one could expect in a normal child of his age'. Yet in *Saleem v Drake*[16] a 6-year-old pedestrian who ran suddenly into the road was held to be entirely to blame for the accident. However, in that case the driver did nothing wrong. Each case, in other words, turns on its own facts.

## 2.5.2   Seatbelts

If a passenger does not wear a seat belt he will usually be found to have contributed to his damage as a result of that negligence. *Froom v Butcher*,[17] is the guideline case on seatbelts and contributory negligence, but it was decided before the law was changed to make the wearing of seatbelts compulsory. Despite this change the guidance given is still good law. Lord Denning MR ruled that:

'Everyone knows, or ought to know, that when he goes out in a car he should fasten the seatbelt. It is so well known that it goes without saying, not only for the driver, but also the passenger. If either the driver or the passenger fails to wear it, and an accident happens – and the injuries would have been prevented or lessened if he had worn it – then his damages should be reduced.'

Rules 99 and 100 of the Highway Code (2007 edition) apply the statutory requirements: Road Traffic Act 1988, ss 14–15; the Motor Vehicles (Wearing of Seat Belts) Regulations 1993;[18] and the Motor Vehicles (Wearing of Seat Belts by Children in Front Seats) Regulations 1993;[19] so that all drivers and front seat passengers must wear seatbelts, where these

---

[14]   [1966] 3 All ER 398.
[15]   [1969] 3 All ER 267.
[16]   [1993] PIQR P129, CA.
[17]   [1976] QB 286.
[18]   SI 1993/176.
[19]   SI 1993/31.

are fitted in the vehicle. There are a number of exceptions (listed in the Motor Vehicles (Wearing of Seat Belts) Regulations 1993 (regs 5–6), applicable to adults and children.

The apportionment of responsibility to a passenger for failing to wear a seat belt when he has been injured by a negligent driver is a three-choice process:

(1)  If the belt would have made no difference at all then no deduction is made. For instance if the driver hits a telegraph pole and it falls and crushes the passenger side, killing the passenger then a seat belt would have made no difference.

(2)  If the belt would have reduced the passenger's injuries then a deduction of 15% is made.

(3)  If the wearing of a belt would have avoided the injuries completely then a deduction of 25% is usually made.

In *Froom*, Lord Denning considered the apportionment of liability thus:

> '... where damage would have been prevented ... I would suggest that damages should probably be reduced by 25% . . . but where the evidence will only show that the failure made a considerable difference, I would suggest that damages attributable to the failure to wear a seatbelt should be reduced by 15%.'

This three-choice test has been challenged over the years – not least by defendants' insurers – to force a reconsideration of the approach outlined in *Froom*, but it has never been overturned. So it was held in *Biesheuvel v Birrell*,[20] that there is nothing, as a matter of logic or public policy, to justify adopting a different standard in relation to rear seat belts.

Another attempt was squashed in *Jones (a child) v Wilkins*,[21] in which the Court of Appeal stated that *Froom* 'can provide valuable guidance' and that there is an advantage to having clear guidelines whatever the range of evidence may be from doctors. This was followed in *Gawler v Raettig*,[22] where it was held that public policy did not require any reconsideration of the approach laid down in *Froom*.

Other examples include: *Salmon v Newland*[23] (20% reduction where the claimant would have sustained less severe facial injuries had she worn a seatbelt); *Devine v Hazlewood*[24] (25% reduction); *Cowler v Ryder*[25] (25%

[20]  [1999] PIQR Q40, QBD.
[21]  [2001] PIQR P179.
[22]  [2007] EWHC 373, QB.
[23]  (1983) *The Times*, May 16.
[24]  (Unreported) (1984), QBD.
[25]  (Unreported) (1986), QBD.

reduction); *Walker v Duck*[26] (15% reduction) and *Palmer v Kitley*,[27] where 15% was deducted where it was 'not an inevitable conclusion that the claimant would have suffered greater injuries had she worn a seatbelt'. In *Pickett v Motor Insurers' Bureau*,[28] the deduction would have been 15%, but for the fact that the claim was dismissed because of the claimant's breach of a term in the 1999 Uninsured Drivers' Agreement.

### 2.5.3 Alcohol/drugs

#### *Drivers*

If a driver is drunk in that he is over the legal limit he will more probably be found to have been negligent and the cause of the accident.

Rule 95 of the Highway Code (2007) states:

> 'Do not drink and drive as it will seriously affect your judgement and abilities. You MUST NOT drive with a breath alcohol level higher than 35 microgrammes/100 millilitres of breath or a blood alcohol level of more than 80 milligrammes/100 millilitres of blood. Alcohol will
> - give a false sense of confidence
> - reduce coordination and slow down reactions
> - affect judgement of speed, distance and risk
> - reduce your driving ability, even if you're below the legal limit
> - take time to leave your body; you may be unfit to drive in the evening after drinking at lunchtime, or in the morning after drinking the previous evening.
>
> The best solution is not to drink at all when planning to drive because any amount of alcohol affects your ability to drive safely. If you are going to drink, arrange another means of transport.'

Rule 96 adds that motorists 'MUST NOT drive under the influence of drugs or medicine'.

#### *Passengers who know the driver is drunk*

Passengers who know that the driver is drunk and yet still get into the car are usually found to have contributed to their damage caused as a result of the drunken driver's negligence. The normal deduction is 20–25%.

In *Owens v Brimmell*,[29] the claimant suffered severe injuries in a road traffic accident, whilst travelling as a passenger in a car driven by the

---

[26] (Unreported) (1987), QBD.
[27] [2008] EWHC 2819, QB.
[28] [2004] EWCA Civ 06.
[29] [1977] QB 859.

defendant, in circumstances where they had been out for an evening together and both drunk 'about 8 to 9 pints of beer'. Watkins J stated (at 866) that:

> 'Thus, it appears to me that there is widespread and weighty authority for the proposition that a passenger may be guilty of contributory negligence if he rides with the driver of a car whom he knows has consumed alcohol in such quantity as is likely to impair to a dangerous degree that driver's capacity to drive properly and safely. So, also, may a passenger be guilty of contributory negligence if he, knowing that he is going to be driven in a car by his companion later, accompanies him on a bout of drinking which has the effect, eventually, of robbing the passenger of clear thought and perception and diminishes the driver's capacity to drive properly and carefully. Whether this principle can be relied on successfully is a question of fact and degree to be determined in the circumstances out of which the issue is said to arise.'

The judge, on the facts of that case, discounted damages on the basis of contributory negligence by 20%.

But the burden of proving that the passenger knew that the driver was drunk and impaired lies on the defendant. In *Malone v Rowan*,[30] a fatal accident claim arising out of a road traffic accident, the deceased was one of five passengers in the defendant's car. The group had visited a public house at various times in the afternoon and early evening, where the driver had consumed 5½ pints of lager. The driver's blood-alcohol reading at the time of the accident was 'at least' 148mg per 100ml. Russell J, having reviewed *Owens v Brimmell*, stated that:

> 'The facts of this case are far removed from those which prevailed in Owen's case. In particular, in this case I have no direct evidence of the deceased's knowledge of what the defendant had consumed. They were not, as in Owen's case, the only two on the scene. Nor have I any evidence of the state of mind of the deceased and whether he ever appreciated, or was reckless, as to any risk that was being run. The burden of proof lies on the defendant. In my judgment, on the facts of this case, he has not discharged, or come anywhere near the discharge of that burden, and I decline to make any reduction in the damages on the grounds of contributory negligence.'[31]

What is the position of the passenger who does not ask? In *Booth v White*,[32] the trial judge held that the claimant was not contributorily negligent for failing to make enquiries as to the amount of alcohol which had been consumed by the driver, despite circumstances where if he had asked the question the answer would have been 'between 10 and 15 pints of lager that day'. Brooke LJ, citing the court at first instance, reluctantly decided (at paragraph 13) that:

---

[30]  [1984] 3 All ER 402.
[31]  Ibid, at 404.
[32]  [2003] EWCA Civ 1708.

'The judge concluded that in all the circumstances he was not persuaded that Mr Booth was negligent in failing to take reasonable care for his own safety by not asking Mr White how much he had drunk. In reaching this conclusion he took into account Mr White's drinking history, the history of the accident and the breathalyser readings. The judge was also unwilling to infer that Mr White's condition was such that Mr Booth was negligent in not making such enquiries. He therefore dismissed the allegations of contributory negligence and found Mr White 100% liable for Mr Booth's injuries.'

Brooke LJ then stated that, 'Although I would not necessarily have decided this case in the same way, I cannot find that Judge Curl was wrong in the way he decided it', and dismissed the defendant's appeal.

Other examples – and these reports all demonstrate that each case turns on its own facts – include:

- *Thomas v Fuller*.[33] The claimant, defendant and a friend spent the evening at a public house, during which they spent about £45 on spirits, before setting off to drive to Scotland on the M1 in a friend's car. The claimant sustained injury when the car ran into the back of a lorry. The court held that the cause of the accident was drink and the parties were on a 'drunken frolic'. The claimant, in putting himself as a passenger in a car driven by his drinking companion, had showed recklessness for his own safety. A fair adjustment 'even though this was a bad case of its type' would be a finding of contributory negligence of 25%.

- *Buckingham v D'Souza*.[34] The claimant aged 16½ and the defendant aged 19 went out together for an evening in which they drank pints of lager as well as vodka and lime over a period of 4 hours. The claimant suffered a catastrophic injury when the car driven by the defendant overturned. Evidence suggested that the defendant's blood alcohol level would have been 'at least 190mg' at the time of the accident. The court held that the defendant's incapacity must have been 'visible to anyone who was watching out for it'. The claimant, accordingly, had to bear some responsibility, and contributory negligence was assessed at 20%. The court noted that 'had it been a case of two boys setting out on a pub crawl a higher degree of contributory negligence might have been appropriate'.

- *Traynor v Donovan*.[35] The claimant suffered severe injuries when travelling in the front passenger seat of a car driven by the defendant. She had met him in a public house only half an hour previously. The defendant was found to have a blood-alcohol level of 168mg. The claimant had not noticed before accepting a lift any sign

---

[33] (Unreported) (1977).
[34] (Unreported) (1978).
[35] [1978] CLY 2612.

that his driving ability might be impaired. The court held that there should be no deduction for contributory negligence to the claimant's damages.

- *Brignall v Kelly*.[36] The claimant was a passenger in the defendant's car and he suffered serious injuries when the vehicle crashed. The defendant provided a blood sample 2½ hours after the accident which showed that his blood-alcohol level was slightly more than twice the permitted maximum for driving. The claimant relied on five witnesses who saw the defendant just prior to the accident and stated that he was behaving normally. The claimant stated that he saw the defendant drink one pint of lager and that he had had a sensible conversation with him when walking towards the car. He saw no adverse signs to suggest that the defendant was drunk. The defendant himself stated that he drank a maximum of four pints of lager in a 2-hour period and that he felt perfectly capable of driving safely. The defendant relied on evidence from a Professor of Forensic Pathology which suggested that at the start of the journey the defendant would have been well into the 'obviously drunk' state. The Court of Appeal held that the trial judge was perfectly entitled to prefer the witness evidence over that of the Professor. McCowan LJ stated:

> 'I refuse to accept the proposition that if a man in a public house observes another man drink one pint of lager and give no sign no intoxication, he cannot accept a lift from him without interrogating him as to exactly how much he has had to drink.'

### 2.5.4  Medical emergency

A sudden, unexpected and unforeseeable onset of a debilitating condition can act as a defence against liability in a consequent accident. Where, in contrast, the driver succumbs to the gradual onset of symptoms, or where he is afflicted by a familiar or foreseeable incapacity, there is no defence, unless it can be demonstrated that the motorist was reasonably unaware of his unfitness to drive.

In *Ryan v Youngs*,[37] a lorry crashed after its driver suddenly collapsed and died of a cardiac arrest. He had appeared to be in good health and medical examination would not have disclosed a defect for liability to sudden collapse. Slesser LJ stated (at 524) that:

> 'To my mind, this case is what has been referred to as an Act of God. An apparently healthy, apparently competent man, in charge of a competent machine, is suddenly struck down, and that is a matter which nobody can reasonably anticipate.'

---

[36]  (Unreported) (1994), CA.
[37]  [1938] 1 All ER 522.

Similar findings were made in *Waugh v James K Allan Limited*,[38] where a lorry driver was struck suddenly by an attack of coronary thrombosis, and *Jones v Dennison*,[39] where the driver lost control of his vehicle following a temporary 'blackout'. It was held that there were no grounds for saying that he ought reasonably to have supposed that he was, or might be, subject to an attack, notwithstanding that 6 years before he had suffered from a coronary thrombosis or slight cerebral thrombosis.

But if the driver knew or should have know he might black out then the defence does not arise. So in *Roberts v Ramsbottom*,[40] a 73-year-old man crashed his vehicle after sustaining a stroke, and *Boomer v Penn*,[41] a Canadian case, which concerned an accident caused by a diabetic driver, both defendants were found liable because they had continued to drive after becoming aware of their unfitness.

These cases can be contrasted with *Mansfield v Weetabix Limited*.[42] Here the motorist was unaware that he suffered from malignant insulinoma, a condition that resulted in a hypoglycaemic state which starved the brain of glucose such that he fell into a semi-conscious state. During the course of a 40-mile journey he was involved in two incidents of driving erratically, one minor accident and, ultimately, a more serious incident that led to the claimant's action. Nevertheless it was held that the condition was such as to exhibit no physical symptoms, or 'signpost', that would have prompted a reasonable driver to abandon his journey. Leggatt LJ stated that:

> 'There is no reason in principle why a driver should not escape liability when a disabling event is not sudden but gradual, provided that the driver is unaware of it. A person with [the driver's] very rare condition commonly does not appreciate that his ability is impaired, and he was no exception.'

Aldous LJ added that:

> 'The standard of care that [the driver] was obliged to show was that which is expected of a reasonably competent driver. He did not know and could not reasonably have known of his infirmity which was the cause of the accident. Therefore he is not at fault. His actions did not fall below the standard of care required.'

## 2.5.5 Ex turpi causa

Ex turpi causa non oritur actio means that 'no court will lend its aid to a man who founds his cause of action upon an immoral or illegal act'. This

---

[38]   [1964] 2 Lloyds Rep 1.
[39]   [1971] RTL 174, CA.
[40]   [1980] 1 All ER 7.
[41]   (1965) 52 DLR (2d) 673.
[42]   [1998] 1 WLR 1263.

defence arises with claimant passengers who are joy riders and/or thieves. It was held in *Gray v Thames Trains Limited*[43] that:

> 'the question was whether the relevant loss was inextricably linked to the claimant's illegal act or so closely connected or inextricably bound up with his criminal or illegal conduct that the court could not permit him to recover without appearing to condone that conduct.'

This ruling has some relevance in road traffic accident claims.

In *Pitts v Hunt*,[44] the claimant was a pillion passenger on the first defendant's motorcycle. The first defendant was not licensed to drive, had no insurance and, whilst in the company of the claimant, had consumed an excessive amount of alcohol. During the course of their journey the first defendant, encouraged by the claimant, had driven in a fast haphazard manner in a deliberate attempt to frighten a number of pedestrians. Eventually the motorcycle collided with a car driven by the second defendant. The court dismissed the claimant's action against this defendant. Bingham LJ found that the maxim ex turpi causa applied as the claimant and first defendant were engaged in a joint illegal enterprise. It was against public policy for the claimant to succeed. The nature of the joint enterprise was such that it precluded the court from finding that the defendant owed any duty of care to the claimant.

A modified principle of ex turpi has been applied to dismiss individual heads of loss and damage tainted by illegality: see, for example, *Hewison v Meridian Shipping*,[45] *Kelly v Churchill Car Insurance*[46] (fraudulent claim for loss of earnings following a road traffic accident) and *Smyly Agheampong v Allied Manufacturing (London) Limited*[47] (vehicle hire charges tainted by illegality where the claimant had used a vehicle on the road without any insurance).

In *Great North Eastern Railway Limited v Hart & Others*,[48] an action which arose out of the Selby rail disaster, it was held that ex turpi had no application to a claim for a contribution brought under s 1(1) of the Civil Liability (Contribution) Act 1978. The claim was brought (by way of subrogation) by the insurers of the motorists whose Land Rover crashed onto the railway line, causing the derailment of two trains, against the Secretary of State for Transport. Morland J stated (at paragraph 84) that:

> 'Almost all litigation arising out of a road traffic accident involves the commission of a criminal offence and almost all of those criminal offences do not involve specific intent but result from carelessness and up to gross

---

[43]    [2008] PIQR P20.
[44]    [1991] 1 QB 24.
[45]    [2002] EWCA Civ 1821.
[46]    [2007] RTR 309.
[47]    (2008) Central London CC, 30 June; LTL 1 September 2008.
[48]    [2003] EWHC 2450 (QB).

negligence. If ex turpi causa were to defeat a claim for contribution, it would seriously affect the whole basis of motor insurance.'

# CHAPTER 3

## LOW VELOCITY COLLISIONS

*Tara Vindis*

### 3.1 INTRODUCTION

Recently there have been a growing number of road traffic accident claims where a defence is raised on causation. In such cases the insurer denies that the accident caused the injuries complained about.

Insurance companies are increasingly mounting these causation defences fearful of the growing number of fraudulent claims made on motor insurance policies.

#### 3.1.1 What is a low velocity collision (LVC)?

It is helpful to refer to vehicles as either 'target' or 'bullet' vehicles. Where a bullet vehicle strikes a target vehicle, the energy of the bullet vehicle will be absorbed by the crumpling of the panels of both cars and/or by there being a change in the velocity of the target vehicle. Where there is such a movement, this change in velocity is referred to as 'Delta Velocity' or 'Dv'.

Accordingly, the speed of the vehicles before the impact is not vitally important. The defence is often raised where the collision involves a very slow moving bullet vehicle and a stationary target vehicle or where the speeds of the vehicles both travelling in the same direction are similar.

For an injury to occur to the occupants there must be some physical movement of the occupant involving force sufficient to cause such injury. There are scientific studies which indicate that adults of normal fortitude ought not to suffer a whiplash injury where the Dv is less than 4mph.

#### 3.1.2 What is the LVC defence?

In such cases the fact of the impact is admitted as is negligence on the part of the bullet vehicle driver but causation is denied. Essentially the defendant asserts that the velocity of the collision was so negligible that it cannot have caused the target vehicle – and thus the claimant – to have moved about with sufficient force to cause an injury.

### 3.1.3   What is delta velocity?

In general terms, the Dv is approximately 50% of the impact speed where the bullet and target vehicles are of the same mass. It is less than the impact speed because some of the energy of the impact will dissipate in panel distortion and the creation of heat and noise. The Dv will be higher where the bullet vehicle has a larger mass than the target vehicle. The Dv is also affected by the point of collision: if the front of the bullet vehicle meets squarely with the rear of the target vehicle then more momentum will be transferred than where the vehicles are misaligned at impact.

Once the Dv of the claimant's vehicle is known, the acceleration forces that are likely to have been exerted on the claimant may be calculated. From that point the likelihood of injury may be assessed.

### 3.2   USE OF EXPERTS

### 3.2.1   Relevance of expert evidence in LVC cases

When considering the question of the sufficiency of the force of the impact to cause injury, the views of both the medical and engineering experts are important.

The Court of Appeal gave general guidance on the use of experts in road traffic cases in *Liddell v Middleton*,[1] suggesting that expert witnesses should be used exceptionally rather than as the rule. Smith LJ observed at p 42, that:

> 'In some cases expert evidence is both necessary and desirable in road traffic cases to assist the judge in reaching his or her primary findings of fact. Examples of such cases include those where there are no witnesses capable of describing what happened ... In such cases the function of the expert is to furnish the judge with the necessary scientific criteria and assistance based on his special skill and experience not possessed by ordinary laymen ...'

In low velocity cases, experts are asked to give their opinion on a matter which has been described by HHJ Stewart QC at first instance in the key authority (which reached the Court of Appeal), *Armstrong and Connor v First York*,[2] Liverpool County Court as 'at the interface between medicine and engineers'.

*Armstrong*[3] was the first LVC case to reach the Court of Appeal. The claimants were sitting in their car waiting at red traffic lights when the defendant's bus tried to pass on their nearside catching the car a glancing blow and causing the claimants to sustain injury (on their case). The

---

[1]   [1996] PIQR P36.
[2]   (Unreported) 27 August 2003.
[3]   [2005] EWCA Civ 277.

paintwork of the car was superficially scratched and there was some paint transference from the bus onto the car's bumper. The claimants gave evidence that they had suffered physical injury and their account was supported by the medical experts instructed (their account of their symptoms was consistent with their description of the accident) and by their medical records showing hospital and GP attendance. The defendant denied that the claimants could have been injured in the impact and relied upon the report of the jointly instructed forensic engineer who concluded that the impact would not have resulted in occupant displacement sufficient for injury to arise for the following reasons:

(1)    unless the occupant of a vehicle was peculiarly vulnerable, the vehicle would have had to move across the road surface in the collision in order to cause an injury;

(2)    there was no evidence that the car had been moved across the road surface;

(3)    the only possibility therefore (given that the claimants had no particular vulnerability) was that the car moved on its springs;

(4)    however, for that to happen, the impact would have had to have been such as to cause some distortion to the panels of the car, and there was no such distortion to the claimants' car.

On the other hand, the trial judge received evidence from the claimants that they were thrown/moved within their seats on impact and experienced spinal pain shortly afterwards. He ruled in favour of the claimants, finding them to have given their evidence honestly and transparently. He found that there must be something inaccurate in the defendant's expert's evidence, although he was not in a position to say what it was.

The Court of Appeal upheld the judge's decision. In relation to engineering evidence each of three Lord Justices had something of their own to say, but essentially they all agreed that it was open to the judge to reject the expert evidence without explaining why he was unable to accept it (provided the judge fulfilled the requirement to give reasons as set out in *English v Emery, Reimbold & Strick*,[4] particularly in a developing or unusual field (see paragraphs 27, 33 and 35 of the judgment).

So the key in such cases is the honesty of the claimant.

If the claimant and the defendant each call expert evidence, then the judge will need to provide sufficient reasons supporting his preference for a

---

[4]    [2002] 1 WLR 2409.

particular expert's evidence. In *Flannery & another v Halifax Estate Agencies Ltd*,[5] 382, Henry LJ stated that

> '... where the dispute involves something in the nature of an intellectual exchange, with reasons and analysis advanced on either side, the judge must enter into the issues canvassed before him and explain why he prefers one case over the other.'

Flannery was considered again by the Court of Appeal in *English v Emery Reimbold & Strick Ltd*,[6] in which Lord Phillips MR at paragraphs 73 and 118 stated:

> 'It is legitimate, where there is a direct conflict of expert evidence, for the Judge to prefer the evidence of one expert to the other simply on the ground that he was better qualified to give it, or was a more authoritative witness, if the Judge is unable to identify any more substantial reason for choosing between them. This should not often be the case. If this is the basis for the Judge's conclusion, he should make it plain ... while it is perfectly acceptable for reasons to be set out briefly in a judgment, it is the duty of the Judge to produce a judgment that gives a clear explanation for his or her order.'

### 3.2.2   Applications for permission to rely on expert evidence

Part 35 of the Civil Procedure Rules (Experts and Assessors) provides at r 35.1 that:

> 'Expert evidence shall be restricted to that which is reasonably required to resolve the proceedings.'

Part 1, the Overriding Objective, is always relevant.

In *Casey v Cartwright*[7] the Court of Appeal gave guidance on the procedure to be followed where a defendant in an LVC case seeks permission to rely on expert evidence as to causation. At paragraph 30, Dyson LJ ruled that a defendant:

(1)   should, within 3 months of receipt of the letter of claim, notify all other parties in writing that he considers this to be a low velocity impact case and that he intends to raise causation as an issue;

(2)   should expressly identify the issue in the defence, supported in the usual way with a statement of truth;

(3)   should, within 21 days of serving the defence, serve on the court and all other parties a witness statement clearly identifying the grounds

---

5   [2000] 1 WLR 377.
6   [2002] 1 WLR 2409.
7   [2007] 2 All ER 78.

on which the issue is raised. This statement should deal with the defendant's evidence relating to the issue, including the circumstances of the impact and any resultant damage.

At paragraph 33, he went on to state that the court:

(1)   will generally give permission for the claimant to be examined by a medical expert nominated by the defendant, if the court receives the defendant's statement and is satisfied that the issue has been properly identified and raised;

(2)   will generally give the defendant permission to rely on such evidence at trial, if the court having received the medical report is satisfied on the entirety of the defendant's evidence that the causation issue has a real prospect of success.

At paragraphs 33–35, the Court also provided examples of when a judge might refuse to give permission for expert evidence, even where the defendant's evidence shows that his case on causation has real prospects of success:

(1)   the defendant did not notify the parties of his intention to raise the causation issue within the required time period (3 months from receipt of the letter of claim);

(2)   there is a factual dispute, the resolution of which is likely to resolve the causation issue;

(3)   the injury alleged and the damages claimed are so small that considerations of proportionality demand that permission be refused.

### 3.2.3   Forensic engineer/accident reconstruction experts

The Court will need to make findings of fact on the speed of the vehicles involved in the collision. Both engineers and accident reconstruction experts can provide expert opinions on this subject although the way they go about this is slightly different.

A forensic engineer will examine the vehicles involved in the collision for signs of damage and draw conclusions from the nature or absence of that damage, considering the various factors (listed below) which affect the likelihood of injury.

An accident reconstruction expert will draw conclusions both from any damage to the vehicles and from inspection of the accident scene.

The passage of time may affect the value of the evidence, but in LVC cases some valuable evidence may be obtained from inspection of a repaired vehicle; the expert will be able to draw conclusions from the repairs carried out, and the traces of a collision on parts that have not been replaced (such as stress fractures in bumpers; crazing to number plates and from the depth of filler used in paint scratches) and may additionally have had sight of relevant photographic evidence.

Imagine the evidential effect at trial if an engineering expert concludes in a soundly reasoned report that the Dv of the target vehicle was equivalent to a car stalling or participating in a fairground ride.

It is not unknown for parties to seek to rely on desk-top reports. These are prepared where the expert has not examined either of the vehicles involved in the collision. Very often, the expert will have been furnished with nothing more than the defendant's written statement. Caution must be exercised in relation to such a report (where there has been no vehicle examination by the forensic engineer) as the expert will be susceptible to rigorous questioning, whether in cross-examination or by way of questions put under CPR Part 35. A report that does not consider all of the factors affecting the likelihood of injury is unlikely to be as persuasive as one that does.

### 3.2.4   Factors affecting the likelihood of injury

As a general rule the less damage there is to the target vehicle, the less likelihood of the claimant being injured. That said, it can also be argued that the more contact energy that is dissipated in crush damage, the less residual energy is left to displace the vehicle occupants. A good example is to consider modern bumpers which are designed to absorb shock and reduce the transfer of energy to the vehicle occupants.

(a)   Vehicle design features are such that some vehicles will sustain more damage from the same impact force than others.

(b)   The relative masses of the two vehicles.

(c)   The position where the target and bullet vehicles come to rest after the impact. If the vehicles were not touching after impact this suggests that the target vehicle was moved and that some occupant displacement occurred.

(d)   Whether the target vehicle had the foot or handbrake applied. If so, this will increase the risk of vehicle damage and reduce the risk of injury.

(e)   Whether the collision was with the target vehicle's tow bar. This is not designed to absorb the energy of a collision, on the contrary, the bullet vehicle's energy will be transferred through the chassis to the car seats thus increasing the risk of injury.

Is it possible to state the minimum delta velocity of the target vehicle before an injury can potentially have been caused, the so-called 'injury threshold'? Certainly some engineering experts instructed by defendants attempt to do this. Those that suggest an injury is impossible below a certain threshold may be found less persuasive by a court than those who suggest that an injury is unlikely to have resulted.

## 3.3 MEDICAL EXPERTS

### 3.3.1 The appropriate medical expert and his instruction

It is important to instruct an expert who understands and has experience of LVC, so lawyers should ensure they have seen the expert's CV (and have details of any research papers written) before instructing the expert. It would be preferable not to instruct a GP. A consultant in A&E medicine or a consultant orthopaedic surgeon will be more persuasive.

As the decision in *Armstrong* underlined, the credibility of the claimant will be a crucial factor in the Court's decision. So the medical expert must be provided with all of the claimant's medical records and instructed to review them carefully. Plainly, if there are no contemporaneous accounts of injury this is likely to support the defendant's case. On the other hand, a claimant will be well served if the medical expert identifies and sets out in the report any contemporaneous complaints and particularly so if an examining medical practitioner noted objective symptoms such as muscle spasm.

In certain cases, it may prove useful to ask the claimant's expert questions pursuant to CPR Part 35 in an attempt to marginalise his view, for example by asking the medical expert to confirm the absence of objective signs of injury on examination. Additionally to identify that the expert's opinion of whiplash injury is based wholly upon the claimant's account, and that the diagnosis of whiplash injury sustained in the accident is dependent on a finding that there was a collision sufficient to move the claimant within the car.

Where the medical records are supportive of the claimant's case, it may also be helpful to get the defendant's expert to agree, through written questions that there was no previous complaint of neck injury or pain in the claimant's medical records, that the medical records include a complaint of injury after the accident and that the records contain reference to no other event or incident likely to have caused the injury complained of.

There is a range of opinion on this subject, which must be identified by the expert pursuant to CPR, r 35.10 and PD35 2.2.

In *Birch v Spirit Group Retail Ltd*[8] the defendant's medical expert was criticised for failing to make reference in his report to the body of opinion in conflict with his thesis, despite having given evidence for over 2 years in this 'hotly disputed area'.

Amongst credible experts who subscribe to the theory of an injury threshold, that threshold is a Dv of around 4mph. Scientific studies have shown that where the delta velocity of the target vehicle is less than 4mph, an adult of normal fortitude should not suffer whiplash injury because the forces generated are insufficient to initiate the biomechanics of a whiplash injury. There is one scientific study (The Brault Study in 1998) which ascertained that whiplash injury could occur in a vulnerable minority of the population where the Dv was as little as 2.5mph, although any whiplash symptoms suffered were said to have resolved within 48 hours of the impact.

However, there are a number of factors which make the risk of injury more likely and therefore every case will need to be assessed on its merits.

### 3.3.2   Semi-medical factors affecting the likelihood of injury

The relevant factors are set out below:

(a)   whether the car occupant braced himself prior to the impact (this reduces the amount of movement of the cervical spine);

(b)   whether there are headrests in the car;

(c)   whether those headrests are positioned correctly;

(d)   the direction that the claimant was looking in at the point of impact. If the passenger was not looking straight ahead then there is a greater likelihood of damage to a greater number of neck structures;

(e)   whether the claimant has any vulnerability or pre-existing injury;

(f)   the claimant's age (the older the spine the more likely the risk of injury);

(g)   the claimant's sex (women are more prone to whiplash injury than men due to less muscle bulk in their necks).

---

[8]   (Unreported) 2 June 2006.

## 3.4 PREPARATION OF LAY WITNESS EVIDENCE

In most road traffic accident cases where only causation is in dispute, the defendant driver would not be expected to give evidence. In LVC cases the evidence of the impact itself is crucial and therefore both drivers will be called. Furthermore, the statements may form the basis of the expert's instruction and should therefore be as detailed as possible.

Additionally, in preparing the statement, the claimant should be asked about the factors affecting the likelihood of injury, as set out above. The sooner this is done the better, not only to avoid memory loss but also to enable a proper assessment of the merits to be conducted, which will include an assessment of the claimant themselves; a claimant who can provide good detail of the mechanics of the impact (speed, movement etc) is more likely to be able to provide evidence of assistance to an expert and be impressive to a judge.

The claimant's credibility is the single most important consideration as the Court of Appeal confirmed in Armstrong. All claimants should be advised at the outset of the task that the Court will undertake in determining causation and the risk of a Court finding the claimant to have been dishonest.

Likewise, if the defendant driver is neither a willing nor convincing witness this will probably extinguish the prospects of defending the claim.

## 3.5 NO NEED TO PLEAD FRAUD

In certain types of LVC claims, the defendant will assert that the claimant is being deliberately dishonest or fraudulent. This arises where the defendant believes that the claimant is either lying about suffering any injury at all, or that the accident was responsible for any actual injury (if for example it is to be alleged that something else specifically was the cause) or lying about both of these matters.

The defendant's representatives should specify in their earliest response to the letter of claim the basis of the defence to be run. If the defence is still not clear, the claimant should ask the defendant to set out his positive case in a CPR Part 18 Request.

In *Kearsley v Klarfeld*[9] the Court of Appeal held that there was no requirement for a defendant to include a substantive allegation of fraud or fabrication in the defence. It was sufficient to set out fully any and all facts from which the defence would be inviting the judge to draw the

---

[9]   [2006] 2 All ER 303.

inference that the claimant had not in fact sustained the injuries as asserted. This could include any reasons given by a medical expert in disbelieving the claimant's account.

# CHAPTER 4

# LIABILITY FOR LEARNER DRIVERS

*Tara Vindis*

## 4.1   INTRODUCTION

The general rule is that provisional licence holders owe the same standard of care to other road users, including those within their vehicle, as holders of full licences, despite being less experienced and therefore less skilful than qualified drivers.

On the other hand, other road users are expected to exercise caution towards learner drivers when encountering the famous 'L' sign on cars on the road.

The Highway Code (revised 7th edition) at rule 204, places learner drivers into that category of road users requiring extra care. Drivers are reminded that it is particularly important to be aware of both learner drivers and inexperienced drivers and riders.

Paragraph 217 of the Highway Code, entitled 'Learners and inexperienced drivers', states that learner drivers may not be so skilful at anticipating and responding to events. Drivers are reminded to be particularly patient with both types of driver.

Where an accident involves a vehicle being driven by a learner driver, consideration may need to be given to bringing an action not only against the driver himself but also against the supervisor or instructor, depending upon the facts and cause of the accident.

## 4.2   LEARNER DRIVER REQUIREMENTS AND PROHIBITIONS

Learners driving a car must hold a valid provisional licence. A learner driver must be supervised by someone who is at least 21 years old who holds a full EC/EEA licence for that type of car (automatic or manual) and has held one for at least 3 years: see reg 16 of the Motor Vehicles (Driving Licences) Regulations 1999[1] and s 87 of the Road Traffic Act 1988.

---

[1]   SI 1999/2864.

Any vehicle driven by a learner must display red 'L' plates, although in Wales the plates can either be red 'D' plates or red 'L' plates or both. The plates displayed must conform to legal specifications and must be clearly visible to others from in front of the vehicle and from behind. When the vehicle is not being driven by a learner driver the plates should either be removed or covered, except when the vehicle in question is a driving school vehicle: see reg 16 of and Sch 4 to the Motor Vehicles (Driving Licences) Regulations 1999.

Before a learner driver is allowed to drive unaccompanied, the driver must have passed the theory test (where required) and the practical driving test for the relevant category of vehicle (Motor Vehicle (Driving Licences) Regulations 1999, reg 40).

Once a driver has passed the necessary tests, he may display a 'new driver' plate or sticker.

Holders of provisional car and motorcycle licences are not permitted to drive these vehicles on motorways.

## 4.3   LEARNER DRIVER DRIVING WITHOUT A SUPERVISOR

In *Verney v Wilkins*,[2] an action was brought by a child passenger who was injured when the adult defendant learner driver overturned the car in which they were both travelling. Winn J held that a breach of the statutory requirements did not give rise to any cause of action on its own, even if a more skilful driver might have avoided the accident but the claimant recovered in full because it was proved that the defendant had driven negligently.

## 4.4   WHAT DUTIES ARE OWED BY A SUPERVISOR?

A precursor to the 1999 regulations was considered by the Kings Bench Division in the case of *Rubie v Faulkner*.[3] There, the appellant unsuccessfully appealed against his conviction by the magistrates for aiding and abetting a driver in the commission of the offence of driving without due care and attention.

The appellant had been a passenger in a vehicle driven and owned by a Mr James who had a provisional licence. The appellant was supervising Mr James' driving. An accident happened when the driver pulled out to overtake a horse and cart on an approach to a pronounced left hand bend. A lorry was approaching in the opposite direction and collided with

[2]   [1962] Crim LR 840.
[3]   [1940] 1 KB 571.

Mr James' vehicle, the engine of which had stopped when the car had reached a point well over the centre of the road.

The appellant, who had no physical control of the vehicle at the time, had said or done nothing to prevent the learner driver's actions although he could see by his position alongside and to the left of Mr James that he was about to drive carelessly in attempting to overtake when he did.

The Court considered that the appellant should have been active rather than passive in his conduct, for example by shouting 'keep in' or 'do not overtake here'.

Hilbery J considered that the relevant regulation (then reg 16 of the Motor Vehicles (Driving Licences) Regulations 1937, now reg 16 of the Motor Vehicles (Driving Licences) Regulations 1999) was framed to make some provision for the protection of the public against the dangers to which they are exposed through a car being driven on the road by a driver who is still a learner and therefore assumed to be not fully competent. The regulation imposed a duty on the supervisor to make up, as far as possible, for the driver's incompetence, unskilful or careless acts. This included participating in the driving of the car where necessary.

*Rubie v Faulkner* was followed in a Scottish Sheriff's Court in *R v Clark*.[4] The supervisor was convicted of being under the influence of drink to such an extent that he was incapable of exercising proper control over the vehicle. The supervisor was under a continuing duty to control the learner driver's driving even when the driver was driving safely.

In *DPP v Janman*,[5] a more recent authority, it was stated that the purpose of the statutory requirement for supervision of a learner driver was the assumption that a provisional driver was not competent to drive alone. The DPP successfully appealed the defendant's acquittal by a magistrates' court. The defendant had been travelling in a vehicle being driven by his partner when it was stopped by police. Because the respondent's breath smelled of alcohol he was asked to provide a breath sample, which was positive. He admitted to the police that he was supervising her driving that night. The Court held that a person supervising a learner will in all probability, save in exceptional circumstances, be in charge of the motor vehicle. A supervisor would have a difficult task in proving that it was not the case that he might take control of the vehicle at any time.

What about in the civil context of a claim for personal injuries as a result of the negligent driving of the vehicle? The key authority, in which the injured claimant was the passenger supervisor is *Nettleship v Weston*,[6] a

---

4   (1950) *The Daily Telegraph*, May 30.
5   [2004] RTR 31.
6   [1971] 2 QB 691.

decision of the Court of Appeal, which sets out the law in relation to the duty of care and standard of care owed by a learner driver.

The defendant asked the claimant to teach her to drive in an informal sense as he was not a professional driving instructor. The first two lessons passed without any incident. However, during the course of the third lesson, the defendant mounted a pavement, struck a lamp post and injured the claimant. Immediately before this happened, the claimant instructor had told the defendant to move off from a halt sign and turn left. The defendant driver was holding the steering wheel and controlling the foot pedals and the claimant was moving the handbrake and the gear lever. Unfortunately the collision occurred despite the claimant using his best efforts to apply the handbrake and straighten up the car, whilst the driver was panicking and despite the slow speed at which the car was travelling at the time. The defendant driver was subsequently convicted of driving without due care and attention.

In the civil action, the defendant denied liability and alleged that the claimant was himself to blame. She also claimed alternatively that the claimant had impliedly consented to run the risk of injury whilst travelling as a passenger in her car.

At first instance, the claimant's claim was dismissed on the basis that he had voluntarily assumed the risk of injury. The judge found that the defendant was not in breach of her duty of care to the claimant which duty was stated to be a duty to 'do her best', the standard of care being reduced by the special relationship between learner driver and instructor. The judge also went on to state that if he was wrong, then he would apportion blame equally.

The Court of Appeal allowed the claimant's appeal and awarded him 50% of his damages, agreeing with the trial judge's apportionment. In relation to the standard of care the Court held that it was the same standard owed by any driver who is sound in mind and is free from infirmity. The standard was not affected or reduced by reason of the instructor's knowledge or the learner's lack of skill.

The same duty is owed to all persons including all passengers. The Court also went on to consider the question of volenti, or consent; the defence could only succeed if the claimant had expressly or impliedly agreed to waive any claim for injury that might befall him. Because Mr Nettleship had enquired and satisfied himself that the car was insured against the risk of injury to passengers before he agreed to provide the lessons, there had been no waiver on his part.

The majority of the Court of Appeal found that on the facts the claimant himself had been 50% to blame for the accident. Instructors and learners were said to be jointly concerned in driving the vehicle and must together maintain the same measure of control over the car as an experienced or skilful driver. In the absence of evidence to distinguish which of them was to blame then the driver and instructor should be found equally to blame.

We have some sympathy for the dissenting view of Megaw J, who found it difficult to attribute any blame to the conduct of the supervisor in this case and would have awarded the claimant 100% of his assessed damages.

*Nettleship v Weston* was considered in a British Columbian case: *Lovelace v Fossum*.[7] The claimant was giving his friend driving lessons. The driver was warned to slow down before approaching a bend in wet and slippery conditions and he followed this instruction. The claimant repeated this instruction when the car was about 90 feet from the bend but the driver did not hear it. The driver lost control of the vehicle which skidded off the road injuring the claimant. The Court held that both the driver and the supervisor were equally to blame for the accident. The instructor was in breach of his duty to instruct his friend in the safe and correct management of the vehicle and the driver was in breach of his duty to use the best skill he possessed to obey the instructor insofar as he possessed the skill to do so.

This is a clearer example of fault on the part of the supervisor. He could or should have repeated his instruction more loudly and/or made it before he got so close to the apex of the dangerous bend.

The same principles would apply where the negligent driving of the vehicle caused injury to the occupants of another vehicle or a pedestrian. Where a driver and a supervisor are covered by different policies of insurance, then depending upon the facts a claim against each as co-defendants is possible.

## 4.5   WHAT DUTIES ARE OWED BY DRIVING INSTRUCTORS?

The duty owed by a driving instructor to a pupil is the same as that owed by a supervisor to his friend. It is important to consider the instructor's role in the accident. Was the leaner driver ready for the driving expected of him? What could or should the instructor have done to have avoided the negligent driving demonstrated?

The key authority is the case of *Gibbons v Priestley and another*[8] which involved a claim brought by the injured learner driver against her driving instructor and the driving school which had employed him. Prior to the accident the claimant, described by the judge as an intelligent, middle aged woman, had received 18 lessons provided by the defendants in a dual

---

[7]   (1971) 24 DLR (3d) 561.
[8]   [1979] RTR 4.

control vehicle. A subsequent lesson with the same instructor took place in the claimant's husband's vehicle which was not fitted with dual controls. The accident happened about 40 minutes or so into that lesson when the claimant turned left out of a junction and started to drive downhill. The claimant let in the clutch sharply and over-steered to the left so that the car was driving towards a tree. The instructor instructed the claimant to brake and pulled up the car's handbrake but the car struck the tree. The claim was dismissed. The judge found that there was no negligence on the part of the defendant in allowing the lesson to take place in a single control car; given the instructor's knowledge of her driving, this was a natural progression. Further, the Court could not criticise the instructor's handling of the five seconds situation between the turn and the collision.

A learner driver's appeal against conviction for driving without due care and attention was dismissed in *R v Preston Justices, ex p Lyons*.[9] In his last lesson before his test, the driving instructor told the appellant to make an emergency stop. The appellant made the stop without looking behind and was struck to the rear by the motorcycle which was following him. The Court found that regardless of directions from his instructor he should have made certain that it was safe to execute the manoeuvre before doing so. If the learner driver had suffered injury and sought to claim against the instructor, we suggest that some element of fault (at least 50%) would be found on the part of the instructor for instructing the driver to perform a manoeuvre which he would or should have seen was unsafe at the time.

## 4.6    WHAT DUTIES ARE OWED BY TEST EXAMINERS?

The duty owed by an examiner to a learner driver or to another road user is not the same as that owed by an instructor or supervisor. An examiner is not there to correct any mistakes that are made by the learner driver as soon as possible, rather to observe whether any mistakes are made. It follows therefore that in most cases an examiner must allow mistakes to be made by the test candidate before taking over the control of the vehicle.

The duty owed by an examiner to other road users was considered by Talbot J in *British School of Motoring Limited v Simms and another*.[10] The claim involved three cars. The claimant's stationary car was struck as a result of a collision between a test car and another car. The test car was being driven by a candidate with the examiner in the front passenger seat. The claimant sued both occupants of the test vehicle. The accident happened when the candidate negligently pulled out from a junction and into the path of a correctly proceeding car without properly giving way to it. The examiner applied the brake when he became aware of the danger from the approaching car so that the test car came to a stop when it was

---

9    [1982] RTR 173.
10   [1971] 1 All ER 317.

more than half way across the road. The Court did not find the examiner to blame. His duty was to assess the learner driver's fitness to hold a full driving licence which included an assessment of any mistakes she might make. He was therefore not to interfere with her driving except when it became necessary to do so to avoid danger to the public or himself or the candidate. This was a specific instruction contained within the Ministry of Transport's manual for examiners which the Court approved. The examiner was found to have applied the brake at a time when he sensed that a real danger was about to take place. In the sudden emergency which arose, in the agony of the moment, although his decision to apply the handbrake was the wrong one, it was still a reasonable decision to have made and he was not negligent.

# CHAPTER 5

## OWNERS' LIABILITY

*Christopher Stephenson*

### 5.1   INTRODUCTION

As a general rule the driver of a vehicle is solely responsible for his driving whether or not he is the owner of the vehicle. That basic principle was summarised by Du Parcq LJ in *Hewitt v Bonvin*:[1]

> 'It has long been settled law that where the owner of a carriage or other chattel confides it to another person who is not his servant or agent, he is not responsible by reason of his ownership for any damage which it may do in that other's hands.'

In most cases, the driver of a car will be insured and so the issue of the liability of the owner of the vehicle (as distinct from the driver) will not arise. However, in some circumstances it may be necessary to consider whether the owner of the vehicle is liable for the negligence of the driver so that the owner's insurer will be liable to indemnify the claimant.

There are well established exceptions to Du Parq LJ's statement of general principle. Where the driver acts as a 'servant or agent' of the owner or the owner otherwise retains a level of control over the vehicle he may be jointly liable for damage caused by the negligence of the driver. Although similar to the general law of vicarious liability, because there is often no employer/employee relationship there are various wrinkles that suggest owner's liability deserves to be treated as a category of its own. This chapter aims to distil the key scenarios in which it is important to consider the particular liability of a vehicle's owner as opposed to its driver.

### 5.2   THE OWNER AS DRIVER – THE REBUTTABLE PRESUMPTION

In *Barnard v Sulley*[2] where the driver of the vehicle was unknown it was decided that there was a rebuttable presumption that the owner of a vehicle, or his servant or agent, was driving it at the time that the damage was caused. The test was that the owner would be liable for the acts or

---

[1]   [1940] 1 KB 188.
[2]   (1931) 47 TLR 557.

omissions of the driver unless he could prove that neither he nor his servant or agent was driving at the time.

If it can be shown that an accident has been caused by an identifiable car but not by an identifiable person there is a rebuttable presumption that it was being driven by the owner, his servant or agent: see *Barnard v Sully*:[3]

> 'ownership of the car was prima facie evidence that it was being driven by the defendant his servant or agent.'

The following principle, deduced from *Barnard v Sully* and *Hewitt v Bonvin* was set out by Lord Donovan in *Rambarran v Gurrucharran*.[4]

> 'An inference can be drawn from ownership that the driver was the servant or agent of the owner, or in other words, that this fact is some evidence fit to go to the jury; this inference may be drawn in absence of all other evidence bearing on the issue, or if such other evidence as there is fails to counterbalance it.'

This principle was applied in the criminal case of *Elliott v Loake*.[5]

An exception to this principle arises where there is evidence that the vehicle has been stolen. In such a case the owner of the vehicle does not owe a duty of care to anyone who may be injured by it as it is driven by a thief.

In a case involving a bus that was stolen by someone who has never been traced and as a result of whose negligence in driving the stolen vehicle the claimant's wife was killed, the bus company were held not to be liable: *Topp v London Country Bus (South West) Limited*[6] following *Denton v United Counties Omnibus Company Limited*.[7]

The presumption was rebutted in *Rambarran v Gurrucharran*.[8] The defendant himself did not drive, but owned a car that his two sons had free use of. There was an accident in which the claimant was injured whilst one of the sons was driving; the defendant proved that he did not know that his son was driving and the son was not on the defendant's business. In finding that the defendant was not liable for his son's driving Lord Donovan (sitting in the Privy Council) concluded that once the owner had discharged his burden of proving he was not the driver and asserted that the driver was not his 'agent' then the burden of proof rested on the party who alleged the driver was driving for the owner's purposes. If he is to make the owner liable, the claimant must then prove that the

---

3  (1931) 47 TLR 557.
4  [1970] 1 WLR 556.
5  [1983] Crim LR 36.
6  [1993] EWCA Civ 15.
7  (Unreported) 1 May 1986, CA.
8  [1970] 1 WLR 556, PC.

driver was driving the car as the servant or agent of the owner or for his purposes, not merely for the driver's own benefit.

In practice there are a number of situations in which an owner may be liable when somebody else is driving their vehicle. Liability does not only emerge from the servant or agent relationship. The important distinction to make in the first instance is whether or not the owner of the car was in the vehicle when the accident occurred.

## 5.3 OWNER AS A PASSENGER – RETENTION OF CONTROL

The mere fact that the owner of a car is a passenger in it at the time at which the driver's negligence causes an accident does not in itself establish liability for the owner, but his presence will give rise to a rebuttable presumption that he retains his right and duty of control.

In *Samson v Aitchison*[9] the owner of a car, Samson, was held to be liable for the negligence of the son of a potential purchaser, Collins, whom he had allowed to test drive it. Samson was present in the car and at trial the judge summarised the liability of the owner thus:

> 'If Collins had been going too quickly, and Samson had told him to go slow, and Collins had persisted in going too quickly, Samson would have had the right to say to him: "If you wish to continue to drive my car you must drive it as I direct and if you will not do so you must cease to drive it". In such circumstances Collins would have had to obey orders or cease driving.'

The Privy Council agreed and said that:

> '... if the control of the car was not abandoned, then it was a matter of indifference whether Collins, while driving the car, be styled as the agent or the servant [of Samson].'

In finding that Samson had not relinquished control of the vehicle, it was his retention of control that gave rise to liability.

The decision in *Samson v Aitchison* was referred to and followed in *Pratt v Patrick*[10] in which it was underlined that the key element to consider is the extent of the owner/passenger's control. Acton J concluded that:

> 'Where the owner of a vehicle being himself in possession of it allows another person to drive, this will not of itself exclude his right or duty of control; and therefore in absence of further proof that he has abandoned that right by contract or otherwise, the owner is liable as principal for damage caused by the negligence of the person actually driving.'

---

[9]  [1912] AC 844.
[10]  [1924] 1 KB 488.

Further, the liability of an owner can be transferred to a bailee. In *Haydock v Brown*,[11] a son borrowed a car from his mother and let somebody else drive him in it. As he had possession of the car he was liable in the same way as an owner. This would be the same if he had paid to hire the car.

## 5.4   OWNER IS NOT A PASSENGER – DRIVER A SERVANT OR AGENT

A closer examination of the servant or agent principle is required where the owner is not travelling in the car and can therefore not simply be held to have retained physical control. *Hewitt v Bonvin*[12] involved a son using his father's car to drive his own friends home after a night out. On appeal the court held that there had been no more than a bailment to the son, he was not acting as a servant or agent of his father and accordingly was not liable. The Court of Appeal's judgment provides a useful discussion of the servant/agent principles of liability.

In his judgment McKinnon LJ acknowledged that a 'servant' style relationship can exist even without any formal employment arrangement. He also made it clear that, even where a formal employment agreement is in place, an employer is not always liable for the acts and omissions of his employee. The judgment said much about the lifestyle of Court of Appeal judges of the day:

> 'A man may, of course, be temporarily employed as a servant without remuneration. If I say to my son, "The chauffeur is ill and cannot come. Will you drive me in my car to the station." He is in no doubt pro tempore my servant, and he is doing my work for me. But even a man who is in every sense a servant, to make his employer liable for his negligent act, must at the moment of his act be doing work for his employer.'

He concluded that for an owner to be held liable when he or she is not in the vehicle, the claimant must show that the driver was engaged to drive the owner's car as a servant and that at the time of the accident he was driving the car as a servant not merely for his own benefit or own concerns.

It is possible to identify a number of common situations where a car is used by someone other than its owner. The question of liability can only be answered by looking at the specific facts of each case. It is necessary to look at the purpose of the journey, and to whom that purpose pertains.

The more recent case of *Candler v Thomas (t/a London Leisure Lines)*[13] highlights the fact that the courts will look at the entirety of a journey to

---

[11]   (1939) *The Times*, May 24.
[12]   [1940] 1 KB 188.
[13]   [1998] RTR 214.

determine whether the driver was using a vehicle for the owner's purpose. In this case the driver had borrowed the owner's van, on the basis that he would use the van to deliver a package for the owner before continuing on to use it for his own purpose. This was enough to fix the owner with liability for the driver's negligence, regardless of whether he had discharged his specific duty to the owner before the accident occurred. We have some doubts about the correctness of the owner being held liable after the driver has finished the owner's delivery.

The judgment in *Candler* refers extensively to the principles set down in *Ormrod v Crossville Motor Services Limited*.[14] In that case the claimants were the driver of a car and his passenger wife, who had an accident whilst driving the car from Birkenhead to Monte Carlo, where they were to meet the owner who was taking part in a motor rally. From there they would proceed with the car to holiday together in Switzerland. The claimant was on his way to Dover for the crossing to France when he had a collision with a bus. He had agreed with the owner that he could use the car to visit friends in Normandy before proceeding to Monte Carlo. It was argued (by the owner in third party proceedings brought by the defendant bus company) that because the claimant had left a few days early for this detour to Normandy the owner should be exempt from liability.

The court found that this did not prevent the owner from being liable as it was held that while the claimant was driving to Dover he was driving in the joint interest of the owner and himself and was accordingly the agent of the owner. The Court of Appeal affirmed Devlin J's finding that:

> 'It is clear that there must be something more than a granting of mere permission in order to create liability in the owner of a motor-car for the negligence of the driver to whom it has been lent. But I do not think that it is necessary to show a legal contract of agency. It is in the area between the two that this case can be found, and it may be described as a case where, in the words of Du Parcq LJ (in *Hewitt v Bonvin*), there is a 'social or moral' obligation to drive the owner's car.'

Lord Denning LJ stated the underlying principle that:

> 'The law puts an especial responsibility on the owner of a vehicle who allows it out on the road in charge of someone else, no matter whether it is his servant, his friend or anyone else. If it is being used wholly or partly on the owner's business or for the owner's purpose, then the owner is liable for any negligence on the part of the driver. The owner only escapes liability when he lends it out or hires it to a third person to be used for purposes in which the owner has no interest or concern.'

In some cases the servant/agent relationship may appear more clear cut but it will always be relevant to ask whether the driver is acting in his own capacity or as an agent of the owner at the relevant time. In *Carberry v*

---

[14]   [1953] 1 WLR 409.

*Davies*,[15] the owner of a vehicle employed a driver. Only he and the driver, who was also related to the owner by marriage, were allowed to drive the family car. When the owner's 16-year-old son wished to go out in the evenings the driver would drive him without receiving payment. On one such occasion the car hit an infant on a motorcycle who subsequently brought a claim against the owner and the driver. The question was whether the driver was acting as an agent for the father or the son. The court found that the proposal that the son should be driven by the driver had originated from the father/owner and as such he was liable for the driver's negligence.

## 5.5  OWNER NOT A PASSENGER – DRIVER ON HIS OWN BUSINESS

In the same way that an employer will not be liable for acts of an employee that do not fall within the scope of 'the course of their employment' the owner of a vehicle will not be liable where the driver borrows it for purely personal reasons, or goes off on a frolic of his own. A clear example of this can be seen in *Hewitt v Bonvin*[16] where the owner's son borrowed his car for his own use without even express permission from his father; the father was not liable for the negligent driving of his son.

The situation is the same when the car is borrowed with the owner's consent. In *Britt v Galmoye and Nevill*[17] the owner of a vehicle lent it to one of his employees so that the employee could take his friends to the theatre after work. Although an employment relationship existed between them, the employer was not in control and the employee was not acting as his servant at the time when the accident happened; therefore the owner was not liable for his employee's negligence.

The same applies whilst the driver is returning the car to the owner. In *Hillman v Walls*[18] the defendant (owner) lent his car to a colleague to return home for lunch and the colleague returned to work after lunch by another means of transport. He brought the car back to work the next morning at the owner's request but on the way injured the claimant. The owner was not liable as the defendant was not in control and the driver was not his servant or agent.

---

[15]  [1968] 1 WLR 1103, CA.
[16]  [1940] 1 KB 188.
[17]  (1928) 44 TLR 294.
[18]  (1938) 5 LJCCR 167.

## 5.6 OWNER NOT A PASSENGER – TAKING THE VEHICLE WITHOUT THE OWNER'S CONSENT

Taking that principle further, it is necessary to consider the liability of an owner when his/her vehicle is taken without consent. Where the owner has not expressly consented to the vehicle being driven, or has no knowledge of a journey that was undertaken, that lack of knowledge or consent is evidence that the driver was not acting as the servant or agent of the owner. That was the basis for the Privy Council's decision in *Rambarran v Gurrucharran*,[19] summarised above.

In *Klein v Caluori*[20] a friend of the owner took his car without his consent and subsequently telephoned the owner to tell him he had taken the car. The owner told him to return it. While driving the car back he had an accident. The court held that the act of borrowing carries by implication a duty to return and there was no distinction between returning a borrowed car and one taken without consent. The order to return the vehicle was merely a reminder of this duty and not sufficient to render the driver of the vehicle an agent of the owner and so the claimant failed to establish a liability against the owner defendant.

## 5.7 OWNER NOT A PASSENGER – FAMILY SITUATIONS

Cars are often borrowed or lent within a family context and this can create difficult liability problems when it all ends in tears. It is astonishing to recall that before the Law Reform (Husband and Wife) Act 1962 there was no tortious liability between spouses and the effect of that is clearly shown by the case of *Smith v Moss*.[21] The claimant was driven home from a party by her husband, in a car owned by her mother-in-law. The couple had attended the party with the mother-in-law and had already dropped her off at home at the time that the accident happened. The claimant was able to recover in full from her mother-in-law as it was held that her husband had been driving in the capacity of agent for his mother. Of course, because of the state of the law as it then was, she was not able to sue her husband.

This case is important in illustrating part of the policy context in which decisions were made about owner's liability. Rightly or wrongly this policy consideration was referred to in the judgment of Charles J:

> 'It is said that the Plaintiff cannot recover against her mother-in-law because the accident was caused by the negligence of her husband, and a husband cannot commit a tort on his wife. Strictly, that is right, but I cannot conceive that, if a husband while acting as an agent for somebody else, commits a

---

[19]  [1970] 1 WLR 556, PC.

[20]  [1971] 1 WLR 619.

[21]  [1940] 1 KB 424.

tort, which results in injury to his wife, the wife is deprived of her right to recover against the principal who is employing her husband as agent.'

Since 1962 spouses have been free to sue each other for tortuous acts. The general rule now is that there is no joint matrimonial responsibility for the driver. So in *Morgans v Launchbery*[22] the Court of Appeal stretched the boundaries of owner's liability in the family context and were knocked back by the House of Lords.

Mrs Morgans was the owner of a car that both she and her husband used. One evening he went out in the car to visit various pubs; he had promised his wife that if he had too much to drink he would get somebody sober to drive. On the night in question, conscious that he had had too much to drink, he asked a friend to drive. Whilst travelling in the car to another town with passengers there was an accident. Mr Morgans and his friend were killed and the passengers were injured. The passengers sued Mr Morgans' estate, Mrs Morgans and the driver. The Court of Appeal held that the wife was liable because as it was a 'family car' the wife had an 'interest and concern' in its use. Lord Denning MR was not unwilling to refer to the broader 'insurance' context in which the decision was made:

> 'When her husband was using it, he was using it as her "agent" in the sense that, if he was involved in the accident, she ought to bear the responsibility, especially as she was the one who was insured.'

His judgment had effectively created the idea of a 'matrimonial car'. The House of Lords did not agree and overturned the Court of Appeal's decision. The House ruled that any development of the law to the extent envisaged by Lord Denning in the Court of Appeal would have to be executed by Parliament. The wife was held not to be liable. As Lord Cross put it:

> 'If one puts out of mind, as one should, all questions of insurance I cannot see why, if the car is in substance owned by the spouses jointly and is more or less a matter of chance that it is registered in the name of one rather than in the name of the other, it is only the spouse that is the registered owner that should be vicariously liable for the driving of the other . . . To my mind the very fact that each joint owner has an equal right to use the car shows that when one is driving it, otherwise than in pursuance of a request by another, he ought to be regarded as driving it on his own behalf.'

In the case of *Norwood v Navan*[23] a wife who only held a provisional driving licence used her husband's car during an afternoon in which she met friends to visit a fortune teller and to go on a shopping trip. The fortune teller did not tell her that on her return (whilst driving without a qualified driver in the car, thus invalidating the insurance policy) she would have an accident in which the claimant would be injured. The

---

[22]   [1973] AC 127.
[23]   [1981] RTR 457.

claimant claimed damages from the wife as driver and her husband as owner on the basis that he was vicariously liable. At first instance he was found to be liable on the basis that the wife had gone shopping for their mutual benefit and that was sufficient to make the wife her husband's agent. The Court of Appeal did not agree and held that the journey was undertaken for the wife's own benefit and any shopping was at most general. This attempt to reintroduce a concept of 'a matrimonial vehicle' as above, therefore, was not successful.

## 5.8 OWNER PERMITTING DRIVING AND AWARE THAT THE DRIVER IS UNINSURED

If an owner allows somebody to use his car in the knowledge that the driver is uninsured they are liable both criminally and civilly. Section 143 of the Road Traffic Act 1988 demands that users of motor vehicles be insured or secured against third-party risks. The section provides that:

'(1) Subject to the provisions of this Part of this Act –
   (a) a person must not use a motor vehicle on a road unless there is in force in relation to the use of the vehicle by that person such a policy of insurance or such a security in respect of third party risks as complies with the requirements of this Part of this Act, and
   (b) a person must not cause or permit any other person to use a motor vehicle on a road unless there is in force in relation to the use of the vehicle by that other person such a policy of insurance or such a security in respect of third party risks as complies with the requirements of this Part of this Act.
(2) If a person acts in contravention of subsection (1) above he is guilty of an offence.'

The extent of the owner's civil liability was considered in *Monk v Warbey*,[24] in which the claimant was injured by a car being driven by an uninsured driver with the knowledge of the owner (the defendant). The claim was based on a similar provision to that provision set out above in the Road Traffic Act 1930. Greer LJ suggested that to recover against the owner direct the claimant had to show that (1) the owner caused or permitted the driving and (2) the uninsured driver was impecunious. That approach has been considered more recently by the Court of Appeal in *Norman v Aziz*,[25] in which Otton LJ expressed the view that the comments of Greer LJ on (2) had been *obiter* and that impecuniosity of the uninsured driver was not a necessary ingredient in a *Monk v Warby* claim against the owner. His analysis was that:

---

[24]  [1935] 1 KB 75.
[25]  [2000] PIQR 72.

'the owner and driver are separate tortfeasors liable in respect of the same damage and their rights between themselves are governed by the Civil Liability (Contribution) Act 1978.'

A useful summary of *Monk v Warby* can be found in the recent Court of Appeal decision of *Bretton v Hancock*.[26] The policy behind this mechanism for owner's liability is clear. It operates to the same ends as the Motor Insurer's Bureau (MIB) to protect claimants from having their claims stifled by the uninsured status or financial circumstances of the driver who causes them injury. The existence of the MIB makes claims for owner's liability rare. But there is still a need for alternative mechanisms for claimants to claim damages for their injuries because there are a number of situations where the MIB are not liable for uninsured drivers, e g where the claimant is a passenger in the car driven by an uninsured driver and he knew that the driver was uninsured. Those exceptions are outside the scope of this chapter.

## 5.9   OCCUPIERS' LIABILITY

A vehicle owner may also be liable under the Occupiers' Liability Act 1957 as in s 3(a) vehicles are expressly included:

'(1)   These provisions shall apply, in like manner and to the same extent as they do in relation to an occupier of premises to persons entering thereon, –

(a)   In relation to a person occupying or having control of any fixed or moveable structure, including any vessel, vehicle or aircraft, and to persons entering thereon.'

This will not give rise to liability where damage is caused by negligent driving but an owner may be liable if the car is in such a state of disrepair that a passenger or somebody who borrows it to drive is injured.

---

[26]   [2005] EWCA Civ 404.

# CHAPTER 6

## PASSENGERS' LIABILITY

*Esther Pounder*

### 6.1 INTRODUCTION

Much of the case law relating to the liability of passengers arising from road traffic accidents has focused on contributory negligence. So as the first part of this chapter we have included consideration of the duty owed by the driver to the passenger. The passenger's negligence can then be considered against the driver's breach.

### 6.2 DUTY OWED TO PASSENGERS

Drivers owe a duty to their passengers to take reasonable care for their safety and not to cause them injury or loss through their negligence. This duty continues while the passenger is travelling in the vehicle. It is, for example, negligent for a lorry driver not to have warned a passenger standing in the back of his vehicle when he knew that they would encounter a low bridge on their journey.[1]

There is also a duty on a driver to stop at the conclusion of the journey at a place where his passenger may safely alight. This duty does not extend, however, to chaperoning passengers across the road on their way to the vehicle.[2]

No higher duty is imposed on the driver in respect of passengers who have been drinking. In *Griffiths v Brown*[3] C was a passenger in a taxi driven by the second defendant. He had been drinking and was intoxicated. The second defendant stopped the taxi across the road from a cash machine for the purpose of allowing C to alight to get money from the machine. As C crossed the road he was struck and injured by a car driven by the first defendant. The court held that the duty of a taxi driver in such circumstances is to take reasonable care (a) to carry his passenger safely during the journey to the stated destination and (b) to stop at the conclusion of the journey, or part of it if the journey is in stages, in a place where the passenger can safely alight. It was held that the taxi driver

---

[1]    *Lewis v Birkett & Dunbar* [1945] 2 All ER 555.
[2]    See *Sweeney v Westerman & Burton Coaches* [1993] CLY 2941.
[3]    [1999] PIQR P131.

owed no additional or special duty to his passenger arising from the fact that the passenger was displaying some effects of having consumed alcoholic drink.

The duty may in certain circumstances, however, extend beyond the period in which the passenger is being carried in the vehicle. In *Hett v Mackenzie*,[4] C had been the offside back seat passenger travelling in a car driven by the defendant's driver. When the vehicle stopped both the driver and C got out. C put his hand on the central column between the two offside doors when the driver slammed his door shut. The edge of the door had a slight lip which protruded over the column and caught C's finger causing him injury. The driver knew of this aspect of the car's construction but C did not. It was held that there was a duty on anyone shutting the door of a motor car, at a time when he knows that others are getting out of the car and may be in close proximity to the door which he intends to shut, to look before he acts. There was found to be no contributory negligence on the basis that the existence of the lip was not something that an ordinary passenger ought to have been aware of. There was no duty on the passenger to examine the construction of the door before placing his hand on the column.

## 6.3　PASSENGER CONTRIBUTORY NEGLIGENCE

Much of the case law concerning passengers relates to the issue of contributory negligence. One of the main reasons for a passenger's claim against a driver, or other road user, to be reduced by reason of contributory negligence is where they failed to wear a seatbelt. In such circumstances passengers should expect their damages award to be reduced by approximately 25% if their injuries would have been avoided or substantially reduced if they had chosen to wear a seatbelt, see *Froom v Butcher*.[5] See Chapter 2 for a full discussion of this topic.

### 6.3.1　Vehicle defects

Passengers will also suffer a finding of contributory negligence where they knew of a defect in the vehicle in which they were being carried where that defect went on to cause an accident. In *Dawrant v Nutt*[6] C was a passenger in a motorcycle side-car combination driven by her husband on a dark stretch of road at night. The lights on the front of the motorcycle combination were not working, a fact known to C. The vehicle came into collision with a car as a result of which C's husband was killed and she was injured. The judge held both C and her husband were guilty of contributory negligence but to different degrees. Both passengers and drivers owe the same duty to other users of the highway to take

---

[4]　1939 SC 350.
[5]　[1976] QB 286.
[6]　[1960] 3 All ER 681.

reasonable care of themselves. The apportionment of blame as between the driver and the passenger would depend on the facts of the individual case.

### 6.3.2   Passenger allows himself to be carried in a dangerous way

Similarly if a passenger allows himself to be carried in a vehicle in a dangerous way he should expect a deduction for contributory negligence where, as result of him being carried in that way, he was injured. In *Madden v Quirk & Another*,[7] C was being carried as a passenger loose in the back of a pick-up van driven by the first defendant, southbound along a main road. The first defendant attempted to overtake a car just as another car had turned from a side road to travel north along the main road. That car swerved out of the way, but the second defendant's vehicle, also pulling out from the side road to travel north, came into collision with the first defendant's van. C was thrown from the back of the van, sustaining serious injuries such that he was left paraplegic. The first defendant was convicted of careless driving and carrying a passenger in a dangerous manner. C accepted that he was 5% to blame for the accident. As between the defendants the judge determined that the first defendant should bear 85% of the blame. He overtook when there was insufficient road width for three vehicles, he was driving in excess of the speed limit and furthermore was additionally negligent for allowing C to be carried in the open-top back of the van. Had the first defendant not allowed C to be carried dangerously the judge concluded that C would not have been injured at all. As for the second defendant, the judge found that he was 15% to blame for the accident as he could and should have seen the first defendant's vehicle in time to take evasive action.

Similarly in *Priestly v McKeown; Burgess v Same*[8] it was held that a 10% deduction for contributory negligence was appropriate where passengers got back into a car which had already been driven dangerously by a sober but reckless driver.

### 6.3.3   Travelling with drunk drivers

This topic is also considered in Chapter 2 on defences. The leading authority, *Owens v Brimmell*,[9] sets out the principles of law for determining whether there should be a deduction for contributory negligence when a passenger is injured while travelling with a driver who has been drinking. D and C were friends who often socialised together. One evening after spending time drinking together in various pubs and a club the two made their way home in a car driven by D. During the journey C sat in the front passenger seat but did not wear a seatbelt. Due

---

[7]   [1989] 1 WLR 702.
[8]   (Unreported) 4 August 1998, LTL.
[9]   [1976] 3 All ER 765.

to D's negligence the car was involved in a collision and C suffered severe and permanent injuries. Watkins J held that C's damages should be reduced by reason of his contributory negligence in allowing himself to be carried in a vehicle knowing that the driver was affected by alcohol. The defendant as the driver should bear the far greater responsibility and C's contribution was assessed at 20%.

The principle was explained as follows:

> 'a passenger may be guilty of contributory negligence if he rides with the driver of a car whom he knows has consumed alcohol in such quantity as is likely to impair to a dangerous degree that driver's capacity to drive properly and safely. So, also, may a passenger be guilty of contributory negligence if he, knowing that he is going to be driven in a car by his companion later, accompanies him on a bout of drinking which has the effect, eventually, of robbing the passenger of clear thought and perception and diminishes the driver's capacity to drive properly and carefully. Whether this principle can be relied upon successfully is a question of fact and degree to be determined in the circumstances out of which the issue is said to arise.'

It is clear that two scenarios were envisaged in the case of *Owens v Brimmell*:

(a)    where a passenger travels in a vehicle when he knows that the driver of that vehicle has consumed so much alcohol as to impair to a dangerous degree that driver's ability to drive properly and safely;

(b)    where a passenger goes out drinking with the driver of a vehicle knowing that he is going to be driven by that driver later when his ability to judge whether his companion can drive properly and safely will be impaired.

The first scenario was considered in the following cases:

•    *Traynor v Donovan*.[10] C was travelling as the front seat passenger in a car driven by D. An accident occurred in which C sustained injury. C had not been wearing a seatbelt; however, the judge accepted that had she been wearing one she would have suffered different but no less severe injuries. At the time of the collision D had been drinking and was subsequently convicted of driving with 168mg of alcohol in his blood. The judge accepted C's evidence that having met D only half an hour previously in a public house she did not observe any indication that his driving ability might be impeded by drink. She called expert police evidence to confirm that symptoms of such excessive consumption of alcohol were not necessarily apparent to a lay person. Accordingly it was held that there should be no deduction for contributory negligence.

---

[10]    [1978] CLY 2612.

- *Malone v Rowan*.[11] A passenger was fatally injured after the driver of the vehicle in which they were travelling was unfit through drink. *Owens v Brimmell* was argued. However, Russel J distinguished *Owens* finding that he had neither direct evidence of the deceased's knowledge of what the defendant had consumed nor any evidence as to the state of mind of the deceased and whether he had ever appreciated, or was reckless as to, any risk that was being run (at p 404E). The burden of proving contributory negligence was on the defendant and he had not come anywhere near discharging that burden. Accordingly there would be no deduction for contributory negligence.

- *Hill v Chivers*.[12] C was a front seat passenger injured when the car in which he was travelling was driven into the path of a bus by D who had been drinking. Primary liability was admitted but D argued that C was guilty of contributory negligence firstly for not wearing a seatbelt and secondly for accepting a lift when he knew or ought to have known that D was under the influence of alcohol. The judge found that had C been wearing a seatbelt he would have suffered lesser injuries and so was satisfied that C's failure to wear a seatbelt amounted to contributory negligence on his part. As for the second argument, the judge found that C had been well aware of D's drinking and ought to have appreciated that he was unfit to drive for that reason. Accordingly C had failed to exercise reasonable care for his own safety and was found to be one-third to blame for the loss, injury and damage he sustained.

See also *Brignall v Kelly*[13] per McCowan LJ:

> 'For my part I refuse to accept the proposition that if a man in a public house observes another man drink one pint of lager and give no sign of intoxication, he cannot accept a lift from him without interrogating him as to exactly how much he has had to drink.'

The second scenario has also been the subject of a number of cases:

- *Stinton v Stinton & MIB*.[14] C was found to be 30% to blame for his injuries when his brother, who was driving the car in which he was travelling, lost control and crashed. C knew that his brother had no insurance and that the pair would both travel in the car after they had been out drinking together. (Note: Although C obtained a judgment against his brother his claim against the MIB failed.)

---

[11]   [1984] 3 All ER 402.
[12]   1987 SLT 323.
[13]   (Unreported) 17 May 1994, CA.
[14]   (1992) *The Times*, August 5.

- *Donelan v Donelan and General Accident Fire and Life Assurance.*[15] C and his then girlfriend, later wife, D, went out for the evening. Both drank a great deal and at the end of the evening C decided that due to his own intoxication D should drive his car. D was an inexperienced driver and had never driven such a powerful car before nor had she ever driven an automatic car. C was aged 38 at the time and D was 23. HHJ Astill held that the authorities, including *Owens v Brimell*, could be distinguished. In the instant case C had instigated and was the cause of D's drunken driving. He was twice her age and was dominant in every way. The judge found that C had put D in a position of great difficulty and no doubt D would not have driven had C not made the decision that she should. D bore some responsibility for the accident, but the minor share at 25%. There was a finding of 75% contributory negligence against C.

- *Booth v White.*[16] The Court of Appeal reaffirmed the principles established in *Owens* and expressly rejected the defendant's attempt to extend the duty imposed on the passenger to require him to interrogate the driver as to his consumption of alcohol. The facts were as follows. At about 12.35pm C and D went to a public house where C bought D a pint of lager. At about 1.15pm D went to play football and C remained in the pub until about 4.30–5pm when D returned. C bought D another pint and he knew that D had won another pint from a game of pool. He otherwise did not pay attention to what D was drinking but he knew that he was habitually a heavy drinker. At around 6.45pm C accepted a lift home from D in his car. During the journey D lost control and crashed causing C very serious injuries. When tested D was found to have been almost twice the legal limit. C admitted that he had drunk between 10 and 15 pints that day and at the time he elected to be driven by D he was incapable of making any reliable judgement for his own safety. It was argued on behalf of D that the world had changed since 1976 when *Owens v Brimmell* was decided; members of the public, the courts and Parliament are very much more stern with those who drink and drive. As people can appear sober when they have in fact had too much to drink, accordingly a passenger who is properly careful of his own safety should not close down the opportunity of obtaining more information by asking the driver how much he has had to drink. The Court of Appeal reaffirmed *Owens* stating that the law requires the passenger to make an assessment of the driver when deciding whether, in the interests of his own safety, he should have a lift. This, their Lordships held, does not extend to requiring an 'interrogation' of the driver by the passenger as to the amount of alcohol he has consumed.

---

[15] [1993] PIQR P205.
[16] [2003] All ER (D) 245 (Nov).

- *Gleeson v Court.*[17] In this recent case, the question of contributory negligence for passengers in cars driven by drunk drivers was considered again. C and four others were passengers late at night in a car being driven by D. C was travelling in the boot of the car underneath the parcel shelf as there were too many passengers for the available seats. Everyone in the car had drunk a considerable amount of alcohol that evening and due to his intoxication D drove too quickly and lost control of the car hitting a safety barrier. As a result of the collision C was thrown out of the boot sustaining serious injuries. D admitted liability but argued that there should be a finding of contributory negligence against C on the basis that:

  (a) he had elected to travel in the car when he knew or ought to have known that D was adversely affected by drink; and

  (b) he was travelling in the boot of the car.

Judge Foster QC found that C knew that D had had far too much to drink to be driving a car. The primary cause of the accident was the behaviour of D: he drove when he was adversely affected by drink, he drove too fast, he failed to control his vehicle and he permitted C to travel in the boot. Travelling in the boot created the mechanism for the injury for which C and D bore some responsibility. If the only element of contributory negligence applicable was choosing to travel with a driver who was adversely affected by alcohol then the appropriate deduction would be 20%, as per *Owens v Brimmell*. Similarly *Froom v Butcher* required a 25% reduction for a passenger who does not wear a seatbelt, where wearing a seatbelt would have prevented the injuries. Travelling in a boot can be distinguished from failing to wear a seatbelt as there is no available restraint in the boot. However, the conduct is otherwise more foolhardy. The judge decided against adding the two figures as both elements flowed from C's impaired decision-making and so there would be an element of double counting. In the circumstances the appropriate reduction was held to be 30%.

---

[17] [2008] RTR 10.

# CHAPTER 7

# DRIVER'S LIABILITY: SPEED AND BRAKING

*Jeremy Ford*

## 7.1  INTRODUCTION

As has been identified in Chapter 2, the general principles of negligence when applied to road traffic accidents mean that a driver should not do or omit to do anything which he should reasonably anticipate might cause injury to other highway users. When assessing whether a driver has fallen below this objective standard it is necessary to consider all of the accident circumstances. The most prominent of these is the reasonableness of the speed at which the driver was travelling.

## 7.2  SPEED

The starting point when considering speed is the applicable speed limit that applied to the material highway at the time of the accident and whether this was being exceeded. The Highway Code includes a useful summary table of the appropriate maximum speed limits for a variety of vehicles on a variety of roads, summarising ss 81, 86, 89 of and Sch 6 to the Road Traffic Regulations Act 1984, see table overleaf:

| | Built-up areas* | Single carriage-ways | Dual carriage-ways | Motorways |
|---|---|---|---|---|
| **Type of vehicle** | mph (km/h) | mph (km/h) | mph (km/h) | mph (km/h) |
| **Cars & motorcycles** (including car-derived vans up to 2 tonnes maximum laden weight) | 30 (48) | 60 (96) | 70 (112) | 70 (112) |
| **Cars towing caravans or trailers** (including car-derived vans and motorcycles) | 30 (48) | 50 (80) | 60 (96) | 60 (96) |
| **Buses, coaches and minibuses** (not exceeding 12 metres in overall length) | 30 (48) | 50 (80) | 60 (96) | 70 (112) |
| **Goods vehicles** (not exceeding 7.5 tonnes maximum laden weight) | 30 (48) | 50 (80) | 60 (96) | 70 (112)** |
| **Goods vehicles** (exceeding 7.5 tonnes maximum laden weight) | 30 (48) | 40 (64) | 50 (80) | 60 (96) |

* The 30mph limit usually applies to all traffic on all roads with street lighting unless signs show otherwise.

** 60mph (96km/h) if articulated or towing a trailer.

Rule 124 of the Highway Code also states:

> 'You **MUST NOT** exceed the maximum speed limits for the road and for your vehicle. The presence of street lights generally means that there is a 30 mph (48 km/h) speed limit unless otherwise specified.'

The fact that a driver was exceeding an applicable speed limit is therefore a fact upon which a party may rely as evidence tending to establish primary liability for an accident but it is not conclusive,[1] exceeding the

---

[1]    Road Traffic Act 1988, s 38(7).

speed limit not in itself being negligence imposing civil liability.[2] This was reiterated in *Quinn v Scott*[3] where Glyn-Jones J stated that:

> 'There are a number of makers of motorcars ... who make their motor cars for the express purpose that, *in appropriate conditions*, they may safely be driven at high speeds – higher indeed than 75 miles per hour. The high speed alone is not evidence of negligence *unless the particular conditions at the time preclude it.*' (my emphasis)

The key question for the court is therefore the reasonableness of the speed taking into account all the conditions prevailing at the time. Consequently, although it may not be negligent to exceed the speed limit, liability will not necessarily be avoided even if a driver was driving within the prescribed speed limit.

Rule 125 of the Highway Code states:

> 'The speed limit is the absolute maximum and does not mean it is safe to drive at that speed irrespective of conditions. Driving at speeds too fast for the road and traffic conditions is dangerous. You should always reduce your speed when
> - the road layout or condition presents hazards, such as bends
> - sharing the road with pedestrians, cyclists and horse riders, particularly children, and motorcyclists
> - weather conditions make it safer to do so
> - driving at night as it is more difficult to see other road users.'

The need to reduce speed to take account of the prevailing conditions is starkly illustrated by cases involving injury to pedestrians, particularly children. Any driver should avoid colliding with pedestrians by travelling at an appropriate speed and in *Daly v Liverpool Corporation*[4] it was held that if the driver sees a pedestrian in time to avoid a collision but does not slow, thinking that the pedestrian has time to move away, he will be liable if owing to age or infirmity the pedestrian does not move.

Another important case on speed is *Moore v Poyner*,[5] in which a driver of a vehicle travelling at 30mph in a residential area, knowing of children playing in the area, was found to be negligent for not slowing down and sounding his horn. Buckly LJ formulated the duty thus:

> '... would it have been apparent to a reasonable man, armed with commonsense and experience of the way pedestrians, particularly children, are likely to behave in circumstances such as were know to the Defendant to exist in the present case, that there was a possibility of a danger emerging, to avoid which he should slow down or sound his horn or both.'

---

[2]  *Barna v Hudes Merchandising Corporation* (1962) 106 Sol Jo 194.
[3]  [1965] 2 ALL ER 588, at 590.
[4]  [1939] 2 ALL ER 142.
[5]  [1975] RTR 127, at 132.

And later:

> 'The question is: what ought the defendant reasonably to have anticipated might happen; and, if it is to be said he ought to have anticipated that a child would run out into the roadway, to avoid an accident happening in those circumstances he would have had to slow down to such an extent that at the moment he passed the front of the coach he could have stopped instantaneously as the child ran into his path, and to do so, I think he would have had to [have slowed] down to something like 5mph.'[6]

*Moore* was cited with approval in *Saleem v Drake*[7] where the Court of Appeal held that a duty in similar circumstances was to slow to a speed that enabled a driver 'to stop instantaneously if a child ran into the road'. On the issue of sounding the horn however, the Court held that in the absence of any indication which should have caused the driver to reasonably anticipate that the child would suddenly come out into the road, he was under no duty to sound his horn on seeing the children. However, where a driver had seen a child 'hovering' at the edge of the road and intent on crossing, it was incumbent upon the driver to reduce speed to a degree sufficient to avoid the accident *and* to sound the horn to warn of likely danger.[8]

A similar decision was reached in *Russell v Smith.*[9]

In summary, the adherence of a driver to the speed limit can be relied upon by parties to assert or deny negligence but ultimately the speed at which a vehicle should be driven must be reasonable in all the circumstances, there being a specific need to reduce speed appropriately to take into account hazards set out in rule 125.

## 7.3   BRAKING

The determination of what a reasonable speed should be taking into account all the circumstances is most often expressed as a duty upon a driver to drive at a speed which enables him to stop within the limits of his vision, taking into account the weather and state of the road.[10] This is encapsulated in rule 126 of the Highway Code:

> 'Drive at a speed that will allow you to stop well within the distance you can see to be clear. You should:
> • Leave enough space between you and the vehicle in front so that you can pull up safely if it suddenly slows down and stops. The safe rule is never to get closer than the overall stopping distance (see typical stopping distances table below);

---

[6]   Ibid, at 133.
[7]   [1993] PIQR P129, at P133.
[8]   *Armstrong v Cottrell* [1993] 2 PIQR P109.
[9]   (2006) Central London County Court; a decision of HHJ Rich QC, Lawtel.
[10]   *Hill-Venning v Baszant* [1950] 2 ALL ER 1151.

- Allow at least a two – second gap between you and the vehicle in front on roads carrying fast traffic and in tunnels when visibility is reduced. The gap should be at least doubled on wet roads and increased still further on icy roads;
- Remember, large vehicles and motorcycles need a greater distance to stop. If driving a large vehicle in a tunnel, you should allow a four-second gap between you and the vehicle in front . . .'

When establishing whether the speed of the vehicle was a reasonable speed for a driver to have been able to stop, it is helpful to rely upon the table of typical stopping distances also within the Highway Code (see below). This is the touchstone for establishing whether a driver would have sufficient thinking and braking time to safely stop his vehicle. Additionally, we recommend consulting other tables of stopping distances (see for example PNBA Facts & Figures, 2008, page 331) when calculating time and distances at trial.

Pursuant to rule 126 it is necessary for the driver of a vehicle to keep a sufficient distance between his vehicle and the vehicle he is following to respond to all traffic exigencies reasonably to be anticipated, as per Lord Cooper in *Brown and Lynn v Western Scottish Motor Traction Co Limited*:[11]

'The distance which should separate two vehicles travelling one behind the other must depend upon many variable factors – the speed, the nature of the locality, the other traffic present or to be expected, the opportunity available to the following driver of commanding a view ahead of the leading vehicle, the distance within which the following vehicle can be pulled up and many other things. The following driver is, in my view bound, so far as is reasonably possible, to take up such a position, and to drive in such a fashion, as will enable him to deal with all traffic exigencies reasonably to be anticipated: but whether he has fulfilled this duty must in every case be a question of fact, just as it is a question of fact whether, on any emergency disclosing itself, the following driver acted within the alertness, skill and judgment reasonably to be expected in the circumstances.'

Exigencies reasonably to be anticipated include a foreseeable emergency.[12] In one case it was held that to say that a bus-driver must always preserve a gap in front of his vehicle, sufficient for him to brake at leisure, was a counsel of perfection which ignored modern traffic conditions.[13]

## 7.4 SUDDEN BRAKING

When dealing with sudden braking, for the driver of the lead vehicle, liability will depend upon whether the sudden stop was owing to that

---

[11] 1945 SC 31, at 35.
[12] *Thompson v Spedding* [1973] RTR 312.
[13] *Wooller v London Transport Board* [1976] RTR 206 as applied in *Parnell v Metropolitan Police District Receiver* [1976] RTR 201.

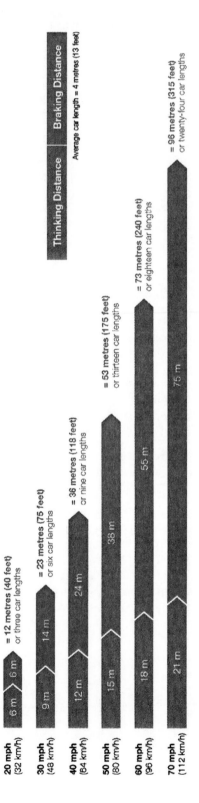

Typical Stopping Distances

| | Thinking Distance | Braking Distance |
| --- | --- | --- |

Average car length = 4 metres (13 feet)

**20 mph**
(32 km/h) — 6 m / 6 m — **= 12 metres (40 feet)** or three car lengths

**30 mph**
(48 km/h) — 9 m / 14 m — **= 23 metres (75 feet)** or six car lengths

**40 mph**
(64 km/h) — 12 m / 24 m — **= 36 metres (118 feet)** or nine car lengths

**50 mph**
(80 km/h) — 15 m / 38 m — **= 53 metres (175 feet)** or thirteen car lengths

**60 mph**
(96 km/h) — 18 m / 55 m — **= 73 metres (240 feet)** or eighteen car lengths

**70 mph**
(112 km/h) — 21 m / 75 m — **= 96 metres (315 feet)** or twenty-four car lengths

driver's negligence or some other cause over which he had no control. So the burden of proving why he stopped suddenly lies on the lead driver.

In *Gussman v Gratton-Storey*[14] a defendant applied her brakes violently in order to avoid hitting a pheasant running across the road, so that the driver behind was unable to stop. The defendant was held liable. We can draw from this that not all extraneous causes for sudden braking will relieve the lead driver of liability.

In *Elizabeth v MIB*[15] a motorcyclist struck the rear of a van that had braked suddenly. The Court of Appeal held that in such circumstances the van driver had the burden of proving why such heavy braking had been required.

For a case where the driver's explanation was sufficient to prevent any inference of negligence arising, see the Privy Council decision of *Ng Chun Pui v Lee Chuen Tat.*[16] However, in *Jungnickel v Laing*[17] it was held that a driver on a motorway who intends to slow down, albeit suddenly, was under no duty to give any warning of his intention because it was the duty of those following behind to keep clear.

## 7.5 SKIDDING

Rule 119 of the Highway Code states:

> 'Skids. Skidding is usually caused by the driver braking, accelerating or steering too harshly or driving too fast for the road conditions. If skidding occurs, remove the cause by releasing the brake pedal fully or easing off the accelerator. Turn the steering wheel in the direction of the skid. For example, if the rear of the vehicle skids to the right, steer immediately to the right to recover.'

Although the law initially regarded a skid as a neutral event, in that it may or may not have been due to negligence,[18] since *Richley v Faull*[19] the burden has shifted in some cases. The defendant skidded onto the wrong side of the road and a collision occurred with a car being driven in opposite direction at a bend on a wet road. The defendant's skid was held to be significant in placing the burden on the defendant to prove that the skid which took him to the wrong place happened without his fault. In *Richley* MacKenna J stated:

---

[14]  (1968) 112 Sol Jo 884.
[15]  [1981] RTR 405.
[16]  [1988] RTR 298.
[17]  (1968) 112 Sol Jo 844.
[18]  *Laurie v Raglan Building Co Limited* [1942] 1 KB 152.
[19]  [1965] 1 WLR 1454, at 1457.

'I respectfully disagree with the statement that a skid by itself is neutral. I think that the unexplained and violent skid is in itself evidence of negligence.'

Effectively therefore the law places a rebuttable presumption of negligence on a skidding defendant and this reflects the uncompromising wording of rule 119 that squarely lays the likely blame for a skid upon the way a vehicle has been driven. One of the rare cases where a defendant successfully rebutted this presumption was in *Custine v Nottingham Corporation*[20] but this related to an accident occurring in snow and ice.[21]

---

[20]   [1970] RTR 365.
[21]   Contrast however the case of *Laurie* [1942] 1 KB 152 where negligence was found in similar road conditions.

# CHAPTER 8

# DRIVER'S LIABILITY: OVERTAKING

*Robert McAllister*

## 8.1  INTRODUCTION

It is not difficult to see how a misjudged overtaking manoeuvre can lead to a road traffic accident. Overtaking will invariably involve the need for proper observation and signalling, for judging distances and speed and will usually require some lane changing or driving in lanes meant for oncoming traffic.

Guidance on overtaking is principally found in rules 162–169 of the Highway Code, although some cross referencing to other rules is given. The rules are relatively detailed and provide ample material for pleading specific particulars of negligence for road traffic cases.

This chapter seeks to highlight the rules of the Highway Code and to give examples of how courts approach the obligations involved in overtaking.

## 8.2  ABSOLUTE PROHIBITIONS ON OVERTAKING

Particular attention should be given to the prohibitions in rules 165 and 191 of the Highway Code. They are complementary in that the third provision of rule 165 is mirrored by part of rule 191:

'**165** You MUST NOT overtake
- if you would have to cross or straddle double white lines with a solid line nearest to you (but see Rule 129)
- if you would have to enter an area designed to divide traffic, if it is surrounded by a solid white line
- the nearest vehicle to a pedestrian crossing, especially when it has stopped to let pedestrians cross
- if you would have to enter a lane reserved for buses, trams or cycles during its hours of operation
- after a 'No Overtaking' sign and until you pass a sign cancelling the restriction'

'**191** ... You MUST NOT overtake the moving vehicle nearest the crossing or the vehicle nearest the crossing which has stopped to give way to pedestrians.'

For completeness, given the cross reference in rule 165, rule 129 provides:

> '**129** Double white lines where the line nearest you is solid. This means you
> MUST NOT cross or straddle it unless it is safe and you need to enter
> adjoining premises or a side road. You may cross the line if necessary,
> provided the road is clear, to pass a stationary vehicle, or overtake a pedal
> cycle, horse or road maintenance vehicle, if they are travelling at 10 mph
> (16 km/h) or less.'

The Highway Code also lists specific statutory material from which the
above prohibitions are derived and reference to those statutes can be
useful for pleading Statements of Case and for investigating potential
criminal liability.

### 8.2.1   Overtaking a vehicle at a pedestrian crossing

This almost invariably leads to liability on the part of the driver if a
pedestrian is hit.

In *Shepherd v H West & Son Ltd*,[1] the pedestrian claimant was struck at a
traffic light controlled crossing by a lorry that was overtaking a waiting
bus. The claimant had started to cross when the lights were green in her
favour. The lorry driver thought that the lights had become green in his
favour by the time that he came alongside the stationary bus. It was held
by Paull J that a reasonable driver would not have let the front wheels of
his lorry get level with the bus until the bus had got half-way across the
crossing; to pass a stationary vehicle under such circumstances was a
dangerous practice that ought to be realised by all motorists. The judge
rejected the argument that the claimant ought to have stopped at the edge
of the bus and said that it was a natural instinct for a pedestrian who had
started to cross, if the lights changed and she heard the bus revving up, to
get out of the path of the bus. In any event, the claimant could have taken
no more than one step forward from in front of the bus and that was not
negligent.

### 8.3   WARNINGS ABOUT OVERTAKING

Rules 166 and 167 of the Highway Code provide warnings against
overtaking, coupled with examples of dangers:

> '**166** DO NOT overtake if there is any doubt, or where you cannot see far
> enough ahead to be sure it is safe. For example, when you are approaching
> •   a corner or bend
> •   a hump bridge
> •   the brow of a hill'

---

[1]   (1962) 106 Sol Jo 391.

'**167** DO NOT overtake where you might come into conflict with other road users. For example
- approaching or at a road junction on either side of the road
- where the road narrows
- when approaching a school crossing patrol
- between the kerb and a bus or tram when it is at a stop
- where traffic is queuing at junctions or road works
- when you would force another road user to swerve or slow down
- at a level crossing
- when a road user is indicating right, even if you believe the signal should have been cancelled. Do not take a risk; wait for the signal to be cancelled
- stay behind if you are following a cyclist approaching a roundabout or junction, and you intend to turn left
- when a tram is standing at a kerbside tram stop and there is no clearly marked passing lane for other traffic.'

There are a number of cases illustrative of the points covered in these rules.

## 8.3.1 Overtaking when passing side roads in urban areas

This manoeuvre is a common occurrence in city streets and yet is fraught with danger. In most cases the overtaking driver is found at least partly to blame.

However in *Tocci v Hankard*[2] a van driver was overtaking a scooter on Balham Hill, London when the driver of the scooter turned to his right across the road to a side road. The van driver avoided hitting the scooter by moving onto the wrong side of road, where he collided with the oncoming claimant. The trial judge found that the scooter driver was almost entirely to blame, but a small part of blame lay with the van driver for not seeing the claimant. As the scooter driver had not been traced, the van driver was liable for the whole of the claimant's claim. On appeal by the van driver Lord Denning MR said that the question had been raised whether the van driver was overtaking at a road junction, and concluded that this was one of those side roads, of which there were many in London, which did not form a road junction in the sense used in the Highway Code and that it was not negligent to attempt to overtake when passing such a side road. Nor was there negligence by the van driver in failing to see the claimant in circumstances where the van driver had acted on the spur of the moment to avoid an accident with the scooter. The claimant recovered damages from the MIB for the untraced scooter driver's negligence (under the Untraced Drivers Agreement), and not against the van driver.

---

[2]    (1966) 110 Sol Jo 835 CA (Lord Denning MR, Danckwerts and Diplock LJJ).

### 8.3.2   Overtaking where view of road hampered by dips in the road

Such manoeuvres usually give rise to liability on the part of the overtaking driver.

In *Goodreid v Ainsworth*,[3] the defendant car driver, after overtaking two cars on a single carriageway road, sought to overtake a further car and a coach in one manoeuvre. The claimant, in an oncoming car, braked hard 'in the agony of the moment' and swerved into a collision with the coach. The defendant was able to brake and pull in behind the coach. The defendant was found negligent for overtaking the coach when unsafe to do so; he should not have attempted the manoeuvre unless he was sure that the road ahead was clear and that he could see the road surface for the full extent of the distance required for safe overtaking. That obligation was all the stronger in the circumstances as the defendant was familiar with the road and knew that it contained hidden dips.

## 8.4   GENERAL GUIDANCE ON OVERTAKING

Rules 162–163 provide more general guidance about overtaking:

'**162** Before overtaking you should make sure
- the road is sufficiently clear ahead
- road users are not beginning to overtake you
- there is a suitable gap in front of the road user you plan to overtake'

'**163** Overtake only when it is safe and legal to do so. You should
- not get too close to the vehicle you intend to overtake
- use your mirrors, signal when it is safe to do so, take a quick sideways glance if necessary into the blind spot area and then start to move out
- not assume that you can simply follow a vehicle ahead which is overtaking; there may only be enough room for one vehicle
- move quickly past the vehicle you are overtaking, once you have started to overtake. Allow plenty of room. Move back to the left as soon as you can but do not cut in
- take extra care at night and in poor visibility when it is harder to judge speed and distance
- give way to oncoming vehicles before passing parked vehicles or other obstructions on your side of the road
- only overtake on the left if the vehicle in front is signalling to turn right, and there is room to do so
- stay in your lane if traffic is moving slowly in queues. If the queue on your right is moving more slowly than you are, you may pass on the left
- give motorcyclists, cyclists and horse riders at least as much room as you would when overtaking a car (see Rules 211–215).'

---

[3]   [2002] All ER (D) 403 (May), Lawtel AC0103256 QBD (Judge Geddes) 27 May 2002.

Again, there are a number of cases that illustrate how motorists should, or should not, overtake that explore the areas covered by these rules. Some are confined to their facts and others are of more general application.

Overtaking drivers should always show consideration for the safety of pedestrians and, where trams are present, the overtaking driver should watch out both for drivers and for pedestrians who are getting on and off: *Christie v Glasgow Corpn.*[4] Similar consideration should be given to buses and taxis.

Ice creams vans give rise to a special danger and a good look out must be kept for adult and children pedestrians who might emerge suddenly from behind an ice cream van: *Gambrino v De Leo.*[5]

Hand signals when overtaking and turning were considered in *Goke v Willett.*[6] Travelling on the A1, a Mini van overtook a slow moving lorry, maintained his offside signal and then slowed to turn into a petrol station on his offside. An Albion van then collided with the rear of the Mini van and an oncoming vehicle, killing the driver. On his own admission, the Mini driver had not seen the Albion before impact. Similarly, the Albion driver had not seen the Mini's signals. The judge held that the Mini van driver was negligent:

(a)   in failing to look, or keep looking properly in his interior mirror;

(b)   in failing to give adequate notice of his intention to turn to his right; and

(c)   in failing to give adequate notice of his intention to pull up and stop.

It was his duty, in the circumstances, to indicate those intentions by a hand signal. The Albion driver was also negligent in failing to keep a proper lookout. Liability was apportioned one-thirds/two-thirds between the Mini van and Albion respectively. The Mini van driver appealed, arguing (i) that he was not negligent and (ii) any negligence was not causative in that the Albion was sufficiently far behind to have avoided the accident if driving properly. The Albion driver's employers cross-appealed arguing for a more favourable apportionment. The Court of Appeal, whilst doubting whether the Mini van driver was held sufficiently to blame by the trial judge, did not interfere with apportionment. According to Edmund Davies LJ:

'I hold that, notwithstanding the use of a trafficator and the operation of brake lights, there may be circumstances when it is still desirable that the

4    1927 SC 273.
5    [1971] 7 DLR 167.
6    [1973] RTR 422 CA (Edmund Davies, Stephenson, Roskill LJJ).

utmost warning to other traffic of one's intentions should be resorted to, and that it may well be that a hand signal, even in these modern days, is called for . . .'

despite the wording of the 1968 edition of the Highway Code pp 7, 35 and

'it was incumbent on [the Mini driver] to take every precaution to see not only that he did not imperil oncoming traffic, but also that following traffic would not be embarrassed . . . one would not expect to find, in the absence of any right-hand turning or similar feature, a stationary, or virtually stationary, vehicle straddling the middle lane . . . The Mini driver's intended manoeuvre was in my judgment of such an unusual character in all the circumstances to call for that extra precaution.'

A classic example of overtaking took place in *Henderson v Cooke*.[7] A car driver pulled from a side road onto a straight unlit section of main road behind a slow-moving van. He indicated and then almost immediately started to overtake the van. A motorcyclist travelling fast in the same direction and from over the brow of a hill sought to overtake the car and the van. He remained on the offside of the road in order to pass the two vehicles. An accident occurred. It was held that although the motor cycle rider throttled back he was going too fast and wrongly concluded that he could get past two vehicles in time. He was not travelling at a speed commensurate with the essential risks, of which he was well aware. He did not take avoiding action, brake or conduct himself as any reasonable, sensible motorcyclist would do in such circumstances. This was partly attributable to the fact that he was just under the alcohol limit. The car driver was also to blame because he could and should have seen the motorcycle approaching fast on his offside as he made his decision to overtake. The Court of Appeal found the trial judge's reasoning and apportionment of 50/50 unassailable.

In *Pell v Moseley*,[8] P was riding his motorcycle along a single carriageway road and sought to overtake a line of three cars, the foremost of which was M. As he did so M turned right to enter a field where a motocross event was taking place and an accident occurred. The trial judge found M 100% liable, holding that she failed to keep a proper look out before executing her turn and that her indication was too late to be of any warning to P, who was executing a safe overtaking manoeuvre within the speed limit on a straight stretch of road and who did not see any indicator. The Court of Appeal apportioned liability 50/50 on the basis that M was at fault for failing to look in her mirror and for indicating late. Also P was liable because he was aware of the motocross event and therefore:

---

[7]    [2002] EWCA Civ 1557, CA (Tuckey and Latham LJJ, Sir Denis Henry) 21 October 2002.

[8]    [2003] EWCA Civ 1533 (Hale, Kay LJJ).

'the judge was bound to ask himself whether, even if there was no indication given with the indicator, there was none the less sufficient material available to the motorcyclist as he rode along for him to realise not merely the possibility that a vehicle was turning right, but the real chance that that was what was happening. I think the only conclusion that one can reach is that the way in which the car was being driven at that point was inconsistent with it simply intending to go straight along the road and anyone behind ought to have been alert to the real possibility that the vehicle would have turned right.' (Kay LJ, paragraph 31)

The court found it impossible to distinguish between the parties' respective faults.

## 8.4.1   Overtaking cyclists and horses

Rule 163 cautions drivers to give cyclists and horses as much room as they would a car when overtaking.

### *Cyclists*

Rule 163 was echoed in *Henry v Santam Insurance Co Ltd*[9] where a motorist was overtaking a cyclist. It was held that he should have allowed for some lateral movement on the part of the cyclist, particularly when the road surface was loose or uneven.

This rule does not mean that cyclists are absolved from blame if they ride in an unpredictable manner and make late turns as they are being overtaken. In *Clark v Wakelin* (Roskill J)[10] the claimant cyclist glanced over his shoulder when on the nearside of the road, put out his right hand, turned across the road and was run into on the crown of the road by the passing defendant motorcyclist. The defendant said that a car had already overtaken the cyclist and that he (the defendant) was about to overtake when the cyclist signalled and pulled out without giving the defendant the chance to avoid the accident. Roskill J said that a driver was entitled to assume that he could overtake without danger if what he was overtaking gave not the slightest sign that it was going to do something other than what an ordinary careful motorcyclist or motorist might expect. The defendant never had a chance of avoiding the accident, for which the claimant was solely to blame.

### *Horses*

Overtaking horses must not be done at speed or too close. If the driver is too close then liability may follow for the horse becoming spooked.

---

[9]   1971 SC 371.
[10]   (1965) 109 Sol Jo 296.

So in *Umphray v Ganson Bros*,[11] a car that injured a led horse when attempting to overtake it was liable when he had not given as much space as possible and had not slowed down sufficiently.

Where a driver seeks to overtake a horse being ridden on a path beside a narrow road, the driver of a vehicle must exercise great caution in passing it; his duty is to slow down and give the horse a wide berth. If he cannot do that because another vehicle is coming from the other direction, then he should wait: see *Burns v Ellicott*.[12] The defendant had brushed the horse, which took fright and reared, resulting in its hoofs being crushed under the front bumper of the defendant's car.

In such cases one should note that a horse rider is not under any absolute duty to prevent the horse from going out of control while it is being properly ridden on a highway: see *Haimes v Watson*.[13] The defendant motorist was overtaking a horse ridden on the highway by the claimant. The horse shied and moved suddenly to the right and the car collided with it. Judgment was given in the defendant's favour upon the basis that fault must attach to a rider who fails sufficiently to control the horse to prevent such a sudden movement. The Court of Appeal allowed the claimant's appeal. Whilst it was incumbent upon the claimant to provide an explanation for the horse's sudden movement, the defendant had to prove negligence and the explanation given had been sufficient to negative any inference of negligence.

Likewise in *Carryfast Ltd v Hack*[14] the defendant, an experienced horsewoman, was riding her horse along a narrow verge adjacent to a main road. The claimant's van was being driven at 30mph. He did not reduce his speed. When the van was close, the horse began to dance or frisk and the driver veered away from the nearside into an oncoming lorry. The defendant admitted that her horse was nervous in traffic but that she could usually keep it under control. The defendant was not held liable in negligence. The sole cause of the accident was the driver's failure initially to slow down, give clearance to the horse and stop if necessary. There may be negligence if there was a reasonable risk of a horse going out of control but no negligence simply for taking a nervous horse on to the highway.

Liability for animals is discussed in detail in Chapter 21.

### 8.4.2   Overtaking large vehicles

The common sense in the guidance on this manoeuvre needs no commentary.

---

[11]   1917 SC 371.
[12]   (1969) 113 Sol Jo 490 (Paull J).
[13]   [1981] RTR 90, CA (Lawton, Templeman, O'Connor LJJ).
[14]   [1981] RTR 464 (Ralph Gibson J).

Rule 164 of the Highway Code provides:

> '**164** Large vehicles. Overtaking these is more difficult. You should
> - drop back. This will increase your ability to see ahead and should allow the driver of the large vehicle to see you in their mirrors. Getting too close to large vehicles, including agricultural vehicles such as a tractor with a trailer or other fixed equipment, will obscure your view of the road ahead and there may be another slow-moving vehicle in front
> - make sure that you have enough room to complete your overtaking manoeuvre before committing yourself. It takes longer to pass a large vehicle. If in doubt do not overtake
> - not assume you can follow a vehicle ahead which is overtaking a long vehicle. If a problem develops, they may abort overtaking and pull back in.

### 8.4.3   Overtaking a line of stationary traffic and related situations

When one party (usually a motorbike) overtakes stationary traffic and comes into collision with another party emerging from a side road the law is complicated. These cases often involve allegations against a vehicle in the line of traffic for encouraging the emerging vehicle to proceed, by waving or flashing his lights. A delicate examination of the facts of each case is required.

The leading case is *Powell v Moody*,[15] in which the claimant motorcyclist overtook a double line of stationary vehicles and suffered an accident when a car came out of a side road. There was a gap in the line of traffic where the side road was and a milk tanker driver beckoned the defendant car driver to come out. The defendant intended to turn right onto the main road and when doing so struck the overtaking claimant. The judge held the claimant motorcyclist 80% to blame and the car driver 20% to blame. The claimant's appeal was dismissed. Sellers LJ said that any road user who jumped a queue of stationary vehicles by going on the offside of a line of stationary vehicles in front of him was undertaking an operation 'fraught with great hazard'. Such an operation had to be carried out with great care because it was always difficult to see the side road gaps from the offside of a queue of stationary vehicles. Danckwerts LJ agreed. But Salmon LJ would have found both drivers equally to blame.

In *Clarke v Winchurch*[16] a car that was parked against the direction of traffic indicated to pull out to travel in the direction that he was facing, thereby needing to cross the lane of oncoming traffic. A bus driver flashed and the car proceeded to pull in front of the bus so that the front of his vehicle protruded by a yard. At the same time, not seen by the bus driver, the claimant moped driver overtook the bus and struck the car. The trial judge found the claimant (overtaking moped rider) two-thirds to blame,

---

[15]   (1966) 110 Sol Jo 215 CA (Sellers, Danckwerts and Salmon LJJ).
[16]   [1969] 1 WLR 69 CA (Phillimore, Wilmer and Russell LJJ).

the bus driver one-third and allocated no responsibility to the car driver. The Court of Appeal changed the apportionment (Russell LJ dissenting) ruling that the claimant was 100% to blame. Phillimore LJ agreed with the trial judge's reasoning for the claimant being substantially to blame:

'If you have a small vehicle like a bicycle or motor cycle, you are in the fortunate position of taking up so little road space that you can slide along the offside, but if you choose to do this, it does seem to me to warrant a very, very high degree of care indeed because you are blinded, to a great extent, to what goes on on the left-hand side of the road.'

He also ruled that when the claimant saw the bus stopped in between regular stops he ought to have realised that there was something going on in front of it. The bus driver's signal to the car driver meant only 'Come on so far as I am concerned' and he could not be criticised for not seeing the claimant. The majority would not interfere with the trial judge's finding that the car driver did all that he could do in proceeding very slowly. Russell LJ, dissenting, would have held the car driver 20% to blame on the basis that he should have only emerged by one foot past the bus before stopping. This case illustrates how difficult these liability situations are.

In *Worsford v Howe*[17] the trial judge absolved a driver of any blame in circumstances not dissimilar to *Clarke v Winchurch* (above). A motorcyclist was overtaking stationary tankers and a car driver relied on the hand signal of one of the tanker drivers to pull across the queue of traffic to continue his journey. The Court of Appeal held that *Clarke* laid down no principle of law and liability should have been apportioned 50/50. This is the apportionment which the trial judge would have found had he not thought Clarke binding on him and absolved the car driver. Browne LJ held:

'It seems to me that the actual decision in [*Clarke*] was simply that this court saw no sufficient reason for disagreeing with the finding of the trial judge that the car driver was not to any extent to blame.'

In *Hillman v Tompkins*,[18] the claimant motorcyclist was overtaking slow moving traffic held up by temporary traffic lights. The defendant car driver reached a turning on her off side that she wished to take. She signalled and, having failed to see the motorcyclist, turned right and into collision with the claimant. The claimant alleged that the defendant started her turn from the line of traffic whereas the defendant said that she was established at the crown of the road and visible. The judge preferred the claimant's version of events, but also found that the defendant was travelling at 30–40mph at or near the centre of the

---

[17]  [1980] 1 WLR 1175, [1980] 1 ALL ER 1028, CA (Megaw, Browne and Donaldson LJJ).
[18]  (Unreported) 22 February 1995, CA (Simon Brown, Ward LJJ) but digested in *Bingham's*.

opposite carriageway in an overtaking position. He found the parties equally to blame. The defendant's appeal was dismissed:

> 'undesirable as it may be, motorcyclists do and can be expected to overtake in circumstances of this kind and in my judgment the defendant was negligent in failing to see the plaintiff as he approached.'

A higher standard of care was expected of the claimant because he was overtaking slow or stationary traffic and approaching a road junction. He was travelling too fast to discharge that standard of care.

Similar issues arose in the following two cases, although they did not involve a line of stationary traffic.

In *Garston Warehousing Co Ltd v O F Smart (Liverpool) Ltd*,[19] a car driver sought to cross a one way main road at a cross roads. A bus was stopped on the main road and the bus driver flashed his headlights at the car because no traffic was about to overtake him. The car came out very slowly and carefully. As he was crossing, the bus driver saw in his mirror the side lights of an approaching overtaking van; sounding his horn, he indicated right and gave a slowing down hand signal to the van. The van collided with the car, which had almost crossed the main road. The judge found that the car driver should have halted immediately after passing the bonnet of the bus, to give a warning of his presence. Because he did not he was held one-third liable. The van was driving at an excessive speed in the circumstances and should have seen the bus driver's signals and the front of the car and was held two-thirds liable. The Court of Appeal refused to interfere with the apportionment. Cairns LJ said that he did not think that *Clarke v Winchurch* laid down any principal of law as to whether or not there was negligence in not stopping when emerging.

In *HL Motorworks (Willesden) Ltd v Alwahbi*,[20] a car driver was held entitled to emerge from a side road as far as the centre line into a main road in response to a signal from one of two stationary cars to his right without having to wait until the road was completely clear in both directions. He was entitled to assume that no vehicle would overtake two stationary cars side by side. Contrary to the finding of the trial judge who apportioned liability equally, the Court of Appeal held that the side road car driver was not negligent but the defendant overtaking car driver, on the wrong side of the road, thereby forming a third lane of traffic, was entirely to blame for the accident.

There are few general principles which we can discern from the case law other than the normal advice that each case turns on its facts.

---

[19]  [1973] RTR 377 (Buckley and Cairns LJJ and MacKenna J).
[20]  [1977] RTR 276 CA (Cairns, Roskill and Bridge LJJ).

## 8.5  BEING OVERTAKEN

The Highway Code gives some guidance to those being overtaken.

Rules 168–169 of the Highway Code provide:

> '**168** Being overtaken. If a driver is trying to overtake you, maintain a steady course and speed, slowing down if necessary to let the vehicle pass. Never obstruct drivers who wish to pass. Speeding up or driving unpredictably while someone is overtaking you is dangerous. Drop back to maintain a two-second gap if someone overtakes and pulls into the gap in front of you.'

> '**169** Do not hold up a long queue of traffic, especially if you are driving a large or slow-moving vehicle. Check your mirrors frequently, and if necessary, pull in where it is safe and let traffic pass.'

Examples of drivers who did not follow this guidance are given below.

In *Miliken v Glasgow Cpn*,[21] a passenger on a tramway car was injured when there was a collision between the tram and a lorry it was overtaking. As the tram overtook and had almost passed a horse-drawn lorry laden with timber the impact occurred. The tramway car was held to have been proceeding carefully and at moderate speed. There was no evidence of any lateral movement on the part of the lorry. It was held that the collision must have been caused by the movement of the lorry and, absent any explanation, it was deemed to have been caused by negligence on the part of the lorryman.

In *Holdack v Bullock Bros (Electrical) Ltd*,[22] a van driver was found negligent when he changed course without warning and struck a scooter driver who had begun to overtake him. The scooter driver was negligent in overtaking without sounding his hooter. The van driver was found two-thirds and the scooter driver one-third liable.

Should the driver being overtaken help the driver overtaking? In *Smith v Cribben*[23] two cars were driving in adjacent lanes of a dual carriageway. C sought to overtake S before the road became a single carriageway but was unable to complete her overtaking manoeuvre in time, lost control and collided with traffic coming in the opposite direction. C alleged that S deliberately accelerated and decelerated to prevent her from completing an otherwise safe overtaking manoeuvre. The trial judge rejected the contention that there had been deliberate prevention of the overtaking manoeuvre, but held that there was negligence in accelerating or continuing at a steady speed rather than easing up or braking. The judge

---

[21]   1918 SC 857 Court of Session.
[22]   (1964) 108 Sol Jo 861 (Hinchcliffe J).
[23]   [1994] PIQR 218, CA (Dillon, Nolan and Roch LJJ).

found C 75% and S 25% liable. On appeal, S (the car being overtaken) was absolved of any responsibility. According to Roch LJ, S was entitled to say:

> 'Any overtaking driver could see my course and speed, could see the road markings and drive his or her vehicle accordingly. Once I start to vary my speed then the risk of collision between my car and the other vehicle is increased.'

Roch LJ further asked whether there was any obligation to watch the rear view mirror so that a driver can slow down so that the car approaching from the rear will not be overtaking at a place of danger and said that:

> 'In my judgment, that places too high a duty on the reasonable driver. The onus upon the driver in [S's] situation is to drive normally at a proper speed and on a proper course. The ordinary reasonable driver is not to be expected to anticipate that the following driver will drive dangerously and to extricate that driver from the dangerous situation that driver creates. In this case, the evidence indicated that [C] had not merely created a dangerous situation but then persisted in it by choosing what was, in my view, an obviously dangerous course of trying to go still faster and complete the overtaking before the dual carriageway ran out.'

Double overtaking is obviously a very hazardous manoeuvre and the courts grant little sympathy when accidents occur as a result. In *Irwin v Stevenson*,[24] the Court of Appeal reversed the trial judge's finding that a tractor driver was negligent in turning right into a field when a collision was caused with a motorcyclist seeking to overtake a van and the tractor sequentially. The judge accepted that the driver had checked his mirror, signalled and then manoeuvred. The judge held that a prudent driver would have looked in his mirror or over his shoulder immediately before manoeuvring and that the motorbike was there to be seen. The motorcyclist was held 50% contributorily negligent by the trial judge for performing a double overtaking manoeuvre of two slowing vehicles, one of which was indicating. The Court of Appeal reasoned from the evidence that the tractor driver had started his manoeuvre before the motorcyclist emerged from behind the van. He had no reason to anticipate that a motorbike would come from behind in a double overtaking manoeuvre and that the rider would fail to see his signal. The driver could not be criticised for concentrating on his manoeuvre once he had begun to turn. In reality, the motorcyclist was 'there to be seen' for too short a time for the tractor driver to have been able to take any avoiding action. Potter LJ (paragraph 18):

> 'the defendant, having indicated his intentions and slowed down in circumstances when the vehicle behind was similarly slowing to allow him to

---

[24] [2002] EWCA Civ 359 (Potter LJ, Sir Anthony Evans), Lawtel AC9900308.

make his turn, should not be regarded as negligent for failing to guard against the possibility of a vehicle appearing at the last moment in a double overtaking manoeuvre.'

What about overtaken drivers who accelerate to avoid being overtaken? In *Ogden & Chadwick v Barber & Higgs*,[25] two motorcyclists, B and O were following a car driven by H. B attempted to overtake H, but H accelerated to prevent the overtake. B therefore decelerated and tucked in behind H. Not put off, B then attempted to overtake again and H again accelerated to prevent the same, whereupon B sought to decelerate and tuck in behind H but was prevented from doing so by H decelerating. As a result, B remained on the wrong side of the road, across the solid white line, over the brow of a hill where there was a slight left bend and he could not avoid riding into collision with C, a motorcyclist who was riding in the opposite direction. O then had a collision with B's motorcycle. The trial judge found H (the car being overtaken) 80% to blame and B (the overtaker) 20% to blame in respect of claims brought by C and O. He ruled that once B realised that H was not going to let him pass he really should not have made the second attempt. H appealed the apportionment and criticised the lack of reasoning given for it. The Court of Appeal affirmed the decision, Rix LJ stating:

> '[H's] driving was truly very, very bad indeed . . . a very serious piece of bad driving on the judge's findings. It was, moreover, a deliberate attempt to keep a motorcyclist on the wrong side of the road approaching a blind brow and bend in the road. On the other hand, [B's] fault was the comparatively less serious and merely negligent as distinct from deliberate fault of attempting any overtaking manoeuvre at all, albeit, on [B's] evidence, which the judge accepted, it started well before the white line . . .'

The Court of Appeal reminded parties that it seldom interferes with issues of apportionment, but hinted that the 20% attribution to B may have been less than some judges would have found.

---

[25]  [2008] EWCA Civ 1113 (Sir Anthony Clarke MR, Rix LJ, Sir Robin Auld).

# CHAPTER 9

# DRIVER'S LIABILITY: TURNING AND SIDE ROADS

*Aileen Downey*

## 9.1   INTRODUCTION

Many road traffic accidents occur as a result of turning into or out of side roads. The process should be easy but the risks and dangers arise because the drivers involved do not look carefully enough or do not judge the speeds and distances involved accurately so that they come into contact.

As with all road traffic cases common sense lies at the heart of the rules governing when and how to turn and to whom the drivers should give way.

## 9.2   THE HIGHWAY CODE

In the Highway Code (2007), rules 179–183 govern turning. They are set out below.

### 'Turning right

**179** Well before you turn right you should
- use your mirrors to make sure you know the position and movement of traffic behind you
- give a right-turn signal
- take up a position just left of the middle of the road or in the space marked for traffic turning right
- leave room for other vehicles to pass on the left, if possible

**180** Wait until there is a safe gap between you and any oncoming vehicle. Watch out for cyclists, motorcyclists, pedestrians and other road users. Check your mirrors and blind spot again to make sure you are not being overtaken, then make the turn. Do not cut the corner. Take great care when turning into a main road; you will need to watch for traffic in both directions and wait for a safe gap.

Remember: Mirrors – Signal – Manoeuvre

**181** When turning right at crossroads where an oncoming vehicle is also turning right, there is a choice of two methods

- turn right side to right side; keep the other vehicle on your right and turn behind it. This is generally the safer method as you have a clear view of any approaching traffic when completing your turn
- left side to left side, turning in front of each other. This can block your view of oncoming vehicles, so take extra care. Cyclists and motorcyclists in particular may be hidden from your view. Road layout, markings or how the other vehicle is positioned can determine which course should be taken

**Turning left**

**182** Use your mirrors and give a left-turn signal well before you turn left. Do not overtake just before you turn left and watch out for traffic coming up on your left before you make the turn, especially if driving a large vehicle. Cyclists, motorcyclists and other road users in particular may be hidden from your view.

**183** When turning
- keep as close to the left as is safe and practicable
- give way to any vehicles using a bus lane, cycle lane or tramway from either direction.'

It can be seen from the above rules that other than the need to indicate, the requirements focus on keeping a proper look out and judging speed and distances so as to avoid inconveniencing other road users.

## 9.3 EMERGING FROM A SIDE ROAD – THE 'SIDE ROAD' RULE

When turning out of a minor road the general rule is that the onus is on the emerging driver to ensure that there is a safe gap in the traffic on the main road in both directions before pulling out. If the emerging driver pulls out when another vehicle is too close for comfort then, generally, he bears the liability for the ensuing accident.

## 9.4 IMPACT WITH OVERTAKING VEHICLES:

For example in *Harding v Hinchcliffe*[1] C was riding a motorcycle along a main road. Ahead of him was a bus travelling in the same direction. The bus signalled to turn left into a minor road, and C overtook the bus as it was turning. D emerged from the minor road in front of the turning bus and collided with C. Neither C or D had seen each other before the impact. At first instance D was found to be wholly to blame. D's appeal was dismissed, and the Court of Appeal found that D had a duty when emerging from a minor road, to wait the extra few seconds to let the bus turn completely into the side road, because there was always a possibility of vehicles travelling behind it, which were masked by the bus.

---

[1]   (1964) *The Times*, April 8, CA.

This 'side road' rule often interacts with other rules, usually those governing overtaking and when it does the accidents involved lead to difficult assessments of responsibility. So cars and motorcycles on a main road must take care when overtaking slow moving or stationary vehicles near side roads because of the risk of emerging drivers.

The overtaking driver was found to blame in the leading case of *Clarke v Winchurch*.[2] D1 was parked on a main road (facing the wrong way against the traffic for the side of the road he was parked on) and wished to emerge from his parking space. He intended to cross the nearest lane of the road (which was oncoming) and travel in the direction in which he was facing. He pulled slightly out with his indicator flashing and a bus driver, D3 (employed by D2) who was travelling towards D1, stopped to let him out. The bus driver looked in his rear mirror, saw nothing coming on his offside and flashed his lights at D1. So the parked car, taking that as an invitation, pulled out in front of the bus and proceeded towards the opposite side of the road. As the front of his car was about a yard beyond the offside of the bus, P (a moped driver who was overtaking the bus) collided with D1. P sued D1, D2 and D3. At first instance the judge found P two-thirds to blame, D3 (the bus driver) one-third and D1 not to blame at all. The judge said that D1 (the parked car) had been just crawling out and was not to blame. On appeal by the bus driver, the Court of Appeal allowed the appeal and found the moped driver wholly to blame because he was overtaking (a very hazardous manoeuvre in stationary traffic) and should have anticipated that something was emerging in front of the bus.

It was held:

(1) that, on the facts, the bus driver, by flashing his lights, meant only "Come on so far as I am concerned," and since he had not seen the plaintiff about to pass him, he was under no duty of care either to the plaintiff or the first defendant and should be acquitted of any negligence in the matter.

(2) (Russell LJ dissenting) That the judge's findings indicated that the first defendant had proceeded slowly and carefully and the suggestion that he should have stopped when the bonnet of his car was protruding only a foot in front of the bus was a counsel of perfection; that in all the circumstances there was no ground for interfering.'

It should be noted that Russell LJ (dissenting) would have found D1 20% to blame, but the Court was unwilling to interfere with the apportionment of liability in relation to D1, given the judge's finding that D1 had come out very, very slowly. So the rules governing pulling out and turning interact with the rules governing overtaking in a subtle way.

---

[2]    [1969] 1 All ER 275, [1969] 1 WLR 69, CA.

However, on different facts the Court of Appeal allowed the 'side road' rule as much strength as the 'overtaking rule' in *Worsfold v Howe*.[3] D was intending to turn right from a minor road, onto the far side, the southbound lane, of a major road. A large tanker stopped (due to heavy traffic) in the northbound lane, leaving a gap and D emerged in front of the tanker proceeding to cross the northbound lane en route to the southbound lane. As the front of D's vehicle emerged beyond the tanker, C, a motorcyclist who was overtaking the tanker, and riding within the northbound lane, collided with D. The trial judge considered C and D equally to blame, on the basis that C was travelling too fast and that D proceeded past the tanker when he could not see. The judge said that despite his own view he was bound by *Clarke v Winchurch* to find that he had to give judgment in favour of D and thereby found C wholly to blame. On appeal by C, the Court of Appeal allowed C's appeal and found D equally to blame.

The Court of Appeal held that *Clarke v Winchurch* laid down no principle of law but was a decision on its own facts so that the judge erred in law in considering himself to be bound by it; that accordingly liability should be apportioned on the basis of the view that the judge originally formed on hearing the evidence, namely, that each party was 50 per cent. to blame. (*Garston Warehousing Co Ltd v O F Smart (Liverpool) Ltd* [1973] RTR 377, CA applied.)

Clearly if the overtaking vehicle on the main road is on the wrong side of the road he will open himself up to potential liability. So in *Dowling v Dargue*[4] D was turning right onto a major road from a minor road. P was on a motorcycle on the main road and was overtaking traffic which had stopped to let D emerge. The front wheel of P's motorcycle hit the front offside door/wing of D's motor vehicle. The trial judge found that(i) P was travelling at 10 mph on the opposite side of the road; (ii) that the accident occurred on the opposite side of the road to P's direction of travel and within the zig zagged area of a pelican crossing; and (iii) D was travelling faster than edging or inching out. P was found to be 80% to blame and D 20%.

Whether or not the emerging side road driver is to be regarded as always to blame or as 'the insurer' for any accident involving overtaking drivers, was considered in *Farley v Buckley*[5] F was driving along a main road, intending to overtake a long wagon travelling in the same direction. The wagon was indicating left and was slowing down and preparing to turn into the side road, thereby creating a gap in the traffic in front of it. As the wagon slowed down, B began to emerge from the said side road, intending to turn right onto the main road. As B emerged beyond the front offside of the wagon, F was completing the overtaking manoeuvre and collided

3    [1980] 1 WLR 1175, CA.
4    (1997) CLY 3769.
5    [2007] EWCA Civ 403, CA.

with B. At trial, the judge found that B had been moving continuously at 5–8mph and that F had been travelling at a speed of 30mph which was reckless, particularly as he could not see to his left past the turning truck when he knew there was a side road to the left. She ruled that despite the finding that the side road driver had not been 'nose-poking' or edging forward bit by bit did not amount to negligence. The overtaking driver was entirely to blame. The Court of Appeal considered that the real issue was as follows:

> 'Was it negligent of B to effect a continuous movement rather than to nose-poke?'

The Court of Appeal ruled that given the short space between the offside of the wagon and the centre of the road, the difference between nose-poking and slow continuous movement was too slight to be of relevance. On the facts the judge was entitled to find that B was not negligent and that F had been reckless whilst overtaking. So here once again the 'overtaking rule' trumped the 'side road' rule. Perhaps the most helpful guidance from this case comes from Pill LJ who noted that it was difficult to see how the judge found that B had proceeded slowly and cautiously when she had also found that B had emerged from a minor road at a speed of 5–8 mph and had been moving continuously. He warned that this case:

> 'was not authority for the proposition that emerging from a minor road at 5–8 mph was an acceptable manoeuvre.'

Nor should it be seen as authority for the proposition that an emerging driver's failure to nose-poke will always avoid a finding of negligence. However, stopping whilst only a few feet out may save the side road driver from liability: an example of this advice is seen in *Bramley v Pipes*.[6] Here the main road driver was going at an excessive speed on a slippery road with good visibility. He collided with the side road driver. The main road driver was held to have been entirely responsible for the accident because the side road driver had barely emerged from a turning before stopping. The detailed facts were that P was a rear seat passenger in a car being driven by the D2. D2 was a young inexperienced driver. There had been an overnight frost and some mud was present on the road leading to potentially slippery conditions in respect of which the local council had erected warning signs. D1 approached from a minor road intending to turn left onto the main road. He stopped the car and looked in both directions. He saw D2 approaching from his right along the main road about 300 metres away and began his manoeuvre. D2 was travelling faster than D1 had estimated and D1 abruptly stopped. At this point the front wheel was just over the give way line marking on the minor road. The major road comprised two carriageways each about 10 feet wide and D1's car did not extend more than about half way into the carriageway. D2

---

6   (Unreported) 29 April 1998, CA.

swerved round D1's car and braked. D2 lost control of the car and P was seriously injured. At first instance the judge apportioned liability 80% to D2 and 20% to D1. D1 appealed successfully. On appeal it was held that:

(1)     The relevant act on which the judge concluded that D1 had been negligent was to allow his car to come into a position where it became stationary with its front wheel on the give way marking. This had been done on a straight road with good visibility after D1 had checked.

(2)     It was harsh to conclude that D1 had acted negligently in mistaking the speed of a car approaching from 300 metres away.

(3)     In view of the distance D1 had pulled out into a straight road with good visibility, it could not be said that he had created a hazard or an obstacle. Any car approaching would not have been presented with any difficulty.

(4)     Since there had been no hazard D1 had not contributed causally, at law, to the accident (although his presence may have been part of the surrounding circumstances).

(5)     The cause of the accident was fully explained by the conduct of D2 who was entirely responsible. This was a seriously inexperienced driver driving at excessive speed under the conditions with a flawed attitude as to safety.

## 9.5    IMPACT WITH SPEEDING VEHICLES ON THE MAIN ROAD

How does the 'side road' rule interact with cars which are speeding on the main road? Clearly if there is evidence that the main road drivers were speeding, and that that speed, contributed to the accident, it is likely that they will be held to be partly to blame. The usual apportionment is 20–25% on the shoulders of the main road driver.

In *Hamied v Estwick*,[7] the claimant was travelling along a wide open road (30mph speed limit), and as he approached a junction with a minor road on his left, D emerged from that side road, intending to turn right onto the main road. A collision occurred, where the front of D's vehicle collided with the nearside of C's car from about half way down to the rear of the car. C could not remember the accident and D was the only eyewitness. His evidence varied as to whether he emerged and then paused, or whether he pulled out slowly. At first instance the judge concluded that D was plainly negligent in the way he emerged from the minor road, but also found that C was partly to blame as he had been

---

[7]     (Unreported) 1 November 1994, CA.

travelling at a speed of 35–40mph. The main road driver had thereby failed to give himself an opportunity to stop/avoid the accident. There was no evidence that C had braked. The judge found C 20% to blame. C (the main road driver) appealed that finding, urging the Court of Appeal to find that driving at a slightly faster speed than the limit on a wide open road with good visibility was not itself negligent and that a driver on such a main road was not obliged to drive on the assumption that drivers on side roads might emerge. The Court of Appeal dismissed the appeal holding that they could not interfere with the trial judge's finding and that by driving faster than he should have done, C deprived himself of the time and opportunity to take evasive action.

This decision seems a little harsh on the main road driver but it is a fine example of how the side road rule, whilst dominant, did not exclude contributory negligence by other drivers.

In *Dolby v Milner*,[8] D was turning right onto a main road and should have given way. M was travelling along the main road in excess of the speed limit and failed to take evasive action. At first instance M (the main road driver) was found 75% to blame and D (the side road driver) 25% to blame. On appeal by M, the Court of Appeal stated that the main road driver was visible to D from 95 yards away and D should have seen M. Thus the apportionment was reversed and the side road driver was found mainly to blame (75%).

In *Paul Farrah Sound Ltd v Rookledge*,[9] S was driving on a minor road and turned right onto a main road. M was travelling at excessive speed towards S on the main road. A collision occurred. Liability was apportioned by agreement 75% against S and 25% against M.

In *Smith v Goss*,[10] S was emerging from a side road onto a main road and a collision occurred with M who was proceeding along the main road. S was found to be 70% to blame, while M was 30% to blame. S's appeal asserting that that M was more blameworthy was dismissed. It was held that S owed a high degree of duty as he was emerging from a side road.

We mentioned the braking and skidding rule in the previous chapter and the side road rule does interact with this. So in *Downes v Crane(1) and Villers(2)*[11] the claimant was driving along when the second defendant (D2), travelling in the opposite direction, turned right from a minor road into the path of D1. D1 braked but skidded out of control and collided with D2 and then collided head on with C on C's side of the road. At first instance the judge found that D2 was wholly to blame (the side road rule).

---

[8]   (1996) CLY 4430.
[9]   (1996) CLY 4431.
[10]  (1996) CLY 4432.
[11]  (Unreported) 13 December 1999, CA.

D2 appealed on the basis that D1 was equally to blame. The Court of Appeal considered that the judge should have asked himself whether D1:

> 'was a sufficient distance away that a reasonable driver, keeping a proper look-out, with full attention on the road ahead . . .. would have been able to brake without losing control of his vehicle?'

The Court of Appeal found when considering the circumstances of the accident that D1 should have been keeping a proper look-out such that he could have braked without skidding and found him 25% to blame and D2 75% to blame.

All cases such as this are fact-sensitive but in general emerging drivers should exercise great care and very slow nose-poking should avoid liability for an impact with an overreacting driver.

## 9.6   ANTICIPATING SIDE ROAD DRIVERS EMERGING

We have already seen above that drivers proceeding along major roads must also drive responsibly and carefully, particularly as they approach junctions with side roads or crossroads. The case law above seems to show that considerable responsibility is laid at the door of main road drivers. They are expected to anticipate the movements of minor road drivers including negligent movements. However, more recent cases suggest that this responsibility has been diluted, perhaps in response to roads becoming busier, and the need to keep traffic moving. So once again it can be said that the 'side road' rule is growing in strength and main road drivers are not required to drive with an 'abundance of caution'.

To see the emergence of the strengthening of the side road rule and the loosening of the main road driver's responsibility see the following cases starting in 1957.

In *Lang v London Transport Executive*,[12] a bus travelled along a main road at a speed of no more than 20mph, approaching a junction with a minor road. The bus driver noticed cyclists on the minor road and the cyclists drove straight out onto the main road ignoring a 'Slow, Major Road ahead' sign. A collision occurred. In considering the question: 'was the possibility of danger reasonably apparent (to the bus driver)?', the judge noted that the bus driver said in evidence that he knew from experience that sometimes persons would emerge from a side road, even when it was not prudent; it seems that the Court found that the bus driver had failed to take reasonable care for the safety of other traffic on the road because of that. The trial judge found him one-third to blame, with the emerging cyclist two-thirds to blame.

---

[12]   [1959] 1 WLR 1168.

In our view this was an unduly punitive finding against the bus driver.

In *William v Fullerton*[13] the side road motorist who emerged at an 'excessive speed' was found to be largely to blame (75%) and the driver on the main road was found also to have contributed to the accident, to the tune of 25%, because he failed to keep a proper look out. He did not see the emerging driver, who crossed the major road at between 30–60mph! This decision has unsurprisingly subsequently been questioned in *Humphrey v Leigh* (see below).

Reaching the 1970s, in *Walsh v Redfern*[14] a car was being driven fast along a side road approaching a T-junction. A lorry was driving along the main road and slowed as he approached the junction, noticing the headlights of the car on the side road, although he could not estimate the speed of the car. The car emerged from the side road into the path of the lorry without altering his speed and a collision occurred. It was agreed that the car driver was to blame but the Court found that the lorry driver was not negligent in any way. On appeal Lyell LJ considered the decision in *Lang*, and at 203 held that:

> 'If the driver on the major road can see, from the way the other driver (on a minor road) is proceeding, that he is not going to give way, it is the duty of the main road driver, to give way if he can, and so avoid an accident.'

In the later case of *Truscott v Mclaren*[15] Latey J considered that this case reflected the correct approach in such cases.

Then in 1971 a real strengthening of the side road rule occurred in *Humphrey v Leigh*[16] where it was held that a driver on a main road had no duty when driving along a main road to slow down and prepare to brake, so as to be ready in case a vehicle emerged suddenly from a side road. The facts were that D2 was driving at a proper speed, keeping a proper look out, approaching a side road junction when D1 emerged from the side road at a speed of 20mph without stopping and a collision occurred. P, who was standing nearby, was injured and sued. The judge found D1 entirely to blame and the Court of Appeal agreed, dismissing D1's appeal.

We accept that no duty is owed by a main road driver to a side road driver whilst driving along the main road within the speed limit and before the side road driver emerges. So there is no duty to slow down at that time. The same cannot be said for a main road driver who sees a side road driver come out. Once the clear danger is presenting itself the main road driver comes under a duty to do his best to avoid the damage. So it is clear from *Walsh v Redfern* and some of the following cases that a main road

---

[13]   (1961) 105 Sol Jo 208.
[14]   [1970] RTR 201.
[15]   [1981] RTR 34, CA.
[16]   [1971] RTR 363.

driver cannot ignore 'emerging dangers' on the road ahead. But what about the driver who has not emerged but is going so fast that he is likely to emerge into the main road when it is not safe?

Coming to the 1980s, in *Truscott v Mclaren*[17] D2 was driving at 40mph along a main road approaching a crossroads. From 75 yards away D2 noticed D1 approaching the crossroads on a minor road at about 50–55mph. D2 carried on without altering his speed and D1 then failed to stop at the crossroads and collided with D2. P, who was standing nearby, was injured. The trial judge found that D2 (the main road driver) should have slowed down and prepared to brake and had he done so the accident would have been avoided. So D2 was found 20% to blame and D1 80% to blame. D2 appealed that finding. The Court of Appeal dismissed the appeal. Stephenson LJ concluded at page 42 that the trial judge:

> '... was entitled to find and indeed was right in finding that, at this crossroads, in the light of what D2 did see, or should have seen if he was keeping a proper lookout, of the way in which D1's car was approaching this crossroads, he should have taken the step which the Judge thought he should have taken, of easing up, taking his foot off the accelerator and covering the brake.If D2 had taken the precaution which, in my judgment was right to hold was a reasonable precaution in the circumstances, the collision would have been avoided and so would the accident to P.'

On some roads, there is confusion as to where priority lies.

In *McIntyre v Coles*[18] an accident had occurred at an unmarked and somewhat confusing Y-junction. A lorry driver was travelling towards an obvious turn to the right and indicated right on his approach. A motorcyclist was travelling in the opposite direction, and drove straight into the path of the lorry as it was turning towards the right hand junction. The motorcyclist was killed. The widow blamed the lorry driver, claiming that the deceased was on the 'main' road, and the lorry should have given way to the motorcyclist. The lorry driver claimed he had priority. At first instance the judge dismissed the widow's claim. On appeal the widow claimed that both the deceased and the lorry driver should be found equally liable. The Court of Appeal dismissed the appeal, while noting that the junction had been called a 'death trap' by the trial judge.

It was held, that, even without traffic signs, there was sufficient indication that the road on which the motor lorry was travelling had priority over the road from which the motor cyclist emerged; that, on the evidence, there was no negligence on the part of the lorry driver and accordingly the appeal must be dismissed.

---

[17]   [1982] RTR 34, CA.
[18]   [1966] 1 WLR 831.

Further it was noted that it is a well-recognised and conventional practice, rather than a rule, that where approaching vehicles are in risk of collision or where there is doubt as to priority, the vehicle which has the other on its right is the 'give-way' vehicle. It may not be established as obligatory but it is a very salutary guiding rule.

## 9.7 TURNING OFF A MAIN ROAD

As a general rule if a driver on a main road intends to turn right into a minor road, across oncoming traffic, it is incumbent upon that driver to ensure that he can execute the manoeuvre safely. This is the same as the side road rule.

So in *Simpson v Peat*[19] a prosecutor appealed to the Divisional Court after the Justices acquitted a defendant driver for committing an error of judgement, which they felt could not give rise to criminal culpability. The defendant had been travelling at a reasonable speed along a main road and had turned right across the path of oncoming traffic into a minor road. A collision had occurred with a motorcycle, which had been travelling in the opposite direction at a reasonable speed. The Justices felt that the defendant had made a simple error of judgement in thinking that there was sufficient room for the motorcycle to pass through and acquitted him on the basis that the defendant could not be guilty on the basis of an simple error of judgement. The Divisional Court remitted the matter to the Justices with a direction to convict because the defendant thought he had left room for traffic coming in the opposite direction to get through, when he had not in fact done so.

> 'The expression "error of judgment" is not a term of art; it is in fact one of the vaguest possible description: it can be used colloquially to describe either a negligent act or one which, though mistaken, is not negligent. When one is considering section 12, the marginal note of which is "careless driving", it is in our opinion clear that a driver may not be using due care and attention although his lack of care may be due to something which could be described as an error of judgment. If he is driving without due care and attention it is immaterial what caused him to do so. The question for the justices is: was the defendant exercising that degree of care and attention that a reasonable and prudent driver would exercise in the circumstances?'

Drivers on a main road should ensure that they do not overtake just before a side turn: so in *Challoner v Williams v Croney*[20] W was the first of a convoy of three cars on an unlit road. Having taken the wrong road W indicated right and moved to the centre of the road and began to turn right into a side road. He was half-way across when he was struck by C. C was travelling behind the other two cars in the convoy and had overtaken

---

[19]   [1952] 2 QB 24, [1952] 1 All ER 447.
[20]   [1975] 1 Lloyd's Rep 124, CA.

the two cars in front when he struck W. At trial the judge found both W and C equally to blame. On appeal C was found wholly to blame.

A recent case concerned cars travelling along a main road, in convoy. In *Hames v Ferguson & Others*[21] C was a back seat passenger in a car driven by F. W was driving another vehicle in convoy behind F's vehicle. Both cars were speeding. As they rounded a bend F collided with a tractor that was turning left into a field. W also collided with the tractor. C was injured. The judge found W 40% liable and F 60% liable. On appeal by W, the Court of Appeal dismissed the appeal and concluded that the judge was entitled to find that if both drivers were driving in close convoy at excessive speed down a country lane, and collided with a turning vehicle, each was bound to be distracting the other.

---

[21]  (Unreported) LTL 16/10/08.

# CHAPTER 10

## DRIVER'S LIABILITY: LIGHTING VEHICLES

*Laura Begley*

### 10.1  INTRODUCTION

This chapter is divided into two main sections, firstly dealing with the obligations of the motorist or vehicle user to light his vehicle and secondly dealing with the powers and limited obligations of the Highway Authority to light roads.

### 10.2  GENERAL OBLIGATION TO LIGHT A VEHICLE

The obligations of vehicle users to light their vehicles are specifically regulated by the Road Vehicle Lighting Regulations 1989[1] to which further reference will be made below. These Regulations are fairly supplemented and to a great extent duplicated by the provisions of the Highway Code in respect of the lighting of vehicles. There is a body of case law which pre-dates the 1989 Regulations and as a result of which general rules have evolved in relation to lighting of moving and stationary vehicles. As one might expect, there is a general rule that driving an unlit vehicle in the dark is prima facie evidence of negligence : see *Baker v E. Longhurst & Sons*.[2] The 1989 Regulations define the 'hours of darkness' at reg 3 as 'The time between half an hour after sunset and half an hour before sunrise.' This rule also applies where weather or other conditions seriously reduce visibility as set out below.

### 10.3  OBLIGATION TO LIGHT A MOVING VEHICLE

Generally speaking headlights should be used in the hours of darkness as defined above, or when visibility is seriously reduced for other reasons, for example weather conditions. The Highway Code provides at rule 113:

'You **MUST**
- ensure all sidelights and rear registration plate lights are lit between sunset and sunrise

---

[1]   SI 1989/1796.
[2]   [1933] 2 KB 461.

- use headlights at night, except on a road which has lit street lighting. These roads are generally restricted to a speed limit of 30 mph (48 km/h) unless otherwise specified
- use headlights when visibility is seriously reduced.'

Regulations 24 and 25 of the Road Vehicle Lighting Regulations 1989 deal with the basic requirement to light a moving vehicle. The rules provide a regime whereby dipped beam headlights are required to be used at all times on vehicles in motion between sunset and sunrise or in seriously reduced visibility, save where the vehicle is on a road with a speed limit of 30mph or less and is illuminated by street lighting (and is thereby a 'restricted road' under s 81 of the Road Traffic Regulation Act 1984). In these circumstances there is no statutory requirement to use headlights. When vehicles which fall under reg 24(7) (including most vehicles for domestic use), are parked they may be left unlit so long as they are legally parked on a road with a speed limit of 30mph or less (cf reg 24(5)). The lighting of parked vehicles is considered further at **10.4**. Regulations 24 and 25 provide:

**'24. Requirements about the use of front and rear position lamps, rear registration plate lamps, side marker lamps and end-outline marker lamps**

(1)    Save as provided in paragraphs (5) and (9), no person shall –
    (a)    use, or cause or permit to be used, on a road any vehicle which is in motion –
        (i)    between sunset and sunrise, or
        (ii)    in seriously reduced visibility between sunrise and sunset; or
    (b)    allow to remain at rest, or cause or permit to be allowed to remain at rest, on a road any vehicle between sunset and sunrise unless every front position lamp, rear position lamp, rear registration plate lamp, side marker lamp and end-outline marker lamp with which the vehicle is required by these Regulations to be fitted is kept lit and unobscured.
(5)    Paragraphs (1), (2), (3) and (4) shall not apply in respect of a vehicle of a class specified in paragraph (7) which is parked on a road on which a speed limit of 30 mph or less is in force and the vehicle is parked-
    (a)    in a parking place for which provision is made under section 6, or which is authorised under section 32 or designated under section 45 of the Road Traffic Regulation Act 1984, or which is set apart as a parking place under some other enactment or instrument and the vehicle is parked in a manner which does not contravene the provision of any enactment or instrument relating to the parking place; or . . .
(7)    The classes of vehicle referred to in paragraph (5) are –
    (a)    a motor vehicle being a goods vehicle the unladen weight of which does not exceed 1525 kg;
    (b)    a passenger vehicle other than a bus;
    (c)    an invalid carriage; and

    (d)    a motor cycle or a pedal cycle in either case with or without a sidecar;

not being –

    (i)    a vehicle to which a trailer is attached;

    (ii)    a vehicle which is required to be fitted with lamps by regulation 21; or

    (iii)    a vehicle carrying a load, if the load is required to be fitted with lamps by regulation 21.

(9)    Paragraphs (1), (2), (3) and (4) do not apply in respect of –

    (a)    a solo motor bicycle or a pedal cycle being pushed along the left-hand edge of a carriageway;

    (b)    a pedal cycle waiting to proceed provided it is kept to the left-hand or near side edge of a carriageway; or

    (c)    a vehicle which is parked in an area on part of a highway on which roadworks are being carried out and which is bounded by amber lamps and other traffic signs so as to prevent the presence of the vehicle, its load or equipment being a danger to persons using the road.

## 25 Requirements about the use of headlamps and front fog lamps

(1)    Save as provided in paragraph (2), no person shall use, or cause or permit to be used, on a road a vehicle which is fitted with obligatory dipped-beam headlamps unless every such lamp is kept lit –

    (a)    during the hours of darkness, except on a road which is a restricted road for the purposes of section 81 of the Road Traffic Regulation Act 1984 by virtue of a system of street lighting when it is lit; and

    (b)    in seriously reduced visibility.

(2)    The provisions of paragraph (1) do not apply –

    (a)    in the case of a motor vehicle fitted with one obligatory dipped-beam headlamp or a solo motor bicycle or motor bicycle combination fitted with a pair of obligatory dipped-beam headlamps, if a main-beam headlamp or a front fog lamp is kept lit;

    (b)    in the case of a motor vehicle, other than a solo motor bicycle or motor bicycle combination, fitted with a pair of obligatory dipped-beam headlamps, if –

    (i)    a pair of main-beam headlamps is kept lit; or

    (ii)    in seriously reduced visibility, a pair of front fog lamps which is so fitted that the outermost part of the illuminated area of each lamp in the pair is not more than 400 mm from the outer edge of the vehicle is kept lit;

    (c)    to a vehicle being drawn by another vehicle;

    (d)    to a vehicle while being used to propel a snow plough; or

    (e)    to a vehicle which is parked.

(3)    For the purposes of this regulation a headlamp shall not be regarded as lit if its intensity is reduced by a dim-dip device.'

Notably, there is no obligation to light a solo motor bike or a pedal bike which is 'being pushed along the left-hand edge of a carriageway or a pedal cycle waiting to proceed as long as it is kept to the near left hand or nearside of the carriageway'. The inference is therefore that motor bikes and pedal bicycles are required to be lit when being ridden in the usual fashion along the road.

## 10.4  OBLIGATION TO LIGHT A PARKED OR STATIONARY VEHICLE

As the regulations cited above demonstrate and the Highway Code provides in rules 248–250, save where a vehicle is in a recognised parking space or parked on a road or layby where the speed limit is 30mph or less, the vehicle must display parking lights. The Code also makes it clear that unless the vehicle is parked in a recognised parking space, the vehicle must face the direction of the flow of traffic.

### 'Parking at night

**248** You **MUST NOT** park on a road at night facing against the direction of the traffic flow unless in a recognised parking space.

**249** All vehicles **MUST** display parking lights when parked on a road or a lay-by on a road with a speed limit greater than 30 mph (48 km/h).

**250** Cars, goods vehicles not exceeding 1525 kg unladen weight, invalid carriages, motorcycles and pedal cycles may be parked without lights on a road (or lay-by) with a speed limit of 30 mph (48 km/h) or less if they are:
- at least 10 metres (32 feet) away from any junction, close to the kerb and facing in the direction of the traffic flow
- in a recognised parking place or lay-by

Other vehicles and trailers, and all vehicles with projecting loads, **MUST NOT** be left on a road at night without lights.'

These rules have developed over time to deal with some of the difficulties which are amply demonstrated by the cases below. The presence of an unlit vehicle in a road is prima facie evidence of negligence. It is for the driver of this vehicle to explain how it came about and why he could not move it out of the way or give warning to oncoming traffic; see the judgment of Denning LJ in *Hill-Venning v Beszant*[3] referred to below. One of the functions of headlights is to demonstrate to other road users the position and speed of a vehicle. If a vehicle is parked on the wrong side of the road with its headlights illuminated this will found an action in negligence – although the driver of the other vehicle may also be found to be negligent for having struck the illuminated vehicle and not stopped in time. See *Chisman v Electromotion (Export) Ltd*,[4] where the defendant lorry driver was considered guilty of 'plain and obvious negligence'. For a more recent case in this regard, see *Tomkins v Royal Mail Group Plc.*[5] In that case the defendant's lorry driver had unhitched the trailer of his

---

[3]   [1950] 2 All ER 1151, CA.
[4]   (1969) 6 KIR 456, 113 Sol Jo 246, CA.
[5]   [2005] EWHC 1902, QB.

Parcelforce lorry at 4am on the offside of the kerb in the road outside the depot facing into the oncoming traffic. The trailer was unlit in any way. The street was lit by street lamps and it was a frosty and clear night with no ice on the road. The claimant had left his night shift as a van driver and drove into the trailer without having appeared to have seen it or slowed down. He was rendered tetraplegic. Judge Eccles QC found that both parties were negligent and apportioned liability 35/65 in the claimant's favour. The defendant was negligent and in breach of the parking and vehicle lighting regulations. Retro reflectors and lighting on the trailer would probably have alerted the claimant in time. The claimant was negligent in not seeing the trailer in spite of the street lighting and driving into collision with it. For cases where this type of collision has arisen because of a malfunction of the lights or a defect in the car or vehicle see below. For further cases which concern a vehicle which has been parked and left unlit see Chapter 22.

## 10.5   FAILURE TO USE HEADLIGHTS

The failure to use headlights in the dark or in adverse weather conditions will give rise to a rebuttable presumption of negligence. As the court in *Wintle v Bristol Tramways and Carriage Co Ltd*[6] commented:

> 'A driver must make allowances for the appearance on the road of lorries and other vehicles, and he must exercise common prudence by showing such an amount of light as would warn an approaching vehicle of the driver and his trolley.'

In thick fog with visibility of 10–15 yards, a motorcyclist who failed to use dipped headlights whilst travelling at 15mph was found to be negligent by the Court of Appeal in *Burgess v Hearn*.[7] The defendant in *Swift v Spence*[8] was guilty of an offence under the Road Vehicles (Use of Lights During Daytime) Regulations 1975 when he drove in slow moving traffic in foggy conditions with only his side lights illuminated rather than his headlights.

## 10.6   MALFUNCTIONING LIGHTS OR DEFECT IN VEHICLE

The presumption of negligence may be rebutted however, if the lights become extinguished or fail through no fault of the driver: see M*aitland v Raisbeck & RT and J Hewitt Limited*.[9] In that case a bus collided with the rear of a slow moving lorry whose rear light had gone out. The driver of the lorry had not known that this was the case and in the Court of

---

6   (1917) 86 LJKB 936.
7   (1965) *The Guardian*, March 25.
8   [1982] RTR 116.
9   [1944] KB 689.

Appeal, Lord Greene MR found that 'accidents can happen ...' commenting that neither party had been negligent nor liable in nuisance. In *Parish v Judd*[10] it was held that although the presence on the road of an unlit vehicle at night is evidence of negligence there is no negligence if the lights failed without negligence on the part of the driver. In that case the defendant had been driving along a road at 10mph when his lights failed though no fault of his own. Nuisance will not be made out in such circumstances because some default on the part of the driver or person responsible for the vehicle is required. See also *Sieghart v British Transport Commission*[11] where a lorry driver, whose lorry had just been checked at the depot and found to be in good order, came to a standstill on a straight road at night to adjust his windscreen wipers. Unbeknown to him, the tail light on the lorry had ceased to work and the claimant and his wife struck the rear of the lorry as they drove along the road at night and came across the unlit obstruction. The lorry driver was not guilty of negligence and nuisance was not made out, there being no fault on his part.

In *Butland v Coxhead*[12] a lorry driver was found to be not negligent where his lorry had broken down and could not be moved and had been left on the London to Portsmouth Road in darkness on the side of the road. The claimant had run into the back of the lorry on his scooter, notwithstanding that rear lamps had been left illuminated at the rear of the lorry. The point was made that it would be a good thing if lorries had to carry warning lights but there were no regulations to that effect. In a similar vein see *Moore v Maxwells of Emsworth Ltd*[13] where a lorry driver was alerted by a fellow motorist that there was a problem with his lorry and discovered that his tail light had gone out. In attempting to check this, he fused all the obligatory lights on the lorry and pulled over on the side of the unlit dual carriage road and attempted to repair the necessary fuse. As he did so, his mate stood at the rear of the lorry to warn approaching vehicles. The claimant did not see the obstruction in time and collided with the rear of the lorry. The driver was found not to have been negligent. The lights had been checked and found to be working normally before he set off. The grass verge to the side of the road was too soft for the heavy lorry to be safely driven on to. He had acted reasonably in assuming he could fix the fuse there rather than driving on to a better lit road. There was no evidence that his employer was negligent in failing to provide torches or warning lights or that it was customary to do so. (In relation to this latter point, things have probably moved on: see *Jordan v North Hampshire Plant Hire Ltd.*[14]) Compare this case with *Hill—Venning v Beszant*[15] where a motor cyclist was found to be negligent in failing to move his motorcycle off the road and on to the verge where his lights had

---

[10]   [1960] 3 All ER 33.
[11]   (1956) 106 L Jo 185.
[12]   (1968) 112 Sol Jo 465.
[13]   [1968] 2 All ER 779, CA.
[14]   [1970] RTR 212, CA.
[15]   [1950] 2 All ER 1151, CA.

failed and after several minutes it had become apparent to him that there
was an electrical wiring fault with the lights rather than just a need for a
light bulb change. The trial judge had found the claimant to be fully
responsible for the accident in failing to see the motorcycle on the side of
the road and colliding with it. On his appeal to the Court of Appeal
liability was apportioned two thirds/one third in the claimant's favour.
The fact that the motorbike could easily have been lifted off the road on
to the level verge just 3 feet away was a key factor. As Denning LJ
explained, the existence of an unlit bike on a fast road at night is prima
facie evidence of negligence and the onus was on the claimant to show
how it came to be unlit and why he could not move it out of the way or
warn oncoming traffic.

In *Fotheringham v Prudence*[16] the defendant's lorry lost a wheel as it was
bring driven along. The defendant pulled in just after a bridge on the
nearside of the road, about 12 yards away from the nearest street lamp on
the other side of the road. The lorry had no rear lights or reflectors. The
claimant who was riding a bicycle collided with the rear of the lorry. The
trial judge found the defendant wholly to blame. Upon the defendant's
appeal to the Court of Appeal that finding was upheld, namely finding
that there was ample evidence of negligence and causation and that the
Claimant was not guilty of contributory negligence. In *Hill v Phillips*[17] the
defendant's lorry trailer had broken down and the driver had pushed it
using his towing lorry on to a grass verge which was 4 feet 6 inches wide.
The trailer was 8 feet wide and therefore protruded into the nearside of
the road. The lorry driver had driven off to find a garage leaving the
trailer unlit. The claimant was a passenger in a car being driven with
dipped headlights. The driver did not see the trailer in time and collided
with it. At first instance the court held the defendant wholly to blame on
the basis that the car driver should not be expected to see what was not
visible. On appeal by the defendant to the Court of Appeal, both parties
were found equally to blame. The defendant ought to have lit the trailer,
whether by leaving the lorry behind it with the lights on, or by carrying a
precautionary lamp which could have been left there. The driver of the car
ought to have driven so that he could see unlit obstructions eg cyclists
without lights or men in dark clothes. Finally in *Lee v Lever*[18] the driver of
a vehicle which developed an electrical fault and lost power was found
50% to blame for the accident when the claimant collided with his car
which had been left unlit on the side of a well lit road which was a
clearway. The defendant had removed the battery and taken it to a garage
on the other side of the road for re-charging. The defendant ought to have
borrowed a warning lamp from the garage and to have pushed the car on
to the verge.

---

[16]   (1962) *The Times*, May 16.
[17]   (1963) 107 Sol Jo 890, CA.
[18]   [1974] RTR 35, CA.

As may be seen from what precedes, these cases are fact sensitive and there may well be room for a substantial finding of contributory negligence on the part of the claimant in running into the stationary vehicle. See in this regard *Henley v Cameron*.[19] For further cases in respect of obstructions in the road please see Chapter 22.

## 10.7  DIPPED HEADLIGHTS

Headlights should always be dipped for overtaking or where there is oncoming traffic or one is driving in a built up area. The reasons for this are so that other road users will not be dazzled or caused discomfort. Rule 113 of the Highway Code provides that:

> 'You should also
> * use dipped headlights, or dim-dip if fitted, at night in built-up areas and in dull daytime weather, to ensure that you can be seen;
> * keep your headlights dipped when overtaking until you are level with the other vehicle and then change to main beam if necessary, unless this would dazzle oncoming road users
> slow down, and if necessary stop, if you are dazzled by oncoming headlights'

This is echoed by the requirements of reg 25 of the Road Vehicle Lighting Regulations 1989 set out above. A driver (the first defendant) was found to be negligent for switching his headlights up to full beam on approaching another driver (the second defendant) which dazzled the second defendant and caused him to collide with the claimant who had been standing with his bicycle at the side of the road in *Saville v Bache*;[20] the first defendant had denied switching his headlights as alleged and not given any explanation for putting them on full beam. Widgery LJ acknowledged that there could be circumstances where a driver had to resort to full beam whilst approaching another and that he would not be negligent if he had a good reason. However, the first defendant had given no explanation and was found to have been negligent.

## 10.8  FOG LIGHTS

Fog lights should not be used unless appropriate for the conditions. They ought to be switched off when conditions improve. If a driver is dazzled by lights he should slow down and if necessary stop. The relevant rules of the Highway Code provide as follows:

> '114 You **MUST NOT**
> * use any lights in a way which would dazzle or cause discomfort to other road users, including pedestrians, cyclists and horse riders

---

[19]  (1949) 65 TLR 17, per Tucker LJ, at paras 18 and 19.
[20]  (1969) 113 Sol Jo 228, CA.

- use front or rear fog lights unless visibility is seriously reduced. You **MUST** switch them off when visibility improves to avoid dazzling other road users (see Rule 226).'

'**226** You **MUST** use headlights when visibility is seriously reduced, generally when you cannot see for more than 100 metres (328 feet). You may also use front or rear fog lights but you **MUST** switch them off when visibility improves (see Rule 236).'

'**236** You **MUST NOT** use front or rear fog lights unless visibility is seriously reduced (see Rule 226) as they dazzle other road users and can obscure your brake lights. You **MUST** switch them off when visibility improves.'

This is supplemented by the requirements of regs 24 and 25 set out above and by the chart in reg 27 of the Road Vehicles Lighting Regulations 1989 which is set out below for ease of reference in relation to warning lights. The Regulations refer to the use of fog lamps where there is 'seriously reduced visibility'. The same considerations as mentioned above in relation to driving in the dark essentially apply to driving in foggy conditions where visibility is significantly reduced. The cases which follow need to be read in the context of the current requirements in respect of the use of correct forms or lighting in foggy conditions on drivers.

The following are examples of cases where fog has reduced visibility and caused difficulties for road users. In *Harvey v Road Haulage Executive*[21] the claimant was riding a motorcycle in foggy conditions along a road with three lanes. Visibility was 11 or 12 yards. As the claimant rode along he suddenly became aware of a lorry straddling the nearside lanes on a diagonal slant which he thought was moving but was in fact stationary. He did not overtake it because he could not see if the opposite carriageway was clear because of the fog. He collided with the lorry. The lorry had been towed into its position on the nearside of the road and the engine was running. There was an issue as to whether its tail lights were illuminated but the trial judge approached the case on the basis that they were. At first instance he dismissed the action on the basis that the motorcyclist had been riding too fast for the conditions. On appeal the Court of Appeal apportioned liability 50/50. The lorry driver should have ensured that the vehicle had been towed fully into the nearside lane rather than straddling two lanes on a diagonal and the motorcyclist was at fault for riding too fast and colliding with the lorry which was stationary. See also *Burgess v Hearn*.[22] In that case the claimant was riding a motorcycle combination with his dipped headlights on whereas the defendant's car was only showing sidelights notwithstanding thick fog which reduced visibility to 10–15 yards. The claimant was riding at 25mph and collided with the defendant's oncoming vehicle which was driving at 15mph. The claimant had just had to swerve to avoid another collision on the nearside of the road which is why he was in the opposite carriageway when the

---

[21]  [1952] 1 KB 120, CA.
[22]  (1965) *The Guardian*, March 25, CA.

collision occurred. The trial judge found the parties equally to blame on the basis that the defendant should have been showing his headlights and the claimant was riding too fast and had blindly pulled out on the wrong side of the road. On appeal by the defendant, it was held that even if the defendant had illuminated his headlights this would not have prevented the accident because the claimant would not have seen them in any event.

## 10.9   DRIVING WITHIN THE LIMIT OF VISION

A driver should proceed at a speed and in a manner that will allow him to pull up and stop within the limit of vision. If a driver drives along an unlit road with dipped headlights then he is:

> ' . . . bound to travel at a speed enabling him to cope with the ordinary trials which occur on the highway.' (Per O'Connor J in *Young v Chester*.[23])

In that case the claimant was driving along the A2 in Kent on a dark clear night with dipped headlights at about 40–50 mph when he saw the rear lights of the vehicle in the lane ahead which then appeared to disappear. He assumed that the other vehicle had taken a slip road off the main road. When he was 30 yards from the defendant's stationary car which was then unlit, he applied his brakes sharply and collided with the rear of the car. If he had seen it in time, he could have avoided colliding with it. The defendant had been driving along the road when his engine suddenly lost power and the car stopped on the nearside of the road. He attempted to re-start the car using the self starter and the car lights 'were dimmed if not put out'. The claimant was found 40% to blame and the defendant 60% to blame for the accident. The defendant's negligence lay in stopping in a position which was dangerous with a car which was not lit. The Court of Appeal declined to interfere with the judge's apportionment. See also in this regard *Hill v Phillips*[24] where Upjohn LJ commented in respect of driving in rural or isolated areas:

> 'So long as motorists drive with dipped headlights in country roads they must drive in a manner as to see unlighted obstructions. Everyone knows there are cyclists who ride their bicycles without lights, or men in dark clothes in country roads, and motorists must appreciate their presence.'

## 10.10   USE OF WARNING LAMPS

Regulation 27 of the Road Vehicle Lighting Regulations 1989 places restrictions upon the use of various types of warning lamps which include headlights, reversing lights and fog lights and is replicated below for ease of reference.

---

[23]   [1974] RTR 70, CA.
[24]   (1963) 107 Sol Jo 890.

**'27 Restrictions on the use of lamps other than those to which regulation 24 refers**

No person shall use, or cause or permit to be used, on a road any vehicle on which any lamp, hazard warning signal device or warning beacon of a type specified in an item in column 2 of the Table below is used in a manner specified in that item in column 3.

| (1) Item No. | (2) Type of lamp, hazard warning signal device or warning beacon | (3) Manner of use prohibited |
|---|---|---|
| 1 | Headlamp | *(a)* Used so as to cause undue dazzle or discomfort to other persons using the road. |
| | | *(b)* Used so as to be lit when a vehicle is parked. |
| 2 | Front fog lamp | *(a)* Used so as to cause undue dazzle or discomfort to other persons using the road. |
| | | *(b)* Used so as to be lit at any time other than in conditions of seriously reduced visibility. |
| | | *(c)* Used so as to be lit when a vehicle is parked. |
| 3 | Rear fog lamp | *(a)* Used so as to cause undue dazzle or discomfort to the driver of a following vehicle. |
| | | *(b)* Used so as to be lit at any time other than in conditions of seriously reduced visibility. |
| | | *(c)* Save in the case of an emergency vehicle, used so as to be lit when a vehicle is parked. |
| 4 | Reversing lamp | Used so as to be lit except for the purpose of reversing the vehicle. |

| (1) | (2) | (3) |
|---|---|---|
| *Item No.* | *Type of lamp, hazard warning signal device or warning beacon* | *Manner of use prohibited* |
| 5 | Hazard warning signal device | Used other than-<br>(i) to warn persons using the road of a temporary obstruction when the vehicle is at rest; or<br>(ii) on a motorway or unrestricted dual-carriageway, to warn following drivers of a need to slow down due to a temporary obstruction ahead; or<br>(iii) in the case of a bus, to summon assistance for the driver or any person acting as a conductor or inspector on the vehicle. |
| 6 | Warning beacon emitting blue light and special warning lamp | Used so as to be lit except-<br>(i) at the scene of an emergency; or<br>(ii) when it is necessary or desirable either to indicate to persons using the road the urgency of the purpose for which the vehicle is being used, or to warn persons of the presence of the vehicle or a hazard on the road. |
| 7 | Warning beacon emitting amber light | Used so as to be lit except-<br>(i) at the scene of an emergency;<br>(ii) when it is necessary or desirable to warn persons of the presence of the vehicle; and<br>(iii) in the case of a breakdown vehicle, while it is being used in connection with, and in the immediate vicinity of, an accident or breakdown, or while it is being used to draw a broken-down vehicle. |

| (1)<br>*Item No.* | (2)<br>*Type of lamp,<br>hazard warning<br>signal device or<br>warning beacon* | (3)<br>*Manner of use prohibited* |
|---|---|---|
| 8 | Warning beacon emitting green light | Used so as to be lit except whilst occupied by a medical practitioner registered by the General Medical Council (whether with full, provisional or limited registration) and used for the purposes of an emergency. |
| 9 | Warning beacon emitting yellow light | Used so as to be lit on a road. |
| 10 | Work lamp | *(a)* Used so as to cause undue dazzle or discomfort to the driver of any vehicle.<br><br>*(b)* Used so as to be lit except for the purpose of illuminating a working area, accident, breakdown or works in the vicinity of the vehicle. |
| 11 | Any other lamp | Used so as to cause undue dazzle or discomfort to other persons using the road. |

## 10.11   USE OF LIGHTS AS SIGNALS

Brake lights can be used to signal that the driver is slowing down or stopping and will be interpreted as such. See in this regard *Flack v Withers*,[25] where the claimant was riding a pedal bicycle behind the defendant's slow moving car. The defendant slowed in the road so as to allow another car coming from the opposite direction to pass. The claimant continued cycling and collided with the rear of the defendant's car before being thrown into the path of the oncoming vehicle and sustaining serious injuries. At first instance the claimant was found 17% to blame, and the defendant was adjudged negligent on the basis that he had not seen the claimant before the accident – he had not checked his wing mirror and had merely glanced in his inside mirror. It was suggested that he ought to have used a hand signal to indicate to other road users his intention to slow down. On appeal by the defendant the Court of Appeal held that there was no evidence of negligence on the part of the defendant. It was said that a driver would not give more than an

---

[25]   (1960) *The Times*, March 22.

occasional glance into his rear view mirror whilst driving. The defendant's vehicle was fitted with the usual red lights which would have illuminated when he put pressure on the brakes. In such circumstances it was not necessary to give a hand signal. The claimant had not discharged the onus of proof and the claim therefore failed.

Indicators are plainly used as signals intended to warn of a change of direction. The Highway Code at rules 170–183 deals with road junctions and the use of indicators for turning. At rules 162–169 the Code deals with overtaking and, finally, at rules 200–203 reversing. It is the duty of the driver who intends to change direction firstly to signal and secondly to see that:

> 'no one was inconvenienced by his change of direction and the duty is greater if he first gives the wrong signal and then changes it.' (Per Streatfield J in *Pratt v Bloom*.[26])

See also *Another v Probert*.[27] In that case the defendant to a charge of careless driving drove along a main road with his left indicator flashing. In reliance on this indication a police car which had been waiting to join the main road moved out but the defendant did not turn as indicated and collided with the police car as it moved out. The defendant defended the charge against him on the basis that the police ought not to have relied on the signal. He was successful at first instance. However, he was convicted on the prosecution's appeal on the basis that it was careless driving to give misleading signals.

Flashing headlights are on occasion used by drivers so as to signal to other road users that there may be a safe passage. However the Highway Code provides:

> '**110** Flashing headlights. Only flash your headlights to let other road users know that you are there. Do not flash your headlights to convey any other message or intimidate other road users.
>
> **111** Never assume that flashing headlights is a signal inviting you to proceed. Use your own judgement and proceed carefully.'

In *Clarke v Winchurch*[28] the first defendant's car had been parked on the nearside of the road in a line of parked cars. He indicated to pull out and needed to cut across the line of traffic approaching from behind him. A bus (the second defendant, driven by the third defendant) travelling in the nearside lane stopped and flashed its headlights. The first defendant driver pulled out from the line of parked cars until the front of his car protruded about a yard from the offside of the bus. As he did so, the claimant, who was riding a moped to the offside of the bus, and whom the

---

[26]   (1958) *The Times*, October 21; Divisional Court.
[27]   [1968] Crim LR 564, Divisional Court.
[28]   [1969] 1 WLR 69.

bus driver had not noticed, collided with the first defendant's car as he drove past the bus. At trial the second defendant bus driver was found to have been one-third liable for the collision and the claimant moped driver was found to be two-thirds liable. There was disputed evidence as to how the first defendant had pulled out. The bus driver said he had done so 'a bit too sharply for my liking' whereas the first defendant said he had pulled out 'very slowly'. On appeal by the second defendant the Court of Appeal held that the flashing headlights should only be interpreted as 'come on so far as I am concerned'. The Court further held that the second defendant was under no duty of care to the driver who responded to the signal. The rationale behind this was explained by Russell LJ who considered that the imposition of such a duty would 'operate as a serious impediment to the courtesies of the road and the proper flow of traffic'. The first defendant was not to blame because the evidence demonstrated that he had inched his way out and this was not negligent. The claimant's claim therefore failed. Phillimore LJ and Russell LJ both, however, noted that if the driver who flashed had observed the presence and approach of the vehicle which collided with the emerging vehicle then this would 'give rise to different considerations'. If the driver who flashes has seen the potential for the collision, then he would owe the emerging motorist a duty to stop him. In such circumstances it may well be negligent for that motorist to flash his headlights in the first place.

In the later case of *Worsfold v Howe*[29] Browne LJ said in the leading judgment that *Clarke v Winchurch* was a decision on its own facts and laid down no principle of law – although in context this related to the apportionment of liability between the parties to the collision rather than the liability of the party which had flashed its headlights.

In *Leeson v Beavis & Tolchard Ltd*[30] the approach in *Clarke v Winchurch* was followed in similar circumstances. The driver of a lorry flashed his headlights at a van driver who was waiting to emerge from a garage exit. A motorcyclist was riding to the offside of the lorry and as the van emerged from behind the lorry, they collided. Stamp J emphasised that if a driver flashes another road user, this ought not to be interpreted as meaning more than:

> 'he, the driver, is not going to run over him or run into him, he does not thereby indicate that, if the other party crosses beyond the shelter of his vehicle it will be safe.'

---

[29]  [1980] 1 WLR 1175.
[30]  [1972] RTR 373.

## 10.12   SIDE LIGHTS AND LIGHTING OF LARGE VEHICLES

Regulation 24 of the Road Vehicle Lighting Regulations 1989 requires vehicles which exceed an unladen weight of 1525 kg to use side marker lamps and an end outline marker lamp to be kept lit and unobscured. There are a number of reported cases dealing with situations whereby a collision has been caused by an ill lit lorry positioned across the highway, whether undertaking a manoeuvre or otherwise. Many of these cases pre-date the Regulations and need to be read in that context. See in particular *Barber v British Road Services*.[31] The defendant was a lorry driver who wanted to back his lorry which was 30 feet long from a road 32 feet wide into the car park at a roadside café at 3am on a wet and rainy dark morning. The manoeuvre took about one and a half minutes. As his lorry was positioned across the A road, the claimant did not see it and collided into the side of the lorry. The Court of Appeal held that permanent side lights were not legal at the time, but the manoeuvre was fraught with danger and some temporary lateral light should have been shown. This was an unlit obstruction across a fast main road and that was prima facie evidence of negligence. The defendant's explanation was insufficient and he was found two-thirds liable for the accident. The claimant was one-third liable for not having seen the obstruction before the collision.

In *Jordan v North Hampshire Plant Hire Limited*[32] the claimant was driving along a major and fast road at about 60mph and was emerging from a slight left hand bend when during the hours of darkness he was presented with the trailer of the defendant's lorry and collided with it. The lorry was 35 feet long and it had a flashing light on the roof of the cab but no side lights although there were three reflectors on the side of the trailer. The defendant had been stationary at a café and had to position his lorry right across the width of the road and go on to the grass verge in order to turn out of his parked position. At first instance liability was apportioned 50/50. On appeal by the defendants the Court of Appeal were unimpressed and thought that if anything the claimant ought to have done rather better at trial. It held that the defendant ought not to have pulled into a café on his offside when the manoeuvre he would have to make to leave would cause grave risks to other road users, further that the lorry was insufficiently lit, the reflectors would not have shown at the moment that the car emerged from the bend and that the flashing cab light may have been confusing. It was also held that the driver's mate could have flashed a torch as a warning (cf *Moore v Maxwells of Emsworth Ltd*, above).

---

[31]   (1964) *The Times*, November 18, CA.
[32]   [1970] RTR 212, CA.

## 10.13   STREET LIGHTING

Section 97 of the Highways Act 1980 provides that:

> '(1)   The Minister and every local highway authority may provide lighting for the purposes of any highway or proposed highway for which they are or will be the highway authority, and may for that purpose –
>   (a)   contract with any persons for the supply of gas, electricity or other means of lighting; and
>   (b)   construct and maintain such lamps, posts and other works as they consider necessary.
> (2)   A highway authority may . . .'

The Highway Authority has a discretion to light a street but no obligation. In Sheppard *v Glossop Corporation*[33] the Court of Appeal was satisfied that the defendant in that case was not liable for an accident which occurred after 9pm at night on a road where in accordance with its practice it extinguished a lamp which it had caused to be placed at what was thought to be a dangerous spot on the road. The defendant had not done anything to make the street dangerous and therefore was under no obligation to light that or any part of the road or to give a warning of the danger. For cases where it may be argued that the highway has created some danger by way of an obstruction in the road see the chapter which deals with obstructions.

Section 39 of the Road Traffic Act 1988 provides that public authorities should take measures to promote road safety; this relates primarily to road signage and layout as opposed to lighting. This is considered further in the chapter which deals with the liability of public authorities. In relation to the provision of traffic lights see s 65 of the Road Traffic Regulation Act 1984 and to their operation see Chapter 11.

---

[33]   [1921] 3 KB 132, CA.

# CHAPTER 11

## DRIVER'S LIABILITY: TRAFFIC LIGHTS

*Linda Nelson*

### 11.1    SIGNIFICANCE OF TRAFFIC LIGHTS

It is a criminal offence for a driver not to comply with traffic lights. The Road Traffic Act 1988 (RTA 1988) provides at s 36(1):

> 'Where a traffic sign . . . has been lawfully placed on or near a road, a person driving or propelling a vehicle who fails to comply with the indication given by the sign is guilty of an offence.'

Section 192(1)(b) of the RTA provides that 'traffic sign' has the meaning given by s 64(1) of the Road Traffic Regulation Act 1984, namely:

> 'any object or device (whether fixed or portable) for conveying, to traffic on roads or any specified class of traffic, warnings, information, requirements, restrictions or prohibitions of any description . . .'

ie including traffic lights.

Although failing to comply with traffic lights constitutes an offence, it does not confer a cause of action. Such a failure may simply be relied upon as evidence of negligence.

The sequence of illumination of traffic lights is stipulated in reg 33(3) of the Traffic Signs Regulations and General Directions 2002[1] (the Traffic Signs Regulations):

(a)    red,

(b)    red and amber together,

(c)    green,

(d)    amber.

Regulation 33(4) provides for the use of green filter arrows.

The significance of traffic light signals is prescribed by reg 36(1):

---

[1]    SI 2002/3113.

- Red means 'do not proceed beyond the stop line' (reg 36(1)(a)) (except in the case of emergency vehicles: reg 36(1)(b) provides that if observing the red signal would be likely to hinder the emergency vehicle, red means 'do not proceed beyond the stop line in a manner or at a time likely to endanger any person or to cause the driver of any vehicle proceeding in accordance with the indications of light signals ... to change its speed or course in order to avoid an accident.' Further discussion of liability in relation to emergency vehicles can be found in Chapter 16.)

- Red with amber denotes an impending change to a green light but conveys the same prohibition as the red signal (reg 36(1)(c)).

- Green indicates that vehicles may proceed beyond the stop line (reg 36(1)(d)).

- Amber conveys the same prohibition as the red signal, except that when a vehicle is so close to the stop line that it cannot safely be stopped without proceeding beyond the stop line, it shall convey the same indication as the green signal which was shown immediately before it (reg 36(1)(e)).

- A green arrow signal means traffic may, notwithstanding any other indication given by the signals, proceed beyond the stop line only in the direction indicated by the arrow (reg 36(1)(f)).

The *Highway Code* provides further guidance for drivers in relation to traffic lights. The current edition (2007) provides at rule 109:

'You MUST obey all traffic light signals and traffic signs giving orders, including temporary signals and signs. Make sure you know, understand and act on all other traffic and information signs and road markings.'

Page 102 of the Highway Code contains pictures of a set of traffic lights and specifies the meaning of each of the light signals (as stipulated in the Traffic Signs Regulations, set out above).

## 11.2   CROSSING AGAINST A RED LIGHT

The starting point is the general principle that a driver is entitled to assume that no traffic or pedestrian will be crossing against a red light.

In *Joseph Eva Ltd v Reeves*,[2] D (an on-duty policeman) approached a junction in his vehicle and when he was 20–30 yards from the traffic lights they turned to green. He overtook three lanes of traffic by driving at 25–30 mph onto the opposite side of the carriageway but had plenty of

---

2    [1938] 2 KB 393, [1938] 2 All ER 115, CA.

time to pull back in before encountering oncoming traffic. He continued through the junction and into collision with C who was crossing from D's left against a red light. D was held not liable:

> '[D] was entitled to assume that traffic approaching the crossing from the west would act in obedience to the statutory regulations and he was not bound to assume or provide for the case of an eastbound vehicle entering the crossing in disobedience to the red light. This does not, of course, mean that, if he had noticed [C's] van in time, it was not his duty to take all reasonably possible steps to avoid coming into collision with it . . .'
> (Greene MR at 401)

and:

> ' . . . it cannot have been negligence on his part to put himself in a position where such traffic, if it existed, would be invisible to him.' (at 402)

However, in every case the particular facts must be taken into account. In *Cullen v Coggins*[3] C drove through a red light. The court rejected a submission that D was contributorily negligent for entering the junction without taking all necessary care but made clear that that decision was made on the facts. At paragraphs 14–15 of the judgment Mance LJ said:

> 'It is right to point out that at page 410 Scott LJ [in *Joseph Eva Ltd*], in reaching the same conclusion, used language which might, on one reading, suggest that there was a public policy element in this ruling, the encouragement of obedience to traffic lights, which precluded any finding of negligence on the part of a driver crossing such lights at green. However the better view is, in my view, that *Joseph Eva Ltd v Reeves* is simply a decision on its particular facts and lays down no rule of law. Every traffic accident case must, it seems to me, be considered in the light of its particular circumstances.'

Case law suggests that the general principle (that a driver is entitled to assume that no traffic will be crossing against a red light) can hold true even where the driver crossing on green saw the other driver approaching the red light. In *Hopwood Homes Ltd v Kennerdine*,[4] C crossed a light on green and waited in the junction to make a right turn. He saw D approaching but as he knew that the lights were red for D and D had time to stop at the lights, C moved forward to make his turn. D did not stop: he continued through the red light and collided with C. The court held D 100% liable; C was not to blame as he had good reason to suppose D would stop at the red light. Buckley LJ (at p 85c) referred to the test put by Lord du Parcq in *London Passenger Transport Board v Upson*[5] as being relevant, namely:

---

[3]  (Unreported) 8 March 2000, CA.
[4]  [1975] RTR 82, CA.
[5]  [1949] AC 155, at 176.

'whether [C] should have appreciated on grounds of experience and common sense that the defendant was likely to drive through the traffic lights when they were against him.'

The court also took into account (at 83H–J) that had D been driving at a suitable speed and steered his vehicle properly, he would have been able to negotiate around the front of C's vehicle.

## 11.3   CROSSING WHEN LIGHTS ARE AMBER/CHANGING

It is possible for a collision to occur even when both drivers have obeyed the traffic signals. In *Godsmark v Knight Bros (Brighton) Ltd & anr*,[6] D1 (a lorry) drove though an amber light (properly) as he was not able to stop safely when it changed from green, and D2 drove through a green light, the signal having just changed from red and amber. When the two vehicles collided in the junction, D1 mounted the pavement and struck C. Barry J held D1 two-thirds to blame on the basis that although D1 was not able to safely stop at the lights, he would have been able to stop before entering the junction as his stop line was set about 40ft back from the junction. It must have been obvious to him that if he proceeded he would block the junction for a considerable time and he should have avoided creating an obstruction to traffic lulled into a sense of security by green lights. One-third liability was apportioned against D2: the lights had just turned green in his favour and there was an obligation to see that no other vehicles had entered the junction while his lights were on amber (particularly given that his view of the junction was almost completely obscured by another vehicle).

## 11.4   CROSSING A GREEN LIGHT

A green light does not give a driver an absolute right to proceed. In *Radburn v Kemp*,[7] C rode his bicycle through a green light onto a large junction. Before he could take his exit the lights changed and D drove through a green light into collision with C. D admitted primary liability. The court held D 100% liable:

' . . . there is, of course, no absolute right to enter a road junction merely because the lights turn in your favour.' (Davies LJ at 1505F)

and:

'[D] had no business, despite the lights being in his favour, to enter the junction at all unless he was satisfied that it was safe for him to do so, and, once he had entered it, no right to proceed farther across the junction

---

[6]   (1960) *The Times*, May 12.
[7]   [1971] 3 All ER 249, [1971] 1 WLR 1502, CA.

without taking the utmost care to save harmless people who rightly were already on the junction before he entered it.' (Davies LJ at 1506H).

A driver about to cross a green light must also ensure that he will not collide with pedestrians crossing the road. The degree of blame attached to the parties will depend on the circumstances, as demonstrated by the following three cases.

In *Connaire v McGuire*,[8] C attempted to cross a dual carriageway (at a point at which it widened to four lanes in each direction) at a light-controlled junction with no pedestrian facilities (such as a marked crossing, pedestrian light phasing etc). He crossed to the central reservation. At that point the traffic lights were red and so C set off across the final four lanes. As he was in lane two the lights turned to green. D had been driving slowly along the fourth lane, waiting for the lights to change so that he could accelerate quickly through them. He did so and struck C. Wright J apportioned liability 60/40 in C's favour: C should have checked that no traffic in the fourth lane was approaching in reliance on the green light and D had a duty to make sure that it was safe to enter the junction. He could not proceed into the junction blind and in total reliance on the green signal.

In *Goddard & Walker v Greenwood*,[9] the apportionment of blame against the driver crossing a green light was only 20%. Both claimants were crossing three lanes of traffic towards a central reservation. The traffic lights incorporated pedestrian lights, but they did not press the button to initiate the pedestrian sequence. The traffic lights had turned green by the time they stepped off the kerb. There was a lorry on the inside lane and they crossed in front of it. D was in the middle lane and maintained his speed of 25mph through the green lights. Although the lorry driver sounded his horn, D was unable to stop in time to avoid a collision with the claimants when they stepped out from behind the lorry. Parker LJ held (at paragraphs 12–13):

> 'The fact that the lights had ... turned to green does not mean, in my judgment, that [D] was absolved from using reasonable care in proceeding across the pedestrian crossing, particularly in circumstances where his view of it was partly obscured. In my judgment a reasonably careful driver in the situation in which [D] was placed would have anticipated that there might be a pedestrian on the crossing.'

At paragraph 15 he stressed that no general rule was laid down in this case.

In *Watson v Skuse*,[10] C was crossing a road and ignored the pedestrian lights, looking only to see that the traffic lights were red. D was driving a

---

8    [1994] CLY 3343, HC.
9    [2002] EWCA Civ 1590.
10    [2001] EWCA Civ 1158, CA.

large lorry and was stationary at the lights. C crossed 'unduly close' to the lorry: he walked to the side of the studs that marked the pedestrian crossing and so close to the lorry (the windows of which were 6 feet 3 inches from the ground) that D would not have been able to see him if he had looked when C was directly in front of the lorry. When the traffic lights turned green D moved off, unaware of Cs presence directly in front of his lorry. The Court of Appeal upheld the finding of liability against D: at paragraph 22 Sedley LJ held that:

> 'the driver of the motor vehicle, never more than when it is configured as this one was so that a person close enough to it will be invisible to the driver, has got to exercise a very high degree of vigilance. Equally, it is well-established that the duty is owed not only to prudent and alert road users, but to the infirm, the young and (albeit within certain limits) the foolish. On any view . . . the claimant was in the last of these categories.'

## 11.5   OPERATION OF TRAFFIC LIGHTS

The courts presume that traffic lights are in proper working order unless there is evidence to the contrary: see *Tingle Jacobs & Co v Kennedy*.[11]

Transport for London, or the local highway authority elsewhere, should be able to provide details of light sequences and whether lights were operating correctly at a given time.

If it is shown that traffic lights were not working at the time of the accident, drivers are not necessarily absolved of liability and there is still room for a finding of negligence in the event of an accident. The Highway Code states at rule 176:

> 'If the traffic lights are not working, treat the situation as you would an unmarked junction and proceed with great care.'

In *Ramoo, son of Erulapan v Gan Soo Swee & anr*,[12] the traffic lights at a crossroads were malfunctioning. C was a passenger in a taxi driven by D1. In their direction of travel the traffic lights were changing in normal sequence but too rapidly. In D2's direction of travel the red phase was omitted from the sequence. Both vehicles had green lights in their favour and drove into the junction and into collision. The PC restored the trial judge's apportionment of liability (set out at p 1018H). Against D1 the finding was 75%:

> ' . . . the crucial question in this case . . . [is] whether either . . . driver or both of them should have realised that the lights were out of order and that whatever colour they might happen to be when they passed them it was their duty to proceed with caution because of the possibility that a vehicle might

---

11   [1964] 1 All ER 888, [1964] 1 WLR 638n, CA, per Lord Denning MR.
12   [1971] 3 All ER 320, [1971] 1 WLR 1014, PC.

enter the crossing from the other road at the same time . . . If [D1] had been keeping a proper look-out he would . . . have realised that the lights were out of order and have slowed down at the crossing . . . In the absence of any evidence from him as to when he first saw the lights and what impression they made on him the natural inference is that he was not keeping a proper look-out . . .' (at 1020F–H).

Against D2 the finding was 25%:

'if [D2] only saw the lights when he was 40 or 50 feet from the junction – which is what he said in his evidence – it is clear that he cannot have been keeping a proper look-out.' (at 1021D–E).

# CHAPTER 12

# DRIVER'S LIABILITY: ROAD SIGNS

*Emily Verity*

## 12.1 INTRODUCTION

Traffic signs are playing an increasingly important role in the prevention of road accidents. The then Transport Minister, Rosie Winterton, launched the largest review of British road signs for 40 years on 13 September 2008. The aims include cutting congestion, emissions, ensuring traffic signs keep apace with the latest technology and keeping traffic moving safely and efficiently.

## 12.2 THE LAW ON TRAFFIC SIGNS

The 1968 Vienna Convention on Road Signs and Signals set out rules for traffic signs across the United Nations. It advocated the use of a triangle shaped sign for warnings and circular signs for regulation of traffic.

Traffic signs in the UK are regulated by ss 64–80 of the Road Traffic Regulation Act 1984.

Essentially, by s 65(1), a highway authority is empowered, at its discretion, to erect traffic signs. A decision not to do so or a failure to consider doing so does not establish negligence unless it can be proved, on the balance of probabilities, that a competent road engineer, exercising reasonable care and skill, would have directed that a sign be placed on the road and that the absence of the sign caused or was a contributory cause of the material accident (see *Burton* and *Lavis* below).

The Traffic Signs Regulations and General Directions 2002[1] (replacing earlier regulations) prescribe the traffic signs for use in Great Britain. The Highway Code Revised 2007 Edition sets out the majority of signs giving warnings, orders, information and directions. If local authorities want to use a sign that is not prescribed in the regulations they must apply to the Department for Transport for special authorisation. The Department provides detailed guidance on the correct design and use of traffic signs through the Traffic Signs Manual (on the website at http://www.dft.gov.uk/pgr/roads/tss/tsmanual). The Department's Manual for

---

[1]  SI 2002/3113.

Streets (LTN 12/07) and Traffic Management and Streetscape (LTN 1/08) provide guidance on design and siting of traffic signs. The principle of these regulations is to use symbols to replace words wherever possible in traffic signs. Pictures using fibre-optic technology have been in use since 2002.

Under the Road Traffic Act 1960, s 54, emergency traffic signs may be erected by the police for up to 7 days indicating prohibitions, restrictions or requirements in extraordinary situations. The Code of Practice 'Safety at Street Works and Road Works' issued pursuant to s 65 and s 124 of the New Roads and Street Works Act 1991 gives guidance on erection of temporary signs at road works.

In 2002, the latest year for which the figures are available, five road workers were killed and 29 seriously injured in the course of their work on highways agency roads. The Handbook of Rules and Guidance for the National Safety Camera Programme for England and Wales 2006/07 sets out guidance for the signing of speed and safety cameras. A driver who fails to conform to any such sign commits a criminal offence under s 36 of the Road Traffic Act 1988.

## 12.3  THE CASE LAW

Generally in civil claims the court apportions liability in accordance with the general rules summarised in earlier chapters on the standard of the driving, rather than any failure by the highways authority to erect a sign.

If a sign is absent, faulty or placed in a hazardous position this may give rise to liability on behalf of the highway authority but the court will usually focus on whether the driver was materially misled.

To understand some of the older cases it is necessary to know that 'Stop' replaces the old 'Halt at Major Road Ahead' sign. This sign appears on minor roads where traffic emerges into major roads and requires every vehicle:

'(a)  to stop at the major road; and,
(b)  not to proceed into the major road in such a manner or at such a time as is likely to cause danger to the driver of any other vehicle on the major road or as to necessitate the driver of any such other vehicle to change its speed or course in order to avoid an accident with the first mentioned vehicle.'

'Give Way' replaces the old 'Slow Major Road Ahead' sign. Its meaning is the same as that of the 'Stop' sign with the omission of requirement (a).

## 12.4 FAILURE TO ERECT ROAD SIGNS

Failure to erect a road sign may lead to liability. But it is difficult to prove: see *Lavis v Kent County Council*[2] in which a motorist's claim in negligence against a highway authority for injury sustained in a road accident failed. He alleged the accident was caused by the authority's failure to erect a road sign in addition to the transverse double broken white lines already provided as a warning of a T junction ahead. It was held (Judge Previte QC, QBD) that in the absence of evidence that a competent road engineer exercising reasonable care and skill would advise the erection of some additional warning sign or other indicator, it had not been established that any additional warning indicator was necessary. The plaintiff was wholly responsible for his accident. Appeal dismissed.

The old rules about local authorities' liabilities arising from mis-feasance, not non-feasance, are relevant in this field. Compare *Burton*, a non-feasance case, with *Bird*, a mis-feasance case.

So in *Burton v West Suffolk County Council*[3] the claimant was injured when his car skidded, without negligence on his part, on road covered at the place of the accident by a thin film of ice. The defendant, who was the highway authority, had carried out some road drainage work some months previously by which the drainage had been improved, but there was still a tendency to flooding and the road surface tended to be damp from water which ran off the adjoining land. If more drainage work had been done this tendency would have been reduced and the accident would probably not have occurred. The claimant claimed damages on the grounds that the failure to complete the drainage work amounted to misfeasance; and, that the defendant failed to give warning of the dangerous state of the road. It was held that if a highway authority does work on a road by way of repair or reconstruction, it must be done properly and in such a way as not to cause danger on the road, but this does not mean that where some work has been done and done properly to improve the drainage of the road the defendant should be held liable for failing to do further work, which would result in further improvement of the drainage. It was not misfeasance but non-feasance. The defendant was under no duty to warn the claimant of the icy conditions of the road.

Covering up road markings leads to liability; so in *Bird v Pearce and Somerset County Council*[4] D1 suffered a crash and sued the highway authority for bad signage. The crash occurred at a crossroads. The first defendant's car, entering the crossroads from one road, was struck by the second defendant's car travelling along the other. Both roads were unclassified. The traffic system was laid out by the highway authority and gave priority to D1 due to double dotted white lines at the mouth of the

---

[2]   (1994) *The Times*, November 24.
[3]   [1960] 2 QB 72, [1960] 2 WLR 745, CA.
[4]   [1979] RTR 369, 77 LGR 753, CA.

side roads. However, at this crossroads the white lines had been obliterated by resurfacing about a month before the accident and had not yet been repainted. As between the defendants the first defendant was found 90% to blame. In third-party proceedings D1 sought contributions from the highway authority. It was held that it was foreseeable that there was a risk of drivers misunderstanding their priorities at a crossroads junction – a greater risk than in the days before there had been any signs at all at the mouths of the side roads along a major road. The highway authority had created a pattern of traffic flow which did not exist before it placed white lines on the roads, a pattern which drivers could be expected to rely on. The highway authority was under a duty of care to the claimant to prevent injury from the potentially dangerous situation resulting from the removal of the white lines. It failed to erect any warning sign. The authority should contribute one-third to the damages paid by the first defendant.

Failing to erect signs where regulations require them leads to liability: so in *Prynn v Cornwall County Council*[5] the plaintiff sustained catastrophic head injuries in a road traffic accident on a section of road which was being resurfaced and was covered in loose chippings. The plaintiff lost control of his car and collided with vehicles travelling in the opposite direction. The trial judge found that three signs warning of the roadworks were not placed in accordance with the guidance given by Traffic Safety Measures for Roadworks. The chippings would have been thicker on either side of the furrows than in the beaten pathway. In consequence, he accepted that to veer from the pathways might have created a risk to a vehicle travelling at speed. There were more chippings than there should have been but these were not sufficient to cause a reasonably competent driver to lose control of his steering nor were they so substantial as to result in a finding that they created a foreseeable danger, breached the defendant's statutory duty or were a nuisance. The judge found that the plaintiff had lost control of his vehicle as a result of his speed, which was excessive in the circumstances. He concluded that the plaintiff had failed to prove that his loss of control was due to the surface of the highway. On appeal it was held that the plaintiff did not lose control because of his excessive speed, but because the chippings made that speed unsafe. He was travelling at that speed because (i) the third warning sign was too close to the beginning of the resurfaced section; (ii) there was no speed warning; (iii) both the third warning sign and the new road surface were in shadow which might have made them less obvious; and (iv) there were slightly too many chippings which made the surface less adherent and the road surface even less stable than it ordinarily would have been during the resurfacing. The defendant had not given enough warning to vehicles travelling in the same direction as the plaintiff of the new road surface on which the safe speed was no more than 20 miles an hour. However, the plaintiff should have realised that his speed was faster than was safe with regard to the state of the road surface and should have taken prompt steps

---

[5]    (Unreported) 1995, LTL 27/4/2001.

to bring his vehicle under control. The expert evidence did not help materially in the resolution of the issues. The use of experts in straightforward running-down cases was to be discouraged.[6] Primary negligence was established against the defendant but the plaintiff was one-third contributorily negligent. Appeal allowed.

However, trying to blame the highway authority where the claimant driver was obviously negligent himself is not a good route to compensation. So in *Hudson v Pirelli Construction Ltd*[7] workmen were carrying out street light works on the central reservation. At the point where they were working the road had been a dual carriageway for about 200 yards, prior to which it had been a single carriageway. They were using two vehicles which had been parked close to the central reservation in the offside lane in an area protected by cones and warning signs. The claimant was driving along the road and was injured when she drove into the back of one of the two vehicles. She was substantially to blame for the accident but sued the highway authority, submitting that the workmen were in breach of the Code of Practice 'Safety at Street Works and Road Works' issued pursuant to s 65 and s 124 of the New Roads and Street Works Act 1991. The claimant alleged that (1) the workmen should have removed their vehicles from the carriageway before removing the cones and warning signs, even if that meant the workmen crossing the busy road to collect the signs and cones; (2) the workmen ought to have placed three warning signs at 200, 400 and 600 yards before the work in accordance with the Code and not relied on one 'men at work' sign at 800 yards before. (3) It was lastly alleged that in removing the signs the defendants ought to have removed the signs closest to the vehicle first. The judge dismissed the claim and held that the placing of the signs had been reasonable in all the circumstances. The judge found a breach of the Code on (3) but held that even if the code had been followed, by the time of the accident all of the signs would have been removed in any event. The sole cause of the accident was the way in which the claimant had been driving: very fast and without keeping a proper lookout. The appeal was dismissed. Where it was necessary to place warning signs under the Code of Practice, but it was not possible to place those signs in accordance with the Code because of the road layout, the workmen were expected to do the best that they could.

Another (rather hopeful) attempt to succeed on this type of claim occurred in *Larner v Solihull Metropolitan Borough Council*.[8] The driver was involved in a traffic accident when she emerged from a minor road onto a major road without stopping at the junction. In doing so she had passed two 'Give Way' signs on each side of the minor road at the mouth of the junction. There was a long history of accidents at this particular junction, and the driver sued the council alleging that the council should

---

[6]   *Liddell v Middleton* (1995) *Times*, July 17, 1995 referred to.
[7]   (2000) LTL 3/4/2000.
[8]   [2001] RTR 469, [2001] PIQR P248.

have provided additional advance warning of the fact that she was required to give way to traffic on the major road and that the absence of such warning meant that the council was negligent and/or in breach of its statutory duty under s 39 of the Road Traffic Act 1988 in failing to provide that additional warning. At trial the judge concluded that no duty was owed to L, either under statute or at common law, and anyway there was no breach or causation. On appeal it was held that although a common law duty of care might in exceptional circumstances be imposed upon the statutory duty under s 39 of the Road Traffic Act 1988, it would have to be shown that the default of the relevant authority fell outside the ambit of the discretion given to the authority by that section, where the authority had acted wholly unreasonably. In this case there was no evidence that the council had ever been other than entirely conscientious in relation to its obligations as to road safety.

The leading modern authority on signs and local authority liability is *Gorringe v Calderdale Metropolitan Borough Council.*[9] In that case the mis-feasance/non-feasance rule was once again confirmed. The facts were: the claimant braked hard and lost control and crashed on a straight road at a hump in the road which obscured her vision of the oncoming vehicles. A sign had previously been marked on the road 'SLOW' but this was no longer visible. She had been driving within the speed limit (at 50mph) but had suddenly braked and skidded into a bus and she blamed the local authority for failing to give her proper warning of the danger involved in driving fast on that stretch of road when she could not see what was coming over the hump.

The judge had held that her accident was entirely the local authority's fault and that, in the absence of any warning, the claimant could not be blamed for driving too fast as the highway was out of repair.

The Court of Appeal overturned the judge and held that the local authority was not in breach of any duty to the claimant and that she was entirely responsible for the accident. Her appeal to the House of Lords was on the basis that the absence of suitable road signage constituted (1) a failure to maintain the road under the Highways Act 1980, s 41; and (2) the local authority's common law duty of care required it to put into effect safety measures that included the positioning of the road signs in order to discharge its duty under the Road Traffic Act 1988, s 39. The House of Lords dismissed the appeal, holding that the defendant local authority did not owe a duty of care to the claimant to paint a marking on the surface of the road or to erect signs warning her to slow down as she approached the crest of the road where the claimant's accident occurred. The provision of road signs or markings was quite different from keeping the highway in repair. The duty under s 41 of the 1980 Act had a fairly narrow scope. The accident was not caused by any defect in the state of repair of the road or by any failure of the local authority to

---

[9]    [2004] UKHL 15, [2004] 2 All ER 326.

maintain the road. If the local authority at common law owed no duty other than to keep the road in repair and even that duty was not actionable in private law, it was impossible to contend that it owed a common law duty to erect warning signs on the road. The imposition of a liability through the law of negligence on the local authority was inconsistent with the well established rules which had always limited its liability at common law. The public interest in promoting road safety by taking steps to reduce the likelihood that even careless drivers would have accidents did not require a private law duty to a careless driver or any other road user. If a highway authority conducted itself so as to create a reasonable expectation about the state of the highway, it would be under a duty to ensure that it did not thereby create a trap for the careful motorist who drove in reliance on such an expectation. However, in the instant case the local authority was not alleged to have done anything to give rise to a duty of care. The complaint was that it did nothing. The mere fact that the local authority had once painted a road sign on that stretch of road did not mean they were under a common law duty to do so, or that they were under such a duty to repaint the sign when it was obliterated. Drivers had to take care for themselves and drive at an appropriate speed, irrespective of whether or not there was a warning sign. The policy of the law should be to leave the liability for the accident on the road user who negligently caused it rather than look to the highway authority to protect him against his own wrong.

## 12.5  WRONGLY POSITIONED SIGNS

If signs are placed on the road to assist drivers but they are put in the wrong place then liability may follow. Also if drivers park in such a way as to obscure signs they may be liable.

So in *Kelly v WRN Contracting Ltd and Burke*[10] a car was parked by the third party opposite a road marking in contravention of reg 23(2)(a) of the Traffic Signs Regulations and General Directions 1964.[11] The presence of the parked car had a causative effect on an accident resulting in injury to the plaintiff who was a passenger in a vehicle driven negligently by the defendant. The defendant admitted liability to the plaintiff but claimed a contribution from the third party for breach of statutory duty in parking in front of the marking. It was held that since the third party's contravention of reg 23(2)(a) of the Traffic Signs Regulations and General Directions 1964 had a causative effect on the accident, a civil cause of action lay against him for breach of statutory duty. Accordingly the third party was liable to make a contribution to the damages payable to the plaintiff.

---

[10]  (Unreported) (1967).
[11]  SI 1964/1857.

In *Levine v Morris*[12] a fatal accident occurred when a vehicle skidded on a bend, left the road and collided with a large road sign mounted on four concrete columns and sited about four feet in from the nearside of the carriageway. The claimant sued the local authority for siting the sign in a dangerous position. It was held that when there were two sites equally good as regards visibility, the highway authority should not select one that involved materially greater hazard to motorists. The road sign constituted a hazard and had been sited without any consideration of an appropriate position.

However placing a sign in the wrong place does not change the speed limit on a section of road – see *Wawrzynczyk v Chief Constable of Staffordshire Constabulary*.[13] The fact that speed restriction signs had been wrongly positioned had not invalidated a speed restriction order and accordingly the justices had been entitled to find that the appellant had driven a motor vehicle in excess of the speed imposed by the order. It was held that:

(1)   The fact that the appellant had known that the signs had been wrongly positioned was of no relevance since the offence with which the appellant had been charged was not one which required mens rea.

(2)   The Order had not been invalidated by reason of the speed restriction signs being wrongly positioned: the positioning of the signs was in order to give adequate guidance to drivers. The appellant had not been misled and accordingly the speed restriction order had been valid at the time he had driven within the restricted area. (*Davies v Heatley*[14] distinguished.)

## 12.6   BADLY DESIGNED ROAD SIGNS

Some desperate claimants have sued local authorities for putting up signs which are not completely within the prescribed sizes in the relevant regulations. Perhaps not surprisingly such cases have been knocked back.

So in *Canadine & Ors v Director of Public Prosecution*[15] it was held that the fact that the black casing around an illuminated terminal sign at the entry and exit of a speed restriction area was visible on close examination did not render the sign non-prescribed within the meaning of the Road Traffic Regulation Act 1984, s 64(1). In all the circumstances, the casing unit used to hold the illuminated terminal sign in place was not an integral part of the sign and the terminal signs complied with the Directions. The lip of the casing to the front of the terminal signs was clearly not a backing board and was not a background against which the

---

[12]   [1970] 1 WLR 71, [1970] 1 All ER 144, CA.
[13]   (2000) 97(12) LSG 40, (2000) 144 SJLB 133.
[14]   [1971] RTR 145.
[15]   [2007] EWHC 383 (Admin).

terminal sign was displayed. Whilst it might have been different had there been a substantial surround that was visible to road users, the judge had concluded that the lip was effectively invisible. The application of reg 42 of the Directions was limited to the requirement that the back of any sign of the type in the instant case had to be grey, black or in a non-reflective metallic finish, and that requirement had been complied with. Accordingly, the signs in question complied with the Directions. In any event, even if the terminal signs did not so comply, there was no question of road users being misled or misinformed. In those circumstances, any deviation from the prescribed form was so minor that it should be disregarded as *de minimis*. (*Cotterill v Chapman*[16] applied). The appeal was dismissed.

## 12.7   FAULTY ROAD SIGNS

Can the police or the local authority been held liable if traffic lights cease to work and they fail to arrange to repair them in good time?

In *Clough v Bussan, ex parte West Yorkshire Police Authority*[17] a collision occurred at a road junction controlled by traffic lights that were malfunctioning. This malfunction had been reported to the police 34 minutes before the collision. The passenger in one of the vehicles sued the drivers of the two vehicles involved in the collision and one of these obtained leave to join the Police Authority as a third party. This was on the basis that the police had not responded as they should have done. The Police Authority applied to the registrar to strike out the third party notice as disclosing no reasonable cause of action. The registrar dismissed the application. The Police Authority appealed. It was held that it was established law that the police are under a duty to preserve law and order and to protect life and property because this is their continuing obligation. However, nothing had happened to give rise to a particular duty of care towards this particular individual which he could rely on in respect of the claim made against him by the injured passenger. The fact that the police were informed of the malfunction was not sufficient to impose upon them a duty of care to every motorist who might subsequently use the junction.

A different result would probably have occurred if the local authority have been told the day before and had done nothing about the defective lights.

---

[16]   [1984] RTR 73.
[17]   [1990] 1 All ER 431, [1990] RTR 178.

## 12.8   FAILURE TO OBEY ROAD SIGNS

As set out above, generally in civil claims the court apportions liability in accordance with the general rules summarised in earlier chapters on the standard of the driving, rather than any failure by the highways authority to erect a sign.

If a sign is faulty, or placed in a hazardous position, this is more likely to give rise to liability on behalf of the highway authority, but the court will focus on whether the driver was materially misled. If drivers ignore warning road signs they do so at their peril.

So in *Buffel v Cardox (Great Britain) Ltd*[18] a cyclist crossing a main road was injured by a lorry on the main road. About 95 yards from the crossing there were three warning signs consisting of studs in the road with the word 'slow', a cross-roads sign and a flashing beacon. The lorry did not slow down on passing any of these. Parker J held the cyclist alone to blame! On appeal the lorry driver was held liable.

> 'It is not easy to define the word 'slow'. Its meaning must depend on a variety of circumstances. That which may appear slow to some motorists may strike a pedestrian as fast. I think the fairest way to look on it is that the sign is an indication to the motorist that he is approaching a place of potential danger and that therefore, he ought to be driving more slowly than he would drive on a normal open road without any such sign. In other words, his speed ought to be such that he can pull up fairly quickly if someone or something appears from one or other of the crossroads.' (Per Singleton LJ)

> 'I do not think that "slow" means any more than "proceed with caution" – proceed at such a speed that you can stop if, when you get to the crossing, you find somebody, or something, in the process of crossing, or about to cross.' (Per Bucknill LJ)

However, a failure to obey a road sign must in fact be a manoeuvre which occurs within the purview of the road which the road sign governs. If the sign does not yet apply the sign is not relevant. So in *Brazier v Alabaster*[19] a motorist approached a roundabout on a dual-track road. The central intersection of the road ended 62ft 9in from the roundabout. Instead of going round the roundabout the motorist made a U-turn between the end of the intersection and the roundabout to get on to the other track of the road. There was a 'Keep Left' sign on the roundabout. He was convicted of failing to conform to an indication given by a traffic signal contrary to s 14 of the Road Traffic Act 1960 (s 36 of the Road Traffic Act 1988). It was held that the conviction could not stand. A traffic sign could only

---

[18] [1950] 2 All ER 878, 114 JP 564, CA.
[19] (1962) *The Times*, January 16, Div Ct, QBD.

indicate that if a motorist were to pass it he must obey it. As there was not a 'No Entry' sign in the intersection the motorist-had the right to use that part of the highway.

# CHAPTER 13

# DRIVER'S LIABILITY: ROUNDABOUTS

*Ed Lamb*

## 13.1 INTRODUCTION

Although the British have always claimed roundabouts as their own invention, the first roundabout was actually French: the road surrounding the Arc de Triomphe, which was built in 1901. The first British roundabout arrived in Letchworth Garden City in 1909.

The roundabout's heyday was the 1960s. During this decade, the UK saw an exponential growth in roundabouts with the advent of motorways and new towns. One particular highlight of the decade was Frank Blackmore's invention: the mini roundabout.

May accidents occur on roundabouts. However few are fatal and the majority involve low speed collisions and whiplash. In line with all of the other areas of driver liability the two main failings govern liability for roundabout accidents: (1) failure to keep a proper look out and (2) speed. They manifest themselves in these accidents in the following ways: (a) failure to wait for traffic to pass before entering the roundabout; (b) failure to keep or move to the correct lane at the correct time thereby causing last minute lane changes; (c) sudden braking.

## 13.2 THE HIGHWAY CODE (2007), RULES 184–190

Rules 184 to 190 of the Code govern traffic behaviour at roundabouts.

'184 On approaching a roundabout take notice and act on all the information available to you, including traffic signs, traffic lights and lane markings which direct you into the correct lane. You should
- use Mirrors – Signal – Manoeuvre at all stages
- decide as early as possible which exit you need to take
- give an appropriate signal (see Rule 186). Time your signals so as not to confuse other road users
- get into the correct lane
- adjust your speed and position to fit in with traffic conditions
- be aware of the speed and position of all the road users around you

185 When reaching the roundabout you should

- give priority to traffic approaching from your right, unless directed otherwise by signs, road markings or traffic lights
- check whether road markings allow you to enter the roundabout without giving way. If so, proceed, but still look to the right before joining
- watch out for all other road users already on the roundabout; be aware they may not be signalling correctly or at all
- look forward before moving off to make sure traffic in front has moved off

186 Signals and position
When taking the first exit to the left, unless signs or markings indicate otherwise
- signal left and approach in the left-hand lane
- keep to the left on the roundabout and continue signalling left to leave

When taking an exit to the right or going full circle, unless signs or markings indicate otherwise
- signal right and approach in the right-hand lane
- keep to the right on the roundabout until you need to change lanes to exit the roundabout
- signal left after you have passed the exit before the one you want

When taking any intermediate exit, unless signs or markings indicate otherwise
- select the appropriate lane on approach to the roundabout
- you should not normally need to signal on approach
- stay in this lane until you need to alter course to exit the roundabout
- signal left after you have passed the exit before the one you want

When there are more than three lanes at the entrance to a roundabout, use the most appropriate lane on approach and through it.

187 In all cases watch out for and give plenty of room to
- pedestrians who may be crossing the approach and exit roads
- traffic crossing in front of you on the roundabout, especially vehicles intending to leave by the next exit
- traffic which may be straddling lanes or positioned incorrectly
- motorcyclists
- cyclists and horse riders who may stay in the left-hand lane and signal right if they intend to continue round the roundabout. Allow them to do so
- long vehicles (including those towing trailers). These might have to take a different course or straddle lanes either approaching or on the roundabout because of their length. Watch out for their signals

188 Mini-roundabouts Approach these in the same way as normal roundabouts. All vehicles MUST pass round the central markings except large vehicles which are physically incapable of doing so. Remember, there is less space to manoeuvre and less time to signal. Avoid making U-turns at mini-roundabouts. Beware of others doing this.

189 At double mini-roundabouts treat each roundabout separately and give way to traffic from the right.

**190** Multiple roundabouts. At some complex junctions, there may be a series of mini-roundabouts at each intersection. Treat each mini-roundabout separately and follow the normal rules.'

## 13.3 CASE LAW

If a driver fails to arrange his position correctly when entering the roundabout so that he is in the wrong lane when approaching his exit he cannot just barge into the adjoining lane and inconvenience other drivers. Liability will follow if an accident occurs as he does so. Thus in *Slater v Bancroft*[1] motorcyclist C and driver D were approaching a roundabout. There were four lanes on the approach to the roundabout, labelled 1 to 4 by the trial judge, with 1 being the nearside lane. D arrived at the roundabout in lane 2 intending to take the final exit (in effect to the right). C was travelling a little behind D on approach to the roundabout. The road markings in lane 2 showed a straight on arrow, in lane 3: a split straight on/right turn arrow. They entered the roundabout and when D failed to leave the roundabout at the exit straight ahead (as suggested by D's road marking), C had to brake sharply which caused him to skid and fall from his motorbike. It was held on appeal that D was in the wrong lane entering the roundabout according to the road markings. C was in the correct lane. Whilst D being in the wrong lane was not alone sufficient to imply negligence, having been in the wrong lane, it was necessary for her to exercise considerable care in adjusting her position. On the roundabout she had failed to do so and was therefore negligent.

It is just as dangerous to fail to turn off a roundabout when a driver is in the 'turn off' lane, as it is to change lanes suddenly on a roundabout. So in *Grace v Tanner*[2] motorcyclist C was travelling southbound on a dual carriageway in the offside lane of two alongside D who was in a car travelling in the nearside lane. Both approached the roundabout intending to continue their journey along the A23 exit. Both parties entered the roundabout. D made an error: having thought the correct exit was straight on, she realised her mistake late, whilst adjacent to the A23 exit. Instead of sharply turning to make the exit, she decided to continue around the roundabout. At this point, C who had begun to turn off at the A23 exit, collided with D's car. At trial the judge found C at fault and dismissed his claim. It was held on appeal that D having 'missed her exit' or failed to turn off where she should have turned off, should have been aware of the potential danger she presented to other road users on the roundabout. In this case she had failed to do so and therefore both parties were 50% liable.

Both the above cases confirm that whilst being in the wrong lane on roundabouts is not conclusive evidence of negligent driving itself, it is

---

[1] (1999) LTL 19/11/99.
[2] [2003] All ER (D) 377 (Feb).

essential that when manoeuvring from an incorrect position on a roundabout the driver/rider takes care not to inconvenience another driver. This also highlights, with particular contemporary relevance to large multi-lane roundabouts, that the roundabout is a fluid beast and rigid adherence to a marked lane will not prevent the driver from a finding of negligence against him.

# CHAPTER 14

## PEDAL CYCLIST'S LIABILITY

*Oliver Millington*

### 14.1 INTRODUCTION

Where cyclists are involved in road traffic accidents, they tend to be the claimant rather than the defendant, because of their inherent vulnerability on the road. However, a cyclist is a road user as much as any motorist or a motorcyclist. A pedal cyclist has a duty of care towards other road users and towards pedestrians.

Whilst claims against cyclists may be comparatively uncommon (perhaps partly because, unlike motorised road users, they are not obliged to have insurance), a claimant cyclist will often face allegations of contributory negligence.

The key principles regarding cyclists' liability are the same as for other road users, save that there are certain circumstances which are particular to cyclists. The two main failures mentioned previously: (1) failure to keep a proper look out and (2) speed, apply equally to pedal cyclists.

Cyclists can cause very serious injuries, particularly nowadays when courier cyclists in big cities ignore red lights and speed through and over pedestrian crossings knocking down pedestrians. Such impacts have caused serious head injuries in the past when pedestrians' heads have hit the ground after impact.

### 14.2 THE CYCLIST'S VULNERABILITY IN RELATION TO OTHER ROAD USERS

After pedestrians, pedal cyclists are the most vulnerable road users to personal injury.

### 14.3 THE HIGHWAY CODE

The Highway Code, rule 205 sets out the general vulnerability of cyclists in relation to other road users:

'The most vulnerable road users are pedestrians, cyclists, motorcyclists and horse riders. It is particularly important to be aware of children, older and disabled people, and learner and inexperienced drivers and riders.'

Rules 211 to 213 set out more specific guidance:

'**211** It is often difficult to see motorcyclists and cyclists, especially when they are coming up from behind, coming out of junctions, at roundabouts, overtaking you or filtering through traffic. Always look out for them before you emerge from a junction; they could be approaching faster than you think. When turning right across a line of slow-moving or stationary traffic, look out for cyclists or motorcyclists on the inside of the traffic you are crossing. Be especially careful when turning, and when changing direction or lane. Be sure to check mirrors and blind spots carefully.

**212** When passing motorcyclists and cyclists, give them plenty of room (see Rules 162–167). If they look over their shoulder it could mean that they intend to pull out, turn right or change direction. Give them time and space to do so.

**213** Motorcyclists and cyclists may suddenly need to avoid uneven road surfaces and obstacles such as drain covers or oily, wet or icy patches on the road. Give them plenty of room and pay particular attention to any sudden change of direction they may have to make.'

In light of the particular vulnerability of cyclists on the road, it does not necessarily follow that any reduction for contributory negligence will be directly proportionate to the apportionment of liability between the parties. If the cyclist is a child the reduction for contributory negligence will be even smaller.

So in *Russell v Smith & Another*,[1] a 10-year-old cyclist was injured when he cycled across a road junction where he should have given way into the oncoming path of a vehicle. The trial judge found that the child was 75% to blame for the accident. However, having regard to s 1 of the Law Reform Contributory Negligence Act of 1945 and to the provisions of the Highway Code on the general vulnerability of cyclists, and children in particular, the Court reduced the claimant's damages by 50% only. It is, of course, to be noted that the claimant in the above case was a child; it is suggested that a court is likely to be less sympathetic to adult cyclists.

## 14.4   IMPACT WITH CAR DOORS

Cyclists, in common with all other road users, are obliged to anticipate the movements of those who share the carriageway with them. One of the most frequently encountered collision situations is where a cyclist collides with a vehicle door opened into his path. In *Burridge v Airwork Ltd*,[2] a

---

[1]   [2003] EWHC 2060 (QB).
[2]   [2004] EWCA Civ 459.

cyclist was injured when the driver of a stationary mini-bus opened his door and knocked the cyclist off his bicycle. On appeal, it was argued that a reasonably careful cyclist should contemplate that the driver of a stationary vehicle might open his door and as a consequence the cyclist should either cycle into the nearside carriageway or stop and wait until it was safe to pass. The Court of Appeal did not agree:

> '(That submission) intrinsically comes close to saying that all or most cyclists who drive into an unexpectedly opening car door will in part be to blame for that accident. In my judgment, this cannot be right. It would be putting the standard of care too high so to hold. Each case will depend on its own facts and it will be for the party alleging contributory negligence to establish particular facts from which the court can find that the cyclist was at fault' (May LJ, para 29).

## 14.5 IMPACTS WITH VEHICLES TURNING ACROSS HIS PATH

Cyclists who undertake slow or stationary traffic need to keep a careful look out for road users ahead who may wish to turn off the main road.

So in *Clenshaw v Tanner*,[3] the claimant was cycling in a cycle lane on a main road and was travelling slightly faster than the cars to his offside, which were moving slowly because of heavy traffic. As the claimant approached the entrance to a petrol station, a breakdown recovery vehicle driven by the defendant turned across the cycle lane to enter the petrol station, having indicated his intention to turn left. The claimant collided with the rear of the defendant's vehicle. The Court of Appeal upheld the trial judge's decision that the correct apportionment of liability was 50/50. Per Kennedy LJ at para 9:

> 'Although I accept of course that a cyclist is more vulnerable than a lorry driver if any collision should occur, any cyclist who is taking reasonable care for his own safety knows that any vehicle turning left ahead of him will endanger him and he should therefore keep a particularly careful look-out.'

## 14.6 IMPACTS WITH VEHICLES EMERGING FROM A SIDE ROAD

The majority of claims involving cyclists involve vehicles turning out of side roads ahead of them without seeing the pedal cycle. The same applies to pedal cyclists on cycle paths which are part of a pavement where residential houses adjoin.

---

[3]    [2002] EWHC 184.

In *Richards v Quinton*,[4] a cyclist was travelling the wrong way along a cycle path between a footpath and a main road. The defendant's car was emerging from his driveway and was crossing both the footpath and the cycle path, when the cyclist collided with his vehicle. The defendant's view to the left and right was obstructed by foliage and the layout of the road. The cyclist had been cycling the wrong way down the cycle path, although the defendant knew that cyclists sometimes did this. The Court of Appeal held that the cyclist was 75% to blame for the accident and the car driver 25% to blame.

## 14.7   IMPACTS WITH PARKED VEHICLES

Vehicles which park in a position which blocks a cycle lane may be found responsible for subsequent accidents involving pedal cyclists.

So in *Billington v Maguire & Irwell Construction Ltd*,[5] a cyclist collided with the rear of a trailer of a van that was stationary in the cycle lane of a dual carriageway. The trailer was illuminated by beacon, hazard and side lights. The van driver was found to be liable to the cyclist in negligence (Aldous LJ dissenting); however the Court apportioned the cyclist's liability at 70% notwithstanding the primary finding.

Vehicles which are not parked in the cycle lane but are parked simply at the side of the road are not likely to be held liable if a pedal cyclist rides into them.

So in *Howelss v Trefigin Oil & Trefigin Quarries Ltd*,[6] the claimant was cycling his racing bicycle at about 25mph when he hit the defendant's lorry which was parked on a bend in the road. The accident happened when it was raining heavily and there was a strong wind. The claimant said that he only saw the lorry at the last minute when it was inevitable that he would crash into it, but that he had been cycling with his head down, against the wind and the rain, and occasionally glancing up to check that the road was clear. The lorry projected into the road some 2–3 feet and was clearly visible from 45 metres away. At trial, the Court apportioned liability 75/25 in the defendant's favour. The defendant appealed successfully against the decision and was found blameless. As Beldam LJ set out:

> 'A road user is not bound to anticipate folly in all its forms, but he is bound to pay regard to carelessness by other road users where experience shows that such carelessness is common. Therefore, the question the Judge had to decide in this case was whether, by leaving the lorry in the position in which it was left so that approximately 2 foot 6 inches of it extended into the

---

[4]   (Unreported) 31 October 2000, CA.
[5]   [2001] EWCA Civ 273.
[6]   (Unreported) 2 December 1997, CA.

carriageway (visible as it was for approximately 60 metres, but obvious as an obstruction for 45 metres) the lorry would present a danger to other road users.'

The Court of Appeal found that the lorry did not present such a danger.

## 14.8 FAILURE TO WEAR A HELMET

The Highway Code rule 59 requires a cyclist to wear (amongst other things) a helmet:

'**59** Clothing. You should wear
- a cycle helmet which conforms to current regulations, is the correct size and securely fastened
- appropriate clothes for cycling. Avoid clothes which may get tangled in the chain, or in a wheel or may obscure your lights
- light-coloured or fluorescent clothing which helps other road users to see you in daylight and poor light
- reflective clothing and/or accessories (belt, arm or ankle bands) in the dark.'

But will a failure to wear a helmet be regarded by the courts as evidence of contributory negligence? So far no such assertion has been successful, but for adult cyclists we predict that liability (contributory negligence) will soon follow.

In *Miles v Parsons*,[7] a newsagent was found liable to a child bicyclist who suffered an accident with a car on his newspaper round. One of the allegations considered was the newsagent's failure to advise the boy to wear a cyclist helmet. The judge accepted the parties' agreement that the failure to wear a helmet had no legal implications for the case but criticised the newsagent for failing to consider advising the wearing of a helmet.

In *A (A Child) v Shorrock*,[8] a 14-year-old child was injured whilst riding a bicycle on a paper round. He was not wearing a helmet at the time. HHJ Brown sitting in the Queen's Bench Division declined to reduce damages for contributory negligence because there was no statutory requirement to wear a helmet and the claimant was not engaged in any particularly hazardous kind of driving for which it might be thought prudent to wear a helmet.

Four years later in *Swinton v Annabel's (Berkely Square) Ltd*,[9] the defendant sought to rely on *Froom v Butcher*,[10] in comparing the failure to wear a helmet to the failure to wear a seatbelt. HHJ Cox QC sitting at

---

[7] (Unreported) 10 February 2000, QBD, David Foskett QC.
[8] [2001] CLY 4466.
[9] [2005] CLY 2842.
[10] [1976] QB 286.

Lambeth County Court declined to make a finding of contributory negligence as, whilst wearing a helmet was recommended by the Highway Code, it was not a legal requirement. Moreover, the accident occurred on a pathway in a park, where there were no vehicles. Had the accident taken place on a road, the decision might have been different.

It follows from the above cases that where a cyclist is engaged in more hazardous cycling (for example, on a busy main road) and where the injury sustained might have been lesser had he been wearing a helmet (for example, a head injury), the courts might be more mindful to make a finding of contributory negligence.

## 14.9   GRATES AND OBSTRUCTIONS IN THE ROAD

Because cyclists are vulnerable to bricks, rocks, grates and obstructions in the road, they are more likely to swerve and wobble as they ride along. As a result Rule 212 of the Highway Code advises drivers to be careful when overtaking pedal cyclists and to grant them a wide berth. Failure to do so may result in liability if the cyclist does have cause to swerve round an obstruction.

# CHAPTER 15

# MOTORCYCLIST'S LIABILITY

*Mark Whalan*

## 15.1  INTRODUCTION

The general principles set out in the earlier chapters apply equally to motorcyclists as they do to car drivers. So there may be no tortious liability for a road traffic accident, but if all of the riders and pedestrians involved were careful then why did the accident occur? In the majority of cases one or other party has lapsed into carelessness. Liability in most cases is founded on a failure to keep a proper look out, speeding, a failure to concentrate or a failure to follow the highway code.

Motorcycles are dangerous beasts. Some people – usually enthusiasts – love them, feel the thrill to ride them and cannot understand why car drivers do not understand the attraction. Others, usually car drivers, find them noisy, dangerous, annoying and cannot see why anyone would want to wear black leathers and slice through the rain on two slim wheels surrounded by deadly car and lorry drivers.

Recently there has been a spate of mid-life crisis personal injury claims, involving well off mid-40s men who went back to riding motorbikes and suffered road traffic accidents. The loss of earnings element is often substantial. Fatal accident claims are more frequent in motorbike impacts.

## 15.2  THE USUAL FAILINGS

In most cases the usual failings of the riders involved are:

(1)  failing to keep a proper look out; and/or

(2)  driving too fast.

These really are the BIG TWO failings in road traffic cases.

All of the other failings feed off these two, so turning into or out of a side road when it is not safe to do so is really part of the first failing – to keep a proper look out. Likewise failing to brake in time or at all is part of the first failing – to keep a proper look out. Likewise overtaking when it is not safe to do so contains part of the first failing and the second – speed. The same principles apply in motorway driving where changing lanes at an unsafe time is really just part of the first failing. So if there is one guiding principle when determining liability in road traffic cases it is to determine whether each party involved kept a proper look out for the other.

In general the duty of a motorbike rider when using the highway is similar to the duty owed in all other areas of life – to take such care as is reasonable in the circumstances to ensure that he does not injure his neighbour.

In *Bourhill v Young*,[1] a case where a motorcycle collided with a tram, Lord Macmillan summarised the duty owed by motorists to other road users, pedestrians and persons occupying property adjacent to the highway:

> 'The duty to take care is the duty to avoid doing or omitting to do anything which may have as its reasonable and probable consequence the injury to others and the duty is owed to those to whom injury may reasonably and probably be anticipated if the duty is not observed.'

The standard of care is that of the ordinary, skilful, average motorist, described in *Nettleship v Weston*[2] as the standard to be expected of a competent and experienced driver.

Yet 'negligence' in RTA cases is as slippery to tie down as an 'eel in grease'. For instance in *Sam v Atkins*,[3] the Court of Appeal made some important observations as to the nature of negligence in the context of a road traffic accident claim, specifically a vehicle-pedestrian collision. In this case the defendant motorist overtook a row of stationary vehicles at 20mph. The traffic had stopped to allow pedestrians, including the claimant, to cross the road. At a point where the defendant drew level with a stationary transit van, which the motorist could not see through, the claimant emerged into the immediate path of the vehicle. The trial judge, finding that both the pedestrian and motorist were negligent, apportioned liability between the claimant and defendant. The Court of Appeal acknowledged that 20mph was too fast for the road and traffic conditions, but declined to make a finding against the motorist, as the accident could not have been avoided unless the defendant had been driving at 1–2 mph, which the court considered to be 'an unreasonable counsel of perfection'. May LJ stated (at paragraph 14) that:

> 'It is common place to analyse a course of action in negligence compartmentally, examining duty of care, breach of the duty, causation and damage. That is convenient, but technically wrong. Negligence is a composite concept necessarily combining all the elements I have mentioned.'

---

[1]　　[1943] AC 92.
[2]　　[1971] 2 QB 691.
[3]　　[2005] EWCA Civ 1452.

It is not enough, in other words, for a litigant to demonstrate that a motorist was at fault. The culpability will not amount to 'negligence' unless all three elements to the cause of action (duty, breach and causation) are satisfied.

## 15.3   THE HIGHWAY CODE

The rules for motorcyclists are contained in rules 83–88 of the Highway Code. These rules are in addition to other sections in the Code which apply to all vehicles.

### 15.3.1   Crash helmets

Motorcycle riders must wear a crash helmet and if they do not and they suffer a crash they will be found liable for contributory negligence.

Rules 88 and 84 of the Highway Code state:

> '**83** On all journeys, the rider and pillion passenger on a motorcycle, scooter or moped MUST wear a protective helmet. This does not apply to a member of the Sikh religion wearing a turban. Helmets MUST comply with the Regulations and they MUST be fastened securely. Riders and passengers of motor tricycles and quadricycles, also known as quad bikes, should also wear a protective helmet. Before each journey check that your helmet visor is clean and in good condition.

> **84** It is also advisable to wear eye protectors which MUST comply with the Regulations. Scratch or poorly fitting eye protectors can limit your view when riding, particularly in bright sunshine and in the hours of darkness. Consider wearing ear protection. Strong boots, gloves and suitable clothing may help to protect you if you are involved in a collision.'

Rule 86 adds that helmets should be 'light or brightly coloured'.

In *DPP v Peter Parker*[4] it was held that these rules also apply to drivers of motorcycles manufactured with a protective cell.

The substantive law on helmets can be found in *the* Road Traffic Act 1988, ss 16, 17 and 18, as amended by the Motor Cycles (Protective Helmets) Regulations 1998.[5]

The two main historic cases on contributory negligence and failure to wear crash helmets are as follows:

---

[4]   [2005] RTR 16.
[5]   SI 1998/1807.

- *O'Connell v Jackson*,[6] in which the claimant sustained a severe head injury when he was knocked off his moped. His injuries would have been less severe had he been wearing a crash helmet. Contributory negligence was assessed at 15%.

- *Capps v Miller*,[7] in which a motorcyclist was wearing a crash helmet, but the straps were unfastened with the result that it came off in an accident. He sustained severe closed head injuries and brain damage. Contributory negligence was assessed at 10%.

### 15.3.2   Speed

Speed and overtaking, side roads and turning cars are the main causes of motorbike crashes. But of these causes speed is the most prevalent fault for motorbike riders because the acceleration of motorbikes is so much higher than most cars.

The Motorcycling Manual (a DSA publication) states that motorcyclists must:

> 'always leave enough time and space to cope with what's ahead,'

taking the road and traffic conditions into account at all times.

Rule 126 of the Highway Code tabulates 'Typical Stopping Distances'. These are 'shown as a general guide'; and the Code acknowledges that:

> 'motorcycles need a greater distance to stop.'

A motorbike rider who is travelling at over the speed limit puts himself at risk of a finding of contributory negligence when a car driver pulls out of a side road. So in *Powell v Hansen & Chin*,[8] an accident occurred at a junction when the defendant motorist turned right across the path of the oncoming claimant motorcyclist. The car driver was held to be at fault as he had failed to observe or heed at all the oncoming motorcycle which was sounding its horn and had its headlights illuminated. The motorcyclist was also held to be at fault because he was travelling just over the statutory speed limit of 30mph. Liability was apportioned as 80% against the motorist and 20% against the motorcyclist.

A classic example of a motorbike rider being held partly to blame due to speed, where a car pulled out of a side road occurred in *Henderson v. Cooke*.[9] The motorcyclist was driving on the main road but collided with a car which emerged from a minor road. The accident took place at

6   [1972] 1 QB 270.
7   [1989] 1 WLR 839.
8   (Unreported) 11 June 2001, QBD.
9   [2002] EWCA Civ 1557, CA.

midnight on an unlit, straight stretch of carriageway. It was held that the motorcyclist was 50% to blame for the collision because he was not 'riding at a speed commensurate with the essential risk'.

Speed can also give rise to liability despite the rider travelling at less than the relevant speed limit for the road. Liability depends on the circumstances. So in *Thomas v Kostanjevec*,[10] a motorcyclist was held liable for a fatal collision with a pedestrian, notwithstanding the fact that he was driving at 10mph under the statutory speed limit. He had driven his motorcycle downhill towards a bend at approximately 50mph. He hit the pedestrian at a point just past the bend where 'there was no good reason' why the pedestrian should not cross the road! It was held that in deciding his speed, the motorcyclist should have taken note of the fact that he was driving a powerful and heavy motorcycle which, when in a banked bend, could not safely brake, as it was necessary first to bring the motorcycle upright. If he was facing an obstacle in his path, such as the pedestrian, his options would have been severely limited. He should have entered the bend at a speed moderate enough to permit him to stop if a pedestrian or some other obstacle turned out to be in his path.

A good example of a case where speed alone was the motorcyclist's error is *Heaton v Herzog*,[11] a motorist emerged from a side road onto a main road in circumstances where his line of sight was reduced by parked vehicles. He was struck by a motorcycle that was travelling significantly in excess of the speed limit. It was held that the motorist was 25% at fault and the motorcyclist was 75% to blame for the collision.

### 15.3.4 Overtaking

Motorcyclists must abide by the rules applicable to all vehicles when overtaking. Those rules are set out at rules 162–169 of the Highway Code. See Chapter 8.

The Motorcycling Manual adds (p 108) that it can be difficult to judge accurately the speed of oncoming traffic, so 'give yourself plenty of time'. Motorcyclists should 'take great care' when travelling on a two-way three-lane road as an 'oncoming vehicle might pull out to overtake while you are overtaking'.

### 15.3.5 Passing slow or stationary vehicles or 'filtering'

Here two of the major principles of liability in road traffic cases clash: the 'side road' rule and the 'overtaking rule'. Who is to blame – the errant

---

[10] [2004] EWCA Civ 1782, CA.
[11] [2008] All ER (D) 125 (Nov).

driver emerging from the side road or the errant overtaking rider passing a queue of slow moving traffic where there is a side road? What apportionment should be made?

The classic case on motorcycles overtaking slow moving traffic (filtering) is *Powell v Moody*.[12] This case has been considered, attacked, upheld and reconsidered countless times by the Court of Appeal and road traffic lawyers over the 40-odd years since it was decided. Yet it stands firm and proud. The claimant approached a stationary line of cars two abreast and decided to overtake them on the offside. The defendant was driving his car out of the side road passing through a gap ahead of the claimant and on his nearside intending to turn right. He was waved out by the driver of a milk tanker in the stationery line. He was 'inching his way out' past the line of traffic and the motorbike hit him. The trial judge apportioned liability 80% to the motorcyclist and 20% to the side road driver. The Court of Appeal upheld the apportionment stating that overtaking a line of traffic was an exercise fraught with great hazard. The car driver had great difficulty seeing to his right when emerging from the gap.

This issue was considered again in *Clarke v Winchurch*[13] where a motorcycle was described as being 'in the fortunate position of taking up so little road space that you can slide along the offside of stationary traffic', but where it was stated that such a manoeuvre 'warrants a very, very high degree of care indeed'.

Filtering, therefore, is a legitimate, but hazardous manoeuvre. Rule 88 of the Highway Code warns motorcyclists to 'look out for pedestrians crossing between vehicles and vehicles emerging from junctions or changing lanes' when overtaking traffic queues. You should 'take care and keep your speed low' when 'filtering in slow moving traffic'.

Numerous judges have held that where a collision occurs between a motorcyclist overtaking a line of stationary traffic and another vehicle which, at the beckon of one of the stationary motorists, was emerging from a side road, the motorcyclist's negligence is usually between 66% and 80%: *Garston Warehousing Co. Limited v OF Smart (Liverpool) Limited*[14] and *Worsfold v Howe*.[15]

Likewise the motorcyclist who is overtaking will usually be found to blame for hitting pedestrians who are crossing between stationery traffic. In *Snow v Giddins*,[16] the claimant had begun to cross the road at a spot near a road junction and not far from a pedestrian crossing which had a central refuge. The claimant threaded his way through the northbound

---

[12]   (1966) 110 Sol Jo 215, CA.
[13]   [1969] 1 WLR 69.
[14]   [1973] RTR 377.
[15]   [1980] 1 All ER 1028.
[16]   (1969) 113 Sol Jo 229, CA.

traffic, which was stationary, and then stood in the middle of the road just over the centre line. He was then struck by a motorcyclist who had been in the process of overtaking the stationary traffic. At first instance the defendant motorbike rider was held wholly to blame. On appeal the Court of Appeal held that whilst the claimant was not negligent in failing to use a pedestrian crossing he was negligent for taking on the risk that he could be marooned in the centre of the road at the mercy of oncoming traffic instead of crossing where there was a central refuge. They held that a:

> 'person who elected not use a crossing took upon himself a higher standard of care.'

The appeal was allowed and a finding of 25% contributory negligence was made.

### 15.3.6 Overtaking on the left

Liability usually rests on the rider's shoulders where an impact occurs with a vehicle as the rider is overtaking on the left. The Motorcycling Manual states (p 108) that overtaking on the left is permissible, but only if the traffic in front is moving slowly in queues, or signalling an intention to turn right, or if the motorcyclist himself is turning left at a junction.

In *Fagan v Jeffers and the MIB*,[17] a motor scooter, travelling on the inside of two lanes of stationary traffic, collided with a car turning right across a gap created by 'Keep Clear' markings painted on the carriageway. It was held that each driver was equally to blame. The motorcyclist was negligent as he had failed to keep a lookout for turning traffic whilst undertaking a dangerous manoeuvre. The motorist was at fault as he should have appreciated that there had been sufficient room for a two-wheeled vehicle to pass between the near-side vehicle and the kerb.

### 15.3.7 U-turns

Although motorcycle riders who are overtaking or filtering are usually held at least partly to blame for impacts, where the car driver is executing a U-turn liability may be avoided altogether. So in *Davis v Schrogin*[18] a filtering motorcyclist was held to be not at fault when he collided with a car which had tried to escape a traffic jam by executing an unexpected U-turn at a point when the motorcyclist was so close to the point of impact that he could not avoid the collision.

---

[17] [2005] EWCA Civ 380.
[18] [2006] EWCA Civ 974.

## 15.4   OVERALL CONCLUSION

It might be though from reading the above text that motorcyclists are found to blame in almost all circumstances. That is of course not the case. Indeed car drivers are advised by the Highway Code to keep a special look out for motorcyclists due to their small size and the ease with which they can be missed.

Rule 211 of the Highway Code states:

> 'It is often difficult to see motorcyclists and cyclists, especially when they are coming up from behind, coming out of junctions or roundabout. Always look out for them when you are emerging from a junction; they could be approaching faster than you think.'

So returning to the side road rule, expressed in an earlier chapter, liability should generally attach to the emerging motorist unless the motorcyclist on the major road is speeding or overtaking a line of stationary traffic, when contributory negligence can be between 50% and 80%.

# CHAPTER 16

## EMERGENCY VEHICLES' LIABILITY

*Raj Shetty*

### 16.1 INTRODUCTION

When an emergency occurs the services are expected to rush to the scene. This rush gives rise to a greater than average chance of a police, ambulance or fire vehicle being involved in an accident.

Emergency vehicles are often driven fast. They often overtake, sometimes in the oncoming lane. On occasion they will execute unexpected manoeuvres. They use their sirens and the blues and twos.

Cases involving emergency vehicles are usually difficult. Issues will arise on the relevant standard of care, the statutory exemptions and on contributory negligence. Factual issues on the use of sirens, warning lights and on speed arise with regularity.

Emergency vehicles do not have carte blanche to ignore traffic signals and speed limits at all times but they do benefit from certain exceptions to the rules governing compliance with speed limits and traffic signals.

### 16.2 STATUTES AND REGULATIONS

Under s 87 of the Road Traffic Regulation Act 1984, police, ambulance and fire services are exempt from compliance with speed limits, traffic signals and signs. However, the exemption is circumstantial:

> 'No statutory provision imposing a speed limit on motor vehicles shall apply to any vehicle on an occasion when it is being used for fire brigade, ambulance or police purposes, if the observance of that provision would be likely to hinder the use of the vehicle for the purpose for which it is being used on that occasion.'

It follows that the speed limit exemption will only apply to emergency circumstances (those requiring the saving of life and limb) rather that to normal regular or off-duty use.

The Traffic Signs Regulations and General Directions 1994[1] at reg 15(2) provide that:

> 'On an occasion where a vehicle is being used for fire brigade, ambulance or police purposes and the observance of the requirement specified in paragraph (1) would be likely to hinder the use of that vehicle for one of those purposes then, instead of that requirement, the requirement conveyed by the sign in question shall be that the vehicle shall not proceed beyond that sign in such a manner or at such a time as to be likely to endanger any person.'

Regulation 33(1)(b) of the Traffic Signs and Regulations and General Directions 1994 concerns the significance of traffic lights and provides an exemption for emergency vehicles:

> '(1)  The significance of the light signals . . . shall be as follows:
>
> (a)  Except as provided in sub-paragraphs (b), (f) and (g) the red signal shall convey the prohibition that vehicular traffic other than tramcars shall not proceed beyond the stop line;
>
> (b)  When a vehicle is being used for fire brigade, ambulance or police purposes and the observance of the prohibition conveyed by the red signal in accordance with sub-paragraph (a) would be likely to hinder the use of that vehicle for the purpose for which it is being used, then sub-paragraph (a) shall not apply to the vehicle, and the red signal shall convey the prohibition that the vehicle shall not proceed beyond the stop line in a manner or at a time likely to endanger any person or to cause the driver of any vehicle proceeding in accordance with the indications of light signals operating in association with the signals displaying the red signal to change its speed or course in order to avoid an accident.'

The Zebra, Pelican and Puffin Pedestrian Crossings Regulations and General Directions 1997[2] also contain exceptions for emergency vehicles with a notably extended definition of emergency vehicles:

> '12(1)The significance of the vehicular light signals . . . for the purpose of indicating a Pelican Crossing shall be as follows –
>
> (a)  the steady amber signal shall convey the same prohibition as the red signal except that, as respects a vehicle which is so close to the stop line that it cannot safely be stopped without proceeding beyond the stop line, it shall convey the same indication as the green signal or, if the amber signal was immediately preceded by a green arrow signal, as that green arrow signal;
>
> (b)  except as provided in sub-paragraph (e), the red signal shall convey the prohibition that vehicular traffic shall not proceed beyond the stop line;
>
> (c)  when a vehicle is being used for fire brigade, ambulance, national blood service or police purposes and the observance of the

---

[1]   SI 1994/1519.
[2]   SI 1997/2400.

prohibition conveyed by the steady amber or the red signal in accordance with sub-paragraph (c) or (d) would be likely to hinder the use of that vehicle for the purpose for which it is being used, then those sub-paragraphs shall not apply to the vehicle, and the steady amber and the red signal shall each convey the information that the vehicle may proceed beyond the stop line if the driver –

(i)   accords precedence to any pedestrian who is on that part of the carriageway which lies within the limits of the crossing or on a central reservation which lies between two crossings which do not form part of a system of staggered crossings; and

(ii)  does not proceed in a manner or at a time likely to endanger any person or any vehicle approaching or waiting at the crossing, or to cause the driver of any such vehicle change its speed or course in order to avoid an accident ...'

Rule 194 of the Highway Code states:

'You should look and listen for ambulances, fire engines, police or other emergency vehicles using flashing blue, red or green lights, headlights or sirens. When one approaches do not panic, consider the route of the emergency vehicle and take appropriate action to let it pass. If necessary, pull to the side of the road and stop, but do not endanger other road users.'

So it is clear that emergency vehicles benefit from various exemptions from the rules governing conformity with road traffic lights and signs. But they are still often sued for failure to drive safely and for ignoring warning signs. We examine the case law below. In summary, most of the cases turn on whether the emergency vehicle was displaying warning lights and providing a warning siren such that the road user should have looked out for it.

## 16.3   CASES INVOLVING EMERGENCY VEHICLES

### 16.3.1   Standard of care

Emergency service drivers are subject to the same standard and duty of care as every other road user; so in *Gaynor v Allen*[3] a pedestrian was injured by a police motorcyclist who was on a road where a 40mph speed limit was in force. The defendant policeman (who died in the collision) had been driving at 60mph. The defendant contended that there was a different standard between a police officer and an ordinary motorcyclist in particular when the police officer was on an emergency call out. It was held that the emergency services owed a duty of care to the public to drive with due care and attention without exposing members of the public to

---

3     [1959] 2 QB 403, [1959] 2 All ER 644.

undue danger. The defendant was guilty of negligence. There was an apportionment of one-third and two-thirds to the claimant and defendant respectively.

However on the facts of *Gaynor* a different decision might be reached today. The leading authority in this field is now *Scutts*. Police drivers are not to be held liable simply because they are travelling over the speed limit. They are expected by the public to race to the scene of the incident and the public must take care when they hear the warning signs of an approaching emergency vehicle. So in *Scutts v Keyse*[4] the claimant suffered catastrophic injuries when he stepped off the kerb and into the path of a police car which was answering an emergency call. The police car was travelling at 50mph on a road subject to a 30mph limit and was displaying its blue lights and a two tone siren. The trial judge held the police driver liable and apportioned liability 75:25 in favour of the claimant. On appeal the Court of Appeal dismissed the claim against the police driver ruling that liability was not established against the police driver as he was entitled to assume that other road users would not ignore the 'unmistakable evidence' of an approaching siren. Further it was said that such was the 'conspicuous warning' afforded by modern lights and sirens that *Gaynor v Allen* (above) was perhaps simply because of the passage of time and advancement of technology no longer to be regarded as good law. Judge LJ held that:

> 'depending on the circumstances, the speed at which such a vehicle may be reasonably driven is likely to be faster either that that of a vehicle not being deployed in an emergency, or in a vehicle in an emergency which does not or cannot highlight that it is being used for such a purpose.'

The older case of *Dyer v Bannell*[5] is more in line with the reasoning of *Scutts*. The defendant was answering a call and was travelling at 45mph in a built up area. He overtook a taxi and in doing so collided with the claimant who was intending to turn right from a main road into a side turning. It was held that it was not negligent of a police officer in the execution of his duty to drive at a fast speed but he must exercise a degree of care and skill proportionate to the speed at which he was driving. The claimant had been entitled to suppose it was safe to turn. Judgment was entered for the claimant without any reduction for negligence.

In *Aldridge v Commissioner of Police for the Metropolis*[6] the claimant was injured on Oxford Street when she stepped into the road from between parked cars to cross the road. She reached the pedestrian refuge island in the middle of the road. She checked for traffic coming in the expected direction of travel. The defendant's police vehicle was driving on the wrong side of the street at about 25mph. It was around 5pm and the street

---

4    [2001] EWCA Civ 715.
5    (1965) 109 Sol Jo 216.
6    [1998] Lawtel 6.3.98 (Court of Appeal).

was packed with shoppers. At first instance the judge found there to be no contributory negligence for failing to look to her right, as the only direction from which traffic should have been coming was the left. On appeal the Court of Appeal held that: (a) the Green Cross Code and the Highway Code set out the general principles of road safety for pedestrians to observe in cases where emergency vehicles are present; (b) although the Court of Appeal would be slow to interfere with the judge's findings, the judge had erred in failing to take into account the fact that the claimant had been aware of the presence of a police car in the vicinity for some 6 seconds before she stepped out into its path; (3) the judge's finding that the claimant had stepped out between parked cars made it incumbent on the claimant, particularly with knowledge of the police car, to exercise caution. In the circumstances the claimant's contributory negligence was assessed at one-third. Brooke LJ stated that:

> 'When the judge said that the parked cars must almost inevitably be in her line of sight as she was passing through, then this made it incumbent on her when she got to the centre of the road, where there was, to her knowledge (although she had only been aware of it when it was a long way away) a car which was sounding its siren and showing its blue lights, to be careful before she stepped out into the road, and the general propositions of the Highway Code and the Green Cross Code, to which I have referred, bear out my view that these were considerations which the judge ought to have taken into account when he determined the issue of contributory negligence.'

## Emergency vehicles and criminals

What is the officer's liability if he is chasing a criminal and an accident occurs during the chase? Can the criminal sue the officer for personal injury?

In *Marshall v Osmond*[7] the claimant was a passenger in a car he knew was stolen and the defendant was a policeman driving a police car chasing the stolen car. The stolen car stopped and the claimant got out to run away but was hit by the chasing police car. At first instance the claim was dismissed on the basis that a police officer on call out does not owe the same duty of care to a suspect as to innocent road users. The Court of Appeal upheld the decision but on different grounds: the duty owed by the police to the suspect is the:

> 'same duty as that owed to anyone else, namely to exercise such care as is reasonable in all the circumstances.' (per Donaldson MR)

The appeal was dismissed because the officer had not been negligent during the chase although he had made an error of judgement.

---

[7]   [1983] QB 1034.

When the officer is injured by a road traffic accident caused by the criminal's negligent driving whilst trying to escape an action and liability follows in the normal course.

### 16.3.2   Speed

Whilst the emergency services are exempt from prosecution for driving faster than the speed limit they must still drive at a speed which allows them to maintain reasonable control. So if the police car skids off the road with no other vehicle involved that is evidence of negligence.

In *McLeod v Receiver of the Metropolitan Police*[8] a police car driven at 70mph in answer to an emergency call skidded into a collision with another car. It was held that whilst a police driver would not necessarily be criticised for driving fast in answering an emergency, he should have driven at such a speed that he maintained control of his vehicle. He failed to do so and was therefore guilty.

### 16.3.3   Duty of motorists to emergency vehicles

Rule 76 of the Highway Code provides:

> 'Look and listen for ambulances . . . or other emergency vehicles with flashing blue lights or sirens. Make room for them to pass (if necessary by pulling to the side of the road and stopping) but do not endanger other road users . . .'

It is also provided in s 38(7) of the Road Traffic Act 1988 that:

> 'A failure on the part of a person to observe a provision of the Highway Code . . . may in any proceedings (whether civil or criminal) be relied upon by any party to the proceedings as tending to establish or negative any liability which is in question in those proceedings.'

So other road users must take great care to look out for emergency service drivers when they 'hear the sirens'. If they fail to do so they will be liable for avoidable collisions. It is more difficult to apportion liability when the emergency service vehicle fails to use its sirens.

The leading case in this field is *Griffin v Mersey Regional Ambulance*.[9] The appellant was proceeding through the green traffic lights and collided with an ambulance on an emergency call with its siren sounding which had passed through a red traffic light. The duties owed by drivers crossing on a green light in circumstances where an emergency vehicle was crossing on a red light were set out in reg 33 of the Traffic Signs Regulations and

---

8    [1971] Crim LR 364.
9    [1998] PIQR 34.

General Directions 1994[10] and rule 76 of the Highway Code. The trial judge found the appellant (car driver) to be 60% contributory negligent. The appellant submitted that the judge had been wrong in his apportionment of liability, contending that the appellant was not liable at all or alternatively could only be said to be 25% liable. The appellant relied on the case of *Eva Ltd v Reeves*[11] which stated that there was no duty owed to other road users in circumstances where, for emergency vehicles, traffic lights effectively became give way signs. The appeal was dismissed. The Court of Appeal held (1) that there was no absolute proposition set out in *Eva Ltd v Reeves*. Each case turned on its own facts – see *Davis v Hassan*.[12] (2) The judge rightly identified that the duty was on the ambulance driver using the junction as he was in an emergency against a red light. He owed a higher duty of care when crossing a red light and recognised it as a duty of care beyond that of the car driver's duty to take reasonable steps to avoid a collision with any vehicles crossing a red light. Simon Brown LJ stated that:

> 'In my judgment, the nature of the duty owed by drivers crossing on green in circumstances where emergency vehicles are crossing on red is illuminated by two further provisions. First, regulation 33(2) of the 1994 regulations:
>
>> "Vehicular traffic proceeding beyond a stop line in accordance with paragraph (1) [ie lawfully crossing on the green light] shall proceed with due regard to the safety of other road users . . ."'

He also relied on rule 76 of the Highway Code which (as stated above) provides that road users must look and listen for emergency vehicles and make room for them to pass, but in so doing not endanger other road users.

What is the position of an emergency service vehicle which is *not* sounding its sirens? The decision in *Griffin* was distinguished in *Purdue v Devon Fire and Rescue Service.*[13] The claimant entered a junction on a green light and was struck by a fire engine travelling at 50mph and crossing on red. The motorist had failed to notice the fire engine, which he would have seen had he glanced to his right, as it was a large red vehicle with three sets of flashing lights flashing, although it was not sounding a siren. The judge entered judgment for the claimant and made no finding of contributory negligence. The defendants appealed. The Court of Appeal upheld the appeal. *Griffin* (above) was distinguished. A driver had a duty to take reasonable steps to avoid a collision with any vehicle that crossed a red signal (see *Griffin*). There was a great deal of sympathy to be had for the claimant who on one view was simply exercising his right of way. However, the Highway Code obliged drivers to look and listen for emergency vehicles. Whilst the facts of this case were exceptional, it would

---

[10]   SI 1994/1519.
[11]   [1938] 2 KB 393.
[12]   (1967) 117 NLJ 72.
[13]   [2003] JPIL C3.

have been expected that whilst he was stationary at the traffic lights, the appellant should have glanced to his right. Whether that expectation could be elevated to a duty was difficult to find since his first need was to look at the signal itself. However, a careful driver would have glanced to his right whilst at the signal. It was difficult to understand how the appellant did not see the oncoming fire appliance with all its lights flashing. A properly observant driver would and should have seen it. The appellant's failure was a want of due care. Whilst satisfied that the fire engine was mainly responsible for the collision, liability was reduced by 20%. May LJ stated:

'In my view . . . This was a case where Firefighter Worth, the driver of the fire engine, did not give way as the regulations and the Service Guide Notes require. He in fact proceeded to cross red traffic lights when it was not safe to do so. On the finding of fact, which in my judgement is unimpeachable, that Mr Purdue moved off more or less at the moment the lights turned green in his favour, there was no proper basis for the assumption that Mr Purdue had seen the fire engine and was waiting for it to pass. Accordingly, and to put it simply, the driver of the fire engine failed to give way in circumstances where he ought to have done so and where it was unsafe not to do so. He had no proper basis for making the assumption that he made. In addition, it does seem to me to justify the recorder's other conclusion. Since there was no proper basis for the assumption that Mr Purdue has seen the fire engine, the wailers ought to have been activated . . . (2) I would have expected Mr Purdue to glance to his right as he was stationery at the traffic lights, perhaps also to his left, except that this was a dual carriageway and traffic from the right was the first possibility. Whether any expectation that he should have glanced to the right is to be elevated on these facts to a duty to do so has given me some thought. His first need and the sensible thing to do was to observe the traffic light which was straight ahead of him. That is plainly what he was doing. I am inclined to think that a careful driver in his situation should have glanced to the right. You do not know that a silent fire engine is a fire engine until you see it, but it is common knowledge that drivers sometimes jump red traffic lights. However that may be, I find it very difficult to understand how Mr Purdue did not in fact see this fire engine in his peripheral vision as it approached with all its lights flashing. With some hesitation, I am driven to conclude that a properly observant driver would and should have so noticed the fire engine and that Mr Purdue failed to do so. I think that this failure amounts to a want of observation and thus a want of due care. Accordingly, in my judgement there was a degree of contributory negligence but, for the reasons advanced by Mr Hillier, I do not think that the degree was great . . . I would assess the degree of contribution as 20 per cent and would allow the appeal to that extent.'

# CHAPTER 17

## PEDESTRIANS' LIABILITY

*Adam Dawson*

### 17.1 INTRODUCTION

The need for car and motorbike drivers to take care not to injure pedestrians whilst they use the highway is self evident. Moving vehicles are lethal weapons. Pedestrians are vulnerable and fragile.

The need for care is perhaps best summarised by the House of Lords in *Nance v British Columbia Electric Railway Company Ltd*[1] where it is stated:

> 'Generally speaking, when two parties are moving in relation to one another as to involve the risk of collision, each owes the other a duty to move with due care, and this is true whether they are both in control of vehicles, or both proceeding on foot, or where one is on foot and the other controlling a moving vehicle.'

Whilst many view the Highway Code as guidance for drivers, the first 33 paragraphs relate to the rights and duties of pedestrians. This chapter will seek to explore the relationship between the pedestrian and the motorist and examine how the courts have dealt with a variety of scenarios where these two parties end up in conflict.

### 17.2 RIGHTS AND DUTIES OF PEDESTRIANS

The starting point in the old times, before pavements and when pedestrians and horses ruled, was that the pedestrian was always right; so for instance in *Craig v Glasgow Corporation*[2] it was held (at 216) that:

> 'A man had an absolute right to be (on the road) and it is a duty of drivers of vehicles not to run him down.'

---

[1] [1951] AC 601, at 611.
[2] (1919) 35 TLR 214.

However, as car travel became the norm this old rule had to wither. The more modern approach was summarised by the House of Lords in *Nance v British Columbia Electric Railway Company Ltd*[3] where a pedestrian's duty was defined as follows:

> 'When a man steps from the kerb into the roadway, he owes a duty to traffic which is approaching him with risk of collision to exercise due care.'

## 17.3   THE HIGHWAY CODE

The first section of the Highway Code provides general guidance for pedestrians. Of general note is the following:

> '**1** Pavements should be used if provided . . .
>
> **2** If there is no pavement, keep to the right hand side of the road so that you can see oncoming traffic . . .
>
> **3** . . . Wear or carry something light-coloured, bright or fluorescent in poor daylight conditions. When it is dark, use reflective materials . . .'

So pedestrians should wear brightly coloured clothing at night. How many people over the age of 21 think of that before they go out to the theatre?

In a situation where for example a pedestrian may be struck at night and the pedestrian is wearing dark clothes without reflective materials, whilst liability will often be found against the driver, a higher level of contributory negligence will undoubtedly be argued for (and probably awarded) where the pedestrian was dressed in a such a way as it would make it more difficult for vehicles to spot him.

Other rules in the Highway Code state that:

> '**9** . . . Where there are barriers, cross the road only at the gaps provided for pedestrians and do not climb over the barriers or walk between them and the road.'
>
> '**14** . . . If you have to cross between parked vehicles, use the outside edges of the vehicles as if they were the kerb. Stop there and make sure you can see all around and that the traffic can see you . . . Never cross the road in front of, or behind, any vehicle with its engine running, especially a large vehicle, as the driver may not be able to see you.'

---

[3]   [1951] AC 601, at 611.

## 17.4   CROSSING THE ROAD

The most famous codification of a pedestrian's duty is contained within the 'Green Cross Code' incorporated as rule 7 in the Highway Code which states:

'(A)   First find a safe place to cross . . .
(B)   Stop just before you get to the kerb . . .
(C)   Look all around for traffic and listen . . .
(D)   If traffic is coming, let it pass . . .
(E)   When it is safe, go straight across the road – do not run . . .'

If a pedestrian breaches this rule and an impact occurs the liability will usually follow.

## 17.5   TRAFFIC LIGHT CROSSINGS

The general rule (Highway Code, rule 21) is that a pedestrian should only cross the road at traffic lights when a constant 'green man' is showing. If the green man starts flashing whilst on the crossing then the pedestrian continues to have right of way and should have sufficient time to complete their crossing before the traffic lights signal green to the traffic. If the green man is already flashing when arriving at the junction to cross, the pedestrian should not begin to cross.

A pedestrian is entitled to assume that motorists will not drive onto a crossing in contravention of a red light. In *Tremayne v Shell*,[4] a pedestrian negotiating a complicated multiple road junction at night was struck by a car that had passed a stop line against red traffic lights. The Court of Appeal held that driving over a crossing against a red traffic light was conclusive against the motorist. The pedestrian, whether or not he looked in the direction of the oncoming car, was entitled to assume that traffic would stop on the light turning red.

But what is the position if the pedestrian crossed when his traffic lights were red? Will he be completely to blame? The leading case on the topic is *Fitzgerald v Lane*[5] in which a pedestrian attempted to cross the road at traffic lights showing green in favour of car traffic. A motorist, who was travelling at excessive speed and was not keeping a proper look out for pedestrians, proceeded through the green light. The House of Lords held that liability should be apportioned evenly between the parties. This case clearly shows that there is still a duty on a motorists to take care (keep a proper look out and maintain a safe speed) when going through a crossing, even if the lights are in the driver's favour.

---

[4]   (1986) *The Times*, December 11.
[5]   [1988] 2 All ER 961.

A clearer case of negligence arose in *Shepherd v H West & Son Ltd*,[6] where a lorry ran down a pedestrian on a traffic light crossing. The traffic lights were showing red for cars as the claimant walked across the road. She was in the process of passing the vehicle closest to her (a bus) on a two-lane road when the lights turned from red to amber for cars. A lorry proceeded (legally) through the amber light in the outside (second) lane, overtook the stationary bus and struck the claimant. The Court of Appeal had no hesitation in saying that the lorry driver was negligent:

> 'A reasonable driver in such circumstances would not have let the front wheels of his lorry get level with the bus until the bus had got halfway across the crossing. To pass a stationary vehicle under such circumstances was dangerous practice.'

There is quite a high standard of care required of drivers at traffic light crossings as was shown in *Watson v Skuse*.[7] The Court of Appeal considered a claimant who attempted to cross the road in front of a large lorry. The judge at first instance found that it would have been impossible for the lorry driver to have been able to see the claimant as the claimant had chosen to cross not at the appropriate markings but very close to the front of the lorry. The claimant failed to clear the junction (or the front of the lorry) before the traffic lights changed and he was struck by the lorry as it pulled away. The claimant was criticised by judges both at first instance and in the Court of Appeal, for what was a foolish course of action. However, the Court of Appeal did not dismiss the claim, preferring to hold contributory negligence (at 80%) and stating that some liability (20%) must still attach to the driver on the basis that:

> 'A driver of a motor vehicle owed a duty of care to other road users including pedestrians and would have to exercise a particularly high degree of vigilance to the young, infirm and foolish people.'

The best general advice to motorists is that they should slow down when approaching traffic light controlled crossings: see *Moore v Poyner*.[8]

In practice it is therefore crucial to determine the factual matrix of the road and the pedestrian's attempted crossing, such as whether the vehicle behind the defendant noticed any brake lights or other cautious behaviour by the driver.

The classic image conjured up when considering possible dangers is of a football being kicked into a residential road by a child and chased, or of children emerging from behind ice cream vans. However, the caution applies to all manner of situations, whether it be driving past a school in the morning or late afternoon, or seeing brake lights ahead of you whilst driving along a motorway.

---

[6]   [1962] Sol Jo 391, at 392, CA.
[7]   [2001] EWCA Civ 1158, CA.
[8]   [1975] RTR 127.

The Highway Code reinforces the need for drivers to pay particular care and drive slowly when passing schools, shopping areas, bus stops or parked vehicles, especially ice cream vans and stationary buses (see rules 204–210).

## 17.6 PEDESTRIAN CROSSINGS

Pedestrian crossings are governed by the little known Zebra, Pelican and Puffin Crossing Regulations and General Directions 1997.[9] Regulation 18 prohibits vehicles stopping on crossings; reg 24 prohibits vehicles overtaking at crossings and reg 25 gives precedence to pedestrians over vehicles at zebra crossings.

### 17.6.1 Zebra crossings

Zebra crossings are uncontrolled by traffic lights. They are identified by white staggered lines across the road often with flashing round yellow lights on either side of the pavement.

The Highway Code, provides:

> '19 Give traffic plenty of time to see you and to stop before you start to cross. Vehicles will need more time when the road is slippery. Wait until traffic has stopped from both directions or the road is clear before crossing. Remember that traffic does not have to stop until someone has moved onto the crossing. Keep looking both ways, and listening, in case a driver or rider has not seen you and attempts to overtake a vehicle that has stopped.'

Whilst pedestrian crossings are clearly the appropriate place for a pedestrian to cross the road, they do not provide an absolute right for the pedestrian to step into the road and there remains an onus, as expressed in the Highway Code above, to be vigilant and check before stepping out. So it is unwise to step out onto a crossing when a car is already clearly going to go over the crossing without stopping. However, the share of blame depends on the speed of the driver and whether he was keeping any proper look out; the range of apportionments is very wide.

Set out below is a selection of cases dealing with apportionment of liability in cases where pedestrians have stepped onto crossings. The oldest decision and the strictest for drivers is *Scott*. In *Scott v Clint*,[10] it was held that reg 4 of the Pedestrian Crossing Regulations 1954 laid down an absolute duty that once a pedestrian was on a crossing the driver of any vehicle approaching that crossing must accord him precedence, however unexpectedly or suddenly he crossed. A lorry was only 10 yards away from a pedestrian crossing and going at 15–20mph when two children walked

9    SI 1997/2400.
10   (1960) *The Times*, 28 October, Div Ct.

out onto the crossing without looking. The defendant was found entirely to blame. Whilst it may appear a harsh decision to find fully against the defendant it underlines the guidance and rules within the Highway Code which warn drivers to be especially careful and slow down when approaching a pedestrian crossing.

In *Kozimore v Adey*[11] the pedestrian 'ran blindly' onto the crossing. Her fault was assessed at 75%.

In *Lawrence v W N Palmer (Excavations) Ltd*[12] a pedestrian proceeded to cross without regard to whether there was traffic on the road and so her negligence was assessed at 33%.

In *Williams v Needham*[13] and *Maynard v Rogers*[14] the pedestrians would have been able to see the cars involved if they had looked, but stepped out without looking, contributory negligence was assessed at 66%.

In *Clifford v Drymond*[15] the pedestrian failed to look to her right before stepping out; had she done so she would have seen a vehicle about 75ft away travelling at approximately 30mph. Negligence was apportioned at 20% against the claimant.

### 17.6.2   Pelican crossings

Pelican crossings are signalled controlled crossings operated by pedestrians. They need to be activated by the pedestrian by pressing the control button in order to trigger the light phasing to change. The general rules of road crossing apply: pedestrians are warned not to cross whilst the green man is flashing (or a red man is shown) (see Highway Code, rule 22).

### 17.6.3   Puffin crossings

Puffin crossings differ from Pelican crossings as the red and green men are above the control box at the side of the road and there is no flashing green stage.

### 17.6.4   Toucan crossings

Toucan crossings are light controlled crossings which allow cyclists and pedestrians to share the crossing space and cross at the same time. They are push button operated. Cyclists are permitted to ride across the crossing and do not have to dismount.

---

[11]   (1962) 106 Sol Jo 431.
[12]   (1965) 109 Sol Jo 358.
[13]   [1972] RTR 387.
[14]   [1970] RTR 392.
[15]   [1976] RTR 134.

## 17.6.5  School crossings

Local authorities are empowered by s 26 of the Road Traffic Regulation Act 1984 to arrange for the patrolling of crossings used by children on their way to and from school. School crossings are identified by a uniformed school crossing patrol (colloquially referred to as lollipop) man/woman.

Section 28(2) of the Act sets out the circumstances under which vehicles can be required to stop by a school crossing patrol:

> 'He shall cause the vehicle to stop before reaching the place where the children are crossing or seeking to cross and so as not to stop or impede their crossing, and the vehicle shall not be out in motion again so as to reach the place in question so long as the sign continues to be exhibited.'

The obligation to stop is absolute and it is no defence in criminal proceedings to show that no one was impeded by the motorist's failure to stop.

However, lollipop men and women owe duties to the children and must take care when the children are under their supervision. So in *Toole v Sherbourne Pouffes Ltd*[16] the Court of Appeal examined the duties of a lollipop man. A six-year-old claimant came out of a school which was close to a main road and was taken by a teacher with other children to a pedestrian crossing. A school crossing patrolman was stationed there. He stood at the side of the road with the children waiting until he could step forward with his sign board to stop the traffic. The first defendant's van was approaching and as he saw that the patrolman and his sign remained at the side of the road, proceeded at around 30mph. Suddenly the claimant darted out across the road and was hit by the van. At first instance the judge held the first defendant free from blame. Instead the local authority was found liable on the basis that they employed the patrolman and were therefore vicariously liable for his negligence in allowing the claimant to dart into the road. On appeal the Court of Appeal upheld that decision stating that the patrolman had failed to do enough to keep the children under control. They stated that had he been really exercising proper charge and keeping them back the claimant would not have made the sudden dart across the road. It is worth noting that the second defendant had chosen not to call the lollipop man to give evidence.

## 17.6.6  Not using crossings

In *Snow v Giddins*,[17] the claimant had begun to cross the road at a spot near a road junction and not far from a pedestrian crossing which had a central refuge. The claimant threaded his way through the northbound

---

[16] [1971] RTR 479, CA.
[17] (1969) 113 Sol Jo 229, CA.

traffic, which was stationary and then stood in the middle of the road just over the centre line. He was then struck by a motorcyclist who had been in the process of overtaking the stationary traffic. At first instance the defendant motorbike rider was held wholly to blame. On appeal the Court of Appeal held that whilst the claimant was not negligent in failing to use a pedestrian crossing he was negligent for taking on the risk that he could be marooned in the centre of the road at the mercy of oncoming traffic instead of crossing where there was a central refuge. They held that a:

> 'person who elected not use a crossing took upon himself a higher standard of care.'

The appeal was allowed and a finding of 25% contributory negligence was made.

When considering whether to cross the road at a particular point, pedestrians must not only look around for traffic and listen:

> ' . . . but should also attempt to assess the speed and therefore, danger posed by any approaching traffic.'

This speed assessment duty was relevant in *Mulligan v Holmes*[18] where a pedestrian claimant crossing the road failed to work out the approximate speed of a car from his view of its headlights! The car was speeding and the court held the pedestrian had contributed negligence for that failure to notice the high speed. This was assessed at 20%.

In the recent case of *Greenwood v Cummings*[19] a motorcyclist struck a pedestrian who had stepped out into the road. The motorcyclist's visibility had been affected by driving towards the sun and he had simply failed to see the claimant. The claimant had not stopped when reaching the kerb and simply stepped out into the road. It was held that had the motorcyclist been paying better attention and driving slower he might have been able to stop in time. Additionally the claimant's actions in failing to stop at the kerb and failing to keep a proper look out were sufficient for a finding of one-third contributory negligence against him.

## 17.7   WALKING ALONG THE ROAD

Pedestrians are entitled to step off the pavement to avoid a hazard or obstruction, such as a projecting building, overhanging trees or hedges, pot-holes, floods or snow. The decision to step off the pavement if compelled by necessity is unlikely to be evidence of negligence. When the court investigates the factual scenario which caused the claimant to step off the pavement it will have to weigh up how compelling the need was and what, if any, checks the claimant made before doing so.

---

[18]   [1971] RTR 179.
[19]   (Unreported) (2008) QBD LTL 18/09/2008.

## 17.8   STANDING ON THE PAVEMENT

If a pedestrian is standing on the pavement, he is entitled to consider himself safe as vehicles have no business on the pavement. A pavement is after all the appropriate and expected place for a pedestrian to be. Cases sometimes arise when part of a vehicle, possibly a lorry wing mirror, overhangs the kerb. Lord Denning MR dealt with this scenario in a claimant friendly way in *Chapman v Post Office*[20] where he concluded:

> 'I see no reason why a person standing on the kerb is guilty of negligence at all; even if she leans out or has her back turned to the oncoming traffic. Even if she went an inch or two into the roadway, I cannot see that would amount to negligence in the slightest. The very fact that a van driver hits with his wing mirror a lady standing legitimately on the kerbside means that he is at fault and she is not.'

## 17.9   DRUNKEN PEDESTRIANS

Drunken pedestrians involved in accidents are usually dealt with by a finding of contributory negligence, where the evidence points to them having contributed to the accident. Apportionment in such cases is very fact specific. The court will need to look at the degree of negligence of the driver and his blameworthiness and then try to establish how the intoxication contributed to the claimant being injured. A couple of examples of how the courts have dealt with drunken pedestrians in the past are set out below.

In *Lunt v Khelifa*[21] (see above for facts) as previously stated in this chapter, the pedestrian (Mr Lunt) who stumbled out into the road three times over the legal drink drive limit, was held one-third liable for the impact.

Lying in the road in a drunken stupor is not a good idea for pedestrians. So in *Green v Bannister*[22] the Court of Appeal heard that the defendant had been reversing her car at night from a parking space outside her home in a cul-de-sac. She had been looking over her right shoulder in order to avoid hitting any parked cars. The defendant continued for around 35 yards when, as she manoeuvred past shrubbery, she reversed over the claimant who was lying in the road in a drunken stupor. The trial judge apportioned liability 60%/40% against the claimant stating that he was more to blame than the defendant driver. The Court of Appeal upheld the first instance decision stating that:

> 'It had been open to the trial judge to conclude that (i) the care needed in travelling down this particular street in reverse gear at night called for particular attention to what might be in the car's path; (ii) that the driver

---

[20]   [1982] RTR 165, CA.
[21]   [2002] EWCA Civ 801.
[22]   [2003] EWCA Civ 1819.

ought to have checked in her nearside mirror as well as over her right shoulder and that (iii) had she done so she would have probably seen the claimant lying in the road. They went on to say however that:

> "Once the driver had been held negligent, the conclusion that the claimant was the more blameworthy of the two and was 60% contributorily negligent had by no means been unfair to the driver.'"

## 17.10   CHILDREN

Children are described by the Highway Code as particularly vulnerable pedestrians. To that extent drivers need to take even more care when they are or are likely to be in the vicinity of children. Although contributory negligence is unlikely against very small children, there are numerous first instance cases with finding of contributory negligence in claimants aged 9 and upwards.

In *Rowe v Clark*[23] the claimant was a 14-years-and-8-months-old schoolboy. He was returning from a shop at lunchtime with four other boys. They all had to cross the road. The defendant was driving her car with her small son strapped into the back seat. The road was painted with the marking 'SLOW' in capital letters, alongside conventional 'school' signs. The claimant, having crossed more than half of the road from the shop back towards the school, was struck by the defendant whilst she was driving on her side of the road. The judge found as a fact that the children were late back to school and were hurrying. The defendant stated that she had seen two of the boys cross the road and three of the boys remained on the pavement. It was held that she had not sounded her horn or slowed down. She did not watch those on the pavement and the judge at first instance found the parties equally to blame. The finding was upheld on appeal. The defendant had failed to keep a proper lookout, had failed to sound her horn and was driving too fast in an area where danger was likely. In justifying the 50% contributory negligence against the child the court stated that:

> 'a boy aged nearly 15 must be expected to take reasonable care of himself. The degree of care varies with the age of the child. There is a distinction to be drawn between a child of 12 and one of 14 and likewise between a boy of 14 and one of 16. He should not have rushed into the road. He was negligent in apparently not seeing the approaching car.'

In *Honnor v Lewis*[24] a finding of 20% contributory negligence was made against an 11-year-old who crossed a road and failed to see the defendant's car approaching. It was held that an 11-year-old should have 'realised the need to look carefully for traffic coming from his right before crossing'.

---

[23]   [1998] Lawtel, C8400268.
[24]   [2005] EWHC 747 (QB).

Assessment of contribution by a child involves two parts in accordance with the Law Reform (Contributory Negligence) Act 1945. The court will assess the causative potency of the lack of care and the blameworthiness. Children shoulder less blame generally the younger they are. So in *Russell v Smith & Another*,[25] a 10-year-old cyclist was injured when he cycled across a road junction where he should have given way into the oncoming path of a vehicle. The trial judge found that the child was 75% to blame for the accident. However, having regard to s 1 of the Law Reform Contributory Negligence Act of 1945 and to the provisions of the Highway Code on the general vulnerability of cyclists, and children in particular, the Court reduced the claimant's damages by 50% only. It is, of course, to be noted that the claimant in the above case was a child; it is suggested that a court is likely to be less sympathetic to adult cyclists.

Whilst there are plenty of cases to support split liability findings in relation to children, the courts have also recognised that children can simply be careless, leaving drivers with no alternative than to come into collision with them. If the driver has kept a proper look out and driven slowly then no negligence arises and no claim can succeed.

In *Carter v Sheath*[26] a 13-year-old pedestrian stepped out onto a pelican crossing when the evidence was that a red man was showing to him. He was subsequently hit by the defendant who passed correctly through a green traffic light. The claim was dismissed with the motorist found to be a 'good, careful driver', and as such she was exonerated of any blame.

The defendant was also successful at first instance in *Lunn v Kilkenny*[27] where a 3-year-old climbed over her garden gate and ran into the road attempting to reach an ice cream van. HHJ Grenfell held that the defendant had taken a great deal of care as she approached the ice cream van, cognisant that children might be in the vicinity. The defendant only had a split second to react and in any event it was unlikely that even if she had sounded her horn the child would have altered course. He stated that:

> 'It was an impossible burden on any motorist to anticipate that a child was going to dash out from any parked van.'

## 17.11  APPORTIONMENT OF LIABILITY

The classic statement of principle for apportionment of liability in pedestrian/car impact running down cases is in *Baker v Willoughby*.[28] The House of Lords recognised that the duties of pedestrians and motorists are necessarily different. Lord Reid held:

---

[25]   [2003] EWHC 2060 (QB).
[26]   [1990] RTR 12.
[27]   (2003) Lawtel AC0108213.
[28]   [1970] AC 467.

'A pedestrian has to look to both sides as well as forwards. He is going at perhaps 3mph. At that speed he is rarely a danger to anyone else. The motorist has not got to look sideways though he may have to observe over a wide angle ahead; and if he is going at considerable speed, he must not relax his observations, for the consequences may be disastrous, and it sometimes happens that he sees the pedestrian is not looking his way and takes a chance the pedestrian would not stop and that he can safely cross behind him. In my opinion, it is quite possible that the motorist may be very much more to blame than the pedestrian.'

The courts rightly place a considerable burden on the driver. This was explored in *Lunt v Khelifa*.[29] A pedestrian was attempting to cross a road and stepped out effectively in front of the defendant's car. It was agreed that at the time the pedestrian stepped into the road the defendant was only 20 to 25 yards away and travelling at 25mph. But the defendant was three times over the legal drink drive limit. At first instance the judge held that the defendant should have been aware that pedestrians were in the area and given that there was no evidence that the defendant had seen the pedestrian prior to impact the defendant should bear the majority of responsibility. He awarded liability two-thirds:one-third in the pedestrian's favour. In the Court of Appeal, Latham LJ giving the leading judgment considered that the first instance judge had been somewhat generous to the pedestrian given that:

'he [the pedestrian] was the one who had created the dangerous position by stepping out into the road'

but refused to interfere with the level of contributory negligence stating:

'. . . this court has consistently imposed upon drivers of cars a high burden to reflect the fact that the car is a potentially dangerous weapon.'

This line appears consistent with much of the recent case law relating to pedestrian accidents. So Hale LJ, giving judgment in the Court of Appeal in *Eagle v Chambers*[30] stated:

'It is rare indeed for a pedestrian to be found more responsible than a driver unless the pedestrian has suddenly stepped out into the path of an oncoming vehicle.'

In *Sahakian v McDonnell & Anor*[31] the first instance judge considered *Eagle v Chambers* and held that liability should be apportioned 50%:50% between the two parties where the claimant had 'hurried across the road from behind a car' but the CCTV evidence showed the defendant was driving: 'too quickly for the conditions and had not seen the Claimant in time to effect any proper braking'.

---

[29]   [2002] EWCA Civ 801.
[30]   [2003] JPIL C151, CA.
[31]   [2007] EWHC 3242 (QB).

See also *Jukes v (1) Etti (2) Motor Insurers Bureau*[32] and *Adeji v King*,[33] where liability was apportioned 60%:40% in the claimant's favour; and *Williams v Needham*[34] where the claimant was held two-thirds liable after stepping into the road without looking.

On occasion pedestrian accidents occur when a vehicle leaves the road and collides with a pedestrian on the pavement. But the vast majority of pedestrian accidents arise when pedestrians are attempting to cross the road. As set out above there are many different types of pedestrian crossings: traffic light controlled junctions, Zebra, Pelican, Puffin, Toucan and special school crossings.

Apportionment is by its nature a fact-sensitive exercise and on that basis there is a reluctance in the appeal courts to alter levels of contributory negligence unless they consider the apportionment to be wholly out of step with reality.

An example of this reluctance is *Ehrari v Curry & Anor*.[35] The claimant was an 11-year-old child who wanted to cross a busy road in order to catch a bus. She stepped out into the road from behind a parked car and was subsequently hit by the defendant's lorry wing mirror. The defendant had previously seen children in the vicinity although he had had only 1 second to register the claimant's presence when she stepped out before the impact took place. The Judge awarded the claimant 70% of the damages. On appeal it was held that the driver should have noted that there was an obvious source of danger on the pavement, namely children and that he should have kept a careful watch. The evidence suggested that even though the defendant only had 1 second to react, a slight movement of the steering wheel would have been sufficient to avoid the claimant. So the appeal was dismissed and judgment remained on the basis of 70/30.

## 17.12  PEDESTRIAN LIABILITY TO MOTORISTS

Whilst the majority of cases within this chapter follow the rule that the motorist is likely to be found more liable than the pedestrian, there are occasions where accidents will be solely the pedestrian's fault and cause the motorist to suffer loss and damage.

So in *Eames v Cunningham and Capps*[36] a motorcyclist's pillion passenger was killed when a pedestrian stepped into the road causing a collision. The motorcyclist gave evidence that the pedestrian had stepped into the road, hesitated and then stepped in front of the motorcycle. The

---

[32]  [2006] EWHC 2493 (QB).
[33]  [2003] Lawtel AC9900497, CA.
[34]  [1972] RTR 387, QBD.
[35]  [2007] EWCA Civ 120.
[36]  (1948) Eastern Daily Press, 1 June, 82 Sol Jo 314.

motorcyclist had also sounded his horn prior to the collision. The court held that the motorcyclist had not been negligent and gave judgment for the motorcyclist.

Similarly in *Barry v MacDonald*[37] the defendant (pedestrian) collided with a motorcyclist who sustained fatal injuries as a result of the accident. The defendant's evidence was that he: 'stepped off the kerb without looking and the next thing I was flying. It was entirely my fault'. Understandably the court held that the defendant was solely liable for causing the accident and entered judgment for the motorcyclist.

---

[37]   (1966) 110 Sol Jo 56.

# CHAPTER 18

## LIABILITY OF CHILDREN AND SCHOOLS

*Shahram Sharghy*

### 18.1 INTRODUCTION

Whilst it is clear that a motorist owes a duty of care to a pedestrian, it is quite often forgotten that there is a similar duty imposed on a pedestrian to exercise due care and attention when crossing a road.

Additionally some pedestrians require from drivers special additional care because of their disability, infirmity or age. The most obvious type of pedestrian who requires special consideration and attention is a child. But blind pedestrians, deaf pedestrians and other disabled members of the public also require special attention from drivers.

Whether driving on a road outside a child's home, in a shopping mall or outside a school, drivers are required to be aware of the special risk created by children in all such situations. Sometimes after an accident it is clear where the responsibility lies, but in most cases it is not easy to strike the balance between the liability of a reasonably prudent and cautious driver and the responsibility of a child.

The purpose of this chapter is to demonstrate how courts have dealt with road traffic accidents where children have been injured or involved and to summarise the guidance which can be gleaned from these judgments.

### 18.2 THE THREE MAIN RULES

We tentatively offer the following three main rules from the cases set out below:

(1) The general standard of care expected of a driver is that of a 'reasonably prudent driver' not a 'perfect driver' who takes every imaginable precaution. And the law expects that a reasonably prudent driver would have the following in mind when driving:
   (a) the likelihood of pedestrians crossing into his/her path; and,
   (b) the increased likelihood of a child pedestrian crossing the road when it is not safe to do so. Furthermore, when driving near a

group of young children, especially young boys playing football, or driving near ice cream vans, a very high standard of caution is required.

(2)   It would be an excessive requirement for the law to expect drivers to sound their horns every time they passed a parked car or saw a child on a pavement. Similarly, although it is going too far to say a prudent driver should start to brake just because he sees a child on a pavement doing nothing out of the ordinary, still the law expects drivers to slow down and keep a careful look out when children are about.

(3)   A judge will only find a child guilty of contributory negligence if he or she was of such an age as to be expected to take better precautions for his/her own safety. There is a distinction to be drawn between a child of 10 and one of 14 and likewise between a child of 14 and one of 16. As a general rule children under 10 are unlikely to be held contributorily negligent. Children between 10 and 12 may well be held contributorily negligent, but this will depend on their understanding of road safety, which will be a question of fact for the judge. It may depend on whether they have been taught the Green Cross Code at school or at home.

In common with all of the other situations in which impacts occur on roads the two main mistakes made by drivers are: failing to keep a proper look out and driving at excessive speed. In child pedestrian cases the additional factor is the unpredictability of the behaviour of children due to their lack of road sense and this impacts on the duty which the courts impose on drivers nearby. Negligence can and has been found against a driver due to driving at excessive speed when he was travelling at only 15 miles per hour!

## 18.3   THE HIGHWAY CODE (2007)

There are plenty of rules in the Highway Code dealing with the driver's responsibility in circumstances where child pedestrians will be present. So for instance:

### 'Crossing the road

7 The Green Cross Code. The advice given on crossing the road is intended for all pedestrians. Children should be taught the Code and should not be allowed out alone until they can understand and use it properly. The age when they can do this is different for each child. Many children cannot judge how fast vehicles are going or how far away they are. Children learn by example, so parents and carers should always use the Code in full when out with their children. They are responsible for deciding at what age children can use it safely by themselves.'

### 'Crossings

**18** At all crossings, when using any type of crossing you should always check that the traffic has stopped before you start to cross or push a pram onto a crossing and always cross between the studs or over the zebra markings. Do not cross at the side of the crossing or on the zig-zag lines, as it can be dangerous.

You MUST NOT loiter on any type of crossing.'

'**29** Crossing controlled by an authorised person. Do not cross the road unless you are signalled to do so by a police officer, traffic warden or school crossing patrol. Always cross in front of them.'

### 'Signals

**105** You MUST obey signals given by police officers, traffic officers, traffic wardens and signs used by school crossing patrols.'

### 'Road Users Requiring Extra Care

**204** The most vulnerable road users are pedestrians, cyclists and motorcyclists and horse riders. It is particularly important to be aware of children, older and disabled people, and learner and inexperienced drivers and riders.

. . .

**208** Near schools. Drive slowly and be particularly aware of young cyclists and pedestrians. In some places, there may be a flashing amber signal below the 'School' warning sign which tells you that there may be children crossing the road ahead. Drive very slowly until you are clear of the area.

**209** Drive carefully and slowly when passing a stationary bus showing a 'School Bus' sign as children may be getting on or off.

**210** You MUST stop when a school crossing patrol shows a "Stop for children" sign.'

## 18.4  CHILDREN NOT FOUND NEGLIGENT

Children do not have the same understanding, experience or appreciation of danger as adults do. So when they are put in potentially dangerous road traffic situations a lower standard of care is expected of them. Indeed when very young no standard of care is expected of them. As they mature the standard is imposed and then raised.

In one example a car driver waved a child pedestrian across a road in front of him and she followed his direction and was run down as she crossed. The crossing was dangerous. An adult in those circumstances would have been found partly to blame. But in *Gough v Thorne*[1] the child was not found to blame. The claimant was aged 13½ and was waiting with her brothers aged 17 and 10 to cross the road. A lorry stopped to allow them to cross. The driver put his right hand out to warn other traffic and beckoned the children to cross. They had crossed to just beyond the lorry when a car driven by the defendant came past the lorry at speed and hit the claimant. The judge held the defendant negligent but also held the claimant one-third to blame for having advanced past the lorry into the open road without pausing to see whether there was any traffic coming from her right. On appeal it was held that the claimant was not to blame at all. Although there was no age below which it could be said that a child could not ever be guilty of contributory negligence, age was a most material fact to be considered. The question whether the claimant could be said to be guilty of contributory negligence depended on whether any ordinary child of 13½ could be expected to do any more than she did. If she had been a good deal older she might have wondered whether a proper signal had been given by the lorry driver and looked to see whether any traffic was coming, but it was quite wrong to suggest that a child of 13½ should go though such mental processes.

Per Lord Denning MR: A judge should only find a child guilty of contributory negligence if he or she was of such an age as to be expected to take precautions for his or her own safety and should only make such a finding if blame could be attached to him. Where a child had no road sense and none of the experience of older people, no blame could be attributed to him or her.

If a child is so young that an understanding of safety cannot reasonably be expected then the child will not be held to have been negligent.

For instance, a child of 3 years old cannot not be held to be negligent on roads. So in *Prudence v Lewis*[2] a child aged just under 3 years old was struck by the defendant's car on a pedestrian crossing. His mother had been waiting to cross, holding her youngest child in a pushchair poised on the edge of the kerb at the crossing. While she looked round for her third child the claimant ran on to the crossing and was hit when he was about 7ft from the kerb. It was held that the defendant was wholly to blame. He had seen the mother and children but, though realising that any child was likely to run out, did not blow his horn thinking that they should wait for him to pass. A child of just under 3 years old was incapable of being guilty of contributory negligence.

The responsibility of a 5-year-old was considered in *M (a child) v Rollinson*.[3] The claimant (aged 5) was taken by her father to purchase an ice cream from an ice cream van. She took the ice cream and went around

---

[1]   [1966] 1 WLR 1387.
[2]   [1966] *The Times*, 21 May, Brabin J.
[3]   [2003] 2 QR 14.

the front of the van whilst her father was paying for it. She then ran into the side of the defendant's vehicle which was driving past at no more than 15mph. It was held that whilst it was generally not negligent to pass a parked vehicle at 15mph, consideration had to be given to the fact that the vehicle was an ice cream van and carried a warning to its rear. Any reasonable person should have been aware of that hazard and 15mph was not slow enough to avoid the impact. The accident occurred in a residential area. The defendant had not been sufficiently careful and was liable to M in damages. This case should be compared to the Court of Appeal decision in the case of *Kite v Nolan*[4] below.

The responsibility of a 6-year-old was considered in *Puffett (a child) v Hayfield*.[5] The claimant aged 6 at the time of the accident was seriously injured after he was struck by the defendant's car. The road was residential and both the claimant and defendant lived there. It was dark although street lights were on. The road was dry and weather conditions were good. At 7pm children regularly played in the street. The claimant emerged between two parked vehicles, one of which was a van, into the path of the defendant's vehicle. The claimant's presence would have been obscured from the defendant behind the van. The defendant was going too fast. The defendant was found liable at first instance and the child was not found at all to blame. On appeal it was held that the judge was right to find the defendant negligent in that her speed was excessive in the circumstances. Per Pill LJ: Had the defendant been driving at a lower speed, she would have had a better opportunity of reacting to an unexpected movement on to the road and thereby avoiding a collision. However, there will be cases where the movement into the road is so proximate to the car's approach that, even at a lower speed, the driver will not be able to avoid a collision.

Likewise in *Jones v Lawrence*[6] a boy aged 7 ran across a street from behind a parked van. The defendant was riding his motorcycle near the crown of the road and was unable to avoid striking the claimant, who had failed to see the motorcycle approaching. There was a 30mph speed limit but the judge found from independent evidence that the defendant's speed was about 50mph. It was held that by travelling at such a speed the defendant had deprived himself of the opportunity to avoid the collision by swerving or braking and was negligent. The claimant's behaviour was such as one could expect in a normal child of his age momentarily forgetful of the perils of crossing a road and no finding of contributory negligence could be made against him.

The Court of Appeal considered the age of responsibility in *Andrews v Freeborough*[7] where Davies LJ held that an 8-year-old child was too young

---

4    [1983] RTR 253, CA.
5    [2005] EWCA Civ 1760, [2005] All ER (D) 256.
6    [1969] 3 All ER 267.
7    [1966] 3 WLR 342.

to be held negligent. The 8-year-old girl and her brother aged 4 were standing on the pavement edge waiting to cross the road. The defendant was driving her car at 15–20mph close to the kerb (because of oncoming traffic) and saw the children when she was about 40 yards away. She thought they were waiting to cross although they did not look in her direction. She did not reduce her speed or sound her horn. As the defendant's car passed the children, the girl's head came into violent contact with the windscreen. At the trial of the action the defendant said she saw the girl step off the pavement into the side of the car but the judge did not accept this evidence. He held the defendant to blame for: (a) not sounding her horn, (b) failing to reduce her speed and if necessary stop on seeing the children, and (c) driving too close to the kerb. He found no contributory negligence on the part of the child. On appeal Willmer LJ said:

> 'I confess I find it quite difficult to appreciate just how the accident happened if the child remained on the kerb throughout. But [the judge's] finding that the child did not step off the kerb was a finding of primary fact, based largely on his view of the quality of the evidence he had heard. In my judgment it is not a finding with which this Court could properly interfere.'

Per Davies LJ:

> 'I am bound to say that I am of the view that it was more probable that the child did step off the kerb into the side of the car. But it is not necessary to express any decided view on this point for the little girl was only 8 years of age. Even if she did step off into the car it would not be right to count as negligence on her part such a momentary, though fatal, act of inattention or carelessness.'

## 18.5   CHILDREN FOUND TO HAVE BEEN NEGLIGENT

Once a child is over 10 he is more likely to be found to bear responsibility for an accident caused by his running out into the road without looking. We set out the cases below in decreasing order of age from 16 to 11.

## 18.6   CONTRIBUTORY NEGLIGENCE

In *Foskett v Mistry*[8] the claimant was a boy aged 16½ years who ran down a parkland slope onto a busy road and collided with the nearside of the defendant's car near the windscreen, sustaining serious injury. The defendant had not seen him before he ran into the car. A driver coming in the opposite direction had seen the claimant and thought he was going to run into the road. The judge at first instance dismissed the claim. On appeal it was held that the defendant taking reasonable care ought to have glanced at the open parkland on his left and should have seen the

---

[8]   [1984] RTR 1, CA.

claimant when he emerged into his view. A reasonably careful driver would have sounded his horn in the circumstances; if the defendant had seen the claimant and sounded his horn the accident would probably have been prevented. The defendant was plainly negligent, though the claimant was guilty of contributory negligence to the extent of 75%.

In *Rowe v Clark*[9] the claimant was 14 years and 8 months of age at the date of the accident and was returning from a shop at lunchtime in the school day. He was with 4 other boys and they all had to cross the road. The defendant was driving along the road which was marked 'SLOW' along with conventional school signs. The accident happened on the defendant's side of the road, the claimant having crossed more than half of the road from the shop back towards the school. The children were late back to school and were hurrying. The defendant had seen two of the boys cross the road and three of the boys remained on the pavement, but had not sounded her horn or slowed down. She did not watch those on the pavement. The judge at first instance found both parties equally to blame for the accident. The defendant appealed on the grounds that she was blameless or alternatively 50% liability was too high. The claimant cross-appealed on the basis that 50% contributory negligence was too high. On appeal it was held that on the facts of the case, the defendant had failed to keep a proper look out in that she had not seen the claimant until the collision, even though she had noticed the boys and seen two of them cross the road. She should therefore have expected the others to cross and therefore was negligent in failing to watch them, to anticipate that they were going to cross the road and sound her horn. The defendant was further negligent in failing to approach a 'danger zone' at a very slow speed and had therefore failed to pay sufficient attention. However, a child of nearly 15 years of age must be expected to take reasonable care of himself. The degree of care varies with the age of the child. There is a distinction to be drawn between a child of 12 and one of 14 and likewise between a child of 14 and one of 16. The claimant should not have rushed into the road and was negligent in not seeing the defendant's approaching car. As such the judge's apportionment of liability could not be criticised. Per Swinton-Thomas LJ: There is a distinction to be drawn between a child of 12 and one of 14 and likewise between a boy of 14 and one of 16. There can be no doubt at all that the claimant ought not to have run out in the road when it was dangerous to do so and that he was negligent in failing to see the defendant's approaching car.

In *Grant v Dick*[10] the claimant who was 14 years old at the date of the accident was hit by the defendant's car whilst crossing a dual carriageway. She was one of a group of 10 children who were attempting to cross a busy dual carriageway. Some of the children had already crossed the road and were gesticulating to the remainder to cross. The defendant had seen the children crossing the road and could also see that some were clearly

---

[9]   (Unreported) (1998) CA.
[10]  [2003] EWHC 441 (QB).

waiting to cross to join their friends, but carried on at the same speed. It was held that applying the standards of a reasonably prudent driver the defendant was at fault because having seen some children cross the road and others poised to do the same, he should have reduced his speed and sounded his horn to halt the progress of the children (including the claimant) who were about to cross the road. However, although the defendant bore primary liability, the claimant was held partly responsible in that she had acted negligently in running in front of the defendant's car. Therefore liability was apportioned 60/40 in the claimant's favour.

In *Ehrari v Curry*[11] the 13-year-old claimant was struck by the defendant's truck when she walked out from behind a parked Volvo with furniture on the roof. The passenger saw the claimant a fraction before impact but the driver did not. It was held that because the passenger saw the claimant prior to the impact, the defendant's attention must have been elsewhere. The defendant's attention did not always have to be fixed in front but had it been, he could have blown his horn which might have avoided such a serious accident. Liability was apportioned 70/30 in the defendant's favour because the primary cause of the accident was the claimant walking into the road.

In *Armstrong v Cottrell*[12] the claimant, aged 12, attempted to cross a road, hesitated and was struck by the defendant's vehicle. The defendant had seen the claimant and her friends 'hovering' at the side of the road. The claimant's claim was dismissed by the trial judge. The appeal was allowed and judgment entered against the car driver, because the defendant had seen the claimant, she should have slowed down and sounded her horn. The claimant's contributory negligence was assessed at 33%.

In *Willbye v Gibbons*[13] the claimant, aged 12, was attempting to cross a road and ran into the side of the defendant's car. The car was travelling at 25mph. Prior to this collision the defendant had driven past a group of jostling boys. He was concerned enough about their behaviour to hoot his horn. The defendant then stopped behind parked cars on his side of the road to allow a car in the opposite direction to pass. As the defendant moved away he saw a child on his left moving in and out of the parked cars. He then saw the claimant standing on the kerb to his right 'poised' as if to run across the road and looking in his direction. The next time the defendant saw the claimant was as the collision occurred. It was accepted on the evidence that the defendant had accelerated to about 25mph over 20–25 yards from his stationary position behind the parked cars. The Recorder found the defendant was not negligent and that the claimant was wholly to blame for the accident. The claimant appealed. On appeal it was held that the Recorder had applied the proper test as follows: Did the defendant's driving fall below the standard of the reasonable driver, not

---

[11]  [2006] EWHC 1319 (QB), [2006] All ER (D) 61.
[12]  [1993] 2 PIQR P109, CA.
[13]  [2003] EWCA Civ 372, CA.

the perfect driver who takes every imaginable precaution, but the reasonable driver judged by reasonable standards of skill and ability? However, the Recorder did not properly assess the evidence of the defendant himself. The defendant was not keeping a proper look out. He failed to see the claimant crossing the road at all despite the fact there must have been at least 2 seconds from the moment that she took off from the kerb until the moment she ran into the side of the car. Secondly, from the stationary position, the defendant took off with greater acceleration than was called for in these particular circumstances. Had the defendant been paying proper attention and accelerated more moderately he could have braked and sounded his horn and, probably, the accident would not have occurred. The defendant was 25% responsible for the accident and the child claimant 75% to blame.

In *Britland v East Midland Motor Services Ltd*[14] the claimant was a 12-year-old boy on his way to school. Mr G was driving the defendant's school bus. The claimant ran along the pavement for 10–12 yards before veering right through parked cars to run across the road into the path of the defendant's bus. On appeal it was held that the claimant would have known that he should not have run into the road. He was thoughtless and reckless for his own safety. He was largely to blame. However the defendant driver ought to have noticed the claimant running along the road for those 10–12 yards and slowed his speed or covered his brakes in anticipation of the claimant running out. The defendant was 25% to blame.

In *Morales v Eccleston*[15] the claimant was an 11-year-old boy who was playing with a football along the pavement adjacent to a busy London road. The traffic was heavy but moving at 20–30mph on both sides of the road. The weather was fine, the road was dry and the visibility was good. The defendant was travelling at 20mph on the opposite side of the road to which the claimant was playing. The claimant lost control of his football and without looking in either direction, followed it across the first carriageway into the path of the defendant's vehicle. The trial judge held that the defendant was 80% to blame. The defendant appealed. On appeal, McCowan LJ said:

> '. . . on the evidence presented to the trial judge the defendant could not have had much more than two seconds in which to see the claimant. Despite this there was some evidence upon which the judge could have arrived at the view that the defendant was not keeping a proper look out. On the other hand the child claimant showed a reckless disregard for his own safety and must bear a higher proportion of blame for the accident than the defendant. Blame was apportioned at 25% to the defendant and 75% to the claimant.'

---

[14]  (Unreported) (1998) CA.
[15]  [1991] RTR 151, CA.

In *Melleney v Wainwright*[16] the claimant aged 11 ran into the path of the defendant's car. The claimant's two friends had already crossed the road and the claimant was attempting to join them. The defendant was travelling on the road with a 60mph limit. He had seen the claimant and braked momentarily to reduce his speed to 30mph. The judge found that the defendant had foreseen the possibility that the claimant might cross and was therefore negligent. Given that he was not aware that the claimant had definitely seen him, he should have taken the precaution of sounding his horn and slowing down substantially. The claimant's contributory negligence was assessed at one third. The defendant's appeal was dismissed:

> 'I do not think it can be overstated, that when motorists are driving near to a group of young children, and especially young boys, a very high standard of caution indeed is required. Here were three 11 year old lads, two had crossed the road, their companion, the plaintiff, was left stranded on the side from which they had come. The risk of him doing something silly in order to rejoin them ought to have been foreseen as a very high risk. The precautions the defendant did take were simply not adequate, in my view, to discharge his duty as a driver of a motor vehicle approaching the situation that he had seen' (as per Sir Richard Scott, VC).

In *Wells v Trinder*[17] the pedestrian claimant was hit by the defendant's car while crossing a road. The claimant's mother had just dropped her off and had seen the approaching defendant's car and shouted to warn the claimant. The judge at first instance found in favour of the claimant. The defendant appealed on the grounds that the judge had failed to attach contributory negligence or should not have found against the defendant at all. On appeal it was held that the judge at first instance had found that the defendant approached the scene very fast. The judge was therefore entitled to find negligence against the defendant on the basis of his speed and failure to have his full lights on. With regards to the issue of contributory negligence, it was held that it was difficult to see how the claimant could be acquitted of all responsibility in the case, as the claimant's mother had seen the oncoming car and therefore there was no reason why the claimant should not have seen it. The claimant was held 25% liable for her own injuries. (Her age is not stated anywhere in the judgment of the Court of Appeal.)

In *Honnor v Lewis*[18] the claimant who was aged 11, almost 12 years old at the time of the accident, was attempting to cross the road to get to school when he was struck by the defendant's car. The school was directly opposite where the claimant attempted to cross the road and the road was known to be highly populated with school children at that time of the morning. It was the defendant's case that he did not see the claimant until immediately prior to the collision and that he was travelling well within

---

[16]   (Unreported) (1997) CA.
[17]   [2002] EWCA Civ 1030, [2002] All ER (D) 122.
[18]   [2005] EWHC 747 (QB), [2005] All ER (D) 374.

the speed limit. The claimant, who had red hair, was seen by a witness who was travelling immediately behind the defendant's car. Although the claimant did not have any recollection of events, the evidence suggested that the claimant had not seen the defendant's vehicle before the collision. It was held that the defendant was negligent for failing to slow down, failing to notice the school warning sign, failing to sound his horn and failing to notice the presence of the claimant. As the claimant stepped out into the road without noticing the presence of the defendant's car the claimant was found to be 20% responsible for his own injuries. Per Silber J: A child of 11 years of age should have realised the need to look out carefully for traffic coming from his right, especially on a busy road. Even if he had seen the car but had misjudged the distance, he would still be negligent.

## 18.7   DRIVER NOT AT FAULT

If the child steps out into the road from behind a van or lorry and walks into the side of a moving vehicle there is no point bringing the claim because unless it can be shown that the car driver did something wrong, no negligence will be found. Unless a child is visible on the approach of the car or a school or ice cream van is visible, the higher duty of care applying in the presence of children does not arise.

In more recent times, the courts have become reluctant to base liability on use of the horn where the car driver has slowed down in response to the risk that a child may run out.

So in *Moore v Poyner*[19] the defendant was driving his car at 25–30mph along a street on a Sunday afternoon. There was no other traffic. A coach 30ft long was parked against the nearside pavement and concealed from the defendant an opening between the houses on that side of the road just beyond the front of the coach. As the defendant's car was passing the coach the claimant, a child of six, ran from the opening across the front of the coach into the defendant's path and was struck by the nearside front of the car. The judge held the defendant liable as he should have slowed down or sounded his horn. On appeal it was held that the defendant was not liable. The test to be applied to the facts was would it have been apparent to a reasonable man, armed with common sense and experience of the way pedestrians, particularly children, behave in certain circumstances to have slowed down or sounded his horn, or both? What course of action would have been taken if he was going to make quite certain that no accident would occur? Ought he to have slowed down to such an extent that there could have been no possibility of a child's running out at any moment in front of him and his being unable to stop without striking the child? In the present case for the defendant to do so he would have had to slow down to something like 5mph. Such a duty of

---

[19]   [1975] RTR 127, CA.

care would be unreasonable; the chance that a child would run out at the precise moment the defendant was passing the coach was so slight as not to require him to slow down to that extent. As for sounding the horn, drivers in traffic are constantly exposed to the danger of pedestrians stepping out in front of parked cars. It would be an impossible burden for drivers to sound their horns every time they passed a parked car.

Another classic case which showed that the fact of an accident involving a child has occurred does not give rise to liability was *Miller v C & G Coach Services Ltd*.[20] The claimant, a 15-year-old schoolgirl, alighted from her school bus and passed behind it to cross the road when she was hit by a coach owned by the defendant. The claimant alleged that the defendant had failed to keep a proper look out, drove too fast and failed to slow down. The defendant's case was that the driver had no reason to expect passengers to run into the road, he slowed down and the accident was caused by the claimant's negligence in not checking that it was safe for crossing. On appeal it was held that it could not be proved that the coach driver had driven negligently. He did not see the claimant before the moment of impact. His speed was appropriate to conditions and he had kept a proper look out. The claimant had stepped out from behind the departing bus into the path of the coach, which she had not previously seen.

> 'On a common sense view this was a tragic accident. The claimant walked out into the front and into the path of an oncoming car and was knocked down by it. It was nobody's fault.' (Per Wall J)

Likewise in *Davies v Journeaux*[21] the claimant aged 11½ was struck by the defendant's car when running across the road from the pavement on the defendant's nearside. She had come down a flight of steps to the pavement, which was 3ft wide. The entrance to the steps was 3 or 4ft wide. She was struck by the offside front of the car which after the accident, was parallel with the pavement and 4ft 9 inches from it. There was a mark on the road behind the nearside rear wheel 22ft long indicating heavy application of the brakes. The passenger in the nearside front seat of the car saw the claimant as she stood momentarily in the entrance to the steps and then dashed across. The defendant did not see her until she was in the act of dashing across; he was then 50 to 60ft away travelling at 20 to 25mph. The judge held him 40% to blame for having failed to see the claimant at the moment when his passenger did and failing to sound his horn. The defendant appealed. On appeal it was held that the fact that the passenger saw the claimant a split second before the defendant did not establish a lack of proper care on the defendant's part; he was driving and needed to switch his eyes from one direction to another. Even if he had seen the claimant at the same instant it could not be said he should then have sounded his horn; what he did do was to apply his brakes heavily.

---

[20]   [2003] EWCA Civ 442.
[21]   [1976] RTR 111, CA.

Having regard to the brake marks he had acted promptly and efficiently. The judge's decision seemed to place a duty on motorists to sound the horn virtually whenever they see a pedestrian, regardless of whether the pedestrian is manifesting an intention of leaving the pavement and dashing across the road. The appeal was allowed.

Despite the presence of an ice cream van the same result occurred in *Kite v Nolan*.[22] The defendant was driving his car on a hot afternoon when he saw an ice-cream van parked on the offside of the road in front of him. He also saw three cars parked on the nearside ahead of the van. He slowed almost to a standstill to allow an approaching car to pass between the van and the parked cars. He then accelerated to about 15mph. The claimant aged 5 ran out in front of him from between the parked cars and was struck by the defendant's car. The judge found that the defendant could not have avoided striking the claimant unless travelling at not more than 5mph. He held that the defendant was not negligent, referring to *Moore v Poyner* (above). On appeal it was argued that the defendant should have realised the serious risk of a child running out bearing in mind the weather and the attraction of the ice-cream van. The appeal was dismissed. The court had to determine what was a reasonable standard of care in all the circumstances of the particular case. It would have regard to many factors including the following: (a) likelihood of pedestrian crossing into the defendant's path; (b) whether the pedestrian concerned was an adult or a child; (c) the degree of injury expected if the claimant was struck; and (d) the adverse consequences to the public and the defendant in taking whatever precautions were under consideration. The application of the principles must always depend on the particular circumstances of the case. Any decision applying the general standard to particular facts is unlikely to produce a precedent.

Despite the presence of children on the pavement the claim failed in *Saleem v Drake*[23] because the driver slowed down in response to the danger. The claimant was a 6-year-old pedestrian who was severely injured, having been struck by the defendant's mini-bus. The claimant had suddenly run out into the road. The defendant had noticed the claimant playing at the side of the road and had slowed down. The defendant had not sounded his horn. The claimant's claim failed and he appealed. The appeal was dismissed. The defendant had satisfied his duty of care towards the claimant by slowing down. There was no indication that the claimant would rush out and, therefore, the defendant was under no duty to sound his horn.

Probably the most favourable case for defendant drivers who have collided with errant children is *Brooking v Stuart-Buttle (deceased)*.[24] The defendant was travelling along a main road at 10:45 pm. It was a fine

---

[22]   [1983] RTR 253, CA.
[23]   [1993] 2 PIQR P129, CA.
[24]   (Unreported) (1995) CA.

night, the road was appropriately lit and the defendant's speed was 30mph which was found to be acceptable in the circumstances. The claimant aged 9 years 8 months and his friend were on their way to a fish and chip shop on the other side of the road. The friend crossed the road first. He ran across the road in front of the defendant's car. The defendant saw him, cried out and tried to take evasive action. The friend made it to the central reservation. The claimant did not, he ran into the path of the defendant's car and was hit and suffered serious injuries as a result. The trial judge found for the defendant on the basis that she could not have been expected to have seen the claimant until shortly before he emerged into the road and as such, the collision was unavoidable. On appeal, the claimant argued that the defendant, having seen the friend run across the road, should have immediately reduced her speed in anticipation of the claimant running out behind him. The Court of Appeal held that this was not reasonable. There was nothing to suggest that the defendant should have anticipated the emergence of a second child. Secondly, the claimant argued that the defendant did not keep a proper look out. The Court of Appeal held that this was not correct. On the facts the defendant could not have been expected to have seen the claimant until shortly before he emerged onto the roadway. In addition, the defendant was faced with the distracting presence of the friend. The fact that the friend had run across relatively close to her oncoming car and only just made it to the central reservation would inevitably lead the defendant to pay attention to the presence of the friend. A motorist is expected to be reasonably prudent, but not expected to be a perfectionist assisted by hindsight. Per Hobhouse LJ: It is always easy to make allegations and to raise hypotheses which are consistent with some want of reasonable care. But those allegations have to be made out on the evidence.

If the driver is keeping a proper look out and travelling well within the speed limit then he will not be held to have been negligent. So in *Ebanks v Collins and Motor Insurer's Bureau*[25] the claimant aged 6, in the company of his uncle, had just bought some sweets. He detached himself from his uncle, ran across the road from between parked cars and was hit by the defendant's car which was travelling in the opposite carriageway. The judge held that the defendant had no opportunity of avoiding the collision and gave judgment for the defendant. The claimant appealed and it was held that the fact that the defendant managed to stop shortly beyond the place of the accident indicated that he was driving at a very moderate speed. The claimant ran out from between parked cars. Children with sweets in their pockets on their way home can run extremely fast. The defendant could not avoid the collision with the claimant. Per Butler-Sloss LJ: The fact that he was unable to stop in time because a child was running out between parked cars, even though he was on the other side of the road, is not in itself a reason for saying that in every case of that sort the driver should have been able to take action to prevent an accident.

---

[25]   [1994] CLY 3401, CA.

Another useful case for defendants is *James v Fairley*.[26] The claimant (aged 8) was struck by a car that the defendant was driving when the claimant crossed the second of two lanes on an A-road. The trial judge found on the facts that the defendant was not negligent. The claimant appealedand it was held that the trial judge's findings of fact were entirely proper. When the claimant was standing on the pavement before crossing the road, she had not been behaving in a manner which would have alerted a prudent driver to the possibility of anything unusual or dangerous occurring. The judge had been entitled to find that the defendant would not have seen the claimant before he collided with her even though she had crossed one of the two lanes of the road. Per Longmore LJ: A prudent driver would, of course, note the presence of children on a pavement once he sees them but it is going too far to say a prudent driver should start to brake just because he sees children doing nothing out of the ordinary on the pavement.

In *Lunn v Kilkenny*[27] the claimant, a 3-year-old, had climbed over the garden gate which had been tied up by her parents and past a mini-van parked on the pavement to reach a parked ice-cream van. The defendant could not and did not see the claimant until she ran out into the road. The defendant had taken care to drive slowly (between 10–15mph) as she was passing the ice-cream van. The claimant submitted that the defendant should have taken greater care and sounded her horn to warn children who may have been thinking about crossing the road, especially given the presence of the ice-cream van. It was held that the defendant had not been negligent as she had reduced her speed to between 10–15mph and had been taking a great deal of care as she approached the ice-cream van. Given the manner in which the claimant stepped out from behind the parked van it was inevitable that the defendant was going to collide with her regardless of her speed. Furthermore, it was unlikely that even had the defendant sounded her horn, the claimant would have stopped and not crossed the road.

## 18.8 CAN A PARENT BE LIABLE FOR A CHILD RUNNING ACROSS THE ROAD?

In *Palmer v Lawley and Another*[28] the claimant car driver brought an action against two defendants following a road traffic accident. The claimant had been driving down a suburban road when the first defendant, who was travelling in the opposite direction, swerved to avoid hitting a 2-year-old child. The child had escaped from a house when her 8-year-old sister failed to properly secure the latch. It was alleged by the claimant that the child's mother (the second defendant) had been negligent in allowing her to escape. The court dismissed the claim. It was

---

[26]   [2002] EWCA Civ 162, [2002] All ER (D) 298.
[27]   (Unreported) (2003) Leeds County Court.
[28]   [2003] CLY 2976.

held that the first defendant had not been driving negligently in swerving to avoid the child. It was further held that if the child's mother were to be found negligent, then this would place too high a burden on parents; therefore nobody was liable.

The suggested higher duty of care set out above in cases where children are on the pavement may not apply if they are accompanied by adults. So in *Goundry v Hepworth*[29] the claimant, who was 4 years old at the time of the accident, attempted to cross the road with a number of adults. The claimant was in the middle of the road when two cars approached. The first car passed by. However, when the second car approached and drew level, the claimant ran out into the road where a collision occurred. At the trial the judge held the defendant liable on the basis that she should have stopped or slowed down to allow the claimant to cross. The defendant's appeal was successful as the court held that the judge's proposition was incorrect as, if the defendant was obliged to stop or slow down, so was the car in front.

> 'In the defendant's position some drivers might have stopped and ushered the group across, or at any rate allowed the group to finish crossing the road. However, with a group of adults, and fully appreciating that it included small children, apparently behaving and patiently waiting beyond the white line, very many motorists driving with reasonable care would not have thought it appropriate to do so.' (Per Sir Igor Judge)

> 'What is the duty of an ordinary, prudent motorist, on seeing a group of people which includes young children standing in the middle of the road waiting to cross? The duty is not to stop and allow the group to cross in front of them. There was nothing unruly about this group. The group as a whole was standing calmly waiting for the defendant's car to pass. To place a duty on a driver in the defendant's position to stop and wave the group across is to place on the driver a 'counsel of perfection.' (Per Hallett LJ)

## 18.9   CHILDREN 'LARKING AROUND'

Another situation where the higher duty of care is likely to be imposed on drivers is where young children are larking about on the pavement. So in *J (A Child) v West*[30] the claimant, aged 9 at the date of the accident, was seriously injured when he jumped off a kerb into the road and into the path of the defendant's pick-up truck. The claimant had been larking about on the pavement with a group of slightly older youths and had spat at one of them who then raised his fist as if to hit the claimant. The claimant's instinctive reaction to this was to jump backwards (into the path of the defendant's truck). The judge at first instance found the defendant wholly liable on the basis that he had been driving too fast and too close to the kerb. The defendant appealed and it was held that the

---

[29]   [2005] EWCA Civ 1738, [2005] All ER (D) 405.
[30]   (Unreported) (1999) CA.

judge had been entitled to find on the evidence before him that the claimant had jumped off the kerb instinctively. Therefore the claimant's involuntary reaction to the perceived threat could not be said to amount to negligence. On the other hand, the defendant who had been driving negligently had been faced with a common situation of a group of children which constituted a well known risk, against which a reasonable motorist should have guarded. Per Sedley LJ: Jumping backwards in the course of horseplay is only as culpable as the horseplay itself, and this was not culpable in a 9 year old, whose capacity for sensible forethought left him short of the necessary standard of disregard for his own safety. Whilst the claimant was guilty of momentary inadvertence, it could not be criticised as negligence given his age.

## 18.10   SCHOOL'S LIABILITY

Schools may become liable if they allow their pupils to escape and run into the road.

So in *Jenney (A Minor) v North Lincolnshire County Council*[31] the claimant was almost 9 years old at the date of the accident and suffered from global development delay and had special educational needs such that he could not safely be let out of school on his own. On the day of the accident the claimant left school during break time via one of the five possible exits and was hit by a car whilst crossing the road. Although every break time was supervised by members of staff, there was no system for ensuring that all the exits were effectively barred at such times. This was particularly important as prior to the claimant's accident other children had left school at break times. Instead there was a 'policy' whereby members of staff were instructed to close any open exit gates which they came across in the course of carrying out their duties. The judge at first instance held that although the degree of supervision provided by the school was adequate, the degree of security was not. It was also held that the risk of an accident as sustained by the claimant was a foreseeable consequence of the failure to provide adequate security. The defendant appealed and it was held that the initial evidential burden was on the defendant to show that there was a non-negligent explanation for how the claimant came to be on a major road when he ought to have been at school. Given the vulnerability of the claimant and the knowledge of the defendant that escape was not difficult, the defendant's 'policy' was somewhat haphazard. The defendant was therefore liable because it had not taken the necessary precautions to address the separate exits and their individual weaknesses.

> 'Given that the defendant knew that escape was not difficult and could happen unobserved, it owed a special duty to their vulnerable pupils such as the claimant. Had the defendant been able to explain how the claimant

---

[31]   [2000] LGR 269, CA.

managed to leave the school the evidential burden would have returned to the claimant to show that the escape was negligent. As the defendant was unable to explain how the claimant left school, it was left to argue that it took all reasonable precautions to keep him in school.' (Per Henry LJ)

# CHAPTER 19

## LOCAL AUTHORITY LIABILITY

*Laura Elfield*

### 19.1 INTRODUCTION

Some road traffic accidents occur because of the condition and layout of the highway. This chapter considers the potential liability of public authorities for such accidents.

The main public authorities involved are the highway authorities and the main statutory provision is s 41 of the Highways Act 1980 (HA 1980), which relates to highway maintenance and repair. Section 41(1) (and its sister provision s 41(1A), which relates to ice and snow) is the only relevant statutory provision expressly to confer a civil right of action to individual claimants.

In this chapter we will also consider claims against public authorities in relation to signage (see also Chapter 12) and claims arising from road layout. In general terms it is much more difficult for injured claimants to succeed in such claims. We also consider claims against statutory undertakers who carry out works on highways.

A public authority may be found liable in the following areas:

- highway maintenance and repair;

- snow and ice;

- signage & road layout;

- street works, including the liability of statutory undertakers;

- negligence;

- nuisance.

### 19.2 PUBLIC AUTHORITIES AND BREACH OF DUTY

It is important to start with an understanding of the framework in which a claim against a public authority for breach of duty exists. This is because there are numerous statutory provisions which are potentially relevant but very few which are of real assistance in relation to civil claims against public authorities for accidents on the highway.

Sections 41(1) and 41(1A) of the HA 1980 expressly confer a civil right of action against a highway authority for breach of the statutory duty.

There are various other provisions contained in the HA 1980 and the Road Traffic Act 1988, which may be relevant to the liability of public authorities for road traffic accidents, but these in general are of limited use to claimants. This is because such provisions in general terms impose upon the relevant public authority a statutory power to act and the courts have held time and again that the exercise of a statutory power involves policy decisions, which can only be challenged if they are 'unreasonable' in a public law sense: see in particular *Stovin v Wise*[1] and *Gorringe v Calderdale Metropolitan Borough Council*.[2]

Moreover, even if the relevant section imposes a statutory duty, this will not normally give rise to a right to sue for breach. So in *Stovin* at 952–953, Lord Steyn stated:

> 'If [a statutory] duty does not give rise to a private right to sue for breach, it would be unusual if it nevertheless gave rise to a duty of care at common law which made the public authority liable to pay compensation for foreseeable loss caused by the duty not being performed. It will often be foreseeable that loss will result if, for example, a benefit or service is not provided. If the policy of the Act is not to create a statutory liability to pay compensation, the same policy should ordinarily exclude the existence of a common law duty of care.'

This will not of course exclude the situation where there has been an assumption of responsibility to or a special relationship with a particular member or category of the public, but such situations will be rare in the context of what Steyn LJ referred to as a 'broad public law duty'.

There are exceptional cases where a duty will arise. In *Gorringe*, Lord Hoffman, at paragraph 43, stated:

> '... I would certainly accept the principle that if a highway authority conducts itself so as to create a reasonable expectation about the state of the highway, it will be under a duty to ensure that it does not thereby create a trap for the careful motorist who drives in reliance upon such an expectation.'

Lord Scott, at paragraphs 65–66, also considered that common law liability might arise:

---

[1]   [1996] AC 923, HL.
[2]   [2004] UKHL 15, HL.

' . . . from acts done on or around the highway that have created a source of danger to users of the highway . . . the principle that a highway authority may be liable if it introduces a new danger to the road is plainly unexceptionable . . .'

Therefore, a duty in negligence may arise where such negligence amounts to a positive act of entrapment or ensnarement: see also *Thompson v Hampshire CC*.[3]

In *Gorringe* the House of Lords made clear that a failure to exercise a statutory power, even if unreasonable in the public law sense, did not mean that the public authority was in breach of any common law duty of care.

Effectively the existence of the statutory power or duty provides only the background against which negligence is considered, rather than any additional assistance to a claimant. If local authorities are negligent in executing their policy then liability may attach but this again does no more than restate the general principles of negligence.

The common law liability of public authorities generally is a complex topic and a detailed consideration is outside the scope of this text.

## 19.3 HIGHWAY MAINTENANCE AND REPAIR

The duty imposed is to maintain and repair the highway and is not concerned with road layout or with signage.

Section 41 of the HA 1980 imposes a statutory obligation on a highway authority to maintain the highway. The highway authority has a defence, under s 58 of the HA 1980, if it can prove that it took such care as in all the circumstances was reasonably required to secure that part of the highway to which the action relates was not dangerous to traffic.

Section 41(1) of the HA 1980 provides:

'The authority who are for the time being the highway authority for the highway maintainable at the public expense are under a duty . . . to maintain the highway.'

Section 58(1) of the HA 1980 states:

'In an action against a highway authority in respect of damage resulting from their failure to maintain a highway maintainable at the public expense it is a defence (without prejudice to any other defence or the application of the law relating to contributory negligence) to prove that the authority had

---

[3]    [2004] EWCA Civ 1016, at [30].

taken such care as in all the circumstances was reasonably required to secure that the part of the highway to which the action relates was not dangerous for traffic.'

Section 58(2) sets out a number of criteria to which the court 'shall have particular regard' namely:

'(a)    the character of the highway, and the traffic which was reasonably to be expected to use it;

(b)    the standard of maintenance appropriate for a highway of that character and used by such traffic;

(c)    the state of repair in which a reasonable person would have expected to find the highway;

(d)    whether the highway authority knew, or could reasonably have been expected to know, that the condition of the part of the highway to which the action relates was likely to cause danger to users of the highway;

(e)    where the highway authority could not reasonably have been expected to repair that part of the highway before the cause of the action arose, what warning notices of its condition have been displayed . . .'

## 19.4   DEFINITIONS

### 19.4.1   Highway

The definition of a highway is contained in s 329(1) of the HA 1980 and means:

'the whole or part of a highway other than a ferry or a waterway.'

In practice, most footpaths, public paths, bridleways, byways open to all traffic and cycle tracks are 'highways' for the purposes of the HA 1980 (and see also s 66(1) the Wildlife and Countryside Act 1981).

For the purposes of the s 41 duty, a highway must also be 'maintainable at the public expense'. There is rarely any dispute about this issue as highway authorities are required to keep and make available at all reasonable hours, free of charge, a list of the highways in their areas which are maintainable at the public expense: see ss 36(6) and (7) of the HA 1980. The list is not determinative. It may be that the highway authority has adopted a highway, for example by undertaking maintenance work upon it.

A detailed consideration of the law relating to adoption of the highway is beyond the scope of this text but is well covered in Halsbury's Laws.

Other roads and walkways remain the responsibility of private owners or may even, in rare cases, be a highway that nobody is liable to maintain.

## 19.4.2   Highway authority

The highway authority is usually the county council or metropolitan district council.

In London, the relevant London borough council is responsible and, in the City of London, the Common Council of the City of London.

The Secretary of State (or, in Wales, the Secretary of State for Wales) is the relevant highway authority for: any trunk road: see s 1 of the HA 1980; any road in respect of which the Secretary of State is appointed highway authority by statutory instrument; and any other highway constructed by him, save where the obligation is delegated to the local highway authority. In practice, the Secretary of State often delegates responsibility in any event to the county or metropolitan district council: see s 6(1) of the HA 1980.

Non-metropolitan district councils can, by giving notice to the county council, opt to undertake the maintenance of footpaths, bridleways, non-trunk urban roads and non-classified urban roads within the district, subject to an obligation to indemnify the county council in respect of any claim arising out of a failure to maintain: see s 50(2) of and Sch 7, Part 1 to the HA 1980. If the county council disagrees, it serves a counter-notice and the minister then determines responsibility for the maintenance.

## 19.5   FAILURE TO MAINTAIN

A three-stage approach is applied to a claim for failure to maintain or repair the highway. In *Burnside v Emerson*,[4] the Court of Appeal set out the approach as follows:

> 'First: the claimant must show that the road was in such a condition as to be dangerous for traffic. In seeing whether it is dangerous, foreseeability is an essential element. The state of affairs must be such that injury may reasonably be anticipated to persons using the highway . . .
>
> Second: the claimant must prove that the dangerous condition was due to a failure to maintain, which includes a failure to repair the highway . . .
>
> Third: If there is a failure to maintain, the highway authority is prima facie liable for any damage resulting therefrom. It can only escape liability if it proves that it took such care as in all the circumstances was reasonable . . .'

Although the case was decided under the old Highways (Miscellaneous Provisions) Act 1961, it has been followed and applied under the HA 1980: see in particular, *Mills v Barnsley Metropolitan Borough Council*.[5]

---

[4]   [1968] 1 WLR 1490, at 1493–1494.
[5]   [1992] PIQR 291, at 293.

Stage 1 refers to the s 41 duty, Stage 2 is simply a matter of factual causation and stage 3 deals with the s 58 defence. Both ss 41 and 58 are considered in more detail below.

### 19.5.1   Section 41 – scope of the duty

The duty under s 41 includes a duty to repair: see s 329 of the HA 1980, the interpretation section, which provides:

> '"maintenance" . . . includes repair, and "maintain" and "maintainable" are to be construed accordingly.'

It is not a duty to improve the highway.

The duty is limited to repair and maintenance of the fabric of the highway. In *Goodes v East Sussex County Council*,[6] the House of Lords held that the duty did not extend to salting, gritting or the removal of ice and snow. Parliament has effectively overruled *Goodes* in relation to ice and snow and this is dealt with below. However, the confinement of the duty to the fabric of the highway remains.

In *Gorringe v Calderdale Metropolitan Borough Council*,[7] it was held that the duty does not include the provision of information by means of street furniture or painted signs. In *Shine v Tower Hamlets LBC*,[8] an unstable bollard was not considered to be part of the fabric of the highway.

### 19.5.2   Ice and snow

In *Goodes v East Sussex County Council*,[9] the House of Lords ruled that the s 41 duty to maintain did not include salting, gritting and removal of ice and snow. This was not politically acceptable so the Government inserted a provision in the Railways and Transport Safety Act 2003 (Commencement No 1) Order 2003,[10] which amended the HA 1980 with effect from 31 October 2003 making these activities part of the local authorities' responsibility. Section 41(1A) of the HA 1980 provides that:

> 'In particular, a highway authority are under a duty to ensure, so far as is reasonably practicable, that safe passage along a highway is not endangered by snow or ice.'

It is often said that s 41(1A) has reversed the decision in *Goodes*: see, for example, the dicta of the Court of Appeal in *Thompson v Hampshire*

---

6    [2000] 1 WLR 1356.
7    [2004] UKHL 15.
8    [2006] EWCA Civ 852.
9    [2000] 1 WLR 1356.
10   SI 2003/2681.

*County Council.*[11] In fact, the duty is different to that set out in s 41, which of course provides an absolute duty to maintain, subject to the s 58 defence.

No guidance has been provided, to date, on the definition of 'reasonably practicable' although the burden is almost certainly on the highway authority to prove this. A first instance decision on the application of s 41(1A) is *Rhiannon Pace v City and County of Swansea.*[12]

Outside of the statutory duty, a claim in negligence is unlikely to assist: see, for example, *Sandhar and another v Department of Transport, Environment and the Regions.*[13] This is so because it is difficult to see how a claim in negligence would add anything to the statutory provisions.

### 19.5.3   Flooding and mud

If water or mud accumulates on the road, for example after heavy rain, the s 41 duty will only be engaged if this has been caused by a failure to maintain. This will usually involve a failure to maintain the drains or a satisfactory system of drainage in the road. The leading case is *Burnside v Emerson.*[14] in which torrential flooding caused the claimant to lose control of his vehicle and collide with an oncoming car. While the Court of Appeal stated that: 'an occasional flood at any time is not in itself evidence of a failure to maintain', on the facts there was a failure to maintain a satisfactory system of drainage so that the claimant succeeded in his claim against the highway authority.

Equally, in *Misell v Essex County Council*[15] it was held that an accumulation of mud on the road, on an ongoing basis, required a regular system of inspection and cleaning. A failure to drain the highway and to take steps to remove the mud or to prevent its accumulation amounted to a failure to 'maintain' for the purposes of s 41.

In *Department of Transport, Environment and the Regions v Mott MacDonald Limited and others*[16] the Court of Appeal confirmed that *Burnside* remained good law, notwithstanding the decision in *Goodes v East Sussex County Council.*[17]

---

[11] [2004] EWCA Civ 1016 at [11].
[12] (unreported) 10 July 2007, Swansea CC, Mr Recorder Andrew Keyser QC.
[13] [2004] EWCA Civ 1440, CA.
[14] [1968] 1 WLR 1490, CA.
[15] (1994) 93 LGR 108.
[16] [2006] EWCA Civ 1089.
[17] [2001] 1 WLR 1356, HL.

### 19.5.4  Reasonable foreseeability of danger

The test for liability is – reasonable foreseeability of danger. Each case will turn on its own facts and the issue of foreseeability is for the trial judge to decide.

In *Rider v Rider*[18] Sachs LJ stated, at 514–515, that:

> 'In every case it is a question of fact and degree whether any particular state of disrepair entails danger to traffic being driven in the way normally expected on that highway. The test is an objective one. To define that degree by using words and phrases suited to a particular case can end by putting an unwarranted gloss on the duty.'

Lord Lawton in the same case, at 518, said:

> 'In most cases proof that there were bumps or small holes in a road, or slight unevenness in flagstones on a pavement, will not amount to proof of a danger for traffic through failure to maintain. It does not follow, however, that such conditions can never be a danger for traffic. A stretch of uneven paving outside a factory probably would not be a danger for traffic, but a similar stretch outside an old people's home, and much used by the inmates to the knowledge of the highway authority, might be.'

All relevant factors should be considered, including whether or not the stretch of road was well lit and the use made of the road. In particular, more will be expected of a highway authority in relation to a busy stretch of road than one less used. Surprises can be dangerous so that, if there is a sudden change in the condition of the road, this might be considered a dangerous defect: see, for example, *Pitman v Southern Electricity Board*.[19]

### 19.5.5  The 'one-inch' rule for pavements

This text is aimed at vehicle accidents not slippers and trippers, but some reference to the law relating to tripping accidents on pavements is necessary.

The main thing to say about the 'one-inch' rule is that it a mere guide and perhaps not even that. In *Littler v Liverpool Corporation*,[20] Cumming-Bruce J stated, in relation to the test concerning a pavement:

> 'A length of pavement is only dangerous if, in the ordinary course of human affairs, danger may reasonably be anticipated from its continued use by the public who usually pass over it . . . Uneven surfaces and differences in level between flagstones of about an inch may cause a pedestrian temporarily off

---

[18]   [1973] QB 505, CA.
[19]   [1978] 3 All ER 901, CA.
[20]   [1968] 3 All ER 343, at 345.

balance to trip and stumble, but such characteristics have to be accepted. A highway is not to be criticised by the standards of a bowling green.'

The Court of Appeal in *Meggs v Liverpool Corporation*[21] made similar comments where a 74-year-old woman tripped over a flagstone that had sunk three-quarters of an inch: see, in particular, Lord Denning at 692 who overturned the first instance decision that this made the pavement unsafe.

In *Mills v Barnsley Metropolitan Borough Council*[22] the Court of Appeal overturned a first instance decision to the effect that a defect some two inches across and 1¼ inches deep was dangerous on the basis that this:

> ' . . . impliedly set a standard which, if generally used in the thousands of tripping cases which come before the courts every year, would impose an unreasonable burden upon highway authorities in respect of minor depressions and holes in streets which in a less than perfect world the public must simply regard as a fact of life. It is important that our tort law should not impose unreasonably high standards, otherwise scarce resources should be diverted from situations where maintenance and repair of the highways is more urgently needed. This branch of the law of tort ought to represent a sensible balance of compromise between public and private interest. The judge's ruling in this case, if allowed to stand, would tilt the balance too far in favour of the [claimant]. The risk was of low order and the cost of remedying such minor defects all over the country would be enormous.'

This passage was approved by the Court of Appeal in *James v Preseli Pembrokeshire District Council*.[23]

### 19.5.6   Section 41 and road traffic accidents

There are no special principles applicable to defects in the carriageway which cause road traffic accidents rather than on the pavement which cause tripping accidents.

In general terms, where highway authorities publish guideline codes for intervention, the actionable limit for a defect in the carriageway tends to be greater than the limit for defects on the pavement. The position however remains fact-sensitive: a defect which would be excused in the main part of the carriageway may, for example, be actionable if on a pedestrian crossing.

In relation to road traffic accidents, there is plenty of case law showing that the courts are willing to apply an equally strict standard of maintenance to the surface of the carriageway as to pavements. The reasoning must, in part, be because the consequences of a road traffic

---

[21]   [1968] 1 WLR 689.
[22]   [1992] PIQR 291, at 293.
[23]   [1993] PIQR P114.

accident can be significantly more severe than a pedestrian tripping accident and also, when at speed that hazards may be less easy to avoid.

For example, liability was established in *Bright v Attorney-General*,[24] when the claimant was thrown from his motorcycle when it struck a 'rough patch of road' consisting of a 'groove' of compacted chippings deposited by workmen. In *Rider v Rider*,[25] the vehicle in which the claimant was travelling as a passenger ran out of control after driving across the 'unsupported, broken and uneven' edges of a narrow unclassified road. In both cases it was held that there was 'ample evidence' to support the view that the road was foreseeably dangerous to reasonable drivers. It is questionable whether, in either case, such defects in a pavement would have been considered actionable.

In *Bramwell v Shaw*[26] the Court of Appeal stated that: 'an extremely high standard of maintenance was necessary' where a road that was used to carry heavy traffic was old and likely to break up.

## 19.6   THE SECTION 58 DEFENCE

Once a claimant has established a breach of s 41 and that the breach caused the road traffic accident, the burden shifts to the defendant to make out the s 58 defence, namely that it took such care as was reasonably required to ensure that the highway was not dangerous to traffic.

The statutory provisions are set out above. The court has to have regard to the list of factors in s 58(2) but the list is not exhaustive and sometimes other considerations may be relevant.

The factors set out in s 58(2) are largely self-explanatory. Many cases will turn on s 58(2)(d) which generally involves consideration of the adequacy of the inspection regime. This will depend upon the nature of the highway and the volume of traffic using it. Most highway authorities adopt the *Local Authority Association Code of Practice for Highway Maintenance*, which contains suggested frequency of inspections for different types of roads. When considering a claim, it is useful to request from the highway authority not only a copy of their inspection regime but also the minutes of the meetings in which the regime was decided. It will not, of course, be sufficient merely to establish a failure to inspect. Such failure must have causative relevance: see, for example, *Day v Suffolk CC*.[27]

It will not be a defence to a claim under s 41 to assert that independent contractors were engaged to carry out the works. The statutory duty is non-delegable. This means that, while the highway authority may wish to

---

24   [1971] 2 Lloyd's Rep 68.
25   [1973] QB 505.
26   [1971] RTR 167.
27   [2007] EWCA Civ 1436, CA.

join the independent contractor to any claim and seek indemnity, a claimant can simply pursue the highway authority.

## 19.7  STATUTORY UNDERTAKERS: WATER, ELECTRICITY, GAS ETC

This chapter is concerned with the duties of public authorities in relation to road traffic accidents. However, the chapter would not be complete without mention of the New Roads and Street Works Act 1991 (NRSWA 1991), which applies to statutory undertakers executing street works. These include for example water, electricity, gas, television and telephone companies.

Claims against contractors carrying out works on the highway, where such works are negligently executed, are of particular use when a highway authority is likely to have a defence under s 58 of the HA 1980. It is worth noting that, unlike under s 58 of the HA 1980, public authorities (and, of greater relevance here, main contractors) can escape liability, in negligence, for the acts of contractors they engage if they can show that they took reasonable care in selecting contractors (or sub-contractors) in the first place. It is therefore sometimes necessary to trace the chain of sub-contractors in order to see who was actually responsible for the default.

By s 50 of the NRSWA 1991, the highway authority has to give statutory undertakers a licence to carry out the works and by s 53(1) and (2), the highway authority has to keep a 'street works register' showing all street works being carried out in its areas, including the dates of the work and the identities of the undertakers. This can be useful to inspect when considering potential defendants to a claim.

Section 65 of the Act provides that any part of the street which is broken up or open or otherwise obstructed must be adequately guarded and lit, with traffic signs placed and maintained where reasonably required.

Section 66 requires undertakers to complete their works with 'all such dispatch as is reasonably practicable'.

Section 67 requires such works to be adequately supervised.

Section 70 requires the undertaker to reinstate the street and to do so with all such dispatch as is reasonably practicable.

As set out above, claimants usually do not have to be concerned about contractors or statutory undertakers as the duty owed by the highway authority under s 41 of the HA 1980 is non-delegable. Equally, as already discussed, there is unlikely to be a civil claim in negligence for breach of the statutory duties under the NRSWA 1991: see *Keating v Elvan Reinforced Concrete Co. Limited*,[28] a case decided under the Act's predecessor, the Public Utilities Street Works Act 1950. However, where works are negligently executed where this creates a danger, then a claimant is likely to have a claim in negligence. This is most useful where a highway authority has a defence under s 58 of the HA 1980, making it necessary to consider pursuing the contractor or undertaker.

## 19.8   ROAD LAYOUT AND SIGNS

This topic is also considered in Chapter 12.

The Road Traffic Act 1988 (RTA 1988), s 39 provides that local authorities must take measures to promote road safety. The relevant provisions are as follows:

> '(2)   Each relevant authority:
>    (a)   if it is a local authority, must prepare and carry out a programme of measures designed to promote road safety; or
>    (b)   if it is Transport for London, may prepare and carry out such a programme . . .
> (3)   Each relevant authority:
>    (a)   must carry out studies into accidents arising out of the use of roads, other than GLA roads or roads for which the Secretary of State is the highway authority . . . within their area; or
>    (b)   if it is Transport for London, on GLA roads or parts of GLA roads.
> (4)   Must, in the light of those studies, take such measures as appear to the authority to be appropriate to prevent such actions, including the dissemination of information and advice relating to the use of roads, the giving of practical training to road users or any class or description of road users, the construction, improvement, mainte-nance or repair of roads for the maintenance of which they are responsible and other measures taken in the exercise of their powers for controlling, protecting or assisting the movement of traffic on roads . . .'

While, on its face, s 39 appears to be mandatory, its scope has been significantly restricted, in relation to individual claimants, by the decisions in *Larner v Solihull Metropolitan Borough Council*[29] and *Gorringe v Calderdale Metropolitan Borough Council*.[30] *Gorringe* has already been considered above in some detail in relation to the general duties of public authorities but it is also the leading case on signage.

In *Larner* the claimant emerged from a minor road on to a major road without stopping and suffered an accident. She brought a claim against

---

[28]   [1968] 1 WLR 722.
[29]   [2001] LGR 255, CA.
[30]   [2004] UKHL 15.

the local authority under s 39 of the RTA 1988 and in particular alleged that, despite having passed two 'Give Way' signs, additional advance warning would have prevented the accident. The Court of Appeal held that the effect of the words 'such measures as appear to the authority to be appropriate' in s 39 meant that this was a discretionary power. Therefore it would have to be shown that the default of the authority was outside the ambit of the discretion or in other words was unreasonable or irrational in the public law sense.

In *Gorringe* the House of Lords went further. The claimant was driving her car up a hill when she was involved in a head-on collision with a bus. The road, at the top of the hill, veered sharply to the left so that it was not possible to see oncoming traffic until almost at the crest. There was an 'uneven road' warning sign marking the area, as well as a painted 'SLOW' sign on the road's surface, although this had worn away to the extent that it was held that it was no longer visible. The claimant blamed the local authority for failing clearly to indicate the dangers of that particular area of road.

The House of Lords held, firstly, that the defendant was not in breach of its duty of care under s 41 of the HA 1980, because a road marking did not constitute part of the physical or structural condition of the roadway. The House of Lords also held that s 39 imposed no common law duty on councils to place warning signs. To the extent that the Court of Appeal in *Larner* had suggested that an authority could be liable if it had acted wholly unreasonably in failing to provide a sign and such default therefore fell outside the ambit of the discretion given to them by the section, *Larner* was wrongly decided.

So the only way a civil claim for breach is likely to be successful against a local authority in relation to road layout and signage is if the local authority has created a danger or a trap. An example given in *Gorringe* by Lord Brown of Eaton-under-Heywood at [102] was as follows:

> 'Although motorists are not entitled to be forewarned of the ordinary hazards of highway use, plainly they must not be trapped into danger. If, for example, an authority were to signal a one-way street but omit to put 'No Entry' signs at the other end, it might well be found liable, not because of any statutory power or duty to erect such signs but rather because it induced a perfectly careful motorist into the path of danger . . . Such cases, however, may be expected to be few and far between.'

The powers of public authorities in relation to traffic signs themselves are set out in s 65 of the Road Traffic Regulation Act 1984 and the regulations made thereunder. These provisions however are, on their face, discretionary and unlikely to be of real assistance in civil claims. Street lights are dealt with in Chapter 10.

## 19.9   NEGLIGENCE

While it is possible to frame a case in negligence against a public authority, the analysis above shows that this is often likely to be difficult. Case law which pre-dates *Gorringe* should be treated with great care.

For an example of a case where negligence was found against a highway authority, see *Shine v London Borough of Tower Hamlets*.[31] Here, the presence of an unstable bollard in the highway did not amount to a breach of s 41 as the bollard was not part of the fabric of the highway. However, in circumstances where the authority knew that the bollard was unstable and had actioned but not carried out repairs, negligence was established. The local authority had a policy of inspecting the bollards and of putting them into a safe state if they were found to be insecure. The case therefore did not challenge the policy of the local authority but only the negligent execution of that policy.

## 19.10   NUISANCE

Claims in public nuisance are often pleaded in the alternative to those for breach of statutory duty and/or negligence in relation to accidents on the highway.

Public authorities and statutory undertakers can be liable for public nuisance where they create a danger or permit an unreasonable obstruction on the highway.

An example is *Hale v Hants & Dorset Motor Services Ltd & Another*[32] where having planted trees a local authority failed to cut them back with the result that a bus collided with an overhanging branch. Lord Greene MR stated:

> 'It does not appear to me to matter very much whether the action is regarded as an action based on breach of statutory duty or merely on nuisance or negligence at common law . . .'

It seems unlikely that public authorities and statutory undertakers will be liable for adopting or continuing a nuisance: see *Marcic v Thames Water Utilities*.[33] For a successful attempt to distinguish *Marcic* at first instance, in a case involving complaints of nuisance against a statutory undertaker in relation to odours emanating from a sewage works, see *Dobson v Thames Water Utilities*.[34]

---

[31]   [2006] EWCA Civ 852.
[32]   [1947] 2 All ER 628, CA.
[33]   [2003] UKHL 66, HL.
[34]   [2007] EWCH 2021.

In *Shine v London Borough of Tower Hamlets*,[35] the Court of Appeal held that liability for injury caused by the introduction of items on to the highway (an unstable bollard), was to be determined according to the law of negligence rather than nuisance: see in particular Buxton LJ at paragraph 16:

> '. . . In modern parlance we would think, as Lord Scott of Foscote thought [in *Gorringe*], that these issues as to liability for injury caused by something that is not the maintenance of the highway but the introduction of items on to the highway are to be determined according to the law of negligence.'

This has led some commentators to suggest that the law of nuisance has effectively been superseded by the law of negligence in relation to the creation of dangers on the highway. This does appear to be based upon a misreading of what Lord Scott actually said at paragraph 51 of *Gorringe*. In considering the nature of the duty imposed by the predecessor to the Highways Act 1980, which was the Highways (Miscellaneous Provisions) Act 1961, Lord Scott stated:

> 'In a case, therefore, where the damage complained of has been caused not by a failure to maintain the highway but by something done by the highway authority, or for which the highway authority have become responsible . . ., liability continued after 1961 as before to be determined by the common law principles of negligence or, as the case may be, public nuisance. It is only where the alleged liability arises out of a failure "to maintain" the highway that the Section 41(1) duty and the Section 58(1) defence come into play.'

The advantage of a claim in public nuisance over a claim in negligence is that a claimant does not have to prove breach of any duty of care. Both causes of action require a claimant to prove causation and foreseeability of harm but, in negligence, a claimant must also prove that the public authority knew or ought to have known of the alleged defect or danger. In public nuisance the public authority would be liable whether it knew or ought to have known of the danger or not: see *Wringe v Cohen*.[36]

In addition to the law of public nuisance, ss 130 and 150 of the HA 1980 impose statutory duties on a highway authority to abate nuisances on the highway. These include duties, by s 130, to prevent the obstruction of the highway and to remove roadside waste. Section 150 deals expressly with the removal of an 'accumulation of snow' from the highway where this causes an obstruction.

It is unlikely that these provisions give rise to civil actions in damages. There has been no authority deciding the point in relation to either section. The provisions are enforceable by enforcement notices and, in the case of s 150, a magistrates' court may, on the complaint of any person, order a highway authority to remove the obstruction.

---

[35] [2006] EWCA Civ 852.
[36] [1940] 1 KB 229, CA.

## 19.11   CONTRIBUTORY NEGLIGENCE OF MOTORISTS

In most cases involving accidents due to a failure to maintain the highway, or arising out of flooding and mud on the highway, some liability has been attributed to the motorists involved.

The Highway Code at rule 124 warns motorists to adapt their driving to the 'appropriate type and condition of road' they are on and to 'be prepared for unexpected or difficult situations'.

In relation to flooding and mud, ice and snow, the Highway Code contains, at rules 201–212, a whole section entitled 'Driving in Adverse Weather Conditions'.

In *Gorringe v Calderdale Metropolitan Borough Council*,[37] Lord Scott, when considering the limited scope of common law remedies against a highway authority, noted, at paragraph 76, that the:

> '. . . overriding imperative is that those who drive on the public highways do so in a manner and at a speed which is safe, having regard to such matters as the nature of the road, the weather conditions and the traffic conditions. Drivers are first and foremost themselves responsible for their own safety.'

So when the motorist suffered a head-on collision at the crest of a hill, in circumstances in which the road was poorly marked, the House of Lords considered that, had primary liability been established, contributory negligence would have been not less than 50%.

In *Tarrant v Rowlands*,[38] the motorist succeeded on primary liability when he lost control of his vehicle in a pool of water. It was held that the local authority should have made special provision to drain the road where there was often a pool of water at this point and the local authority should reasonably have known about it. However, the motorist was found 50% to blame. It was found that a motorist was under a duty to drive at such a speed and in such a manner that he could reasonably expect to see obstructions which would be expected, such as flooding on roads in wet weather. Equally, the claimant in *Burnside v Emerson*[39] was found two-thirds to blame for driving 'far too fast in the circumstances'.

---

[37]   [2004] UKHL 15.
[38]   [1979] RTR 144.
[39]   [1968] 1 WLR 1490.

# CHAPTER 20

## ROADSIDE NEIGHBOURS' LIABILITY

*Christopher Wilson*

### 20.1  INTRODUCTION

The actions and omissions of owners and occupiers of land adjoining the highway may cause road traffic accidents. A structure or tree on their land may fall onto the highway, either striking a road-user or creating a danger on the highway. The state of their premises may cause injury to road users, for example: spikes on a boundary fence or a trench excavated next to a footpath. In these cases, an injured road-user may have a claim against the owner and/or occupier of the relevant land as well as any contractor who constructed the nuisance.

In this chapter we consider the basis of liability of owners and occupiers of neighbouring land to road-users and the extent of that liability. We do not deal with cases involving things put on the highway by adjoining owners or occupiers, for example skips or parked cars. Liability in those situations is covered in Chapter 22, 'Spillages and Obstructions'.

### 20.2  BASIS OF LIABILITY

Liability for dangers created to users of the highway may be founded in the torts of nuisance, or negligence. The latter requires proof of a breach of duty of care, whereas the former does not.

### 20.3  NUISANCE

Nuisance is an act or omission which interferes with, or disturbs or causes annoyance to, a person's enjoyment of a public right (or rights in connection with private land).

The action for private nuisance was developed in the fifteenth century to protect the right of an occupier of land to enjoy the land without substantial and unreasonable interference, and is not dependent on the nature of the conduct giving rise to that interference. Public nuisance was developed to protect the community at large from acts and omissions which are socially objectionable. Conduct of this kind came to be treated as criminal and punishable as such, but a civil action could be brought on behalf of the community by the Attorney General. In addition, where a member of the public suffered particular damage over and above that suffered by the public at large, he was entitled to sue for public nuisance.

The crime of public nuisance at common law has recently been held to be alive and well,[1] but has been superseded by statute in the case of highways.[2] The Highways Act 1980 also makes provision for statutory control of works carried out on or near the highway.[3]

The standard of duty in nuisance depends on the particular situation. In *Overseas Tankship (UK) Ltd v The Miller Steamship Co Pty (The Wagon Mound No 2)*,[4] Lord Reid stated that:

> 'Nuisance is a term used to cover a wide variety of tortious acts or omissions and in many, negligence in the narrow sense is not essential ... although negligence may not be necessary, fault of some kind is almost always necessary and fault generally involves foreseeability.'

Lord Wilberforce subsequently explained that:

> 'the tort of nuisance, uncertain in its boundary, may comprise a wide variety of situations, in some of which negligence plays no part, in others of which it is decisive.'[5]

This protean[6] nature of the forms of nuisance gives rise to cases in which it has been said that the duty of an occupier towards his neighbour is strict, yet in others the duty is said to be based on reasonable foreseeability of harm. The essence of a claim in private nuisance 'is the unreasonable user by a man of his land to the detriment of his neighbour'.[7] In *Cambridge Water Co Ltd v Eastern Counties Leather plc*,[8] Lord Goff observed that there was a difference between nuisance which has arisen through natural causes, or by the act of a person for whose actions the defendant is not responsible, where the applicable principles in nuisance have become closely associated with those applicable in negligence, and nuisance which has been created by one for whose actions he is responsible. In the latter type of case:

> 'It is still the law that the fact that the defendant has taken all reasonable care will not of itself exonerate him from liability, the relevant control mechanism being found within the principle of reasonable user'.

But, he continued:

---

[1]   *R v Rimmington, R v Goldstien* [2006] 1 AC 459, HL.
[2]   See now Highways Act 1980, s 130.
[3]   Highways Act 1980, Part IX.
[4]   [1967] 1 AC 617, PC.
[5]   *Goldman v Hargrave* [1967] 1 AC 645, PC.
[6]   *Sedleigh-Denfield v O'Callaghan* [1940] AC 880, per Lord Wright at 903.
[7]   *Miller v Jackson* [1977] QB 966, per Lord Denning MR at 980.
[8]   [1994] 1 SC 264, at 300.

'it by no means follows that the defendant should be held liable for damage of a type which he could not reasonably foresee; and the development of the law of negligence in the past 60 years points strongly towards a requirement that such foreseeability should be a prerequisite of liability in damages for nuisance, as it is of liability in negligence.'

He concluded that the decision in *The Wagon Mound No 2* essentially settled the law to the effect that foreseeability of harm is indeed a prerequisite of the recovery of damages in private and public nuisance.

Actions and omission that cause accidents on the highway are in a special category:

'The law of England has always taken particular care to protect those who use a highway. It puts on the occupier of adjoining premises a special responsibility for the structures which he keeps beside the highway. So long as those structures are safe, all well and good; but if they fall into disrepair, so as to be a potential danger to passers-by, then they are a nuisance, and, what is more, a public nuisance; and the occupier is liable to anyone using the highway who is injured by reason of the disrepair. It is no answer for him to say that he and his servants took reasonable care; for, even if he has employed a competent independent contractor to repair the structure, and has every reason for supposing it to be safe, the occupier is still liable if the independent contractor did the work badly.'[9]

The tort of nuisance may be developing to the point at which it is no longer relevant where damage results in personal injury. In *Hunter v Canary Wharf Ltd*,[10] Lord Goff observed:

'I wish to draw attention to the fact that although, in the past, damages for personal injury have been recovered at least in actions of public nuisance, there is now developing a school of thought that the appropriate remedy for such claims as these should lie in our now fully developed law of negligence, and that personal injury claims should be altogether excluded from the domain of nuisance.'

## 20.4 CONDUCT

'The result of ... cases cited to us is that a person is liable for a nuisance constituted by the state of his property: (1) if he causes it; (2) if by the neglect of some duty be allowed it to arise; and (3) if, when it has arisen without his own act or default, he omits to remedy it within a reasonable time after he did or ought to have become aware of it.'[11]

A defendant causes a nuisance by deliberately or recklessly using his land in a way which he knows will cause to his neighbour harm that amounts to an unreasonable interference with the neighbour's enjoyment of his

---

[9] *Mint v Good* [1951] 1 KB 517, per Denning LJ at 526.
[10] [1997] AC 655.
[11] *Noble v Harrison* [1926] 2 KB 332, per Rowlatt J at 338.

land. In such a case, it does not matter that the defendant took all possible steps to prevent his actions amounting to a nuisance to his neighbour.[12]

A defendant allows a nuisance to arise by neglect if he knew or ought to have known that, by reason of his conduct, harm that was reasonably foreseeable would be caused to his neighbour. In that case the defendant is regarded as negligent in his act or omission, giving rise to a difference in semantics as to whether the claim is in nuisance or negligence.

A defendant adopts a nuisance if he knows or should have become aware of the nuisance and fails to abate it. He is under a general duty of care, in relation to hazards to his neighbour occurring on his land, whether natural or man-made, to remove or reduce such hazards; and the duty is based on knowledge of the hazard, ability to foresee the consequences of not checking or removing it, and the ability to abate it. The standard of care required of the occupier is founded on what it was reasonable to expect of him in his circumstances.[13]

## 20.5   WHO IS LIABLE?

The person who actually creates the nuisance is liable, whether or not he is or was the owner or occupier of the land. If he is the owner, his liability continues even if he sells or leases it, so that it is no longer in his power to prevent the nuisance from continuing. Likewise, a contractor who constructs a building on land belonging to another is liable if the building is a nuisance.

A person may create a nuisance personally or by authorising or allowing third parties to do so. Accordingly, an owner who licenses another to burn bricks in a brick kiln on his land is liable in nuisance to neighbouring cottages.[14] He may also be liable in nuisance if he allows to remain present on his land persons whose actual or apprehended activities include, to his knowledge, harmful acts repeatedly committed by them on a neighbour's land.[15] He is not liable for the acts of a trespasser on his land 'unless he knows or ought to have known of the nuisance in time to correct it and obviate its mischievous effects'.[16]

The occupier of land is liable for a nuisance emanating from it because, by virtue of his occupation, he has it in his power to prevent or eliminate the nuisance. He has sufficient control over the hazard which constitutes the

---

[12]   *Read v Lyons* [1947] AC 156, per Lord Simmons at 183.
[13]   *Goldman v Hargrave* [1967] 1 AC 645, PC.
[14]   *White v Jameson* (1874) LR 18 Eq 303.
[15]   *Lippiatt v South Gloucestershire County Council* [2000] 1 QB 51, CA.
[16]   *Sedleigh-Denfield v O'Callaghan* [1940] AC 880, per Lord Wright at 904.

nuisance for it to be reasonable to make him liable for the foreseeable consequences of his failure to exercise that control so as to remove the hazard.[17]

At common law, a non-occupying owner is liable if he has the power to enter the premises to stop the nuisance. In the case of a landlord, that power will arise where the lease expressly or impliedly reserves a right to enter to repair, or in the absence of a strict right, he has been given permission to enter whenever he asked.[18] A landlord's immunity against claims in negligence in respect of the state of the premises has been removed at common law,[19] and by the Defective Premises Act 1972.

The owner or occupier may also be liable for the acts of an independent contractor. The general rule is that the person engaging an independent contractor is not liable for the negligence of that contractor. Exceptions to that rule include operations that the contractor is instructed to carry out that are particularly hazardous,[20] or that involve the creation of a danger on the highway.[21] In the latter type of case, the law imposes for the protection of those using the highway a direct and personal duty on the employer to see that due care is taken in performing work carried out on the highway, usually under statutory authority, so that if things go wrong he cannot avoid liability on the ground that the direct cause of the injury was the act of the contractor. The exception does not extend to works carried out on land near to the highway: in such a case the employer is liable only if the contractor's work involves some special risk or hazard, or the employer is under a positive and continuing personal duty that cannot be delegated.[22] Even then, the employer is not liable if the injury was not caused by negligence directly arising from the work that the contractor was engaged to perform but rather from the contractor's collateral negligence; for example, leaving a tool on a window sill which is blown off by the wind onto a pedestrian below.[23]

It seems that if the owner sells the land or the tenant assigns the lease, they will no longer be liable for a nuisance that exists on the land which they did not create.[24]

---

[17]  *Jones (Insurance Brokers) Ltd v Portsmouth City Council* [2003] 1 WLR 427.
[18]  *Mint v Good* [1951] 1 KB 517, per Denning LJ at 527.
[19]  See *AC Billings & Sons v Riden* [1958] AC 240.
[20]  Eg *Honeywill & Stein Ltd v Larkin Bros, (London's Commercial Photographers) Ltd* [1934] 1 KB 191.
[21]  *Holliday v National Telephone Co* [1899] 2 QB 392.
[22]  *Salisbury v Woodland* [1970] 1 QB 324, CA.
[23]  *Padbury v Holliday & Greenwood Ltd* (1912) 28 TLR 494.
[24]  *Attorney General v Tod Heatley* [1897] 1 Ch 560.

## 20.6   TREES AND NATURAL GROWTHS

A tree or other natural growth may become a danger to users of the
highway by falling onto it, or by projecting over it at a height that
interferes with traffic. A tree that has grown in a way that causes an
obstruction to traffic should be obvious: more difficult is an apparently
healthy tree that falls without warning.

In *Noble v Harrison*,[25] as a result of a latent crack that was not
discoverable by any reasonably careful inspection, a branch of an old
beech tree growing on the defendant's land and overhanging a highway
suddenly broke and damaged the claimant's vehicle. The Court of Appeal
held that the mere fact that the branch overhung the highway did not
make it a nuisance, since it did not obstruct the free passage of the
highway, and although the branch proved to be a danger the defendant
was not liable because he had not created the danger and neither knew
nor ought to have been aware of the secret and unobservable operation of
nature that caused the defect and subsequent fall.

In *Cunliffe v Bankes*,[26] an elm tree was infected with honey fungus, a
disease that attacks the roots and may cause the tree to deteriorate and
fall. The owner of the land had the trees inspected each summer and the
disease was not apparent before the tree fell in January 1944, causing a
fatal accident when a motorcyclist collided with it. The court held that the
owner was not liable in negligence or in nuisance, on the ground that
reasonable examinations of the tree that had been carried out and did not
disclose the disease.

In *Caminer v Northern & London Investment Trust Ltd*[27] an elm tree fell on
a windy day, wrecking a car and injuring its passengers. The tree was
about 130 years old and had a large, but not abnormally large, crown. Its
roots were found to have been diseased for many years, although there
was no indication above ground of its condition. The defendant did not
have the tree inspected nor lopped, topped or pollarded. In the House of
Lords the claimants did not pursue the claim that the disease should have
been discovered, but contended that the defendant should have reduced
the size of the tree, such that it would not have fallen. The House held that
the test was what a reasonably prudent landowner would have done in the
circumstances and decided that, on the facts, the defendant was not liable:
in particular, there was no duty to lop or top all well grown elms in or
near public places. However, as Lord Normand observed:

> 'The test of the conduct to be expected from a reasonable and prudent
> landlord sounds more simple than it really is. For it postulates some degree
> of knowledge on the part of the landlords which must necessarily fall short

---

[25]   [1926] 2 KB 332.
[26]   [1945] 1 All ER 459.
[27]   [1951] 1 AC 88, HL.

of the knowledge possessed by scientific arboriculturists but which must surely be greater than the knowledge possessed by the ordinary urban observer of trees or even of the countryman not practically concerned with their care.'

In *British Road Service v Slater*,[28] an oak tree stood on the verge of a highway, about 3 ft 6 ins from the metalled surface, with a substantial branch coming out of its trunk and going at right angles towards the road for about 2 ft before turning straight upwards. The verge belonged to the defendants but the oak had grown before they bought the land, although after the dedication of the highway. Neither the defendants, nor the highway authority, nor the claimant's lorry driver, who frequently used the road, had ever considered the branch to be a hazard; but on one occasion after dark, the lorry driver had to drive close to the edge of the road to allow an on-coming lorry to pass, the branch knocked some packing cases off the back of the lorry and caused an accident. The branch was held to be a nuisance, because it prevented the convenient use of the highway and was not there by virtue of statute or other lawful authority; but the defendants were not liable because they had not created the nuisance and neither knew or had any reason to believe that it constituted a nuisance.

In *Quinn v Scott*,[29] the National Trust owned land with a belt of trees, including a number of beech trees, bordering a road for distance of about a mile. One of those trees fell, causing a collision between two vehicles and significant injury to the claimant. The judge held that, in the circumstances, the Trust had complied with its duty to provide itself with skilled advice about the safety of the trees but that signs of disease in the beech tree had been missed. In finding liability in nuisance, he imputed to the Trust knowledge of the poor condition of the tree and decided that a reasonable landowner would have had the tree felled without delay.

In *Salisbury v Woodland*,[30] the occupier of a house engaged an apparently competent tree felling contractor to remove a large tree standing in the front garden adjoining the highway. The contractor brought down the tree negligently, causing an accident on the road. The occupier was held not liable for that negligence under the general rule that an employer of an independent contractor is not responsible for his contractor's acts or omissions, because the removal of the tree was not work of an inherently dangerous nature, nor was it work carried out on the highway to bring it within those exceptions to the general rule.

---

[28]   [1964] 1 WLR 498.
[29]   [1965] 1 WLR 1004, QBD. See also *Brown v Harrison* [1947] WN 191, CA (dying condition of a tree was apparent in the dead branches at the top).
[30]   [1970] 1 QB 324, CA.

Once a tree has fallen into the highway without negligence on the part of the occupier, it seems that the occupier is not obliged to warn road users of its presence and is not liable if a motorist collides with it.[31]

## 20.7   SNOW AND BIRDS

The above stated principles are not limited to trees:

In *Slater v Worthington's Cash Stores (1930) Ltd*,[32] the claimant was window-shopping when snow, that had accumulated to a depth of 18 ft on the sloped roof of the shop in unusually severe storms ending 4 days before, fell and injured her. The defendants knew from inspecting the roof that the snow had accumulated but did nothing to remove it or warn pedestrians below. The court held that the accumulation amounted to a public nuisance that the defendants had continued, and that the defendants were in breach of their duty of care in negligence also.

In *Wandsworth London Borough Council v Railtrack plc*,[33] pigeons roosted under a railway bridge and fouled the pavement below, causing inconvenience to pedestrians. The council brought proceedings for order requiring the defendant to 'pigeon-proof' the bridge and pay for the increased costs of cleaning the pavement. The Court of Appeal held that a claim in public nuisance could, unlike a case of private nuisance or negligence, be established without proving the existence and breach of a duty of care, and that if the owner was aware of the existence of a nuisance created by natural causes and had the means and opportunity to abate it and had failed to do so, he was liable in public nuisance if the interference was with the right of the public in general to enjoy the use of the highway in reasonable comfort and convenience.

## 20.8   ARTIFICIAL STRUCTURES

Artificial structures may be constructed over, next to or under the highway. They may be constructed in a manner that creates a danger to users of the highway, or they may become dangerous as a result of an act or omission by the owner or occupier, or as a result of a latent defect or act of a third party. In this context, an artificial structure includes a building, a projection from a building and a wall or fence.

Where a structure is constructed in such a way that it is a danger to users of the highway, it is in law a nuisance.

---

[31]   *Hudson v Bray* [1917] KB 520, DC: dealing with provisions now contained in ss 136 and 137 of the Highways Act 1980.
[32]   [1941] KB 488, CA.
[33]   [2002]1 QB 756, CA.

In *Fenna v Clare & Co*,[34] the owners of a shop had, in front of a receding window and abutting the footway, a low wall that was 18 ins high, on top of which was a row of sharp, 4½ in iron spikes. A child aged 5 was found near the wall with injuries consistent with having stumbled on it. The Divisional Court upheld the jury's verdict that the owners were liable in public nuisance.

In *Morrison v Sheffield Corporation*,[35] the council planted trees in the highway, protected by guards comprising iron posts some 5 ft high, with spikes on the top bent downwards to prevent children climbing them. During a wartime blackout, the claimant walked into the spike, causing serious injury to his eye. The Court of Appeal upheld the judgment for the claimant, holding that, although the guards were authorised by statute, the council was under a continuing duty to take reasonable care to prevent them from becoming a danger under altered conditions.

In *Jewson v Gatti*,[36] there was a cellar beside the highway in which scene-painting was being carried out. The opening was unprotected except for a bar; a passing child looked down to see and leant on the bar which gave way, and she fell into the cellar. The Court upheld the child's claim because it would have been known that children would naturally look down and lean against the bar.

On the other hand, in *Morton v Wheeler*,[37] the owners of a shop near the entrance to a football ground fitted an iron bar with 'sharp fearsome-looking spikes' along the sill to a window adjoining the highway, so as to prevent people waiting to enter the ground sitting on the window sill. A man walking along the highway suddenly felt ill and fell onto one of the spikes, which fatally injured him. The Court of Appeal held that, taking into account all the ordinary chances of life, the injury could not reasonably have been foreseen and therefore the spikes were not a danger such as to constitute a nuisance.

Likewise, in *Liddle v Yorkshire (North Riding) County Council*,[38] workmen excavating a trench in the road piled earth against a retaining wall, which children could climb to get to the top of the wall. One child fell and injured himself, but the court held that, amongst other things, the temporary heap of soil did not constitute a nuisance.

Where the structure was not a nuisance when constructed but a person on the highway is injured as a result of a failure on the part of the owner or occupier to repair the structure, or of a positive act to the structure that

---

[34]   [1895] 1 QB 199, DC.
[35]   [1917] 2 KB 866, CA.
[36]   (1886) 2 TLR 441.
[37]   (1956) *The Times*, February 1.
[38]   [1934] 2 KB 101, CA.

creates a danger, the defendant will be liable in nuisance whether or not he knew or ought to have known of the relevant defect.

In *Tarry v Ashton*,[39] the claimant was walking along the Strand in London when a large lamp, which had been suspended from the front of the defendant's house and projected several feet over the highway, fell on her. Some 3 months before, knowing that the lamp was old, the defendant had employed an experienced contractor to examine the lamp and put it into repair, but the contractor failed to do so properly. The Divisional Court upheld the claim that the defendant was liable, on the ground that a person who has a lamp projecting over the highway is under a duty to maintain it so as not to be dangerous and is not absolved from liability if he employs a competent person to repair it. Contrary to the headnote in the report of the case, Blackburn J did not base his decision on the ground that the defendant knew of the disrepair, but he did note that the occupier would not be liable for a latent defect or act of a trespasser without knowledge.[40]

In *Mullan v Forrester*,[41] the defendants took down parts of their old building but left a street wall standing without support, which fell in a storm and killed three people. On the jury finding that there had been no negligence on the part of the defendants the trial judge dismissed the claimants' claim, but the Court of Appeal in Ireland remitted the case for a new trial on the ground that if the wall was found to be a nuisance the claimants were entitled to succeed even if the defendants had not been negligent.

In *Harrold v Watney*,[42] a 4-year-old child tried to climb over a fence abutting the highway to join children playing on the other side. The fence was rotten and he fell, injuring himself. The court held that a rotten fence close to a highway is an obvious nuisance and that an adult who became tired and leaned against the fence would have been lawfully using the highway and entitled to recover. It held that the accident had not been caused by any misconduct of the child because climbing fences is what children do.

In *Macfarlane v Gwalter*,[43] a pedestrian's leg went though an old grating in the pavement that was out of repair. The occupier of the cellar was required by statute[44] to keep the grating in repair and on his failure to do so, the grating constituted a public nuisance for which he was liable.

---

[39]  (1876) 1 QBD 314, DC.
[40]  See the analysis of this case in *Wringe v Cohen* [1940] 1 KB 229, CA.
[41]  [1921] 2 Ir R 412.
[42]  [1898] 2 QB 320, CA.
[43]  [1959] 2 QB 332, CA.
[44]  Public Health Acts Amendment Act 1890, s 35(1); see now Highways Act 1980, s 180(6), below.

A similar result can be arrived at in a claim based on negligence. In *Kearney v London & Brighton Railway*,[45] the railway company was liable when a brick fell from a wall supporting a bridge built 3 years before onto the claimant on the highway below, not on the basis of an absolute duty in nuisance but rather in negligence on the principle of res ipsa loquitur.[46] However, liability under this principle will not be established if the defendant proves that precautions were taken that rebut the presumption of negligence.[47]

In *Wringe v Cohen*,[48] a case involving a claim in private, rather than public, nuisance, the Court of Appeal reviewed the authorities and concluded that if, owing to want of repair, premises on a highway become dangerous and constitute a nuisance, so that they collapse and injure a passer-by or an adjoining owner, the occupier of the premises, or owner if he has undertaken the duty to repair, is liable, whether he knew or ought to have known of the danger or not, but where the nuisance is created not by want of repair, but by the act of a trespasser or by a secret and unobservable operation of nature (such as subsidence under or near the foundations of the premises), he is not liable in the absence of knowledge or means of knowledge, because he did not cause the nuisance by any act or breach of duty. The court agreed with Rowlatt J, who in *Noble v Harrison* had held that the absolute duty in *Tarry v Ashton* did not apply to trees.

Accordingly in *Barker v Herbert*,[49] the defendant owned a vacant house with an area fenced off from the street by railings. One of the railings had been broken by children, leaving a gap through which the claimant, aged 3 or 4 years, climbed and fell from a parapet on the other side. The jury found that the area behind the railings was a nuisance but the defendant did not know nor ought to have known that the railing had been removed and could not reasonably have foreseen that a child might be injured if the railing was gone. The Court of Appeal held that the defendant was not liable in nuisance and, in any event, the child had not been injured by falling through the gap while using the highway but had fallen inside the area.

In *Cushing v Peter Walker & Son (Warrington & Burton) Ltd*,[50] the blast from an enemy bomb loosened a slate on the roof of a pub in Liverpool, and 16 days later the slate fell in high wind onto the claimant on the highway. The wind would not have dislodged the slate by itself and a reasonable inspection of the roof after the blast did not detect the loosened slate. The occupier of the pub was held not liable, on the ground

---

[45]  (1871) LR 6 QB 759.
[46]  See Chapter 2.
[47]  Eg *Walsh v Holst & Co Ltd* [1958] 1 WLR 800, CA.
[48]  [1940] 1 KB 229, CA.
[49]  [1911] 2 KB 633, CA.
[50]  [1941] 2 All ER 693.

that the nuisance had been caused by a third party and the occupier neither knew nor ought to have known that the roof was unsafe.

In contrast, in *Leanse v Egerton,*[51] on a Tuesday the claimant was injured while on the highway when a piece of glass fell from a window in the defendant's house that had been damaged in an air-raid on the night of the previous Friday. Because the defendant's agents were closed over the weekend and it was difficult to get labour, the defendant did not instruct a builder to carry out repairs until Monday and no work was done before the accident. The court held the damage created a danger to people passing along the road which the defendant was presumed to know about on Saturday but did nothing until after the weekend, such as pull out the glass or have the area cordoned off; therefore he had continued the nuisance and was liable for the claimant's injury.

Cellar flaps, plates and doors let into the surface of the highway are not nuisances in themselves, so the owner is not liable if a highway user is injured when they are suddenly opened by someone for whom he is not responsible.[52] The occupier, on the other hand, is likely to be responsible for the carelessness of the person who opened the door. Where the door over an opening in the highway is left open, so as to render the opening dangerous, primary liability rests on the person opening the door but the occupier may also be liable.

In *Pickard v Smith,*[53] the tenant of refreshment rooms at Manchester railway station arranged for delivery of coal, and a passenger fell in when the trap door was left unguarded. The court held that the contractor had been engaged by the tenant to open the cellar door and trusted to guard it while open. The act of opening the door was treated as the act of the tenant and, having thereby caused danger, the tenant was bound to take reasonable means to prevent injury. In such circumstances the independent contractor would be also liable in negligence, as would his own employer on ordinary principles of vicarious liability.[54]

*Wilson v Hodgson's Kingston Brewery Co Ltd,*[55] a brewery engaged an independent contractor to deliver beer to a public house. The occupier opened the cellar flaps on the highway, which were left unguarded and the claimant was injured. The occupier was held liable but not the brewery, because its contractor had not been engaged to work on the highway and the contractor's failure to guard the opening was collateral negligence.

By s 180(6) of the Highways Act 1980, the owner or occupier is under a statutory duty to keep in repair all vaults, arches and cellars under the

[51] [1943] KB 323.
[52] *Evans v Edinburgh Corporation* [1916] 2 AC 45.
[53] (1861) 10 CB(NS) 470.
[54] *Whiteley v Pepper* (1876) 2 QBD 276.
[55] (1915) 85 LJKB 270.

street, the openings and coverings, lights, and gratings in the surface of the highway and any landings, flags or stones of the street by which the above are supported. The duty is not absolute and does not by itself give rise to a cause of action: nuisance or negligence is necessary to found liability.[56]

If the structure in or over the highway is interfered with by a third party without the knowledge or consent of the occupier, the occupier is not liable provided he made the structure reasonably secure against accidental, as opposed to intentional, interference, unless he ought reasonably to have anticipated intentional interference.

In *Braithwaite v Watson*,[57] a coverplate normally secured by a crossbar and weight was left loose and was dislodged. It was held to be a danger and the occupier was liable when the claimant fell in.

In *Wells v Metropolitan Water Board*,[58] the coverplate of a valve box was left open, presumably by a child, and the claimant tripped over it. The Board was held liable in nuisance and negligence because the cover could easily be opened by a child and no locking device had been fitted. However, without evidence that the interference could or ought to have been foreseen and guarded against, liability would not be established.[59]

In *Wheeler v Morris*,[60] two men jumped up to a sunblind fixed outside a shop and brought it down on a pedestrian. The occupier was not liable, on the ground that the blind was not a nuisance and that he had taken such precautions as were reasonable to avoid the result of accidents that might reasonably be foreseen.

## 20.9  DANGERS ON PREMISES

A public nuisance arises if premises adjoining a highway are dangerous to users of the highway, and the occupier is liable if he creates or continues that nuisance. Examples of dangers on land adjacent to the highway are:

- an unfenced excavation next to the highway;[61]

- an unfenced area within the curtilage of a house at a lower level than the adjacent footpath;[62]

---

[56]  *Scott v Green & Sons* [1969] 1 WLR 301, CA.
[57]  (1889) 5 TLR 331.
[58]  [1937] 4 All ER 639.
[59]  *Mileham v Marylebone Corporation* (1903) 67 JP 110.
[60]  (1915) 84 LJKB 1435, CA.
[61]  *Barnes v Ward* (1850) 9 CB 392.
[62]  *Coupland v Hardingham* (1813) 3 Camp 398.

- an unfenced hoist-hole about 14 ft from the highway;[63]

- an unfenced chalk pit varying from 14–50 ft, into which pedestrians might fall on dark nights or in foggy weather.[64]

The danger must be sufficiently close to the highway:

> 'so that a person walking on it might, by making a false step, or being affected with sudden giddiness, or in the case of a horse or carriage way, by the sudden starting of a horse, be thrown into the excavation'.[65]

If it is not, the claimant is not using the highway and may be a trespasser who is owed limited duties by the defendant.[66] Examples are:

- a pit 36 ft away from the highway;[67]

- an unfenced canal separated from a towpath by a 24 ft strip of land;[68]

- an unfenced aperture in a wall $3\frac{1}{2}$ ft up, to which a boy climbed and put his head through, to be struck by a lift;[69]

- an unfenced dock 47 ft from the highway;[70]

- a defective wall separating a yard from the highway. A heavy stone fell on a child playing in the yard: the court held that the wall was a public nuisance but that the landlord was not liable because the claimant was not injured while using the highway.[71]

## 20.10  DANGEROUS ACTIVITIES ON PREMISES

An occupier of land is under a duty to take reasonable care that persons using the highway are not injured as a result of activities carried out on that land. Examples are:

- Quarry blasting a short distance from a main road:[72] the occupier was liable when a pedestrian was struck on the head with a stone,

---

[63]  *Hadley v Taylor* (1865) LR 1 CP 53.
[64]  *Carshalton Urban Council v Burrage* [1911] 2 Ch 133 (a case decided under the Public Health Acts Amendment Act 1907, s 30).
[65]  *Hardcastle v South Yorkshire Railway* (1859) 4 H&N 67.
[66]  See the Occupiers' Liability Act 1984.
[67]  *Blithe v Topham* (1607) Cro Jac 158.
[68]  *Binks v South Yorkshire Railway* (1862) 3 B&S 244.
[69]  *Stiefsohn v Brooke* (1889) 53 JP 790.
[70]  *Caseley v Bristol Corporation* [1944] 1 All ER 14.
[71]  *Bromley v Mercer* [1922] 2 KB 126. For the liability of the defendant landlord, see now the Defective Premises Act 1972.
[72]  *Miles v Forest Rock Granite Co* (1918) 34 TLR 500.

fracturing his skull. The court held that the facts were sufficient evidence on the part of the occupier.

- Opaque clouds of steam and smoke periodically billowing across the highway for about 1½ minutes as a result of quenching coke in ovens. The occupier was held liable in nuisance and also in negligence in failing to post a man at each end of the highway to warn oncoming traffic as soon as a discharge was imminent.

- Fat on the pavement outside a butcher's shop, which caused the claimant to slip.[73] The fat got there either as the butcher was chopping meat and it flew onto the pavement or it got onto the floor in the shop and was carried outside on a customer's shoe. There was no evidence that the butcher was aware that it had got to the pavement but he was liable both for causing a nuisance and in negligence by conducting his business in a way that fat could get onto the pavement or onto the floor in his shop and carried outside.

Sporting activities near the highway can result in liability for the occupier:

- A golf ball struck from the 13th tee hit the windscreen of a taxicab, injuring the driver. The directors of the club were liable in nuisance on the ground that they knew or ought to have known that balls from the 13th tee frequently landed on the road.[74]

- A cricket ball struck from a cricket ground hit the claimant in the street. There was evidence that it had been an exceptional hit by the batsman and that a ball had been struck onto the road six times in the previous 28 years, without incident. The possibility of the ball being hit on to the highway might reasonably have been foreseen but the committee and members of the club were not liable in negligence (and, by concession, nuisance also), since the risk of injury to anyone in such a place was so remote that a reasonable person would not have anticipated it.[75]

- Young children were playing a game of football on grassland adjoining a busy highway when one kicked the ball into the highway causing a passing motorcyclist to fall off and suffer fatal injuries. The defendants, who were the owners and occupiers of the land and who allowed the children to play there, were held liable in negligence because a reasonable man in their position would have concluded that there was a risk of damage to persons using the highway as a

---

[73]   *Dollman v Hillman Ltd* [1941] 1 All ER 355.
[74]   *Castle v St Augustine's Links* (1922) 38 TLR 615.
[75]   *Bolton v Stone* [1951] AC 850, HL. Compare *Miller v Jackson* [1977] 1 QB 966.

result of the children's activities; the risk was not so small that it could be safely disregarded, and they had failed to take reasonable care in all the circumstances.[76]

## 20.11  CONCLUSION

A claimant injured on, or next to, the highway may have an action in nuisance as well as one in negligence. The common law has developed a collection of rules to protect users of the highway from the acts and omissions of occupiers, owners and their employees, licensees and contractors, under which proof of negligence is not always required.

The development of this area of the law will continue and personal injury claims may be taken out of the tort of nuisance altogether.

---

[76]  *Hilder v Associated Portland Cement Manufacturers Ltd* [1961] 1 WLR 1434.

# CHAPTER 21

# LIABILITY FOR INJURIES CAUSED BY ANIMALS IN ROAD TRAFFIC ACCIDENTS

*Giles Mooney*

## 21.1 INTRODUCTION

Actors are warned never to work with children and animals. In light of the complexity of the legislation, lawyers might consider a similar strategy: 'never litigate with cars and animals'.

Unfortunately, accidents involving motorists and the millions of animals in the United Kingdom are all too frequent and often result in civil proceedings in the courts. The sheer size and weight of many farm animals and the unpredictability of their behaviour when loose on the roads means that accidents do happen and are often serious.

Prior to 1971 the common law included a number of special rules relating to harm done by animals. Given the huge change in the volume of traffic on roads through the last century, some of those rules, including the ancient immunity from liability for animals straying onto the highway, were subject to increasing criticism. As a result of the 1967 Law Commission report on Civil Liability for Animals, the Animals Act 1971 was passed. The purpose of the Act was to update and simplify the patchwork of common law rules that had grown up in relation to liability for animals.

Whilst the resulting legislation may have updated the law it remains arguable whether it simplified matters.

## 21.2 COMMON LAW LIABILITY

### 21.2.1 Negligence

Before turning to the Animals Act 1971, it is worth looking at how the common law still applies to accidents on the road involving animals. Plainly, the owner or person with responsibility for an animal will be held liable for any damage done by an animal if he acts negligently. For example, where a farmer negligently fails to repair broken fencing thus allowing cows to stray onto the road he will be liable for damage caused by the straying cows. Similarly, a horse rider riding along a highway will be liable if he negligently fails to control his horse allowing it to collide with a car.

Historically the courts have been happier to find negligence in claims involving straying animals than for in claims involving horses ridden on the roads.

In *Donaldson v Wilson*[1] the court found a farmer liable where his cows strayed onto the road. The facts of the case reveal that the court considered the farmer to be under a relatively high duty of care. The claimant was driving his motorcycle in North Yorkshire when he collided with cows that had escaped from the defendant's field. The field was properly fenced but had a footpath running through it. A walker had left the gate open and the cows had escaped from the field. The cows then made their way through a dilapidated farm next door and onto the road. The aptly named Mr Recorder Bullock found that it was foreseeable that the gate could be left open by walkers and that given the dilapidated state of the next door farm it was foreseeable that the cows could end up on the road. The defendant was found not to have done enough to secure the field despite evidence that he or his son checked the cows regularly. The decision was appealed on the basis of the far-reaching consequences for farmers across the land but the Court of Appeal upheld the first instance decision.

The reluctance to find riders to blame is highlighted in *Haimes v Watson*.[2] The claimant was driving along a road and attempted to overtake a horse being ridden by the defendant. The horse shied at something at the side of the road into the path of the claimant's vehicle. The judge found that although the horse's movement across the road gave rise to an inference of negligence, this was negated by the rider's explanation that the horse had unforeseeably shied. In light of this the defendant was not negligent.

## 21.2.2   Nuisance

The authors of *Clerk and Lindsell* suggest that where animals are present on the highway they could amount to a public nuisance. The first instance decision of *Livingstone v Armstrong*[3] seems at odds with this proposition. A cow was on the highway and a road traffic accident occurred. The judge did not consider nuisance having noted that counsel had agreed that nuisance had no application to animals. Unfortunately the report is silent as to why counsel reached this agreement. In the absence of any legislative provision or higher authority we suggest that there is no reason why nuisance should not apply. The argument may be somewhat academic because to be guilty of a public nuisance the tortfeasor must commit an

---

[1]   [2004] EWCA Civ 972.
[2]   [1981] RTR 90.
[3]   (2003) LTL 24/2/2004.

act or omission. In light of this any act or omission which allows animals to be loose on the highway is likely to amount to negligence.

## 21.3    THE ANIMALS ACT 1971

### 21.3.1    Straying animals: sections 4 and 8

One of the key changes made by the Act was to abolish the old rules relating to straying animals and to put in place a regime of strict liability for straying livestock. The two relevant provisions are ss 4 and 8. Unfortunately for claimants in road traffic claims, as is discussed below, the provisions will rarely assist in practice.

Section 4 creates the strict liability for straying livestock:

> '(1) Where livestock belonging to any person strays on to land in the ownership or occupation of another and –
> (a)    damage is done by the livestock to the land or to any property on it which is in the ownership or possession of the other person; or
> (b)    any expenses are reasonably incurred by that other person in keeping the livestock, while it cannot be restored to the person to whom it belongs or while it is detained in pursuance of section 7 of this Act, or in ascertaining to whom it belongs;
> the person to whom the livestock belongs is liable for the damages or expenses, except as otherwise provided by this Act.'

It is clear from the wording of s 4 that only the owner or occupier of the land onto which livestock has strayed can bring an action for damages. Furthermore damages are only recoverable for damage to land or property, not for personal injury. In light of this prohibition, the section will have limited use in road traffic claims. Indeed the only potential application in the field of public highways would be an action by a highway authority in circumstances where straying animals had damaged the road.

Section 8 abolishes the old immunity for straying animals, but the Act goes on in s 8(2):

> 'Where damage is caused by animals straying from unfenced land to the highway a person who placed them onto the land shall not be regarded as having committed a breach of the duty to take care by reason only of placing them if –
> (a)    the land is common land, or is land situated in an area where fencing is not customary, or is a town or village green; and
> (b)    he had a right to place the animals on that land.'

The effect of s 8 is not to create any statutory liability, but to allow a negligence action and then provide a defence to such an action where animals have strayed by reason of lack of fencing.

### 21.3.2   Section 2 – keepers

Given the very clear limitations relating to straying animals, the vast majority of road traffic litigation involving animals is based on strict liability under s 2. This sets out the circumstances in which 'the keeper' of an animal will be strictly liable for damage caused by that animal.

Keeper is defined in s 6(3):

> 'A person is a keeper of an animal if –
> (a)   he owns the animal or has it in his possession . . .'

A potential problem arises where there is more than one keeper. For example a rider of a horse, who does not own it, has the horse in his possession and hence he is the keeper. If that horse happens to bolt whilst out on the road and injures the rider, that rider would be entitled to sue the owner. In other words one keeper can bring an action against another keeper of the same animal. This was exactly the situation in *Flack v Hudson, Hudson and Custance*.[4]

The courts appear to take a rather broad approach to the definition of possession and in the first instance decision of *Hole v Ross-Skinner*[5] a livery yard owner was found to be in possession of horses which were kept on his land and which had escaped and caused an accident on the road.

### 21.3.3   Dangerous animals

The Act splits animals into two categories; dangerous and non-dangerous. Dangerous animals are defined in s 6(2):

> 'A dangerous species is a species –
> (a)   which is not commonly domesticated in the British Islands; and
> (b)   whose fully grown animals normally have such characteristics that they are likely, unless restrained, to cause severe damage or that any damage they do is likely to be severe.'

All the rest are therefore non-dangerous animals.

Where a dangerous animal causes damage the position is clear and liability is strict under s 2(1):

> 'Where any damage is caused by an animal which belongs to a dangerous species, any person who is the keeper of the animal is liable for the damage, except as otherwise provided by this Act.'

---

4   [2001] 2 WLR 982, CA (Civ Div).
5   [2003] All ER (D) 272 (May).

Thus where a rhinoceros escapes from the zoo and onto the road causing a traffic accident the keepers will be strictly liable for that damage. It should be noted that liability does not rest on the characteristic which makes the animal dangerous under s 6(2) being the causative factor in the damage. Thus where a lion escapes onto the road and causes a road traffic accident, liability would be strict even though the lion's dangerousness may be considered focused on pedestrians being eaten rather than cars being hit.

### 21.3.4   Non dangerous animals

The legal situation is not nearly so straightforward in relation to non-dangerous animals which account for the vast majority of accidents in this country.

Section 2(2) creates a 'strict' liability where certain criteria are met:

> 'Where damage is caused by an animal which does not belong to a dangerous species, a keeper of the animal is liable for the damage, except as otherwise provided by this Act, if –
> (a)   the damage is of a kind which the animal, unless restrained, was likely to cause or which, if caused by the animal, was likely to be severe; and
> (b)   the likelihood of the damage or of it being severe was due to the characteristics of the animal which are not normally found in animals of the same species or are not normally so found except at particular times or in particular circumstances; and
> (c)   those characteristics were known to that keeper or were at any time known to a person who at the time had charge of the animal as that keeper's servant or, where that keeper is the head of household, were known to another keeper of the animal who is a member of that household and under the age of sixteen.'

Section 2(2) sets out a conjunctive tripartite test. The legislation has been subject to extensive litigation and whilst this work is primarily concerned with liability in road traffic situations some consideration of more general animal litigation cases is necessary fully to explain the effects of the Act.

### 21.3.5   Section 2(2)(a) – 'the likelihood test'

Section 2(2)(a) is split into two limbs. The first asks the question: was the animal unless restrained likely to cause damage of this kind? The second asks: when damage has actually been caused, is it likely to be severe?

'Likely' was defined in the case of *Smith v Ainger*[6] as 'such as might happen'. It is clear that such a test is lower than a balance of probabilities.

---

[6]   (1990) *The Times*, June 5.

Historically s 2(2)(a) did not cause very much controversy in road traffic cases because it was normally accepted that when livestock was involved in a road traffic accident damage was either likely or likely to be severe. This approach changed after *Mirvahedy v Henley*[7] (see below). Whilst that case was primarily concerned with the construction of s 2(2)(b) (s 2(2)(a) had been conceded by the keepers), in a dissenting judgment Lord Scott considered the meaning of s 2(2)(a) and speculated that it had not necessarily been satisfied in *Mirvahedy*. This dissenting judgment led to s 2(2)(a) becoming the new battleground in Animals Act cases. The current approach to the two limbs of s 2(2)(a) is summarised below.

### 21.3.6   The first limb

The first limb will not always be easily satisfied in road traffic cases. It is a rather general question about the animal itself. If a domesticated animal is left unrestrained is it likely to cause damage (ie personal injury or damage to property) in a road traffic accident? Although the answer may depend on the particular animal it is arguable that most domestic animals are not likely to cause personal injury or damage to property simply because they are left unrestrained.

It is possible that an unrestrained animal may find its way to a highway and cause damage but it is not necessarily likely.

### 21.3.7   The second limb

The second limb has been the subject of recent consideration in the Court of Appeal in *Freeman v Higher Park Farm*.[8] The keeper of a horse which had caused personal injury argued that the second limb of s 2(2)(a) should be looked at in relation to all the potential damage that an animal might cause and not with reference to the accident itself. The Court of Appeal rejected this approach, finding that when looking at the likelihood of damage being severe the court had to look at the particular characteristic that the animal was displaying and the circumstances of the accident.

In light of this decision it seems that the relevant question for s 2(2)(a) in a road traffic accident will be: 'was damage likely to be severe when this animal collided with a car on the road?'

In RTA cases the answer will usually be yes.

---

[7]    [2003] UKHL 16.
[8]    [2008] EWCA Civ 1185.

## 21.3.8    Section 2(2)(b) – 'the characteristic test'

Section 2(2)(b) is split into two parts. The first part asks whether the likelihood of damage or of damage being severe was due to the animal displaying a characteristic which was unusual for the species. In other words was the animal unusual for its species.

The second part asks whether the likelihood of damage or of damage being severe was due to a characteristic that animals of the species do exhibit but only at particular times or in particular circumstances.

The first part should not cause many problems. For example a cow that exhibited a habit of attacking cars whenever it saw one would clearly fall into the first category.

It is the second part which has caused the most difficulty. Prior to *Mirvahedy* there were two competing Court of Appeal authorities on what the second part of s 2(2)(b) required. The first school of thought set out in *Cummings v Granger*[9] appeared to be true to the wording of the legislation in that it held that a normal characteristic of an animal would suffice if it was only a normal characteristic in particular circumstances or at particular times. The second approach set out in *Breedon v Lampard* CA 1985 unreported,[10] insisted on the animal displaying an unusual characteristic so that proof of a normal characteristic of the species in whatever circumstances would not suffice.

In *Mirvahedy v Henley,* shortly after midnight on the night of 28–29 August 1996 the claimant was driving home along a dual carriageway in Devon. His car crashed into horses which were loose and running across the road. He suffered serious injuries. The horses belonged to the defendants. They had escaped from a field by stampeding through the fencing. Something had clearly terrified the horses although it was never established what. An action was commenced by the claimant in negligence and under the Animals Act 1971. The negligence claim failed on the basis that the fencing had been adequate. The statutory claim failed at first instance but succeeded on appeal to the Court of Appeal and then in the House of Lords. The defendants argued that bolting when terrified was a normal characteristic of horses and hence not caught by the Act. The House preferred the *Cummings* approach and found that whilst bolting was a normal characteristic it was only found in particular circumstances, when horses were terrified.

*Mirvahedy* was greeted with dismay by insurers and in the equine industry generally. However, in the 5 years since the decision it is clear that it is far more limited in scope than some at first thought. What is often forgotten is that s 2(2)(b) has retained some content. A claimant must identify a

---

[9]    [1977] QB 397.
[10]    (Unreported) 1985, CA.

relevant characteristic. It is not enough to simply argue that livestock is on the road and hence *Mirvahedy* applies.

A classic example of this can be found in *Livingstone v Armstrong*[11] where a motorist drove into a cow standing in the road. There was no evidence that the cow was doing anything other than standing. In light of this the court found that the cow was not displaying a relevant characteristic for the purposes of s 2(2)(b).

### 21.3.9   The link

The wording of s 2(2)(b) plainly links it with s 2(2)(a). So the likelihood of damage in s 2(2)(a) must be due to the characteristic in s 2(2)(b).

The link between the two sections was examined in the case of *Bowlt v Clark*.[12] The claimant was driving his car along a road in Northumbria when the defendant, riding her pony moved across from the verge and into the path of the claimant's vehicle resulting in the defendant and the pony landing on the roof of the claimant's car. The claimant and the defendant both sustained personal injuries and the claimant sued for damages in negligence and under the Act. The defendant counterclaimed in negligence. At first instance HHJ Walton found neither party negligent but found for the claimant under the Animals Act 1971 claim. The judge reasoned that s 2(2)(a) was met because damage was likely, and likely to be severe because the horse was large and heavy and in close proximity to traffic. Further s 2(2)(b) was met because the horse had a characteristic to move in a direction other than directed by its rider. The defendant appealed on the basis that the judge had failed to identify a true characteristic or a circumstance which had triggered the characteristic for the purposes of s 2(2)(b). The Court of Appeal agreed but went further finding that there must be a link between s 2(2)(a) and s 2(2)(b) and that the characteristic identified for the purposes of s 2(2)(b) must be the same characteristic as the one which gave rise to the finding that the damage was likely for the purposes of s 2(2)(a). In this case the reason that damage was likely or likely to be severe was because the horse was heavy. All horses are heavy and hence there was no relevant characteristic.

### 21.3.10   Section 2(2)(c) – 'the knowledge test'

Readers will be relieved to know that s 2(2)(c) is the least controversial of the subsections. Unlike the other subsections its drafting leaves little room for argument. It has produced two notable cases.

---

[11]   (Unreported) 11 December 2003.
[12]   [2006] EWCA Civ 978.

In *Welsh v (1) Stokes (2) Stokes*[13] the Court of Appeal looked at s 2(2)(c) and considered what degree of knowledge was necessary. The facts of the case involved a rider falling from a rearing horse whilst the horse was being ridden along a road. The defendants argued that the horse had never reared before and that they did not have the requisite knowledge that the horse had a characteristic of rearing. The expert evidence in the case was that all horses might rear in certain circumstances. Dyson LJ held that knowledge of the general characteristics of horses to rear in certain circumstances was sufficient to satisfy the Act. There was no requirement to know that the particular animal would behave in that way.

Whilst it might have been thought that *Welsh* had ended any scope for argument over s 2(2)(c) the case of *McKenny & Anor v Foster (T/A Foster Partnership)*[14] decided less than 12 months later provided a chink of light for defendants when considering s 2(2)(c). A cow which had been separated from its calf became distressed and escaped from its field colliding with a car. To escape the field the cow had jumped over extensive fencing. In the collision the passenger in the car died. The court held that the cow had reacted in an exceptional manner to separation from her calf. Whilst it was expected that a cow's maternal instinct might cause it to react when separated from its calf, this cow had reacted in such an extreme and unexpected manner that the defendant was held not to have the requisite knowledge for the purposes of s 2(2)(c).

## 21.3.11   Statutory defences

Section 5 of the Act sets out the defences to liability. In the sphere of road traffic litigation, the only one likely to be of relevance is s 5(1):

> 'A person is not liable under sections 2 to 4 of this Act for any damage which is due wholly to the fault of the person suffering from it.'

Whilst s 5(1) provides a total defence it is clear from s 10 that blame can be apportioned under the Law Reform (Contributory Negligence) Act 1945.

## 21.3.12   Conclusion

The Law Commission draft bill for the Animals Act was far less complicated than the legislation that was eventually enacted by parliament. As a result of the opaque language of the Act accidents involving animals on roads will continue to provide scope for uncertain litigation.

---

[13]   [2007] EWCA Civ 796.
[14]   [2008] EWCA Civ 173.

Unless the accident involves a clear case of negligence by the animal's keeper, practitioners should be prepared to read and consider and then re-read and reconsider the Animals Act 1971.

# CHAPTER 22

## LIABILITY FOR SPILLAGES AND OBSTRUCTIONS ON THE HIGHWAY

*Laura Begley*

### 22.1 INTRODUCTION

When ruling on cases involving highway obstructions the courts have tended to look carefully at the weight of the negligence of the motorist and balanced that against the 'obstructer'. The cases often involve apportioning blame. As a result of this approach few definitive rules have emerged.

Some highway obstructions are an inevitable part of life and the courts recognise that sweeping rules governing the liability of those responsible for the obstructions would be unjust. For instance the judge in *Perkins v Glyn*[1] said:

> 'a motorist on the highway had to be expected to be obstructed occasionally.'

When assessing the merits of a claim:

- A detailed assessment of the facts is needed taking into account factors such as the weather conditions, the lighting and the specific characteristics of the road.

- The case law is generally more useful as a guide to the factors which the court will take into account in deciding liability rather than a way to determine who will win.

- The Highway Code provides useful guidelines for motorists when dealing with obstructions and failure to act in accordance with the Code is prima facie evidence of nuisance according to the Road Traffic Act, s 38(7).

- Highway authorities have a bundle of statutory duties and powers in relation to the maintenance of the highway. Where there is a

---

[1]    (1976) CLY 1883.

statutory duty or power, the courts have generally been reluctant to find a co-existent common law duty unless the exercise of the power has created a trap or danger.

## 22.2 NUISANCE OR NEGLIGENCE

Damage caused by a highway obstruction may give rise to a cause of action in negligence and/or nuisance. A public nuisance is incapable of exact definition but is:

> 'an act or omission which is an interference with, disturbance of or annoyance to, a person in the exercise or enjoyment of a right belonging to him as a member of the public.'[2]

In contrast to the common law duty in negligence, the existence of a public nuisance has been said to give rise to strict liability when it can be shown that an individual has suffered particular harm notwithstanding that the nuisance did not present a foreseeable danger. As Denning LJ said in *Morton v Wheeler*,[3] quoted by Edmund Davies LJ in *Dymond v Pearce*:[4]

> 'In an action for private damage arising out of a public nuisance the court does not look at the conduct of the defendant and ask whether he was negligent. It looks at the actual state of affairs as it exists in or adjoining the highway, without regard to the merits or demerits of the defendant. If the state of affairs is such as to be a danger to persons using the highway ... it is a public nuisance. Once it is held to be a danger, the person who created it is liable unless he can show sufficient justification or excuse.'

In *Dymond v Pearce*,[5] a lorry driver parked his lorry on the shallow bend of a road on an August bank holiday evening with the intention of making an early start in the morning. At 9.45pm a motorcyclist collided with the lorry. His pillion passenger brought a claim against the driver and owner of the lorry. The lorry was parked under a street lamp and was visible from 200 yards and both at trial and on appeal it was held not to be parked negligently. The Court of Appeal considered nuisance; Sachs LJ said:

> 'The leaving of a large vehicle on a highway for any purpose for a considerable period (it is always a matter of degree) otherwise than in a lay by prima facie results in a nuisance being created, for it narrows the highway ... But the mere fact that a lorry was a nuisance does not render its driver or owner liable to the Claimant in damages unless its being in that position was the cause of the accident.'

---

[2]   According to *Clerk & Lindsell on Torts* (19th edn at paragraph 20-01).
[3]   (1956) *The Times*, 1 February 1956.
[4]   [1972] 1 QB 496.
[5]   [1972] 2 WLR 633.

Edmund Davies LJ, whilst agreeing with the other judges in dismissing the appeal, reiterated his finding in *Parish v Judd*[6] that in order to become a nuisance an obstruction in the highway had to be shown to be dangerous and in some way that the danger was the fault of the person responsible for it.

It is a fact that some of the cases concerning nuisance assert that the duty is strict as above, while others assert that the duty is based on foreseeability of harm ie negligence. As per Lord Wright in *Sedleigh-Denfield v O'Callaghan*:[7]

> 'The forms which nuisance may take are protean. Certain classifications are possible, but many reported cases are no more than illustrations of particular matters of fact which have been held to be nuisances.'

In these circumstances the sensible approach is to look at the different types of situation which arise and to ascertain the appropriate standard of duty in each type of situation. It is probably also worth bearing in mind as Lord Goff of Chieveley said (obiter) in *Hunter v Canary Wharf*:[8]

> '... although in the past, damages for personal injury have been recovered at least in actions of public nuisance, there is now a developing school of thought that the appropriate remedy for such claims as these should now lie in our fully developed law of negligence and that personal injury claims should be excluded from the domain of nuisance.'

The cases cited below should therefore be read in this context.

## 22.3  VEHICLES CAUSING OBSTRUCTION

Claims for damage may be brought by the owners of the obstruction, or those who collide with the obstruction.

The owner or driver of an obstructing vehicle will not successfully avoid liability merely because an oncoming vehicle was speeding or otherwise being driven carelessly. The courts will assess the causative potency of the actions or omissions of all of the parties when considering contribution. Assessments of a driver's recklessness will be made in the context of the road and the weather conditions and the degree of visibility of the obstruction.

So in *Rouse v Squires*,[9] a lorry had jack-knifed across a motorway at night and a car collided with the lorry in the middle lane and stopped with its rear light on. Subsequently, seeing the obstruction, another lorry stopped

---

[6]  [1960] 1 WLR 867.
[7]  [1940] AC 880, at 903.
[8]  [1997] AC 655.
[9]  [1973] 1 QB 889.

15 ft short of the jack-knifed lorry and used its headlights to illuminate the scene. A third lorry driver, D, failing to appreciate that the various vehicles were stationary, collided with the parked lorry pushing it forward and killing R who was helping at the scene. Following a claim by R's widow against him, D brought third party proceedings against the owners and driver of the jack-knifed lorry and this driver was found one-quarter to blame. As Buckley LJ stated:

> 'If a driver so negligently manages his vehicle as to cause it to obstruct the highway and constitute a danger to other road users, including those who are driving too fast or not keeping a proper lookout, but not those who deliberately or recklessly drive into the obstruction, then the first driver's negligence may be held to have contributed to the causation of an accident of which the immediate cause was the negligent driving of the vehicle which because of the presence of the obstruction collides with it or with some other vehicle or with some other person.'

Where an oncoming vehicle is driven recklessly in all of the circumstances it may be found that the obstructing vehicle played no part in causing subsequent accidents. So in *Wright v Lodge*,[10] a lorry hit a broken down Mini in the nearside lane of a dual carriageway and proceeded to swerve across the central reservation into the path of other vehicles. The lorry driver was found wholly liable to the vehicles in the oncoming lane on the basis that it was his reckless speed on a foggy night that was to blame for his loss of control, not the stationary Mini.

Where the prima facie cause of an accident was debris left in the road following a previous accident the tortfeasor in the original accident may still be liable for further damaged caused by his original negligence. The test in *Rouse v Squires* was applied by the Court of Appeal in *Clift v (1) Hawes (2) The MIB*.[11] In this case the claimant was riding a motorcycle along the A12 road on a dark clear night on which an accident caused by the first defendant's careless driving had just occurred. There was debris in the road and on seeing it the car in front of the claimant's motorcycle, (the second defendant), braked sharply causing a collision. At trial the first defendant was held wholly liable. On appeal by the first defendant and the MIB the Court of Appeal upheld a finding of primary liability against the first defendant applying the rule in *Rouse v Squires*. The claimant's driving was within the range of what was to be expected from other road users and so the relevant collision could be regarded as having been caused by the first defendant. However it made a finding of 30% contributory negligence as the claimant was driving too closely to the vehicle in front and was therefore not 'prepared for foreseeable emergencies'.[12] For another more recent application of *Rouse v Squires* see *Parsons v Western National Limited*.[13]

---

[10]  [1993] 4 All ER 299.
[11]  (Unreported) 24 November 1999.
[12]  Per Diplock LJ in *Thompson v Spedding* [1973] RTR 312.
[13]  (Unreported) (1999), CA.

## 22.4   VEHICLES WHICH HAVE BROKEN DOWN

See also Chapter 10 on liability for lighting vehicles.

The Highway Code offers useful guidelines for motorists whose vehicles break down at rule 274:

> 'If your vehicle breaks down, think first of all other road users and
> - get your vehicle off the road if possible
> - warn other traffic by using your hazard warning lights if your vehicle is causing an obstruction
> - help other road users see you by wearing light-coloured or fluorescent clothing in daylight and reflective clothing at night or in poor visibility
> - put a warning triangle on the road at least 45 metres (147 feet) behind your broken-down vehicle on the same side of the road, or use other permitted warning devices if you have them. Always take great care when placing or retrieving them, but never use them on motorways
> - if possible, keep your sidelights on if it is dark or visibility is poor
> - do not stand (or let anybody else stand) between your vehicle and oncoming traffic
> - at night or in poor visibility do not stand where you will prevent other road users seeing your lights.'

If a vehicle has broken down with no provable fault on the part of its driver and (depending on the conditions), it is reasonable to expect any oncoming traffic to see the obstruction in time to take steps to avoid it, then the person causing the obstruction may escape liability. The following cases demonstrate the factors which the courts have taken into account when assessing liability.

### 22.4.1   Whether the stationary vehicle was appropriately lit

In *Moore v Maxwells of Emsworth Ltd*[14] it was held that an unlit vehicle on the highway called for an explanation. The fact that the lighting system had failed was an acceptable explanation. There was no liability for failing to supply flashing lights as it was not customary to do so. Things have probably moved on since this case: see *Jordan v North Hampshire Plant Hire Ltd*[15] and Chapter 10 on lighting vehicles generally in respect of the current obligations to light a vehicle.

In *Parish v Judd*[16] the defendant avoided liability. He had stopped the unlit vehicle that he was towing just beyond a street light thus ensuring it was illuminated. However, in *Fotheringham v Prudence*,[17] the defendant

---

[14]   [1968] 2 All ER 779.
[15]   [1970] RTR 212, CA.
[16]   [1960] 3 All ER 33.
[17]   [1962] CLY 2036.

was found wholly liable when his lorry broke down in darkness just beyond a bridge where the nearest street lamp was 12 ft away on the other side of the road.

### 22.4.2  Use of hazard lights

If the obstruction is lit with hazard lights it is not a good idea to crash into it. So in *Houghton v Stannard*[18] the defendant was driving a vehicle that collided with the claimant's broken down vehicle. It was held that the defendant was negligent in not having taken heed of the claimant's hazard lights that had been visible from 200 to 250 yards away.

### 22.4.3  Whether the break-down in the carriageway was foreseeable

In *Lloyds Bank Limited v Budd*,[19] a lorry broke down in a carriageway. It had previously broken down in a lay-by. It was a foggy day and the driver was held liable in negligence for deciding to move the vehicle in such conditions whilst knowing there was a risk it might break down again.

### 22.4.4  Combined factors

In some cases a combination of factors will be considered to contribute to a finding of negligence. In *Lee v Lever*[20] the defendant's vehicle broke down in a clearway because of an electrical fault. The defendant was held 50% liable for the resulting collision with the claimant's car, for not borrowing a lamp to light his car, for not recognising the risk that his car might break down by the red light on his dashboard and for failing to push the car off the road and on to the verge. The claimant was also held liable for not keeping a proper look out. The judge reiterated the point that it was unsafe for a driver to assume that no vehicle would be parked or stopped in a 'clearway'.

## 22.5  PARKED VEHICLES

The Highway Code sets out detailed guidelines about where a driver may or may not park their vehicle. At rule 242 it states the general principle:

> 'You **MUST NOT** leave your vehicle or trailer in a dangerous position or where it causes any unnecessary obstruction of the road.'

Danger may also be assessed in terms of visibility and the Highway Code and the Road Vehicle Lighting Regulations 1989 outline situations in which a parked vehicle should be lit. It should be noted that in cases

---

[18]   [2003] EWHC 2666 (QB).
[19]   [1982] RTR 80, CA.
[20]   [1974] RTR 35.

involving parked vehicles the courts have had a keen regard to whether the driver of the vehicle or bicycle that hit the parked vehicle was keeping a proper look out at the time. Findings of liability are often accompanied by sizeable findings of contributory negligence. So in *Billington v Maguire*[21] the defendant parked his trailer in the cycle lane of a clearway; it was raining heavily and passing vehicles were creating clouds of spray. The defendant was held negligent for stopping. In order for the cyclist to avoid the trailer she had to ride onto the grass verge or into oncoming traffic. But contributory negligence was assessed at 70% as the cyclist had failed to see the parked trailer or take any steps to avoid it.

The fact that a vehicle is parked illegally will not prevent a court from finding that the vehicle that collided with it was mainly to blame. In *Hannam v Mann*,[22] an unlit car was parked 5m from a road junction contrary to reg 4 of the Road Vehicles Lighting (Standard Vehicles) (Exemption) (General) Regulations 1975.[23] A motorcyclist collided with the parked car and brought a claim against the owner. The court found for the claimant but held that he was 75% to blame for failing to keep a proper lookout. The Court of Appeal upheld the judge's findings and his apportionment.

In *Howells v Trefigin Oil and Trefigin Quarries Limited*,[24] a cyclist collided with the rear of a lorry that was parked on a bend, sustaining serious injury. Beldam LJ said:

> 'As was once said by a distinguished Judge, a road user is not bound to anticipate folly in all its forms, but he is bound to pay regard to carelessness by other road users where experience shows that such carelessness is common. Therefore, the question the Judge had to decide in this case was whether, by leaving the lorry in the position in which it was left so that approximately 2 foot 6 inches of it extended into the carriageway (visible as it was for approximately 60 metres, but obvious as an obstruction for 45 metres) the lorry would present a danger to other road users.'

On the facts of the case the lorry was not to blame. The accident was wholly the fault of the cyclist who was travelling at speed and failing to keep a proper look out. Despite this tendency in relation to contribution there is a long line of case law to support the submission that parking on a bend is dangerous and as such prima facie negligent and/or a nuisance. Salmon LJ put the responsibility of a motorist in this respect simply in *Waller v Levoi*:[25]

> '[The motorist] . . . was also negligent because parking a car on a bend was unwise. He should have foreseen that someone might come along rather

---

[21]   [2001] EWCA Civ 273.
[22]   [1984] RTR 252.
[23]   Now see reg 24(5) of the Road Vehicle Lighting Regulations 1989, SI 1989/1796.
[24]   [1997] EWCA 2874.
[25]   (1968) 112 Sol Jo 865.

quickly or without keeping a proper look out and that such a person would
be put in an extremely difficult position if there were a car parked on the
bend.'

This approach was adopted by the Privy Council in *Chop Seng Heng v
Thevannasan son of Sinnapam*[26] where the driver of a lorry parked on a
bend was 75% to blame; see also the case of *Stevens v Kelland*[27] where it
was held not to matter whether the vehicle was parked on the inside or
outside of a bend.

## 22.6   MANOEUVRING VEHICLES

A driver may be liable for damage where he or she undertakes a
manoeuvre which in the circumstances creates a foreseeable danger to
other road users. The case law suggests lorry drivers are most likely to
incur this liability due to the size of their vehicles and the fact that they
can single handedly obstruct the whole carriageway. So in *Lancaster v HB
and H Transport Limited*,[28] a lorry attempted to cross a dual carriageway
in foggy conditions where visibility was restricted to 100 yards. The lorry
driver was held wholly liable as his decision to execute that manoeuvre
was described by Geoffrey Lane LJ as 'little short of lethal' in the
circumstances. Dunn J stated:

'The driver of a heavy goods vehicle owes a high duty of care to other road
users.'

Factors including the weather, the lighting and the type of road are
relevant in assessing whether the decision to undertake a manoeuvre was
negligent. In *Jordan v North Hampshire Plant Hire Limited*[29] a lorry was
attempting to turn into a road from a cafe. It was held that it was
negligent to manoeuvre an ill lit lorry onto a busy main road. In *Barber v
British Road Services*[30] the driver of a lorry was negligent in attempting to
turn his lorry in the road at 3am on a dark and rainy morning. The
manoeuvre took one and a half minutes to complete and whilst executing
it he was hit by another lorry, the driver of which sustained serious
injuries. It was held that an obstruction across a fast main road at night
was prima facie evidence of negligence and it was for the person who put
it there to explain how it came there without negligence.

Outside the context of heavy goods vehicles the courts have taken a less
aggressive and more circumspect view of liability. In *Bramley v Pipes and
Another*[31] the first defendant's car stopped with its wheels over the line

---

26   [1976] RTR 193.
27   [1970] RTR 445.
28   [1979] RTR 380.
29   [1970] RTR 212.
30   (1964) *The Times*, November 18, CA.
31   (Unreported) 29 April 1998, CA.

with a junction to a main road having not appreciated until late on the excessive speed of the second defendant's car which was approaching him. The second defendant swerved around the first defendant's car (which protruded less than half way across the carriageway), lost control and slid around before landing upside down in a ditch. The court at first instance found the first defendant 20% to blame and the second defendant 80% to blame. The first defendant successfully appealed the apportionment and finding of liability against him. The Court of Appeal agreed that to characterise his actions as negligence, in the context of the difficulties in assessing the speed of the second defendant's vehicle was harsh. Further, that since it had been a straight road with good visibility he had not as a matter of fact created a hazard or obstacle. The cause of the accident was the second defendant's excessive speed and flawed attitude to safety (he was a very inexperienced driver having just passed his test).

Similarly, in *Thrower v Thames Valley Bus Company Ltd*[32] a bus company was not liable for failing to provide specialist training or give a warning of its approach when their bus was forced to cross the centre lines on a narrow road because the road could still have accommodated two passing vehicles.

## 22.7   OTHER OBSTRUCTIONS

The most likely prospective defendants in such claims will be:

(a)   the highway authority, or

(b)   the owner or controller of the obstruction itself (this may be the highway authority), or

(c)   occupiers of land adjoining the highway.

As to the liability of highway authorities generally and in relation to highway maintenance and repair, snow and ice, signage and road layout and liability of adjoining owners, see Chapters 19 and 20.

### 22.7.1   Highway authority liability – spillages

The highway authority is responsible for taking measures in relation to spillages on the motorway but a driver may be responsible if he knew of the spillage but failed to do anything about it. In *Pope v Fraser and Southern Rolling and Wire Mills Ltd*[33] sulphuric acid spilled from a carboy on a lorry onto the highway. The driver became aware of the spillage but did nothing about it; a motorcyclist was hurt when he skidded in it and fell. The defendants were liable as the driver could have returned to warn

---

[32]   [1978] RTR 271.
[33]   (1938) 55 TLR 324.

other traffic having discovered the leak. The police are not liable for damage caused by spillages that they are aware of following an accident.

In *Ancell v Mc Dermott*[34] the police knew that there was diesel fuel on a road following an accident, a car skidded on the fuel and had a head on collision with a lorry. The police were found not to owe a duty to warn road users about this hazard. (See further Chapter 16).

### 22.7.2    The owner or controller of the obstruction

The most common circumstances in which obstructions are caused are road works and construction works.

It is important for those wishing to undertake road works to have regard to the safety of road users. The question whether the safety precautions that they took were sufficient to avoid liability will be a matter of fact to be looked at in the context of risk presented by the works. In respect of the road user's approach to road works, the Highway Code gives guidelines as follows pursuant to rule 288:

> 'When the 'Road Works Ahead' sign is displayed, you will need to be more watchful and look for additional signs providing more specific instructions. Observe all signs – they are there for your safety and the safety of road workers.
> * you MUST NOT exceed any temporary maximum speed limit
> * use your mirrors and get into the correct lane for your vehicle in good time and as signs direct
> * do not switch lanes to overtake queuing traffic
> * take extra care near cyclists and motorcyclists as they are vulnerable to skidding on grit, mud or other debris at road works
> * where lanes are restricted due to road works, merge in turn (see Rule 134)
> * do not drive through an area marked off by traffic cones
> * watch out for traffic entering or leaving the works area, but do not be distracted by what is going on there. Concentrate on the road ahead, not the road works
> * bear in mind that the road ahead may be obstructed by the works or by slow moving or stationary traffic
> * keep a safe distance – there could be queues in front.'

### 22.7.3    Road works

In *Murray v Southwark Borough Council*[35] the defendant was undertaking an excavation in the road in an area where vandalism was common. The works were covered with a trestle and lamps to make it visible. Vandals removed the trestle and the lamps and the claimant drove through the work site until his front wheels fell into the excavation. The defendants

---

[34]    [1993] EWCA Civ 20.
[35]    (1966) 65 LGR 145.

were held to be liable for not providing enough watchmen in an area where they knew vandalism was common.

Contrast this with *Lilley v British Insulated Callenders Construction Co Ltd*[36] where an obstruction was left by builders in a quiet road surrounded by barriers and lit. There was no periodic inspection of the site overnight as it was a small site and in a quiet road; the same builders did carry out inspections of their larger sites. It was held that the precautions taken were reasonable in the circumstances and the defendant was not liable.

The court will have regard to usual systems of work and the type of precautions that are customary when deciding whether sufficient steps have been taken: see *Maher v Hurst*.[37]

### 22.7.4   Builder's skips

A skip in the road may, by its very nature as a heavy immobile obstruction, constitute a nuisance but in order for an action in public nuisance to succeed it must also be shown that the obstruction was dangerous. The Highways Act 1980, s 139 and s 65 of the Road Traffic Regulations Act 1984 provide a statutory framework governing the placement and lighting of skips. They provide that a skip shall be deposited on the carriageway outside the premises and shall be positioned so that it does not impede the surface water drainage of the highway nor obstruct access to any manhole or the apparatus of any statutory undertaker or the local council. Each skip or group of skips shall while on the highway be marked and lit such that the ends of each skip (that is to say the sides of the skip facing in both directions) are painted yellow and marked in accordance with the Builder's Skips (Markings) Regulations 1984.[38] Each skip shall be guarded by at least three traffic cones placed on the carriageway in an oblique line on the approach side of the skip. At night (that is to say, between half an hour after sunset and half an hour before sunrise), a danger lamp shall be placed against or attached to each corner of the skip or the end corners of the row of skips where two or more skips are deposited in a row and the distance between adjacent skips does not exceed 2m and shall also be placed between each cone and the next: s 139(4) of the Highways Act 1980. Each lamp shall be of the nature as prescribed on para 40 of the Traffic Signs Regulations and General Directions 1981[39] and shall remain lit through the night. Finally, s 139(10) of the Highways Act 1980 provides that nothing in this section shall be authorising the creation of a nuisance or of a danger to users of a highway or as imposing on a highway of the skip to which the permission relates.

---

[36]   (1968) 67 LGR 224.
[37]   (1969) 113 Sol Jo 167.
[38]   SI 1984/1933.
[39]   SI 1981/859.

In some cases it may appear that the burden on those who use skips is a heavy one. In *Saper v Hungate Builders Ltd*[40] a builder's skip was placed outside a house 60 yards from the blind crest of a hill, it was bright yellow in colour, positioned under a street lamp and had two builder's lamps on top of it. Before the accident in question two other motorists had been forced to swerve to avoid it. The defendants were held liable in nuisance and negligence as the skip was not adequately lit by the two builder's lamps but the claimant was 40% negligent on the basis that motorists should be alert when driving at night through residential areas.

This can be contrasted with *Wills v TF Martin (Roof Contractors) Ltd*[41] in which the skip was well lit but located on a poorly lit residential street. The claimant approached in an unlit vehicle and failed to keep a proper look out. It was held that the placing of a skip, properly lit, in the highway cannot amount to negligence. Although the skip was a nuisance regardless of whether it was lit, in this case the defendant was not liable, as the sole cause of the accident was the claimant's failure to keep a look out.

Even where the controllers of a skip have failed to take any steps to ensure its safety, if the oncoming driver is found to not have been paying adequate attention the courts are willing to make heavy findings of contributory negligence. In *Drury v Camden Borough Council*[42] the skip in question was unlit and so dirty that it looked the same colour as the road. It was hit by a scooter driver. The defendant was held liable in negligence and nuisance as the skip was an obstruction and a source of danger with 50% contributory negligence on the part of the claimant for failing to keep a proper look out.

---

[40]   [1972] RTR 380.
[41]   [1972] RTR 368.
[42]   [1972] RTR 391.

# CHAPTER 23

## PUBLIC SERVICE VEHICLE LIABILITY

*Christopher Stephenson*

### 23.1 INTRODUCTION

Buses have accidents. So do coaches and mini cabs. The normal principles of negligence apply. The injured passengers and other persons affected by such negligence can sue the Public Service Vehicle ('PSV') provider for the negligence of its employee.

### 23.2 NO EXCLUSION OF LIABILITY ALLOWED

When we buy a ticket for a journey on a PSV, we are entering into a contract for carriage. We look at the small print on the back of the ticket and we will find all sorts of terms and conditions. However, contracts for carriage cannot seek to limit the liability of the service provider for death or personal injury caused to a passenger. That is no more than a statement of the words set out in s 2(1) of the Unfair Contract Terms Act 1977, which provides that *no* contract is capable of limiting such a liability.

That provision is replicated in specific terms in relation to contracts of carriage by PSV by s 29 of the Public Passenger Vehicles Act 1981, which states that insofar as any contract for the conveyance of passengers by PSV seeks to limit such a liability, it shall be void.

A PSV is defined in s 1 of the Act as any motor vehicle, save for a tram, which:

> '(a)   being adapted to carry more than eight passengers, is used for carrying passengers for hire or reward, or (b) being a vehicle not so adapted, is used for carrying passengers for hire or reward at separate fares in the course of a business of carrying passengers.'

This chapter is not limited to accidents which occur on public transport; the principles also apply to a private hire coach or London buses.

A similar provision is set out in s 149 of the Road Traffic Act 1988 which makes it clear that liability for death or personal injury cannot be limited, even where the passenger has 'willingly accepted as his the risk of negligence on the part of the user'.[1]

## 23.3   THE DUTY OF THE DRIVER

In common with the theme we have elicited from all of the areas of liability for road traffic in this text, the two main failings of PSV drivers are the same as the main failings of all other drivers: failing to keep a proper look out and driving too fast.

The driver's duty to his passengers is no more or less than any driver's duty to any passengers – one to take such care as in all of the circumstance was reasonable to avoid injuring the passengers.

## 23.4   EMERGENCY BRAKING

One fairly common occurrence is injury sustained as a result of the driver's reaction to an extraneous event. If the driver fails to see the car in front braking and brakes suddenly and late such that passengers are thrown about and injured then the bus company will be held liable. Passengers are often injured when a bus stops too suddenly whilst they are standing, ready to alight at an upcoming bus stop.

On a face value reading of the cases set out below one might gain the impression that the courts lean over backwards to protect PSV drivers from legal actions.

In *Wooler v London Transport Board*,[2] the claimant had been injured when the bus that he was travelling on stopped suddenly and he was thrown to the floor. The bus had been travelling behind a lorry and was about 150 yards away from a bus stop, at which passengers were preparing to alight. A pedestrian stepped off the kerb in front of the lorry, which stopped suddenly. The bus driver stopped, avoiding a collision with the lorry, but the claimant was injured. At first instance, the judge held that the bus driver was two-thirds to blame, for driving too close to the lorry. On appeal, the Court of Appeal absolved the bus driver of any blame. They accepted that the bus was a reasonable distance behind the lorry, by simple virtue of the fact that the driver was able to stop without colliding with it. It was expecting too much of the bus driver to travel sufficiently far behind the lorry so as to avoid a collision *and* be able to stop so that none of the passengers (who were standing in anticipation of alighting)

---

[1]    Road Traffic Act 1988, s 149(3).
[2]    [1976] RTR 206n.

were injured. To demand otherwise ignored the realities of modern driving in busy rush hour conditions, the accident happening on Lewisham Way in London.

A similar approach was taken by the Court of Appeal in *Barry v Greater Manchester Passenger Transport Executive*,[3] when on similar facts it was held that passengers on public transport take the risk that the driver of a bus may have to brake in an emergency and that might cause inconvenience. That such stops might also cause injury does not of itself result in a finding of negligence against the driver, if he has simply reacted in the way that a reasonable driver would have done in similar circumstances.

As we can see not all such incidents lead to liability, so for example in *Parkinson v Liverpool Corporation*,[4] the claimant was injured when the driver of the bus on which he was travelling suddenly braked to avoid a dog that had run into its path. The driver had seen the dog about 20 yards in front of him and took his foot off the accelerator to allow the dog to pass. As the bus passed behind the dog, so the dog suddenly swerved back into the path of the bus and the driver slammed on the brakes. The claimant was thrown over. At first instance the judge held that the driver had not been negligent and that the test was whether he had acted as a reasonable driver would have done in a similar circumstance. The claimant appealed and the Court of Appeal held that the judge had applied the proper test, namely how the reasonable driver would have reacted. The claimant had sought to rely upon the earlier case of *Glasgow Corporation v Sutherland*,[5] in which the House of Lords held that the driver of a tram had been liable to a passenger who had been knocked over when he applied the brakes of his tram very suddenly in a similar situation, before the claimant had a chance to take her seat. In *Parkinson* the court distinguished that case on the basis that the passengers in *Sutherland* had not had a chance to take their seats before the driver applied the brakes. Further, the driver of the bus had given an explanation for his actions (namely the dog running back into his path) and it was accepted that any reasonable driver would have reacted in the same way, so the claimant's appeal failed.

## 23.5 PULLING AWAY PRECIPITOUSLY

A common complaint of passengers is that bus drivers pull off from bus stops before passengers are seated. That was the complaint in *Phillips-Turner v Reading Transport Limited*,[6] where the claimant alleged that she was injured because the driver pulled away with a sudden jerk without ensuring that she was seated. The claim failed, on the basis that

---

[3]    (Unreported) 19 January 1984.
[4]    [1950] 1 All ER 367.
[5]    [1951] WN 111
[6]    [2000] CLY 4207.

there was no duty on a bus driver to ensure that all passengers were safely seated before pulling away. However, the court indicated that different considerations might apply if the claimant had been elderly and/or infirm, such that an injury was reasonably foreseeable (see also *Glarvey v Arriva North West Limited*,[7] where a similar approach was adopted).

The leading case is *Fletcher v United Counties Omnibus Co Ltd*.[8] The claimant boarded the bus and was making her way to the rear when the driver pulled away at a reasonable speed. Just after he had done so, however, he was required to perform an emergency stop and the claimant fell and was injured as a result. At first instance the court held the driver 70% responsible, but the Court of Appeal disagreed, stating that bus drivers do not owe a duty that extends as far as ensuring that all passengers are safely seated before pulling off.

## 23.6   THE PUBLIC SERVICE VEHICLES (CONDUCT OF DRIVERS, INSPECTORS, CONDUCTORS AND PASSENGERS) REGULATIONS 1990

The Public Service Vehicle Regulations (PSV Regulations)[9] establish a statutory regime that imposes certain requirements on the drivers and conductors of PSVs (as defined in s 1 of the Public Passenger Vehicles Act 1981, see above). Breach creates a civil liability, although arguably they do not take the duties on drivers much further than the basic common law.

Regulation 4 deals with the basic conduct of drivers, inspectors and conductors, for example stipulating that a driver shall not hold a microphone when a vehicle is in motion, unless in an emergency (reg 4(1)), nor shall he speak to passengers (reg 4(2)), again unless in an emergency. The basic duty is imposed by reg 5(1) which demands that:

> 'A driver and a conductor shall take all reasonable precautions to ensure the safety of passengers who are on, or who are entering or leaving, the vehicle.'

That is perhaps no more than a statement of the common law, but it emphasises that there is a statutory basis to the duty of drivers to their passengers.

Interestingly, the PSV Regulations also impose duties upon passengers. Regulation 6 sets out various duties, ranging from only using specified doors for specified reasons to not putting other passengers at risk or unreasonably impeding or causing discomfort to them. In rush hour on a busy bus it is always useful to have a copy of these regulations to hand.

---

[7]   [2002] CLY 3263.
[8]   [1998] PIQR P154.
[9]   SI 1990/1020.

The duties upon passengers are important to consider, however, if an injury is caused by a fellow passenger. Regulation 5(2) requires that a driver, inspector or conductor shall:

'... take all reasonable steps to ensure that the provisions of these Regulations relating to the conduct of passengers are complied with.'

Therefore, a claimant who is injured by another passenger in circumstances where the behaviour complained of could reasonably have been prevented *may* have a cause of action against the driver, inspector or conductor and hence his or her employer.

# CHAPTER 24

## ROAD TRAFFIC ACCIDENTS ABROAD

*Raj Shetty*

### 24.1 INTRODUCTION

When an English domiciled pedestrian, cyclist or motorist has an accident abroad, a common question which arises during the initial interview with the lawyer is:

> 'Do the English Courts have jurisdiction or will the victim will have to go to the time, inconvenience and expense to bring an action abroad?'

Practitioners may ask themselves: 'what is the applicable law?'

This chapter will deal with some general principles that arise in relation to motor accidents which occur in Europe and other jurisdictions.

### 24.2 GENERAL RULES ON JURISDICTION AND FORUM

In many claims arising from accidents abroad there will be a choice of forum. There may be tactical advantages and disadvantages in pursuing a claim in one of the alternative relevant courts. Issues of quantification, costs and funding, limitation and the use of experts may be important considerations.

There has been an incremental development of jurisdiction in Europe. The Brussels Convention 1968, the Lugano Convention on Jurisdiction and the Enforcement of Judgments in Civil and Commercial Matters 1988 were previously the two most important conventions to consider. The Brussels Convention has now been updated by the Council Regulation (EC) 44/2001 ('the Judgments Regulation') which applies across all EU states with the exception of Denmark which is still covered by the older Brussels Convention. The Judgments Regulation was recognised domestically in the Civil Jurisdiction and Judgments Order 2001[1] which made consequential amendments to the Civil Jurisdiction and Judgments Act 1982.

The rules determining jurisdiction are governed by the law of the country where proceedings are commenced.

---

[1] SI 2001/3929.

As a general rule a claim for damages for personal injuries arising from tortious conduct can be brought in a country where:

(1)   one or more defendants is domiciled; or

(2)   where the accident occurred; or

(3)   where a defendant submits to the jurisdiction of the court.

However, there has been an important recent development in this area of law insofar as accidents that occur in the European Union are concerned.

## 24.3   ACCIDENTS IN EUROPE (EU STATES)

The most significant jurisdictional rules for English victims of accidents are contained within Regulation 44/2001/EC and are embodied within the Civil Jurisdiction and Judgments Order 2001.

Article 2 provides the presumption action in the defendant's country of domicile. The defendant should normally be sued in the place in which he is domiciled.

### 24.3.1   Domicile

The domicile of an individual is held to be within England and Wales if he is resident here and the nature and circumstances of the residence indicate that he has a substantial connection with England and Wales (Art 9).

A substantial connection is presumed if there has been residency for the last 3 months or more (Art 9(6)).

Article 9(1)(b) states that:

> 'An insurer domiciled in a member state may be sued in another member state, in the case of actions brought by the policyholder, the insured or a beneficiary, in the Courts for the place where the Plantiff is domiciled.'

The Fourth Directive (2000/26/EC of 16 May 2000), also known at the 'Visiting Victims Directive' requires the UK and other member states in the European Economic Area (the 'EEA') to implement provisions making it easier for residents of the UK and other states in the EEA to pursue an insurance claim if they have a motor accident in an EEA state other than their state of residence.

The Fourth Directive was implemented on 19 January 2003 by the Motor Vehicles (Compulsory Insurance) (Information Centre and Compensation

Body) Regulations 2003,[2] by the European Communities (Rights against Insurers) Regulations 2002,[3] by Regulations under the Financial Services and Markets Act 2000 and by amendments to Regulations under that Act.

Article 1 of the Visiting Victims Directive applies to victims of any accidents which occur:

(i)   in a member state other than the state in which the victim is resident; and

(ii)  is caused by a vehicle insured and normally based in a member state.

Member states means the EU states and other states within the EEA (Norway, Iceland and Liechtenstein).

### 24.3.2   The Fourth Motor Insurance Directive

The Framework of the Fourth Directive provides the following:

(a)   Each member state has to establish a Motor Insurers Information Centre (MIIC). This is intended to enable an injured party to identify the insurer of a vehicle involved in an accident from the vehicle's registration plates.

(b)   The MIIC will provide details of the vehicle's insurer's appointed claims representatives in the UK.

(c)   The MIIC has a Motor Insurance Database (MID) to which the police have access. The Motor Vehicles (Compulsory Insurance) (Information Centre and Compensation Body) Regulations 2003, reg 4 sets out the information which has to be notified by each insurer to the Information Centre and which the latter has to hold.

(d)   Information on policies is to remain on the MID for 7 years after the expiry of the policy. Data protection takes precedence over the implementation of the Directive and direct disclosure of information is restricted to certain parties, namely the police, UK insurers, MIB and MIIC in strictly controlled circumstances.

(e)   Claims Representatives must be appointed in each member state. The Fourth Directive requires the insurer to nominate a Claims Representative in the injured party's own country who has sufficient powers to settle the claim.

---

[2]   SI 2003/37.
[3]   SI 2002/3061.

(f) The representative has 3 months to make an offer of compensation or deny liability (there must be a reasoned offer or reasoned reply to the points made in the claim).

(g) Victims of accidents have a direct right of action against the insurer providing cover to the party who caused the accident.

(h) Each EU state has to establish or approve a Compensation Body (in England and Wales it is the Motor Insurers Bureau or 'MIB') which will compensate the injured parties where either:
   (i) an insurer has failed to appoint a Claims Representative in the member state of residence; or
   (ii) the insurer or its Claims Representative has failed to provide a reasoned response within 3 months from the date when the injured party presented its claim for compensation to the insurer of Claims Representative.

(i) The injured party's right to present a claim to the Compensation Body is lost if the injured party has taken legal action directly against the insurer.

(j) Where there is an unidentified vehicle which injures a person resident in England and Wales, the claim is to the MIB who reclaim the money from the relevant guarantee fund in the member state where the accident occurred.

(k) This Directive does not apply where both parties are from the same country, even if the accident occurred outside their home country.

### 24.3.3  The Fifth Motor Insurance Directive

The Fifth Directive was implemented on 11 June 2007. The framework of the Fifth Directive provides for the following:

(1) An increase in the minimum levels of insurance coverage to 1 million euros per person or 5 million euros per accident.

(2) Parties injured in an accident abroad will be able to sue a liability insurer in their home court.

There has been academic debate about whether or not an English court has jurisdiction to hear claims brought by English claimants against motor insurers based outside England and Wales but within the EU. Following *FBTO Schadervezekeringen NV v Jack Odenbreit*,[4] the European Court of Justice has definitively ruled that the insurance

---

[4]    (Case C-463/06) [2008] 2 All ER (Comm) 733.

provisions of the Brussels Regulation[5] are to be interpreted to permit victims injured in road traffic accidents in another member state to bring direct actions against European domiciled insurers in the courts of the victim's own domicile.

This decision confirms the interpretation of the Brussels Regulation required by the Fifth Insurance Directive[6] which came into force on 11 June 2007. The European Court ruled that:

> 'The reference in Article 11(2) of Council Regulation (EC) No 44/2001 of 22 December 2000 on jurisdiction and the recognition and enforcement of judgments in civil and commercial matters to Article 9(1)(b) of that regulation is to be interpreted as meaning that the injured party may bring an action directly against the insurer before the courts for the place in a Member State where that injured party is domiciled, provided that such a direct action is permitted and the insurer is domiciled in a Member State.'

Article 6(1) of Regulation 44/2001/EC provides that a defendant domiciled in a member state may also be sued:

> '... where he is one of a number of Defendants, in the Courts for the place where any one of them is domiciled, provided the claims are so closely connected that it is expedient to hear and determine them together to avoid the risk of irreconcilable Judgments resulting from separate proceedings.'

Regulation EC 864/2007 of the European Parliament and the Council of 11 July 2007 which dealt with the law applicable to non-contractual obligations ('Rome II'), are intended to prescribe uniform choice of law rules throughout the EU regarding the applicable law for non-contractual obligations. Article 4 is the relevant article dealing with torts which states:

### 'General Rule

1.  Unless otherwise provided for in this Regulation, the law applicable to a non-contractual obligation arising out of a tort/delict shall be the law of the country in which the damage occurs irrespective of the country in which the event giving rise to the damage occurred and irrespective of the country or countries in which the indirect consequences of that event occur.
2.  However, where the person claimed to be liable and the person sustaining damage both have their habitual residence in the same country at the time when the damage occurs, the law of that country shall apply.
3.  Where it is clear from all the circumstances of the case that the tort/delict is manifestly more closely connected with a country other than that indicated in paragraphs 1 or 2, the law of that other country shall apply. A manifestly closer connection with another country

---

5    Regulation EC 44/2001.
6    Directive 2005/14/EC, 11 May 2005.

might be based in particular on a pre-existing relationship between the parties, such as a contract that is closely connected with the tort/delict in question.'

This Directive will take effect from 11 January 2009. Under the Fifth Directive proceedings commenced after 1 November 2009 for accidents occurring after 20 February 2007 will not be bound by the decision in *Harding v Wealands*[7] which applied the traditional categorisation of choice of law: quantum is procedural and not substantive. Instead under 'Rome II' assessment of quantum is to be governed by substantive law. So in *Maher v Groupama Grand*,[8] Blair J held that the assessment of damages was a matter for English law because the Fifth Directive did not apply because this was a pre-directive case. It would have been a matter for French Law if the case had occurred after the Fifth Directive. The judge also considered interest on damages – a matter outside the scope of this text.

## 24.4   ACCIDENTS OUTSIDE THE EU

Where the RTA occurs outside the EU different rules apply.

The national laws and rules of private international law of the courts seized of the case will determine whether that court has jurisdiction.

The courts of England and Wales will have jurisdiction where:

(a)   the defendant submits to the jurisdiction;

(b)   the defendant is validly served with the initiating process within the territorial jurisdiction of the English court and
    (i)    the defendant does not apply for, or
    (ii)   the defendant is refused a stay of proceedings on the grounds that England is not the most suitable forum;

(c)   the court is satisfied that it is a proper case to give permission for service of the proceedings out of the jurisdiction.

If the defendant is outside the jurisdiction, practitioners should have regard to the now simplified rules concerning service outside the jurisdiction contained in the recently amended Civil Procedure Rules (CPR, r 6.30) and the new Practice Direction 6B that is applicable.

The guiding principle is that the court will adopt a view on forum as to where the case can most suitably be tried in the interests of justice and all the parties.

---

[7]    [2006] UKHL 32,
[8]    [2009] EWHC 38.

## 24.5 THE APPLICABLE LAW

If the proceedings can take place in England and Wales, s 11 of the Private International Law (Miscellaneous Provisions) Act 1995 applies. The general rule is that the applicable law is the law of the country in which the harmful event occurred.

So for instance, if an accident occurs in Spain but the case is brought in an English court without objection, the general rule is that Spanish law applies but with matters of evidence and procedure governed by English law.

This rule can be displaced by s 12 of the Act which provides that where it is 'substantially more appropriate' for the law other than the law of the place where the harmful event occurred to be applied. In deciding this, the factors are:

(1)    factors relating to the parties (nationality, domicile, residence and language);

(2)    factors relating to events (where the happening of the harmful event in one jurisdiction rather than another was purely coincidental);

(3)    factors relating to the circumstances or consequences of those events (the interests of justice or administrative convenience).

An example of the exercise of displacement is as follows. In *Edmunds v Simmonds*[9] the claimant was on holiday with the defendant in Spain when the claimant was injured by the defendant's negligent driving. Both were English and the claimant returned to be cared for in England and would suffer her losses in England. It was held that the general rule would be displaced and English law would be applied.

In *Lauren v Mark B*,[10] the court was required to determine as a preliminary issue whether English or Spanish law should be applied to issues in an action for damages for personal injury brought by the claimants against the defendant, which arose out of a road traffic accident in Spain. The parties were a British family resident in Britain. The first claimant and the defendant (D) were husband and wife and the second and third claimants were their children. They had arranged car hire for a holiday in Spain through a British company. The car was Spanish and was provided by a Spanish company; the rental agreement was between D and the rental company and was subject to Spanish law. Shortly after leaving the Spanish airport in the car, it collided head-on with another vehicle as D was driving on the wrong side of the road. The claimants were all injured, the second claimant very seriously, and claimed damages. D

---

9    [2001] 1 WLR 1003.
10   [2008] Lawtel 1 October 2008 (QBD).

admitted liability but contended in his defence that pursuant to the Private International Law (Miscellaneous Provisions) Act 1995 the applicable law was that of Spain. Judgment was entered against D, leaving the issue of quantum, in particular whether the second claimant, a minor, could claim damages for future loss of earnings as a head of loss under Spanish law. Weighing up the factors in s 12 of the Act, an important factor in favour of Spanish law was that the accident had occurred in Spain. In addition the claimants suffered their immediate losses there, in that they were injured there, and the first and second claimants were treated there for some days. Less important factors were that the other vehicle in the accident was Spanish, and that the hire agreement and the hire car were Spanish. The fact that the insurers were Spanish was not of overwhelming weight: who was liable to pay for the claimants' damage through a contract of insurance was one step removed from the immediate consequence of the tort. Factors in favour of English law were that all the parties were English nationals resident in England, and had only been in Spain for a week's holiday. The tortious act was that of D, an English national, and the consequences of it, as far as the instant claim was concerned, were visited upon English nationals. As far as the second claimant was concerned and, to a lesser extent, the first claimant, the consequences of the tort would be felt for a significantly longer period in England than in Spain; for the second claimant, for the rest of his life. In relation to the main issue, that of the second claimant's future loss of earnings, it was undoubtedly a loss that would be suffered in England. It was relevant that, although the hire and insurance contracts were Spanish, the arrangements for the hire were made in England through an English broker and paid for with English currency. Those factors meant that it was inevitable that the Spanish car hire company and its insurers must have been aware of the possibility, if not the likelihood, that an English family in those circumstances would use a Spanish car for their holiday in Spain. Weighing up all those factors in the balance, there was no doubt that the general rule should be displaced in favour of English law

## 24.6   PROVING FOREIGN LAW

Foreign law is a matter of fact and expert evidence must be called to prove it. The expert's role of course, is not to get involved in issues of determination of fact according to foreign law.

## 24.7   FOREIGN LIMITATION PERIODS

In respect of limitation, the Foreign Limitation Periods Act 1984, s 1 states that:

> '... where in an action or proceedings in a court in England and Wales the law of any other country ... fall to be taken into account in the determination of any matter–

(a)  the law of that other country relating to limitation shall apply ... and
(b)  except where the matter falls within subsection 2 below, the law of England and Wales relating to limitation shall not so apply.'

The English courts can disapply a foreign limitation period if unjust.

Some limitation periods are interrupted by negotiation or criminal proceedings. Not all countries suspend limitation whilst the claimant is a minor.

Some limitation periods are set out in the table below:

| Country | Limitation period |
|---|---|
| Austria | 3 years |
| Belgium | 5 years for road traffic accidents |
| Cyprus | Fatal accidents 2 years |
| | Claims against insurers 2 years |
| Denmark | 5 years |
| | 2 years against insurers |
| Finland | 3 years for road traffic accidents |
| France | 10 years |
| | 3 years if the claim involved a criminal act or the driver was untraced |
| Germany | 3 years |
| Greece | 5 years |
| | 2 years against insurers/MIB equivalent |
| Italy | 5 years |
| | 2 years for road traffic accidents |
| Netherlands | 5 years |
| | 2 years against a road traffic accident insurer |
| Russia | 3 years |
| Spain | 1 year from the conclusion of criminal proceedings or investigation if no proceedings or from resolution of the injury. Limitation can be extended for a year on an annual basis. The same limitation period applies to adults and minors. |
| Switzerland | 1 year from knowledge with a 10 year maximum |
| Turkey | 1 year |

Where proceedings take place in a court in England and Wales, damages are decided as follows: substantive matters are determined by the foreign law and the procedural matters are determined by English law (ie the actual quantum).

An illustration of this is the leading House of Lords case of *Harding v Wealands*[11] which involved an accident in New South Wales, Australia in February 2002 in which H was a passenger in a car driven by W. H was an English national and W was an Australian national but both were living together in England. H was rendered a C5 tetraplegic after the vehicle in which he was the passenger overturned as a result of the negligent driving of W. The High Court of England and Wales accepted jurisdiction and liability was admitted. The issue before the Lords was which law applied to assessing H's damages. The law in New South Wales (NSW) and in particular the Motor Accidents Compensation Act 1999 (MACA) placed certain caps on awards which would have meant a reduction of his damages by around £1.2 million (a 30% reduction). The House of Lords held that damages must be assessed in accordance with English law. When referring to the limiting provisions of the NSW law Lord Rogers explained that:

> '76. Undoubtedly, in practice these and other provisions can be expected to govern the amounts for which claims are settled outside the courts. But that does not make them substantive. It merely means that litigants, who know what the court can and cannot award, will settle their claims accordingly. More particularly, it does not mean that the provisions are to be regarded as substantive rather than procedural for purposes of private international law. In that context, the brocardi ubi remedium ibi ius would be an unsafe guiding principle.

> 77. I would accordingly hold that the provisions of Chapter 5 of MACA [on which the defendant relies] relate to the remedy which the courts of New South Wales can award and are procedural for the purposes of section 14(3)(b) of the 1995 Act. That being so, they fall to be ignored when the English court awards damages for the claimant's injuries. I recognise that this means that the defendant's insurers may have to meet a higher claim for damages than would be the case if the provisions of MACA applied. I recognise also that making a higher award would conflict with certain of the overall objects set out in section 5 of MACA. But I do not regard that as a compelling consideration since, as defendant's counsel was careful to acknowledge, the impact on the scheme of applying a different scale of damages in claims litigated in this country is unlikely to be anything other than marginal.'

After *Harding v Wealands*, the position on accidents abroad is as follows:

(1)   The foreign law will be applied by the UK court to determine issues of liability and the recoverable heads of damage.

---

[11]   [2006] UKHL 32.

(2) The assessment, measure or quantum of damage will be governed by UK law.

(3) The level of assessment will be unaffected by foreign law. It is irrelevant whether a foreign court would award more or less than a forum court in the UK.[12]

(4) Furthermore it should be irrelevant that the foreign court may have a cap or restriction on compensation.

(5) Conditions precedent to successfully pursuing a claim in a foreign jurisdiction (and there were such precedents in the case of *Harding*) such as first making a claim to an insurer, subjecting to Alternative Dispute Resolution etc are questions of procedure and not to be treated as substantive under the 1995 Act.

(6) If the personal injury claim in tort is not actionable in the foreign country but has been replaced by a compensation scheme such as a no-fault scheme implemented in New Zealand, then no claim for damages can be brought in the UK if that foreign law remains the applicable law. This is because there is no action that exists in law. However, displacement under s 12 of the 1995 Act could cure this.

Substantive liability and damage rules (ie the rules to be applied from foreign jurisdictions) would be rules which:

(1) exclude damage from the scope of liability on the grounds that it does not fall within the ambit of the liability rule;

(2) exclude damage from the scope of liability because it does not have the prescribed causal connection with the wrongful act;

(3) require that the damage should have been reasonably foreseeable;

(4) provide for mitigation of damages;

(5) provide for contributory negligence to be taken into account in assessing damages;

(6) provide for the defence of the voluntary assumption of risk;

(7) provide for, or deny, the existence of a particular head of damage.[13]

---

[12] See Andrew McPharland 'Foreign Compensation Systems and Personal Injury Claims' [2007] JPIL 273.

[13] [2006] UKHL 32, per Lords Hoffman and Rodger at [24] and [74] respectively.

## 24.8  LAW APPLICABLE IN FOREIGN STATES

It is for the lawyer representing each party to investigate the foreign law.

Many European jurisdictions involve a reverse burden of proof for passengers or pedestrians in road traffic accidents. Some jurisdictions are largely no fault or strict liability based.

Insurance liability is capped in some systems.

Contributory negligence is not always an available defence or argument in some systems.

Costs orders in foreign jurisdictions are not always the standard 'costs follow the event' orders that English and Welsh practitioners are used to. For example in Denmark, in an out of court settlement, usually each side bears their own costs.

Disclosure in some foreign jurisdictions is simply limited to those documents on which the party intends to rely.

Legal/professional privilege may not exist.

The following are examples of some of the procedural/jurisdictional differences in other systems:

- **Spain**

(1)   There is a one year limitation date for adults and minors. This can be extended but only for one year at a time.

(2)   No costs are recovered even for a successful claimant unless he or she is awarded exactly for what it claimed for.

(3)   Criminal courts can award civil damages but there is a 6-month window in which to commence criminal proceedings.

(4)   The awards are based on prescribed rates according to statutory tables.

(5)   Damages for fatalities are frequently higher than England.

(6)   Third Party insurers will discuss a claim over the telephone but will not correspond as this will extend the limitation date.

- **France**

(1)   There is a ten year limitation period.

(2) Medical experts have to be court appointed. These tend to assess general damages in seven different categories, awarding percentage points to some parts, marks out of seven in others and assessing periods of disability.

(3) There is virtual strict liability for the assistance of pedestrians.

• **USA**

(1) Individual state laws are applicable.

(2) Some states such as Florida and New York have no fault laws although there is no right to sue for minor general damages as opposed to significant, serious and permanent injuries.

(3) There is an expedited system for recovery of economic loss from his own motor insurer.

(4) Contingency fees charged by US lawyers are usually 33% up to trial and 40–50% if the case goes to trial.

• **Malta**
No awards for general damages.

• **Greece**
Damages for fatalities in Greece are much higher than England.

# CHAPTER 25

## THE INSURER'S LIABILITY

*Andrew Ritchie*

### 25.1    UNDER A CONTRACT OF INSURANCE

An insurer's primary liability arises in contract under the contract of insurance which it has issued.

#### 25.1.1    The need for compulsory insurance

Drivers of motor vehicles on public roads in England and Wales are required by law to have 'third party' risk insurance.

Third party risk insurance is cover against liability for personal injury or death caused to other persons arising from the use of a motor vehicle on a road (or other public place) in England or Wales.

Section 143(1) of the Road Traffic Act 1988 provides that every person who 'uses'[1] or 'causes or permits another person to use'[2] a motor vehicle on 'a road' or other public place,[3] must have a policy of insurance covering third party risks as set out in Part VI of the Act.

A policy covering Road Traffic Act 1988 liabilities is known as a Road Traffic Act (RTA) policy.

In practice most RTA insurance policies offer more comprehensive protection than the statutory minimum. Some cover not only third party risks but also the insured's own car against damage (comprehensive). Others cover not only the car but also allow the policy holder to drive any car under RTA insurance.

---

[1]    Road Traffic Act 1988, s 143(1)(a).
[2]    Ibid, s 143(1)(b).
[3]    By a recent amendment.

'Part VI Third-Party Liabilities

*Compulsory insurance or security against third-party risks*

**143 Users of motor vehicles to be insured or secured against third-party risks**

(1)   Subject to the provisions of this Part of this Act –
    (a)   a person must not use a motor vehicle on a road unless there is in force in relation to the use of the vehicle by that person such a policy of insurance or such a security in respect of third party risks as complies with the requirements of this Part of this Act, and
    (b)   a person must not cause or permit any other person to use a motor vehicle on a road unless there is in force in relation to the use of the vehicle by that other person such a policy of insurance or such a security in respect of third party risks as complies with the requirements of this Part of this Act.

(2)   If a person acts in contravention of subsection (1) above he is guilty of an offence.

(3)   A person charged with using a motor vehicle in contravention of this section shall not be convicted if he proves –
    (a)   that the vehicle did not belong to him and was not in his possession under a contract of hiring or of loan,
    (b)   that he was using the vehicle in the course of his employment, and
    (c)   that he neither knew nor had reason to believe that there was not in force in relation to the vehicle such a policy of insurance or security as is mentioned in subsection (1) above.

(4)   This Part of this Act does not apply to invalid carriages.'

## 25.1.2   The required terms of the policy

Section 145 of the Road Traffic Act 1988, sets out the requirements for all RTA policies.

Under s 145(3)(a) it is necessary for the policy to cover any liability which may be incurred in respect of the death of or bodily injury to any person or damage to property caused by, or arising out of, the use of the vehicle on a road in Great Britain.

Additionally the policy must be issued by an authorised insurer and must also cover driving in all of Europe and must also insure against the cost of emergency treatment.

**'145 Requirements in respect of policies of insurance**

(1)   In order to comply with the requirements of this Part of this Act, a policy of insurance must satisfy the following conditions.

(2)   The policy must be issued by an authorised insurer.

(3) Subject to subsection (4) below, the policy –
    (a) must insure such person, persons or classes of persons as may be specified in the policy in respect of any liability which may be incurred by him or them in respect of the death of or bodily injury to any person or damage to property caused by, or arising out of, the use of the vehicle on a road in Great Britain, and
    (b) must insure him or them in respect of any liability which may be incurred by him or them in respect of the use of the vehicle and of any trailer, whether or not coupled, in the territory other than Great Britain and Gibraltar of each of the member States of the Communities according to the law on compulsory insurance against civil liability in respect of the use of vehicles of the State where the liability may be incurred, and
    (c) must also insure him or them in respect of any liability which may be incurred by him or them under the provisions of this Part of this Act relating to payment for emergency treatment.

(4) The policy shall not, by virtue of subsection (3)(a) above, be required –
    (a) to cover liability in respect of the death, arising out of and in the course of his employment, of a person in the employment of a person insured by the policy or of bodily injury sustained by such a person arising out of and in the course of his employment, or
    (b) to provide insurance of more than £250,000[4] in respect of all such liabilities as may be incurred in respect of damage to property caused by, or arising out of, any one accident involving the vehicle, or
    (c) to cover liability in respect of damage to the vehicle, or
    (d) to cover liability in respect of damage to goods carried for hire or reward in or on the vehicle or in or on any trailer (whether or not coupled) drawn by the vehicle, or
    (e) to cover any liability of a person in respect of damage to property in his custody or under his control, or
    (f) to cover any contractual liability.

(5) In this Part of this Act "authorised insurer" means a person or body of persons carrying on insurance business within Group 2 in Part II of Schedule 2 to the Insurance Companies Act 1982 and being a member of the Motor Insurers' Bureau (a company limited by guarantee and incorporated under the Companies Act 1929 on 14th June 1946).

(6) If any person or body of persons ceases to be a member of the Motor Insurers' Bureau, that person or body shall not by virtue of that cease to be treated as an authorised insurer for the purposes of this Part of this Act –
    (a) in relation to any policy issued by the insurer before ceasing to be such a member, or
    (b) in relation to any obligation (whether arising before or after the insurer ceased to be such a member) which the insurer may be called upon to meet under or in consequence of any such policy or under section 157 of this Act by virtue of making a payment in pursuance of such an obligation.

---

[4] This was raised to £1,000,000 in June 2007.

**146 Requirements in respect of securities**

(1)    In order to comply with the requirements of this Part of this Act, a security must satisfy the following conditions.

(2)    The security must be given either by an authorised insurer or by some body of persons which carries on in the United Kingdom the business of giving securities of a like kind and has deposited and keeps deposited with the Accountant General of the Supreme Court the sum of £15,000 in respect of that business.

(3)    Subject to subsection (4) below, the security must consist of an undertaking by the giver of the security to make good, subject to any conditions specified in it, any failure by the owner of the vehicle or such other persons or classes of persons as may be specified in the security duly to discharge any liability which may be incurred by him or them, being a liability required under section 145 of this Act to be covered by a policy of insurance.

(4)    In the case of liabilities arising out of the use of a motor vehicle on a road in Great Britain the amount secured need not exceed –

(a)    in the case of an undertaking relating to the use of public service vehicles (within the meaning of the Public Passenger Vehicles Act 1981), £25,000,

(b)    in any other case, £5,000.'

## 25.1.3    Liability which an RTA policy is not required to cover

Section 145(4) provides five examples of liability which the policy of insurance is NOT required to cover, namely:

*   **Property damage over £1,000,000**
    An RTA policy does not need to provide insurance exceeding £1,000,000 in respect of property damage from one accident caused by the vehicle. This restriction was raised from £250,000 by the Motor Vehicle (Compulsory Insurance) Regulations 2007.[5]

*   **Comprehensive cover**
    An RTA policy does not need to provide cover in respect of damage to the owner's vehicle.

*   **Hire goods**
    An RTA policy does not need to cover damage to goods carried for hire or reward in or on the vehicle or in or on any trailer drawn by the vehicle.

*   **Personal property**
    An RTA policy does not need to cover any liability to a person in respect of damage to property in his custody or under his control.

---

[5]    SI 2007/1426.

Any liability which is not covered by the compulsory insurance requirements cannot be recovered from the insurer unless the policy specifically covers it. Likewise a liability which is not covered by the RTA is not recoverable from the insurer under s 151 of the RTA 1988 or from the MIB, see *Lees v MIB*.[6]

### 25.1.4    The exclusion of claims by employees

An RTA policy does not have to cover liability in respect of the injury to or death of a person employed by the policyholder providing that the injury or death arose in the course of the person's employment. However by virtue of s 145(4)A, this provision does not apply where the injury is to a person carried in or upon the vehicle, or entering or getting on to or alighting from that vehicle *unless* cover in respect of that liability is in fact provided pursuant to a requirement of the Employers' Liability (Compulsory Insurance) Act 1969. This will be considered in more detail below.

Section 145(4) excludes claims by injured employees because they are not required to be covered in Road Traffic Act policies.

'The policy shall not, by virtue of subsection (3)(a) above, be required –
to cover liability in respect of the death, arising out of and in the course of his employment, of a person in the employment of a person insured by the policy or of bodily injury sustained by such a person arising out of and in the course of his employment, ...'

The logic behind this exclusion is clear. Employers' liability policies are meant to cover claims for damages by employees arising from accidents at work whether or not they involve mechanically propelled vehicles.

The problem with the wording of the Act is that it allows some claims to slip between both forms of insurance. If an employee of the insured is run down by the insured's company vehicle the claimant will not recover if the company vehicle was being driven by a thief or a non employee.

So in *Miller v Ensign Motor Policies*,[7] a decision of Jack J, the claimant would have lost against the insurers who issued a certificate on the police car but for a neat point taken that a police officer is not an employee of the police force but instead a constable seconded to Her Majesty the Queen.

The exception in s 145A was intended to close this gap, but only did so for passengers not pedestrians.

---

[6]    [1952] 2 QB 511.
[7]    [2006] EWHC 1529.

By s 145(4A) passengers in employer's vehicles who were injured were brought back into the RTA policy if, and only if, the employers' liability policy did not cover them. So the wording of the section states that the RTA policy does cover the claim where the injury is to a person carried in or upon the vehicle, or entering or getting on to or alighting from that vehicle *unless* cover in respect of that liability is in fact provided pursuant to a requirement of the Employers' Liability (Compulsory Insurance) Act 1969.

This leaves a gap in the insurance cover for employees who are simply walking around, for instance on a pedestrian crossing, and are run down by a vehicle owned by their employers and driven by a thief or a non employee.

Legislation is needed to close this gap.

### 25.1.5   Bodies excluded from the requirement for RTA insurance

Certain bodies are not required to have RTA insurance on their motor vehicles. It appears that the basic premise was that because they were rich they did not need to take out insurance. But the legislation and the MIB agreements have been drafted in such a way that this exemption is now causing problems. When thieves and uninsured drivers drive vehicles owned by such bodies, the Uninsured Drivers' Agreement 1999 excludes the MIB from paying out where an RTA policy is not required so the MIB may refuse payment to an innocent victim.

Section 144 of the RTA provides:

**'Exceptions from requirement of third-party insurance or security**

(1)     Section 143 of this Act does not apply to a vehicle owned by a person who has deposited and keeps deposited with the Accountant General of the Supreme Court the sum of £500,000, at a time when the vehicle is being driven under the owner's control.

(1A)   The Secretary of State may by order made by statutory instrument substitute a greater sum for the sum for the time being specified in subsection (1) above.

(1B)   No order shall be made under subsection (1A) above unless a draft of it has been laid before and approved by resolution of each House of Parliament.

(2)     Section 143 does not apply –
    (a)   to a vehicle owned –
        (i)   by the council of a county or county district in England and Wales, the Broads Authority, the Common Council of the City of London, the council of a London borough, a National Park authority, the Inner London Education Authority, the London Fire and Emergency Planning

Authority, or a joint authority (other than a police authority) established by Part IV of the Local Government Act 1985,

(ii) by a council constituted under section 2 of the Local Government etc (Scotland) Act 1994) in Scotland, or

(iii) by a joint board or committee in England or Wales, or joint committee in Scotland, which is so constituted as to include among its members representatives of any such council,

at a time when the vehicle is being driven under the owner's control,

(b) to a vehicle owned by a police authority or the Receiver for the Metropolitan Police district, at a time when it is being driven under the owner's control, or to a vehicle at a time when it is being driven for police purposes by or under the direction of a constable, or by a person employed by a police authority, or

(ba) to a vehicle owned by the Service Authority for the National Criminal Intelligence Service or the Service Authority for the National Crime Squad, at a time when it is being driven under the owner's control, or to a vehicle at a time when it is being driven for the purposes of the body maintained by such an Authority by or under the direction of a constable, or by a person employed by such an Authority,

(c) to a vehicle at a time when it is being driven on a journey to or from any place undertaken for salvage purposes pursuant to Part IX of the Merchant Shipping Act 1995,

(d) to the use of a vehicle for the purpose of its being provided in pursuance of a direction under section 166(2)(b) of the Army Act 1955 or under the corresponding provision of the Air Force Act 1955,

(da) to a vehicle owned by a health service body, as defined in section 60(7) of the National Health Service and Community Care Act 1990 by a Primary Care Trust established under section 16A of the National Health Service Act 1977 by a Local Health Board established under section 16BA of that Act or by the Commission for Health Improvement, at a time when the vehicle is being driven under the owner's control,

(db) to an ambulance owned by a National Health Service trust established under Part I of the National Health Service and Community Care Act 1990 or the National Health Service (Scotland) Act 1978, at a time when a vehicle is being driven under the owner's control,

(e) to a vehicle which is made available by the Secretary of State to any person, body or local authority in pursuance of section 23 or 26 of the National Health Service Act 1977 at a time when it is being used in accordance with the terms on which it is so made available,

(f) to a vehicle which is made available by the Secretary of State to any local authority, education authority or voluntary organisation in Scotland in pursuance of section 15 or 16 of the National Health Service (Scotland) Act 1978 at a time when it is being used in accordance with the terms on which it is so made available.'

Vehicles owned by the Crown, NHS Trusts, Health Services bodies, education authorities, primary care trusts, the police, local councils, the ILEA, the army, the fire services, the City of London, the National Parks Council etc, etc are not required to have an RTA policy of insurance covering the use on a road or other public place 'at a time when' they are under the control of the owner. What does that mean? It appears to mean that they are required to have RTA insurance at times when they are not under the owner's control.

That is all well and fine but if a thief steals such vehicles and runs a person down or if any non-employee is driving, the relevant body will not be liable vicariously at common law and the MIB may seek to exclude liability under clause 1 'definitions' of the Uninsured Drivers' Agreement 1999 because RTA insurance was not required for the car. Complicated arguments will ensue about the exclusion for RTA insurance not being applicable as soon as the thief got into the car. The victim will or may go uncompensated.

Any lack of cover for victims would be in breach of the Fifth Directive – see recital (7) and Article 1.

### 25.1.6   The insurance certificate

The insurer must issue a certificate to the insured when issuing an RTA policy. The certificate is in a prescribed form. Section 147 of the Road Traffic Act 1988 governs the form and content.

**'Issue and surrender of certificates of insurance and of security**

(1)   A policy of insurance shall be of no effect for the purposes of this Part of this Act unless and until there is delivered by the insurer to the person by whom the policy is effected a certificate (in this Part of this Act referred to as a 'certificate of insurance') in the prescribed form and containing such particulars of any conditions subject to which the policy is issued and of any other matters as may be prescribed.

(2)   A security shall be of no effect for the purposes of this Part of this Act unless and until there is delivered by the person giving the security to the person to whom it is given a certificate (in this Part of this Act referred to as a 'certificate of security') in the prescribed form and containing such particulars of any conditions subject to which the security is issued and of any other matters as may be prescribed.

(3)   Different forms and different particulars may be prescribed for the purposes of subsection (1) or (2) above in relation to different cases or circumstances.

(4)   Where a certificate has been delivered under this section and the policy or security to which it relates is cancelled by mutual consent or by virtue of any provision in the policy or security, the person to whom the certificate was delivered must, within seven days from the taking effect of the cancellation –

(a)   surrender the certificate to the person by whom the policy was issued or the security was given, or
(b)   if the certificate has been lost or destroyed, make a statutory declaration to that effect.
(5)   A person who fails to comply with subsection (4) above is guilty of an offence.'

## 25.1.7   The insurer's contractual liability

Under an RTA policy of insurance the insurer will be contractually liable to indemnify the defendant driver who caused a road traffic accident which damaged the claimant's person or property. The insurer may also be contractually liable to indemnify the insured owner where he is jointly liable with the defendant driver (see above).

Once the claimant has obtained judgment against the insured defendant driver, then the latter will be able to enforce the indemnity provisions in the insurance policy and force the insurer to pay out on the judgment.

Most RTA policies contain a clause allowing the insurer to take over the defence of any claim made against the driver so that the insurer will be able to defend its interests.

If, for any reason, the defendant does not satisfy the judgment which the claimant obtains then the claimant may declare the defendant bankrupt. The intended advantage of this was that once bankrupt the claimant gained the insured defendant's rights under the policy of insurance and could enforce them pursuant to the Third Party (Rights Against Insurers) Act 1930. This right only arises after the judgment has been obtained against the defendant: see *Post Office v Norwich Union*.[8]

There were and are many problems with the alleged security provided by the 1930 Act, not the least of which was that the claimant cannot get his hands on the insurance policy until he has obtained judgment, which puts the egg before the chicken (or vice versa). Also, if the defendant failed to notify his insurers – in breach of the terms of the insurance policy – the claimant could gain no better rights than the defendant had under the policy. The breach would deprive the claimant of the fruits of his judgment: see *Pioneer v National*.[9] The Act was firmly criticised by the Law Commission in its report issued in 2001, No 272. Nothing has been done about it in England.

[8]   [1967] 2 QB 363.
[9]   [1985] 2 All ER 395.

### 25.1.8   Issuing proceedings against the insurer

As a result of the problems outlined above the European Communities
(Rights Against Insurers) Regulations 2002[10] were passed. These provided
that:

> **'Right of action**
>
> 3.– (1)Paragraph (2) of this regulation applies where an entitled party has a
> cause of action against an insured person in tort or (as the case may
> be) delict, and that cause of action arises out of an accident.
>
> (2)   Where this paragraph applies, the entitled party may, without
> prejudice to his right to issue proceedings against the insured person,
> issue proceedings against the insurer which issued the policy of
> insurance relating to the insured vehicle, and that insurer shall be
> directly liable to the entitled party to the extent that he is liable to the
> insured person.'

It is therefore wise for lawyers acting for claimants to sue the contractual
insurers as the second defendant in RTA cases.

### 25.1.9   The insurer's solvency

Should the defendant's insurer become insolvent the claimant has no need
to worry. The Financial Services and Markets Act 2000 provides in ss 213
and 214 that the insurer's liabilities will be met in full by a compensation
scheme.

### 25.1.10   Definition of a motor vehicle

RTA cover deals only with accidents involving motor vehicles. So what is
a motor vehicle? Section 185(1) of the Road Traffic Act 1988 defines
'motor vehicle' as:

> '... a mechanically propelled vehicle intended or adapted for use on roads.'

This phrase has been considered in a number of cases. The issue of
whether any particular vehicle comes within the definition is usually
determined by an analysis of whether (1) the vehicle has mechanical
propulsion and (2) whether the use for which the vehicle was 'intended or
adapted' included use on a road.

Mechanical propulsion appears to mean 'capable of being mechanically
propelled if the vehicle was properly maintained'.

---

[10]   SI 2002/3061.

In *Lawrence v Howlett*[11] a first instance judge held that a pedal cycle with a partly deconstructed engine was not a mechanically propelled vehicle. This decision was doubted in *Floyd v Bush*[12] in which a motorised pedal cycle was held to be a mechanically propelled vehicle despite the fact that it was being pedalled by a thief as he tried to escape. In *Newbury v Simmonds*,[13] a car with no engine was held to be a mechanically propelled vehicle. The case concerned road tax and the court considered that the engine could have been put back in. The issue of whether a car from which the engine has been removed and into which it cannot be put back was left open.

The law on intention or adaptation has developed over the years. The early cases are now doubtful authority.

In *Daley v Hargreaves*,[14] the question in issue was whether or not dumper trucks were vehicles 'intended or adapted for use on the roads'. The particular dumper truck was not found to be motor vehicle within the meaning of s 33 of the Road and Rail Traffic Act 1933 and s 1 of the Road Traffic Act 1930. This was because whilst the truck was a 4-wheeled, mechanically propelled vehicle, it was not fitted with a windscreen, lamps, reflectors, horns, wings, number plates, indicators, speedometers or driving mirrors.

The same conclusion was reached in *Burns v Currell*,[15] in which a mechanically propelled Go-Kart had been used on a road but was not found to have been 'intended or adapted for use on roads' pursuant to s 253(1) of the Road Traffic Act 1960. Whether or not a vehicle was 'intended' to be used on a road depended on whether a reasonable person looking at the vehicle would say that one of its uses would be on a road. Whilst the Go-Kart was capable of being used on a road, there was insufficient evidence to suggest that it was fit or apt for such use in that case.

The intention issue was reconsidered in *Chief Constable of Avon and Somerset v Fleming*,[16] a case concerning a motorcycle which had been adapted for scrambling. Whether a motor vehicle fell within the definition provided by s 190 of the Road Traffic Act 1970 depended upon whether a reasonable person, looking at the vehicle, would say that its general use encompassed possible road use. The particular use to which the person put the vehicle was irrelevant. Substantial alterations to a vehicle intended originally to be used on a road could prevent that vehicle any longer from being a motor vehicle.

[11] [1952] 2 All ER 74.
[12] [1953] 1 WLR 242, CA.
[13] [1961] 2 QB 345, CA.
[14] [1961] 1 All ER 552.
[15] [1963] 2 All ER 297.
[16] [1987] 1 All ER 318.

In *Chief Constable of the North Yorkshire Police v Saddington*,[17] the divisional court decided that a petrol driven micro scooter was a 'vehicle' within the definition of the Road Traffic Act 1988. It was noted that there was no other obvious terrain upon which such a scooter could be used. As the test was whether a reasonable person would say that one of the scooter's uses would be some general use on the road, and given that the purpose of using such a scooter was to beat traffic and time pressures, general use of the scooter on a road could be contemplated. The manufacturer's advice that the scooter was not intended to be used on a road would, in practice, be ignored to a considerable degree. Accordingly, users of such scooters on the road need a driving licence and third party insurance.

In *Winter v DPP*,[18] the judge held that a 'city bug' was a mechanically propelled vehicle and concentrated on the purpose of the Road Traffic Act 1988 which was to protect injured victims from worthless judgments.

The more modern and more substantive approach in *Winter* is the one which would make more sense in future.

### 25.1.11  The definition of 'use or arising from the use'

It should be remembered that RTA policies cover liability arising from or out of the 'use' of motor vehicles not just the driving of them.

So what is use?

Section 145(3) of the RTA 1988 states:

> '(3)  Subject to subsection (4) below, the policy –
>    (a)  must insure such person, persons or classes of persons as may be specified in the policy in respect of any liability which may be incurred by him or them in respect of the death of or bodily injury to any person or damage to property caused by, or arising out of, the use of the vehicle on a road in Great Britain, and ...'

Driving a car is using it. Walking across the road to get petrol for a car when it has run out of petrol is also using the car: see *Dunthorne v Bentley*.[19] Owners who are passengers are using cars because they retain control. Owners who ask others to deliver goods in their vehicles are using them. Car thieves who all go joy riding are all using the car together.

'Use' is interpreted quite broadly. However the limit was reached in *Brown v Roberts*.[20] The passenger in a van opened the door and injured the

---

[17]  [2001] RTR 227, CA.
[18]  [2003] RTR 210.
[19]  [1996] PIQR P323, CA.
[20]  [1965] 1 QB 1.

claimant who was a pedestrian. The claimant sued the passenger who had been negligent. The driver had not been negligent. The latter was insured. The passenger was not. The issue was whether the passenger was using the van and whether the driver had caused or allowed the passenger to 'use' the van whilst uninsured. Megaw J held that the passenger was not 'using' the van within the meaning in the RTA and the driver had not caused the use of the van whilst uninsured because the passenger did not have control over the driving.

One major problem with the current Road Traffic Act 1988 is the fact that s 151 liability (which is dealt with below) is restricted to 'the use' set out in the policy. This gap in the cover is outdated and difficult now to justify. However, until the law is changed the use clause must be considered carefully.

The only 'use' which is covered by the contract of insurance is the use which the insured has purchased. Policies are usually sold covering: (1) social and domestic use or (2) business or work use; (3) use for hire or reward. If the accident occurs whilst the defendant is using the vehicle outside the policy then the insurer will not be bound to indemnify the driver under the policy or under s 151.

### 25.1.12   The definition of 'road or other public place'

RTA policies only cover liabilities arising from accidents on roads or in other public places. The injury or damage must arise from the use of the vehicle on a road in Great Britain. What is a road?

'Road' is defined in s 192(1) of the Road Traffic Act 1988 as:

> 'any highway and any other road to which the public has access, and includes bridges over which a road passes.'

In *Cutter v Eagle Star Insurance Company Ltd* and *Clarke v General Accident*,[21] the House of Lords was asked to decide, in a conjoined appeal, whether two different car parks fell within the definition of 'road' in s 192(1) of the Road Traffic Act 1988. After deciding that the question: 'is a place a road?' was one of fact to be determined after consideration of the physical character and the function which the place existed to serve, the House of Lords found that neither car park could be said to be a road and accordingly the insurance company in one case (*Cutter*), and the MIB in the other (*Clarke*) were not liable to satisfy the judgment obtained because the liabilities were excluded from s 145(3)(a). In neither case had the use of the car occurred on a road.

Clearly, the law needed to be changed and the Motor Vehicles (Compulsory Insurance) Regulations 2000, came into force on 3 April

---

[21]   [1998] 1 WLR 1647.

2000, to effect the change. This inserted the words 'or other public place' after the word 'road' in the following sections of the Road Traffic Act 1988:

- s 143(1)(a) and (b) (users of motor vehicles to be insured against third party risks);

- s 145(3)(a) (requirements in respect of policies of insurance);

- s 146(4) (requirements in respect of securities);

- s 165(1)(b) (obligation to provide names and addresses and produce documents to a constable); and

- s 170(1) (duty to stop and report an accident); and inserted 'or place' after 'the road' in s 170(1)(b)(iii).

These words were inserted to implement three European Directives 72/166/EEC, 84/5/EEC and 90/232/EEC which required that member states took all appropriate measures to ensure that civil liability in respect of the use of motor vehicles normally based in their territory was covered by insurance. The requirement in the directives is not restricted to use on 'roads'.

So the first effect of the Motor Vehicle (Compulsory Insurance) Regulations 2000[22] has been to extend the requirement of insurance so that it now applies to the use of vehicles in public places as well as to roads.

The second effect has been to make provision for the reporting of accidents and the production of insurance documents where an accident occurs in a public place.

The words 'public place' are not defined in the Road Traffic Act 1988 or the regulations and difficulties are arising in practice over whether insurance in necessary in respect of private roads, private driveways and places to which the public have access but over which the owner retains control. There is no jurisprudence on these issues yet. If the insurance industry takes the point that victims of accidents involving motor vehicles which happen to occur on private land are excluded then an argument will arise that Government has failed to implement the directives and a *Francovich*[23] claim will be possible.

---

22  SI 2000/726.
23  [1993] 2 CMLR 66.

### 25.1.13   The criminal offence of 'no insurance'

Pursuant to s 143(2) of the Road Traffic Act 1988, failure to comply with the compulsory insurance provisions amounts to an offence, although s 143(3) provides certain defences to someone so charged.

A defendant can escape conviction if he is able to establish that the vehicle did not belong to him or he was using the vehicle in the course of his employment and in either circumstance that he did not know or had no reason to believe that the required policy of insurance was not in force.

Likewise it is a criminal offence to cause or permit a person to drive a car without insurance.

### 25.1.14   Assault with a car

Does compulsory RTA insurance cover assault with a car?

In *Hardy v MIB*,[24] the claimant security officer had sustained injuries whilst trying to stop a vehicle being driven from his works. The court was concerned with s 201(3)(a) of the Road Traffic Act 1960. It was held that the compulsory insurance requirements under that Act required a policy of insurance to cover liability to a third party arising from intentional criminal use of the vehicle on a road. The injured third party could recover from the defendant's insurers under such a policy even though the driver, by reason of his intentional criminal act, could not have enforced it.

This was confirmed in *Churchill v Charlton*.[25]

Lawyers should bear in mind that the limitation period is now 3 years in such assault claims: see *A v Hoare*.[26]

### 25.1.15   The excess under the policy

In the past the insurer could refuse to pay the excess under the policy where the insured made a claim. This continues to be the case. However, the injured claimant who suffers a road traffic accident and sues the insured cannot be met by the answer from the defendant driver's insurers that the excess must be taken off his claim. This is now enshrined in the Fifth Motor Insurance Directive – see recital 20 and Article 4.

---

[24]   [1964] 2 QB 745.
[25]   [2001] EWCA Civ 112.
[26]   [2008] UKHL 6.

The paragraphs in the MIB Uninsured and Untraced Drivers' Agreements which seek to impose an excess are in breach of this directive and there may be a *Francovich*[27] claim against Government for failing to implement the directive.

## 25.2   INSURER'S LIABILITY UNDER THE ROAD TRAFFIC ACT 1988

### 25.2.1   Section 151 of the Road Traffic Act 1988

Section 151 provides as follows:

**'Duty of insurers or persons giving security to satisfy judgment against persons insured or secured against third-party risks**

(1)     This section applies where, after a certificate of insurance or certificate of security has been delivered under section 147 of this Act to the person by whom a policy has been effected or to whom a security has been given, a judgment to which this subsection applies is obtained.

(2)     Subsection (1) above applies to judgments relating to a liability with respect to any matter where liability with respect to that matter is required to be covered by a policy of insurance under section 145 of this Act and either –

    (a)   it is a liability covered by the terms of the policy or security to which the certificate relates, and the judgment is obtained against any person who is insured by the policy or whose liability is covered by the security, as the case may be, or

    (b)   it is a liability, other than an excluded liability, which would be so covered if the policy insured all persons or, as the case may be, the security covered the liability of all persons, and the judgment is obtained against any person other than one who is insured by the policy or, as the case may be, whose liability is covered by the security.

(3)     In deciding for the purposes of subsection (2) above whether a liability is or would be covered by the terms of a policy or security, so much of the policy or security as purports to restrict, as the case may be, the insurance of the persons insured by the policy or the operation of the security by reference to the holding by the driver of the vehicle of a licence authorising him to drive it shall be treated as of no effect.

(4)     In subsection (2)(b) above "excluded liability" means a liability in respect of the death of, or bodily injury to, or damage to the property of any person who, at the time of the use which gave rise to the liability, was allowing himself to be carried in or upon the vehicle and knew or had reason to believe that the vehicle had been stolen or unlawfully taken, not being a person who –

    (a)   did not know and had no reason to believe that the vehicle had been stolen or unlawfully taken until after the commencement of his journey, and

---

[27]   [1993] 2 CMLR 66.

(b)  could not reasonably have been expected to have alighted from the vehicle.

In this subsection the reference to a person being carried in or upon a vehicle includes a reference to a person entering or getting on to, or alighting from, the vehicle.

(5)  Notwithstanding that the insurer may be entitled to avoid or cancel, or may have avoided or cancelled, the policy or security, he must, subject to the provisions of this section, pay to the persons entitled to the benefit of the judgment –

(a)  as regards liability in respect of death or bodily injury, any sum payable under the judgment in respect of the liability, together with any sum which, by virtue of any enactment relating to interest on judgments, is payable in respect of interest on that sum,

(b)  as regards liability in respect of damage to property, any sum required to be paid under subsection (6) below, and

(c)  any amount payable in respect of costs.

(6)  This subsection requires –

(a)  where the total of any amounts paid, payable or likely to be payable under the policy or security in respect of damage to property caused by, or arising out of, the accident in question does not exceed £1,000,000, the payment of any sum payable under the judgment in respect of the liability, together with any sum which, by virtue of any enactment relating to interest on judgments, is payable in respect of interest on that sum,

(b)  where that total exceeds £1,000,000, the payment of either –

(i)  such proportion of any sum payable under the judgment in respect of the liability as £1,000,000 bears to that total, together with the same proportion of any sum which, by virtue of any enactment relating to interest on judgments, is payable in respect of interest on that sum, or

(ii)  the difference between the total of any amounts already paid under the policy or security in respect of such damage and £1,000,000, together with such proportion of any sum which, by virtue of any enactment relating to interest on judgments, is payable in respect of interest on any sum payable under the judgment in respect of the liability as the difference bears to that sum,

whichever is the less, unless not less than £1,000,000 has already been paid under the policy or security in respect of such damage (in which case nothing is payable).

(7)  Where an insurer becomes liable under this section to pay an amount in respect of a liability of a person who is insured by a policy or whose liability is covered by a security, he is entitled to recover from that person –

(a)  that amount, in a case where he became liable to pay it by virtue only of subsection (3) above, or

(b)  in a case where that amount exceeds the amount for which he would, apart from the provisions of this section, be liable under the policy or security in respect of that liability, the excess.

(8)  Where an insurer becomes liable under this section to pay an amount in respect of a liability of a person who is not insured by a policy or

whose liability is not covered by a security, he is entitled to recover the amount from that person or from any person who –

(a) is insured by the policy, or whose liability is covered by the security, by the terms of which the liability would be covered if the policy insured all persons or, as the case may be, the security covered the liability of all persons, and

(b) caused or permitted the use of the vehicle which gave rise to the liability.

(9) In this section –

(a) "insurer" includes a person giving a security,

(b) "material" means of such a nature as to influence the judgment of a prudent insurer in determining whether he will take the risk and, if so, at what premium and on what conditions, and

(c) "liability covered by the terms of the policy or security" means a liability which is covered by the policy or security or which would be so covered but for the fact that the insurer is entitled to avoid or cancel, or has avoided or cancelled, the policy or security.

(10) In the application of this section to Scotland, the words "by virtue of any enactment relating to interest on judgments" in subsections (5) and (6) (in each place where they appear) shall be omitted.'

## 25.2.2  The insurer can avoid contractual liability

Usually a claimant who sues an insured defendant can gain no better rights against the defendant's insurer than the defendant himself had. So if the claimant sues and obtains judgment but the defendant has broken a condition of his contract of insurance then indemnity can be refused by the insurance company and the claimant will be left whistling for his money. This usual rule is set aside in RTA cases by s 151 of the 1988 Act.

If there is a contract of RTA insurance in place at the time of the road traffic accident covering either the driver or the car (the distinction is relevant because the MIDIS data base only searches for insurance for the car) then the injured claimant can recover damages from the insurer despite the insurer being entitled to refuse to indemnify the defendant driver for breach of some term or other in the insurance policy.

Section 151(5) of the RTA 1988 states:

'(5) Notwithstanding that the insurer may be entitled to avoid or cancel, or may have avoided or cancelled, the policy or security, he must, subject to the provisions of this section, pay to the persons entitled to the benefit of the judgment –

(a) as regards liability in respect of death or bodily injury, any sum payable under the judgment in respect of the liability, together with any sum which, by virtue of any enactment relating to interest on judgments, is payable in respect of interest on that sum,

(b) as regards liability in respect of damage to property, any sum required to be paid under subsection (6) below, and

(c)    any amount payable in respect of costs ...'

The effect of s 151 of the Road Traffic Act 1988 is to restrict the circumstances in which an insurer can avoid liability to a victim even it if can refuse to indemnify the insured.

Provided there is an insurance certificate covering the car even if the driver was not covered by the certificate, the injured claimant can enforce against the insurer.

Alternatively if the driver had an insurance policy covering him to drive any car then the claimant is granted relief even if some other term has been breached.

Under s 151(5) of the Road Traffic Act 1988, the insurer who issued the certificate must satisfy a judgment obtained by an injured claimant for damages for personal injuries and for damage to property (the property damage can only be up to £1,000,000) against the defendant driver even when the policy entitled the insurance company to avoid or cancel indemnity because of breach of some condition or other. However the gap in this protection for injured claimants relates to the 'use' clause. This is dealt with below.

### 25.2.3    The MIDIS database of insurance certificates

In the distant past claimants were often faced with difficulty in finding out whether there was in fact a certificate of insurance covering the car at the time of the accident. Car thieves were unlikely to be forthcoming and DVLA searches did not provide the answer. Even if the vehicle owner was identified, there was no certainty that the owner would respond to correspondence, particularly where the owner was to some extent at fault in allowing the vehicle to be driven by an uninsured motorist. Sometimes problems would be encountered in dealing with the vehicle's insurers. A lack of understanding of s 151 could lead to a claims handler wrongly informing the claimant that the vehicle was not covered. Nor did the claimant have a right to see the policy of insurance in place. These problems have been partially relieved by the Motor Vehicles (Third Party Risks) (Amendment) Regulations 2001.[28]

When a vehicle is insured the insurer must by law notify details of the policy to the Motor Insurance Database (MID). This is managed by the Motor Insurers' Information Centre (MIIC). The purpose of the MID is to permit the identification of insurers by reference to a vehicle's registration number, thereby making it easier for accident victims to claim compensation and for the police to enforce the obligation of all motorists to insure in compliance with the Road Traffic Act 1988. The defect in the

---

[28]    SI 2001/2266.

system is that it does not record the names of drivers who are covered third party to drive any car by certificates.

The Motor Insurance Database Information System (MIDIS) can be used by registered users to make enquiries of the MID and the MIIC. Other enquirers can obtain this information by contacting the MIIC. The names of EU Claims Representatives of UK Insurers can be viewed on the screen.

Implementation of the EU Fourth Motor Insurance Directive (PDF) has, from 19 January 2003 resulted in the victims of accidents in the European Economic Area (EEA) having the right to pursue their claims against the local representative of a foreign insurer. (The Regulations which apply this Directive in the UK also allow UK citizens to obtain insurer information from the MIIC in respect of accidents in the UK where no foreign vehicle is involved.) Details of those non-UK insurers and their representatives can be obtained from MIIC, on provision of the relevant registration number. These rights only apply in respect of accidents abroad after 19 January 2003.

The Fourth Directive was introduced to make it easier for those injured in accidents whilst visiting another EU state to receive compensation by:

- requiring there to be an Information Centre who can identify the insurer of the other party from the registration plate;

- allowing the injured party a direct right of action against the insurer;

- requiring the insurer to nominate a representative in the injured party's own country who has sufficient powers to settle the claim;

- ensuring that there is a compensation body to pay the claim in the event that the insurer cannot be identified or is manifestly dilatory in settling a claim.

These measures introduced by the directive compliment the arrangements of the Green Card system which ensures the ready settlement of claims in the injured party's own country where the other party comes from a different country.

For 7 years after the accident, the claimant has the right to request from either the information centre in his home state, or from the information centre where the other party's vehicle is based, or from the information centre of the state in which the accident occurred the following information:

- the name and address of the insurer;

- the number of the insurance policy;

- the name and address of the insurer's claims representative in the home state;

- the name and address of the registered keeper (in special cases).

The insurer of the party that caused the accident or their claims representative is required to make a reasoned response or offer within 3 months of the claim being presented. This will be regulated, for UK insurers, by the FSA. Moreover, interest will be payable on any settlement unnecessarily delayed beyond 3 months.

The Directive requires data protection to take precedence over the implementation of the directive. MIIC has regular meetings with the Information Commissioner to ensure that the Data Protection Act is complied with fully. MIIC will not disclose the personal details of policyholders or registered keepers where the insurer has been identified and is dealing with a claim. Should a vehicle not appear on the MID, MIIC will consider whether an enquirer needs the personal details of the registered keeper in order to pursue a claim for compensation.

MIIC is the Information Centre in the UK. They can be contacted on 0845 165 2800 or e-mail: information@miic.org.uk or by post.

The Motor Insurers' Bureau is approved as the UK's Compensation Body. Contact MIB by telephone: 01908 830 001 or at www.mib.org.uk.

### 25.2.4   The liability covered by section 151

Section 151(2) of the Road Traffic Act 1988 provides that where judgment is obtained which relates to a liability required to be covered by a policy of insurance pursuant to s 145 of the Act, namely personal injury or death caused by the use of a motor vehicle on a road or other public place; and where the liability is covered by the terms of the policy; and judgment is obtained against the person insured by the policy, or it is a liability which would be so covered if the policy insured all persons and the judgment is obtained against any person other than one who is insured by the policy, then the insurer has a duty to satisfy such a judgment.

Therefore every excluded body which does not need to insure under the RTA 1988 is not bound by s 151. This creates a problem with vehicles stolen from those like the Crown, who do not need a policy of insurance, because s 151 does not bind the owner to pay out in the same way as it binds the insurer to pay out. This is a breach of the Fifth Directive – see recital (7) and Article 1. If a victim of an accident suffers loss as a result of this breach a *Francovich*[29] claim will arise.

### 25.2.5   Interest and costs

Section 151 requires the insurer to pay the judgment compensation including interest on the judgment sum and costs.

### 25.2.6   All drivers are covered

Under the Road Traffic Act 1972 if the tortfeasor driver was not a named driver under the policy the insurance company was under no obligation to meet any judgment entered against the driver. The Road Traffic Act 1988 changed that rule.

Judgment must be obtained against the defendant driver. The driver need not be an insured person under the policy and even if the policy excludes cover for the driver, the liability for the purposes of s 151 is assumed to cover 'all drivers' pursuant to s 151(2)(b).

Accordingly thieves who crash stolen cars are covered by s 151 and the insurer which issued a certificate covering the car will be liable.

### 25.2.7   Drivers with no driving licence are covered

It does not matter that the RTA policy excludes cover to persons without a driving licence, s 151 still applies by virtue of s 151(3). This section states that in deciding whether a liability is or would be covered by the terms of a policy:

> '... so much of the policy ... as purports to restrict ... the insurance of the persons insured by the policy ... by reference to the holding by the driver of the vehicle of a licence authorising him to drive it shall be treated as of no effect.'

Accordingly, thieves with no driving licences are covered and the insurer which issued a certificate covering the car is bound to satisfy the judgment against the thief under s 151.

### 25.2.8   Use inside or outside the terms of the RTA policy

The RTA insurance policy must actually cover the use to which the car was being put at the time of the accident for s 151 liability to arise (see s 151(2)(a)). If the use was outside the permitted use in the RTA policy

---

then the insurer can avoid liability under the policy and under s 151. This is a gap in the protection provided to innocent accident victims and needs to be closed with altered legislation.

Accordingly, the claimant's lawyers should ask the proposed defendant what use he was putting the car to when the accident occurred and should ask for a copy of the description of use clause in the policy! This is quite impossible in most uninsured drivers' cases and so claimant lawyers work on inferences.

Theft constitutes 'social and domestic use' under this bizarre rule although you might think that professional thieves would consider theft to be business use. Be that as it may a victim who is run over by a thief is covered by RTA insurance and s 151 applies.

The problem with this section relates mainly to mini cab drivers. A victim who is run down by a mini-cab driver who is insured only for social driving is not covered by s 151. This problem was highlighted in *Albert v MIB*,[30] in which a passenger in a car was fatally injured in a road traffic accident. His widow sued the negligent driver and the insurer refused indemnity under the contract and under s 151 because the driver was being paid by the passenger to take the passenger to their place of work. The policy was only to cover social and domestic use. The House of Lords upheld the insurer's position. The reasoning for the exclusion from the s 151 cover of the 'wrong kind of use' is now wholly artificial and out of date. For an analysis of the justification – Lord Donovan's reasoning at page 1352D is instructive.

The words 'social or domestic use' were considered by Roskill LJ in *Seddon v Binions*.[31] He ruled that the essential character of the journey in the course of which the accident occurred had to be evaluated.

A classic example of how bizarre this drafting error is now becoming was provided in the Court of Appeal in *Keeley* where the Court was prepared to hold that 'social use' could be flicked on and off like a light switch during the course of a single journey. So in *Keeley v Pashen*,[32] the mini-cab driver with social and domestic insurance who ran down a person who had just got out of his cab was held to have been using the cab for social purposes because he was on his way home when he decided to run down the annoying ex-passenger. This is wholly artificial and the Act needs to be rewritten. It only arose in that case because the claimant failed to bring the MIB into the proceedings and lost the right to do so.

---

[30]   [1971] 2 All ER 1345, HL.
[31]   [1978] 1 Lloyd's Rep 381.
[32]   [2004] EWCA Civ 1491.

## 25.2.9  Shared journey costs

The unfairness created by the *Albert* decision set out in the paragraph above was partially cured by s 150 of the RTA 1988 which states:

**'Insurance or security in respect of private use of vehicle to cover use under car-sharing arrangements**

(1)   To the extent that a policy or security issued or given for the purposes of this Part of this Act –

    (a)   restricts the insurance of the persons insured by the policy or the operation of the security (as the case may be) to use of the vehicle for specified purposes (for example, social, domestic and pleasure purposes) of a non-commercial character, or

    (b)   excludes from that insurance or the operation of the security (as the case may be) –

        (i)    use of the vehicle for hire or reward, or

        (ii)   business or commercial use of the vehicle, or

        (iii)  use of the vehicle for specified purposes of a business or commercial character,

then, for the purposes of that policy or security so far as it relates to such liabilities as are required to be covered by a policy under section 145 of this Act, the use of a vehicle on a journey in the course of which one or more passengers are carried at separate fares shall, if the conditions specified in subsection (2) below are satisfied, be treated as falling within that restriction or as not falling within that exclusion (as the case may be).

(2)   The conditions referred to in subsection (1) above are –

    (a)   the vehicle is not adapted to carry more than eight passengers and is not a motor cycle,

    (b)   the fare or aggregate of the fares paid in respect of the journey does not exceed the amount of the running costs of the vehicle for the journey (which for the purposes of this paragraph shall be taken to include an appropriate amount in respect of depreciation and general wear), and

    (c)   the arrangements for the payment of fares by the passenger or passengers carried at separate fares were made before the journey began.'

So environmentally friendly, non profit making, passenger car sharing arrangements are not a different kind of 'use' from social and domestic anymore.

## 25.2.10  The insurers right of indemnity from the blameworthy insured

The Road Traffic Act insurer can seek an indemnity from the insured or the tortfeasor driver in certain circumstances.

Section 151(7) provides that where an insurer becomes liable under s 151 to pay an amount in respect of a liability of a person insured by a policy, the insurer is entitled to recover the amount paid from the insured or the uninsured driver either in respect of any liability incurred solely under s 151(3) (the driver having no driving licence provision), or, in a case where the amount paid exceeds the amount for which he would, apart from the provisions of s 151, be liable under the policy to pay, the balance of the two amounts.

Section 151(8) provides that where an insurer becomes liable under this section to pay an amount in respect of a liability of a person not insured by the policy, the insurer is entitled to recover the amount paid from that person or from any person who is insured by the policy which would, by its terms, have covered the liability if the policy insured all persons and that person caused or permitted the use of the vehicle which gave rise to the liability.

This means that where the owner of a car allows an uninsured person to drive it, even after asking questions about insurance and being given assurances about the existence of insurance, the owner will be liable to the insurers for the judgment sum. Most often what this means is that where the (drunk) owner allows an uninsured person (mate) to drive him home and the driver crashes, the injured owner has no worthwhile claim against the driver despite the driver's negligence, because the insurer will not satisfy the judgment he will obtain because it will claim a full indemnity from the owner.

An example is *Lloyd-Wolper v Moore*,[33] where the claimant was injured when a car driven negligently by the first defendant caused an accident. The second defendant (the father) owned the car and was insured to drive it. The first defendant (his son) was not insured because he did not possess a valid driving licence and the engine of the car was bigger than he was certified to drive. The second defendant permitted his son to drive and gave evidence that he believed that his son was insured. The second defendant was found liable for causing or permitting the first defendant to drive without insurance and so the indemnity applied. This case may be challenged when a more worthy claimant emerges.

### 25.2.11   Excluded liability: passengers with knowledge

Section 151 does not apply to any 'excluded liability' which is defined in s 151(4). This subsection removes s 151 cover from any victim who was at the time of the use of the vehicle giving rise to the liability allowing himself to be carried in or upon the vehicle or was entering or alighting from the vehicle and knew or had reason to believe that the vehicle had been stolen or unlawfully taken.

---

[33]   [2004] EWCA Civ 766.

'(4)  In subsection (2)(b) above "excluded liability" means a liability in respect of the death of, or bodily injury to, or damage to the property of any person who, at the time of the use which gave rise to the liability, was allowing himself to be carried in or upon the vehicle and knew or had reason to believe that the vehicle had been stolen or unlawfully taken, not being a person who –

(a)  did not know and had no reason to believe that the vehicle had been stolen or unlawfully taken until after the commencement of his journey, and

(b)  could not reasonably have been expected to have alighted from the vehicle.

In this subsection the reference to a person being carried in or upon a vehicle includes a reference to a person entering or getting on to, or alighting from, the vehicle.'

If the passenger can establish that he did not know or did not have reason to believe that the vehicle was stolen or unlawfully taken until after the commencement of his journey then he will recover under s 151 unless he could reasonably have been expected to have alighted from the vehicle before the crash.

The exclusions only bites on passengers with knowledge that the car was stolen or unlawfully taken, not knowledge that the driver was uninsured. Compare this with the Uninsured Drivers' Agreement 1999 which has a much wider exclusion.

This section affords a 'petrol station' defence to insurers. Stopping at a petrol station would enable the victim, newly appraised of information that the car was stolen, to get out. Failure to do so would prevent recovery in the event of a subsequent accident and injury caused to that passenger.

This situation occurs often in road traffic accidents and usually involves young persons and drink. One example is *McMinn v McMinn*.[34]

It is noteworthy that there is no presumption of knowledge in the Act. This lack of presumption should be contrasted with the MIB's knowledge exclusions in the Uninsured Drivers' Agreement 1999 which include presumptions of knowledge. This should also be compared with the decision in *White v White and the MIB*.[35]

More importantly these exclusions, based on knowledge in the RTA 1988, mirror the European directives. They are narrower than and are to be compared with the knowledge based exclusions in the Uninsured Drivers' Agreement 1999. The MIB exclusions are much wider because they exclude passengers who know or are assumed to know that the driver is uninsured or 'the vehicle is being used in the course or in furtherance of a crime'. The extension by the MIB in their agreements of this knowledge

---

[34]  [2006] EWHC 827 (QB).
[35]  [2001] PIQR P281.

based exemption from compensation is in part outside the European Directives and so is a breach of the main principle that compensation paid to victims of uninsured drivers should be the same as that paid to victims of insured drivers.

### 25.2.12 The notice requirement

To enforce a judgment gained against a defendant driver, against the insurance company which issued a certificate covering the car which the defendant was driving pursuant to s 151, the insurer must have been given notice of the bringing of proceedings, either before or within 7 days of commencement of proceedings: s 152(1)(a).

This provision is sometimes mistakenly assumed to apply to the Uninsured Drivers' Agreement 1999. It does not.

Safe practice requires that the notice should be in writing and should be clear.

The form of the notice has been the subject of various judicial decisions. In *Harrington v Pinkey*,[36] the Court of Appeal ruled that a letter stating that the claimant would be advised to sue without further notice if the defendant did not admit liability was not sufficient to satisfy s 152. In *DeZousa v Waterlow*,[37] the Court of Appeal ruled that the notice did not have to be in writing and could be delivered by phone. This was confirmed in *Nawaz v Crowe*.[38] In *Wake v Page*,[39] the claimant's solicitors made an assertion in the initial letter of claim that they were giving notice pursuant to ss 151 and 152 of the RTA 1988. Eighteen months later and without further notice the action was issued. The Court of Appeal held that the earlier letter was not sufficient notice under s 152.

### 25.2.13 Cancellation

Pursuant to s 152(1)(c), the insurer can avoid liability if the policy was cancelled before the accident, provided that:

- before the happening of the event giving rise to liability, the certificate was surrendered to the insurer or the person to whom the certificate had been delivered had made a statutory declaration stating that the certificate had been lost or destroyed; or

- after the happening of the event but before the expiry of 14 days from the taking effect of the cancellation of the policy, the certificate

---

[36] [1989] 2 Lloyds Rep. 310, CA.
[37] [1988] PIQR P87.
[38] [2003] EWCA Civ 316.
[39] [2001] RTR 291.

was surrendered to the insurer or the person to whom the certificate had been delivered made a statutory declaration that the certificate had been lost or destroyed; or

- either before or after the happening of that event, but within that period of 14 days the insurer has commenced proceedings under the provisions of the Road Traffic Act 1988 in respect of the failure to surrender the policy.

Section 147(4) of the Road Traffic Act 1988 provides that the certificate holder must, within 7 days from the taking effect of the cancellation, either surrender the certificate to the person by whom the policy was issued or make a statutory declaration that the policy has been lost or destroyed. Pursuant to s 147(5), any person failing to comply with s 147(4) is guilty of a summary offence punishable with a level 3 fine (see the Road Traffic Offenders Act 1988, Sch 2, Part 1).

Where the owner has sold the car before the accident and the new owner is driving uninsured the old certificate does not cover the car and s 151 will not assist. This gives rise to many assertions by shady car owners that they sold the car on to a man in a pub, before the crash.

### 25.2.14   Non-disclosure

Section 152(2) provides that the insurer can avoid payment where the insurer has obtained a declaration:

> 'that he is entitled to avoid the policy on the ground that the policy was obtained by non-disclosure of a material fact or by a representation of a fact which was false in some material particular; or

> if he has avoided the policy on that ground, that he was entitled so to do, providing the declaration was obtained within 3 months of the commencement of proceedings giving rise to the judgment.'

Furthermore, the insurer must give notice to the claimant of the declaration proceedings.

It is not clear how this sort of declaration helps an insurer when Article 75 of the MIB's articles will make the 'insurer concerned' the one to carry the liability under the MIB's Agreements in any event.

# CHAPTER 26

## THE MOTOR INSURERS' BUREAU'S LIABILITY

*Andrew Ritchie*

### 26.1 THE MIB'S LIABILITY

The MIB may become liable for a tortfeasor involved in a road traffic accident under two agreements: the Uninsured Drivers' Agreement 1999 and the Untraced Drivers' Agreement 2003.

Below we will provide a brief summary of the 1999 Agreement. However, practitioners are directed towards the *Guide to MIB Claims* published by Jordans, which provides full commentary with appendices.

### 26.2 THE 1999 UNINSURED DRIVERS' AGREEMENT

The Uninsured Drivers' Agreement 1999 (the 1999 Agreement) is the fifth in a line of agreements between the Minister for the Department of the Environment, Transport and the Regions (and his predecessors in office) and the Motor Insurers Bureau (MIB). It deals with claims arising from the negligence of uninsured drivers who can be identified and sued. It does not deal with untraced drivers. A new Agreement will be published in 2009.

The 1999 Agreement applies to all claims relating to uninsured drivers arising from accidents occurring in England, Wales or Scotland on or after 1 October 1999.

The 1999 Agreement is altered by the Guidance Notes which must be read alongside the text of the Agreement.

The 1999 Agreement was the first of the five uninsured drivers' agreements to need amending Guidance Notes because it was so poorly drafted. The Guidance Notes have been revisited. A new, second version came into effect on 15 April 2002. In the main, the new notes affect the interpretation of the 'conditions precedent' parts of the 1999 agreement although some provide clarification of the intended effect of the agreement. They apply to all unissued claims regardless of the date of the accident. Just to make life even tougher, the original guidance notes still apply to any claim issued before 15 April 2002.

### 26.2.1    European law and the 1999 Agreement

Europe has issued five Motor Insurance Directives: 72/166/EEC; 84/5/EEC; 90/232/EEC; 2000/26/EEC; 2005/14/EC. Their aim is to provide the same compensation for victims of uninsured drivers as already exists for victims of insured drivers. The UK was bound to implement each.

The Fifth Directive has not been implemented by the Government and the MIB as it should have been on 11 June 2007 and the situation is becoming problematic. Some of the earlier directives are also breached by the 1999 Agreement. In summary the following points need to be addressed:

(1)    The limit on property damage which the MIB should cover should be £1,000,000. The Agreement limits it to £250,000.

(2)    By clause 6, the MIB exclude claims by passengers who knew or are assumed to know that the vehicle is being used in the course of or in furtherance of a crime. The Directives do not allow that exclusion.

(3)    By the procedural strike out clauses 7–11 the MIB exclude claimants who fail to delivery certain notices to the MIB. Under the CPR no other claimant is struck out. So the victim of an uninsured driver is worse off than the victim of an insured driver and this breaches the basic principle of the five motor insurers' directives.

(4)    By clause 6 the MIB exclude passengers who are drunk and should have known matters about the driver which the MIB regard as guilty knowledge. The Fifth Directive provides that such an exclusion is unlawful – see recital (15) and Art 4.

(5)    By clause 1 the MIB deduct an excess of £300 from every claim. The Fifth Directive makes this unlawful – see recitals (13) and (20) and Art 2.

There have been only a few successful challenges in the courts so far. One related to the 1988 Agreement, see *White v White and the MIB*.[1]

One of the bases for complaint about the 1999 Agreement is that clause 6 of the 1999 Agreement (the passenger exception) does not comply with Council Directive 84/5/EEC. Paragraph 4 of Art 1 of the Directive provides that member states may exclude the payment of compensation by any body set up for the task of providing compensation in respect of persons who voluntarily entered the vehicle which caused the damage or injury when the body can prove that those persons(s) knew it was uninsured. Clause 6 goes beyond this. Until the 1999 Agreement is altered

---

[1]    [2001] 1 WLR 481.

so that it does comply with European law it may be possible for an individual claimant to claim damages from the UK Government for preventing that claimant from being able to rely upon his European legal rights. Despite the House of Lord's guidance on the 1988 Agreement and its criticism of the breadth of the exclusion in the 1988 Agreement the MIB drafted the 1999 Agreement to include wide presumptions of 'knowledge' on the part of the injured passenger which are contrary to the injured claimant's interests and wholly absent from the Directive. And the Minister allowed these presumptions into the 1999 Agreement without advice from groups representing victims.

It has been held on a number of occasions that the Uninsured Drivers' Directives do not have direct effect so victims cannot sue for breach of them: see *White v White*. However, in *White*, it was said that it is an established rule that even when a European Directive does not have direct effect, it is the duty of the UK to construe domestic legislation in any field covered by it so as to accord with the Directive.

It follows that if a victim is deprived of part or all of his compensation by the technical strike out provisions of the Uninsured Drivers' Agreements, he may have a remedy against the Government for failing properly to implement the EEC directives. This is because the CPR contain no such strike out provisions so victims of insured drivers face no such deprivation.

The precedent for such actions is contained in the cases: *Francovich v Italy*[2] and *Brasserie du Pecheur v Germany*.[3]

A similar case, *Evans v The Secretary of State for the Environment Transport & the Regions*[4] went to the ECJ in respect of the terms of the Untraced Drivers' Agreement.[5] No case has yet been brought against the Government arising from the strike out provisions in clause 6 of the Uninsured Drivers' Agreement 1999.

### 26.2.2 Privity of contract

There is no privity of contract between the victim seeking the benefit of the 1999 Agreement (or indeed any of its predecessors) and the MIB. This anomaly has been the subject of considerable judicial comment.[6] In practice the MIB never takes the point that a victim cannot obtain the benefit of the various agreements into which the MIB has entered with

---

[2]   [1991] ECR 1-5357.
[3]   [1996] ECR 1-1029.
[4]   [2006] EWHC 322 (QB).
[5]   See Connor Quigley 'EC law and the MIB agreements' [2001] JPIL 422 for a more detailed view on this.
[6]   *Hardy v MIB* [1964] 2 QB 745 and *Albert v MIB* [1972] AC 301.

the Secretary of State. The court has raised the matter independently[7] and obiter and directed the MIB not to take the point.

### 26.2.3 Joinder of the MIB as a second defendant

Actions started under the 1988 Agreement usually led to an application by the MIB pursuant to RSC Ord 15, r 6 which provided that anyone could be joined in an action where their presence was necessary to ensure that all matters in dispute would be effectively determined. CPR, rr 19.2 and 19.4 are now the appropriate provisions for actions to which the 1999 Agreement applies.

A joinder application is unnecessary if the claimant seeks a declaration against the MIB from the outset. It is good practice so to do.

*Albert v MIB*[8] is an example of the MIB being sued as defendant. The MIB accepted liability to satisfy judgment in a claim brought by the widow of a victim of an uninsured driver on condition that the defendant's liability was one which was required to be covered by a policy of insurance pursuant to the Road Traffic Act 1960. The question for determination was whether at the time of the accident the defendant's vehicle was being used for hire or reward.

Under the 1999 Agreement the MIB will almost always become a party to the proceedings as a second defendant. This will arise either upon the application of the MIB (the claimant cannot refuse such a request because to do so would mean that the MIB had no obligation to satisfy any judgment the claimant might subsequently obtain) or increasingly commonly by the inclusion of the MIB as second defendant by the claimant at the outset. The advantage of joining the MIB from the start is that the MIB have indicated in the Amended Guidance Notes that if the claimant adopts this approach they will waive some of the more draconian notice requirements within the 1999 Agreement.

The Amended Guidance Notes state that the MIB should be joined as a defendant unless there is good reason not to do so. A form of words is provided for the joinder of the MIB. The notes state that these words should be used. Given that the MIB are only prepared to make concessions, albeit somewhat limited, where they are joined at the outset, it is prudent to include the MIB as defendant in every claim. If they are not included much of the benefit of the Amended Guidance Notes is lost.

---

[7]  *Coward v MIB* [1963] 1 QB 259, *Gurtner v Circuit* [1968] 2 QB 587 per Diplock LJ at 599. Unless the point was specifically raised, the court was 'entitled to proceed on the assumption that the Bureau has, before action is brought, contracted for good consideration with the plaintiff to perform the obligations specified in the contract with the Minister or has by its conduct raised an estoppel which would bar it from relying on absence of privity of contract.'

[8]  [1972] AC 301.

## 26.2.4 Child claimants and claimants not of full capacity (clause 3)

Clause 3 provides that where any act or thing is done to or by someone on behalf of the claimant (whether that person is the claimant's solicitor or not) and where any decision is made by or in respect of a solicitor or other person acting on behalf of a claimant, or where any sum of money is paid to the claimant's agent, then that act, thing, decision or sum shall be treated as if done to or by, or made in respect of or paid to a claimant of full age and capacity.

It seems upon reading this clause that it provides a 3-year limitation period upon child claimants and those under a disability. As a matter of civil law no such limitation period may apply. In the case of children the 3-year limitation period starts to run when the child reaches 18 years of age and in the case of patients at the end of a period of mental disability (defined in the Mental Health Act 1983), namely, when they become able to manage their property and affairs.

The MIB have denied this to be the intention behind the wording of clause 3 and have indicated in the course of negotiation that the normal limitation periods apply under the 1999 Agreement. Indeed this concession has now found its way into the Amended Guidance Notes. At 2.3 the notes state that 'nothing in this Agreement is intended to vary the limitation rules applying to claimants of full age or capacity. Limitation for personal injury remains 3 years from the date of age or capacity'.

Practitioners are, however, reminded that a strict 3-year time limit applies under the 1996 Untraced Drivers' Agreement regardless of the claimant's age or capacity. If a child victim were injured on his 10th birthday, proceedings would have to be commenced before his 13th birthday. This was successfully attacked as conflicting with the purpose of the European Directives in *Byrne v MIB*.[9] The unnecessary bar no longer stands.

## 26.2.5 MIB's obligation to satisfy compensation claims (clause 5)

The MIB's obligation under clause 5 of the 1999 Agreement is to satisfy outstanding judgments in cases where Part VI of the Road Traffic Act 1988 (RTA 1988) requires that a relevant liability be insured by the user of the vehicle.

The obligation is far from absolute. There are a number of conditions precedent in clauses 6–17 which must be satisfied and a number of new limitations on the MIB's liability.

---

[9] [2008] EWCA Civ 574.

### 'MIB's obligation to satisfy compensation claims

5.1 Subject to clauses 6 to 17, if a claimant has obtained against any person in a Court in Great Britain a judgment which is an unsatisfied judgment then MIB will pay the relevant sum to, or to the satisfaction of, the claimant or will cause the same to be so paid.

5.2 Paragraph (1) applies whether or not the person liable to satisfy the judgment is in fact covered by a contract of insurance and whatever may be the cause of his failure to satisfy the judgment.'

It is noteworthy that the obligation is only to satisfy a liability which is required by the RTA 1988. So if the liability is not required by Part IV of the Act then the MIB does not have to pay it out. Therefore bodies such as the Crown and local authorities who do not have to insure create a problem. If a motor vehicle is stolen and injures a person that claimant cannot sue the Crown because there is no vicarious liability for thieves. Section 151 does not cover the case and the MIB will refuse to pay out because – so they say – no compulsory insurance was required. This situation, when it arises, would be a breach of the Fifth Directive which expressly requires the Government to ensure that even where there is no requirement to insure, victims are compensated – see recital (7) and Art 1.

Where a claimant has obtained judgment in a court in Great Britain against any person (this includes foreign defendants), and that judgment sum remains unsatisfied, the MIB will pay that sum to the claimant. This applies whether or not the person liable is in fact covered by a contract of insurance and regardless of the reasons why that person has been unable to satisfy judgment. The requirement to satisfy only arises on the expiry of 7 days after the date when the claimant could first seek to enforce the judgment against the defendant. In circumstances where the MIB decides that it is not going to satisfy a judgment or where it wishes to apply to have the judgment set aside the claimant should be informed of this as soon as possible.

This requirement to satisfy judgments applies unless certain exceptions contained within clause 6 apply. In those exceptional circumstances the MIB has no obligation to do so.

### 26.2.6   The driver intended to cause harm (clause 5)

The MIB will satisfy judgments which have been entered against uninsured drivers who intentionally caused the victim harm. The adoption of the Cassell principle in the preamble to the MIB agreements supports the courts' contention that to deprive the claimant of his right of indemnity against the MIB would be contrary to the policy of the agreement itself. Examples of this approach are to be found in *Hardy v MIB*,[10] *Gardner v Moore*[11] and *Charlton v Fisher and Another*.[12]

*Gardner v Moore* has recently been considered by the Court of Appeal in *Charlton v Fisher and Another*.[13]

### 26.2.7 What liability is covered? RTA liability (clause 5)

The MIB is required to compensate the claimant if, at a time when the claimant has become entitled to enforce the judgment, the sum remains unsatisfied. Under the 1999 Agreement the obligation bites upon the expiry of 7 days after the date when the claimant could enforce the judgment (see clause 1 and the definition of 'unsatisfied judgment' therein).

The 1999 Agreement covers any liability in respect of which a policy of insurance must insure a person in order to comply with Part VI of the RTA 1988. Any liability which is not covered by the compulsory insurance requirements cannot be recovered from the MIB. So if the insurance is not required by Part IV of the Act then the MIB does not have to pay out. Therefore bodies such as the Crown and local authorities who do not have to insure create a problem. If a motor vehicle is stolen and injures a person that claimant cannot sue the Crown because there is no vicarious liability for thieves. Section 151 does not cover the case and the MIB will refuse to pay out because – so they say – no compulsory insurance was required. This situation, when it arises, would be a breach of the Fifth Directive which expressly requires the Government to ensure that even where there is no requirement to insure, victims are compensated – see recital (7) and Art 1. This needs to be redrafted to accord with European Law.

### 26.2.8 Exclusion of employees injured at work

For example, in *Lees v MIB*[14] the MIB were not liable to satisfy a judgment where an employee, in the course of his employment, negligently drove a lorry on a road killing another employee whose death also arose in the course of his employment. This was because ss 35 and 30(1)(b)(i) of the Road Traffic Act 1930 did not require insurance to cover 'liability in respect of the death arising out of and in the course of his employment of a person in the employment' of the insured.

---

[10]   [1964] 2 All ER 742.
[11]   [1984] AC 548.
[12]   [2001] PIQR P314.
[13]   [2001] PIQR P314.
[14]   [1952] QB 511.

### 26.2.9   Use of a motor vehicle

It should be remembered that RTA policies cover liability arising from or out of the 'use' of motor vehicles not just the driving of them. So what is use? Section 145(3) of the RTA 1988 states:

> '(3)   Subject to subsection (4) below, the policy –
>        (a)   must insure such person, persons or classes of persons as may be specified in the policy in respect of any liability which may be incurred by him or them in respect of the death of or bodily injury to any person or damage to property caused by, or arising out of, the use of the vehicle on a road in Great Britain, and ...'

Driving a car is using it. Walking across the road to get petrol for a car when it has run out of petrol is also using the car: see *Dunthorne v Bentley*.[15] Owners who are passengers are using cars. Owners who ask others to deliver goods in their vehicles are using them. Car thieves who all go joy riding are all using the car. 'Use' is interpreted quite broadly. However the limit was reached in *Brown v Roberts*.[16]

If the defendant driver's insurance cover was for social use and the driver was driving for hire and reward the RTA 1988 will not apply and the RTA insurers will escape liability. But they will be held liable as the MIB agent (under Article 75 of the Memorandum and Articles of Association of the MIB) under the Uninsured Drivers' Agreement 1999. There have been several cases dealing with the question of whether a vehicle was being driven for hire and reward at the time of the negligent driving when the insurance policy only covered social and domestic use (see *Coward v MIB*,[17] *Connell v MIB*[18] and *MIB v Meanan*[19] and *Albert v MIB*.[20]

The problem relates mainly to mini cab drivers. A victim who is run down by a mini-cab driver who was insured only for social driving is not covered by s 151 of the RTA 1988. This problem was highlighted in *Albert v MIB*, and in *Keeley v Pashen*.[21] However the MIB will pick up the tab where the RTA insurer can escape liability under s 151 of the RTA 1988.

---

[15]   [1996] PIQR P323, CA.
[16]   [1963] 1 QB 1.
[17]   [1963] 1 QB 259. The pillion passenger was not being carried for hire or reward. Therefore as the defendant driver was not required to insure his passenger, the MIB had no obligations to satisfy the judgment.
[18]   [1969] 2 QB 494. Although the claimant was being carried for hire or reward, he was not being carried in a **vehicle** in which passengers were carried for hire or reward as he was being carried in a private motor car.
[19]   [1971] 2 All ER 1272.
[20]   [1971] 2 All ER 1345, HL.
[21]   [2004] EWCA Civ 1491.

This major problem with the current RTA 1988 – the fact that MIB liability is restricted to the use set out in the policy, is outdated and difficult now to justify. However, until the law is changed the use clause must be considered carefully.

The only 'use' which is covered by the contract of insurance is the use which the insured has purchased. Policies are usually sold covering

(1)   social and domestic use; or

(2)   business or work use;

(3)   use for hire or reward.

If the accident occurs whilst the defendant is using the vehicle outside the policy then the insurer will not be bound to indemnify the driver. However, the MIB will be liable.

### 26.2.10   The driver cannot recover

It is not possible for an injured driver to recover against the MIB for his own negligence as this is not an obligation required for compulsory insurance under the RTA 1988.

### 26.2.11   Excluded vehicles (clause 6)

Some vehicles do not have to be covered by a Road Traffic Insurance policy:

- **Crown vehicles**
  The MIB are not liable where certain vehicles are responsible for the personal injury and/or damage claimed for. Where the responsible vehicle is owned by or in possession of the Crown or a vehicle not required to be covered by virtue of s 144 of the RTA 1988, then the agreement does not apply. If the crown vehicle is insured then the MIB agreement does apply.
  Where a vehicle has been unlawfully removed from the possession of the Crown the vehicle is deemed to continue to be in the Crown's possession whilst it is kept so removed. So, if the Queen's car is stolen and the claimant is run down by it she must pay not the MIB!

- **Local council, police, and NHS vehicles**
  The 1999 Agreement does not apply:
  -   where an owner of a vehicle has deposited £500,000 with the Accountant-General of the Supreme Court, providing that that person was driving the vehicle at the relevant time;

- to vehicles owned by a council or county district or London borough established by Part VI of the Local Government Act 1985;
- to vehicles owned by a regional, islands or district council in Scotland;
- to vehicles owned by a joint board or committee in England and Wales or joint committee in Scotland, which is so constituted so as to include amongst its members representatives of any such council;
- to a vehicle owned by a police authority of the Receiver of the Metropolitan Police;
- to a vehicle owned by a health service body; or
- to an ambulance owned by a National Health Service Trust;
- to stolen police cars.

There are exceptions to the exceptions! The 1999 Agreement does apply if, in respect of the vehicles named above, the vehicle was not being driven under the control of the owner at the relevant time and additionally in the case of police vehicles if they were not being driven for police purposes at the time.

- **Other exempt vehicles**

  Vehicles being driven to or from any place undertaken for salvage purposes pursuant to Part IX of the Merchant Shipping Act 1894 or being used for the purpose of its being provided in pursuance of a direction under s 166(2)(b) of the Army Act 1955 or under the corresponding provisions of the Air Force Act 1955 are also exempt, as are vehicles made available by the Secretary of State to any person, body or local authority pursuant to ss 23 or 26 of the National Health Service Act 1977 or s 15 or 16 of the National Health Service (Scotland) Act 1978, at a time when the vehicle was being used in accordance with the terms on which it was made available.

If the RTA liability is not required to be covered by Part IV of the Act for these bodies then the MIB does not have to pay out where their motor vehicles cause accidents. Therefore bodies such as the Crown and local authorities who do not have to insure create a problem. If a motor vehicle is stolen and injures a person that claimant cannot sue the Crown because there is no vicarious liability for thieves. Section 151 does not cover the case and the MIB will refuse to pay out because – so they say – no compulsory insurance was required.

This situation, when it arises, would be a breach of the Fifth Directive which expressly requires the Government to ensure that even where there is no requirement to insure, victims are compensated – see recital (7) and Art 1. The solution is in the wording of the Act which deals with no insurance requirement when the vehicle is in the possession of the above stated bodies. When it is not in their possession then insurance is required and the MIB are therefore liable again. The wording is far too obscure for plain English or plain Englishmen to understand.

## 26.2.12    Subrogated and assigned claims (clause 6)

The 1999 Agreement does not apply where a claim is made by or for the benefit of a person (not the injured person) either in respect of a cause of action or judgment which has been assigned to the beneficiary or pursuant to a right of subrogation or contractual or other right belonging to the beneficiary. The amended Guidance Notes make it clear at paragraph 3.4 that clause 6(1)(c) of the 1999 Agreement does not have the effect of excluding claims for the gratuitous provision of care and travel expenses by family members or friends or miscellaneous expenses incurred on behalf of the claimant in circumstances where the claimant would otherwise be able to claim such heads of damages.

The MIB sometimes argue that this excludes claims for medical expenses where the claimant had BUPA or other medical expenses insurance. This is not the interpretation which a plain reading of the text would produce.

## 26.2.13    Exclusion by knowledge – the passenger exception

Under clause 6(1)(e) of the 1999 Agreement, the exceptions from the 1988 Agreement have been extended so the MIB will avoid liability if the injured passenger:

> '6(1)(e) ... knew or ought to have known that:
> (i)    the vehicle had been stolen or unlawfully taken,
> (ii)   the vehicle was being used without there being in force in relation to that use the required policy of insurance,
> (iii)  the vehicle was being used in the course or furtherance of a crime, or
> (iv)   the vehicle was being used as a means of escape from, or avoidance of, lawful apprehension.'

The four situations described above are alternatives to each other.

The burden of proving that the claimant knew or ought to have known of any of the matters set out above falls upon the MIB.

The effect of the words 'ought to have known' which appear in both the 1988 and 1999 Agreements and in the Untraced Drivers' Agreement 1996 was considered by the House of Lords in *White v White*.[22] The court held that the 1988 Agreement was intended to give effect to the terms of the European Council Directive No 84/5/EEC, which allowed member states to exclude payment of compensation to passenger claimants who voluntarily entered the vehicle 'knowing' that it was not insured. The Directive covered cases of actual knowledge and cases where the claimant

---

[22]    [2001] 1 WLR 481.

deliberately refrained from asking questions lest his suspicions should be confirmed. The words in the 1988 Agreement (and ergo, the 1999 Agreement) should be read restrictively as they were intended to bear the same meaning as 'knew' in the Council Directive. So claimants who are negligent or careless about the state of their knowledge are not exempted from recovering. This decision may be very difficult to apply in practice.

Despite the House of Lords the MIB and the Minister drafted the 1999 Agreement to include a lot of presumptions on knowledge against passenger victims. The amended Guidance Notes now make mention of *White v White* as providing 'an interpretation' of the words 'knew or ought to have known'. However there has been no change made or concession agreed by the MIB in relation to clause 6.

The question of whether the passenger possessed the relevant actual or constructive knowledge will be for the judge to decide as a matter of fact (and law) based on the evidence heard at trial (see *Cullen v Harman and MIB and North East Lincolnshire District Council*).[23]

The guilty knowledge of the passenger does not affect a claim made by his dependents. The 1999 Agreement was drafted differently from the 1988 Agreement and does not exclude a Fatal Accident Act 1976 claim by dependents of a fatally injured passenger against a negligent driver: see *Phillips v Rafiq*.[24]

### 26.2.14   Use in furtherance of a crime (clause 6)

There is no sufficient justification for this exclusion. The RTA 1988 does not exclude injured persons with such knowledge. The European Directives do not permit such an exclusion.

What about a vehicle that is being driven in a careless manner? Does this amount to the vehicle being used in the course or furtherance of a crime? The MIB may well argue that careless driving of the vehicle can exempt them from liability.

What about persons who get into cars with drivers who may be drunk. Drunk driving is a crime. The Fifth European Directive expressly debars government and the MIB from excluding such claimants – see recital (15) and Art 4.

This clause is liable to be found to be a breach of the directive and an action against government for damages will follow.

Moreover, whilst cases of actual knowledge cause little problem morally, difficulties arise from the presumed knowledge alternative. Whilst the

---

[23]   (Unreported) 18 February 2000, CA.
[24]   [2007] EWCA Civ 74.

burden of proof of such knowledge is on the MIB it may prove difficult to obtain evidence to support the claimant's assertion that he neither knew or ought to have known (in the *White* (above) sense) of the relevant matters.

### 26.2.15   Constructive knowledge (clause 6.3)

The 1999 Agreement set out circumstances in which the passenger is assumed to have guilty knowledge.

> '**6.3** The burden of proving that the claimant knew or ought to have known of any matter set out in paragraph (1)(e) shall be on MIB but, in the absence of evidence to the contrary, proof by MIB of any of the following matters shall be taken as proof of the claimant's knowledge of the matter set out in paragraph (1)(e)(ii) –
> (a)   that the claimant was the owner or registered keeper of the vehicle or had caused or permitted its use;
> (b)   that the claimant knew the vehicle was being used by a person who was below the minimum age at which he could be granted a licence authorising the driving of a vehicle of that class;
> (c)   that the claimant knew that the person driving the vehicle was disqualified for holding or obtaining a driving licence;
> (d)   that the claimant knew that the user of the vehicle was neither its owner nor registered keeper nor an employee of the owner or registered keeper nor the owner or registered keeper of any other vehicle.
>
> **6.4** Knowledge which the claimant has or ought to have for the purposes of paragraph (1)(e) includes knowledge of matters which he could reasonably be expected to have been aware of had he not been under the self-induced influence of drink or drugs.'

So for example if the injured person was also either the owner of the vehicle or the registered keeper or had caused or permitted the use of the vehicle, without there being in force in relation to such use a contract of insurance as would comply with Part VI of the RTA 1988, he will be deemed to have the requisite knowledge so that the MIB will not be liable.

Whilst the moral justification behind (b) and (c) is apparent, the fourth deeming provision at (d) is too wide. A claimant who had been assured by the driver of the vehicle that although the vehicle was not his it belonged to his wife, would (in the absence of evidence to the contrary), be deemed to 'know' that the vehicle was not insured after he had been injured as a result of the driver's negligence. The position would be the same if the driver had assured the claimant that he was insured to drive his wife's car.

This section goes a lot further than the European Directives and may be struck down as a result. See *White v White*.[25] The guilty knowledge of the

---

[25]   [2001] 1 WLR 481.

passenger does not affect a claim made by his dependents. The 1999 Agreement was drafted differently from the 1988 Agreement and does not exclude a Fatal Accident Act 1976 claim by dependents of a fatally injured passenger against a negligent driver: see *Phillips v Rafiq*.[26]

### 26.2.16  Drink and drugs

Clause 6(4) provides that the effect of self-induced drink and/or drugs is irrelevant for the purposes of the claimant's knowledge (actual or presumed). Aside from the drink or drugs if the claimant could reasonably be expected to have been aware of certain matters this can amount to the relevant knowledge. This clause is new and so was not considered in *White* (above). It will be held now to be incompatible with the Fifth European Directive.

### 26.2.17  Application form (clause 7)

Clause 7 of the 1999 Agreement provides a new strike out provision. Clause 7 provides that the MIB, or in the case of proceedings in respect of a relevant liability which is covered by a policy of insurance with an insurer whose identity can be ascertained, that insurer, must be provided with an application made in such form, 'giving such information' about the relevant proceedings and 'other matters' relevant to the agreement and accompanied by such documents as the MIB may reasonably require.

Failure to do so may result in the MIB obtaining a declaration that they are not liable to meet the judgment sum entered against the negligent driver.

It is not good practice simply to issue proceedings against the negligent driver and/or the MIB without filling in an MIB application form. The MIB require pre-issue notification. If it is not received and/or is received in inadequate form then they will argue that the clause 7 condition precedent has not been met.

It is very unlikely that the MIB will agree to accept a claim submitted on the basis of anything other than its official claim form even if all the information required to be given in the claim form was provided to the MIB. The new form can be obtained from the MIB and downloaded from the website (www.mib.org.uk).

---

[26]   [2007] EWCA Civ 74.

### 26.2.18  Procedural conditions precedent to the MIB's liability

The 1999 Agreement sets out a large number of complex procedural steps which do not exist in the CPR and which if broken provide the MIB with a right automatically and without any proof of any prejudice, to strike down the claim.

If the procedural requirements are not met in time then the MIB will escape the liability it would otherwise have under clause 5 – the liability which the European Directives require the MIB to fulfil.

In such circumstances the claimant's solicitor is likely to face a professional negligence suit.

### 26.2.19  Service of proceedings

Because both the 1988 and the 1999 Agreements require the claimant to serve the defendant driver (or car owner) rather than, as some might expect, the MIB, there is a very real risk that as time goes by it will become more difficult to properly effect service upon the defendant. For example, the defendant's original address may no longer be the defendant's place of residence and the chances of a forwarding address being made available are slim when the defendant was an uninsured driver.

There is no obligation upon the MIB to provide the claimant with any details regarding the defendant's whereabouts. On the contrary it is not in their interests to proffer such information. This of course causes problems where the limitation period is shortly to expire.

In practice the solution is to require the MIB from the outset to agree to accept service on the defendant's behalf. However, if the MIB has not been able to obtain signed authority from the defendant to accept service on his behalf then it is the claimant's solicitor's responsibility to ensure that contact is maintained with the proposed defendant. This might involve the early issue of proceedings.

If the defendant cannot be found then pursuant to CPR Part 6 an application should be made for an alternative method of service (CPR, r 6.8). The application must be supported by a witness statement setting out the attempts that have been made to trace the defendant and whether it is believed that the defendant is trying to evade service.

*Gurtner v Circuit*[27] provides an example of the difficulties that might be experienced in practice in locating a defendant for service.

---

[27]  [1968] 2 QB 587.

Service at the defendant's last known address is now an acceptable method even if the claimant knows the defendant does not live there any more. See *Smith v Hughes*, part of the multiple cases reported in *Cranfield v Bridgegrove Ltd*,[28] in which the Court of Appeal held that services at the defendants last know address was good service under the CPR despite both the claimant and the MIB knowing that the defendant had left that address. This position is a departure from the previous rule set out in the Supreme Court Rules and exemplified in *Yiannacou v Rehal*.[29]

### 26.2.20  Method of service of notices

The 1999 Agreement provides a limited number of ways in which service can properly be effected. This does not apply to the service of the initial application form but does apply to the giving of notice of issue of the relevant proceedings, notice of service of the proceedings, the provision of further information, the supply of any documentation and notice of intention to apply for judgment (clauses 9 to 12 inclusive).

The terms of the agreement make it permissible to use only three methods of service:

(1)   facsimile transmission, or

(2)   registered delivery, or

(3)   recorded delivery post to the MIB's registered office.

If another method is used, for example service by Document Exchange ('DX'), first or second class post, by e-mail or by hand, then the documents provided are deemed insufficiently served.

This clause appears to have been drafted to avoid difficulties previously encountered where the claimant alleged that a certain thing had been sent to the MIB but the MIB were without a record of receiving the item or items. In effect, this clause puts the onus on the claimant to satisfy himself that the notice or document has been received by the MIB. Using the permitted methods enables the sender to prove service by reliance upon the facsimile transmission report or postal receipt. The MIB prefers service by fax as it is almost instantaneous.

However, clause 8 imposes a great burden upon claimants' solicitors in terms of expense and time.

Whilst the MIB prefer service by facsimile, the large numbers of pages that the MIB require to be provided to them makes this unrealistic.

---

[28]   [2003] EWCA Civ 656.
[29]   (Unreported) 20 June 1997, CA.

Further problems will arise if, for example, the MIB's fax number is engaged or their lines are down as is often the case according to claimants' solicitors.

The postal alternatives are equally unattractive. They require that someone from the solicitor's office attend the post office. There may well be queues. Given the volume of pages the costs of recorded or registered mail will be relatively high.

Moreover, the exclusion of immediate service by e-mail is arbitrary given that the sender receives notification if the message is not received by its intended recipient.

Given the onerous nature of this condition precedent, there is every chance that claimant lawyers will fall foul of this requirement and fail to comply.

The requirement was also difficult to justify by reason of its uniqueness. Nowhere in the CPR is there such a requirement for service of documents.

The Guidance Notes at note 5.6 spelled out what was obvious from clause 8, namely that it placed the onus upon the claimant to satisfy himself that notice has been received. The Notes do however allow for service by alternative methods providing that the claimant is able to prove that. So service by DX, First Class Post, Personal Service or any other form of service allowed by the CPR is satisfactory and the MIB will accept that such notice has been served. The CPR also allow for service to be effected by leaving the document at a place specified in r 6.5 (residence, place of business, the business address of a party's solicitor), by means of electronic communication (other than fax) or pursuant to r 6.8 by any alternative method approved by the court.

### 26.2.21  Notice of issue of relevant proceedings (clause 9)

Clause 5(1)(a) of the 1988 Agreement provided that the MIB could avoid its obligation to satisfy judgment unless:

> '... notice in writing of the bringing of proceedings is given within 7 days after the commencement of proceedings ... such notice shall be accompanied by a copy of the writ, summons, or other document initiating proceedings ...'

Clause 9(1) of the 1999 Agreement provides for 14 days rather than 7.

These clauses have always been interpreted strictly see: *Cambridge v Callaghan*,[30] and *Silverton v Goodall*.[31]

---

[30]  [1998] RTR 365.
[31]  [1997] PIQR P451.

The 'strict interpretation' approach has been no different under the 1999 Agreement.

Earlier and later notice will continue to be found to be irrelevant, as will the fact that the MIB have been in lengthy negotiations with the claimant's solicitor or have been provided with the claimant's evidence. Even if the MIB makes an offer to settle prior to the failure to give notice, this will have no effect in interpreting the clause. Prejudice will also be irrelevant.

Given the risk of letters becoming lost in the post in the past, the safest route is for the claimant to issue the Claim Form and personally serve the MIB with the stamped Claim Form and Particulars of Claim at their offices in Milton Keynes.

Under the 1999 Agreement as amended by the Guidance Notes, this will suffice. Personal service is a breach! However an amendment has been made to the Guidance Notes to the 1999 Agreement applying to all applications made after 15 April 2002 so long as the claim is unissued. The new notes permit service by all CPR approved methods. This allows personal service to amount to proper service.

Solicitors will not have complied with the condition precedent in clause 9 if they give the MIB notice as required by s 151 of the RTA 1988 rather than as required under the 1999 Agreement.

### 26.2.22    Discontinue and reissue

If the limitation period has not expired then a failure to comply with the notice requirements can be cured by withdrawing proceedings and issuing afresh, this time giving proper notice to the MIB. This can even be done where judgment had been entered and damages are being assessed; see *O'Neill v O'Brien*.[32]

Sometimes, in previous instances of default where the limitation period had not expired, the MIB would waive its right to rely upon clause 5(1)(a) of the 1988 Agreement rather than making the claimant's solicitors reissue. It is probable that this practice will continue on occasions under the 1999 Agreement. However, caution must be exercised here because it is by no means certain that even where the limitation period is extant the MIB will waive its right. Nor may a claimant be told of the default at once. Strangely it often happens that by the time the claimant becomes aware of a problem with the giving of notice the limitation period has expired.

---

[32]    [1997] PIQR P223.

If the proceedings are issued at the eleventh hour and the notice provision is not complied with then the focus of the claimant's claim will be upon the solicitor's professional indemnity insurers.

If the limitation period is passed the claimant can still discontinue and reissue. In the past the second set of proceedings would have been struck down under the rule in *Walkley v Precision Forgings*,[33] but this case was overruled (in so far as one House of Lords can overrule another) by *Horton v Sadler*.[34] So now the second set of proceedings can be allowed to go ahead out of time if the conditions in s 33 of the Limitation Act 1980 are satisfied. That decision is a matter of discretion for the court. This line of authority has been strengthened by *Richardson v Watson*.[35]

### 26.2.23 Service of documents to accompany notice of issue (clause 9(2))

In order to incur liability the MIB or relevant insurer must have been given proper notice of the bringing of relevant proceedings not later then 14 days after the commencement of those proceedings. By Clause 9(2) of the 1999 Agreement 'Proper Notice' means:

- 'notice in writing that proceedings have been commenced by claim form, writ or other means'; and

- 'A copy of the sealed claim form, writ or other official document providing evidence of the commencement of the proceedings and, in Scotland, a statement of the means of service'; and

- 'a copy of the details of any insurance policy providing benefits ...' (where the claimant is insured and the policy of insurance provides benefits in the case of death, personal injury or damage to property to which the proceedings relate, a copy or details of that insurance policy); and

- 'copies of all correspondence in the possession of the Claimant ...' (which had passed between the claimant and the defendant relevant to the injury or damage sustained by the claimant and which the defendant is held responsible for and any policy of insurance which is or is claimed to be available to the defendant and which is said to or does cover the defendant's liability for the damage and/or injury); and

- '... A copy of the Particulars of Claim ...' unless those Particulars have not been served with the Claim Form, in which case the

---

[33] [1979] 1 WLR 606.
[34] [2006] UKHL 27.
[35] [2006] EWCA Civ 1662.

Particulars of Claim must be served not later than 7 days after
service of them upon the defendant; and

- 'A copy of all other documents which are required under the
appropriate rules of procedure to be served on the Defendant ...
with the claim form, writ, originating process or Particulars of
Claim' (for instance the medical evidence and Schedule of Special
Damage); and

- 'Such other information about the relevant proceedings as the MIB
may reasonably specify.' This might, for example, include the medical
notes.

The 14 day period runs from the date of issue not the date of service. The
Amended Guidance Notes provide no respite from the enormous scope of
this provision. So solicitors must copy the whole bundle of
correspondence with the defendant, all of the claimant's relevant
insurance policies, and any documents served with the Particulars of
Claim.

If the claimant issues proceedings but does not serve them until up to 4
months later the claimant must still send all the above information to the
MIB within 14 days of issue but can delay serving copies of the
Particulars of Claim [and Claim Form] until 7 days after service rather
than 14 days after issue (clause 9(3)). The Amended Guidance Notes give
relief from this provision.

Where the MIB is joined as second defendant at the outset of the
proceedings, the Amended Guidance Notes state (at clause 5.3) that
clause 9(3) of the 1999 Agreement does not apply. Accordingly it is no
longer necessary to serve the Particulars of Claim upon the MIB within
seven days of service upon the negligent driver. This is because the court
will serve the proceedings upon the MIB as second defendant when it
serves upon the first defendant.

However all of the other requirements in clause 9 about notice of issue
*must* be complied with.

If a document has already been supplied to the MIB pursuant to clause 7
then there is no need to send the document again.

The Amended Guidance Notes have make it clear that it is not necessary
to send the Response Pack or Notice of Issue to the MIB in addition to
all of the other documents required.

This technical and complicated clause provides numerous opportunities
for default. Imagine, for example, forgetting to send to the MIB one letter
that had earlier been sent to the defendant. This failing may not be

discovered by the MIB until after judgment has been entered or worse, until after the expiry of the primary limitation period. The MIB would be able to rely upon this failure to avoid satisfying judgment even if the letter was irrelevant. If, however, the undisclosed letter was irrelevant the MIB have indicated that they may not take a point on failure to supply items of non-material correspondence; only material correspondence will be required to be provided. Of course, this raises a new dilemma as to what constitutes material correspondence. The Amended Guidance Notes are ambiguous about this clause.

Even if the MIB are joined as a defendant at the outset, they have indicated that compliance with clause 9 would still be necessary. Indeed, the MIB are reluctant to agree to any generic waiver of clauses 9, 10, 11 and 12.

### 26.2.24   Notice of service of proceedings (clause 10)

Where proceedings are commenced in England or Wales, the MIB will incur no liability under its Clause 5 obligation unless the claimant has notified either the MIB or the relevant insurer, in writing, of the date of service of the claim form or other originating process in the proceedings, either:

- not later than 7 days after the date when the claimant received notification from the court that service has occurred; or

- received notification from the defendant that service has occurred; or

- the date of personal service; or

- 14 days after the date when service is deemed to have occurred in accordance with CPR Part 6,

whichever of those four events occurs first.

It is difficult to see why this provision is necessary because the MIB will have been given notice of the date of issue within 14 days of the issue. This will enable them to apply to join the proceedings and exercise the defendant's rights in defending the merits or quantum. The claimant cannot usually oppose an application made by the MIB to join the proceedings.

A limited concession is made in the Amended Guidance Notes. The MIB will accept notice of the date of the service of proceedings within 14 days of the date of the four events set out above and at clause 10(a) and (b) of the 1999 Agreement. In other words notice must be given within 21 days of the claimant receiving notification from the court that service has occurred, or from the defendant that service has occurred or from the date of personal service, and within 28 days of the date of deemed service. This notice requirement applies whether the MIB are joined as a second defendant or not. In other words the claimant must comply with clause 10 of the 1999 Agreement in its entirety. No benefit is to be had by reason of the fact that the MIB is joined as a party at the outset and would of course have received notice of service together with the Particulars of Claim from the court.

To avoid non-compliance claimants must take steps to ensure that the court or the defendant's legal representatives inform them of the date of service as soon as possible. There is a very real risk that service may be deemed to have occurred without a claimant knowing of it until some time afterwards and after the expiry of the relevant period.

The safest option is for the claimant to serve the defendant personally and then tell the MIB within 14 days by recorded delivery or faxed letter.

### 26.2.25    Notice of other steps in the action (clause 11)

The MIB will not be liable to satisfy a judgment under the terms of the agreement where the claimant fails to give notice to the MIB of any one of a number of other steps in the action not less than 7 days after the happening of the events.

Accordingly, pursuant to clause 11 of the 1999 Agreement, not later than 7 days after the following events, the claimant must give notice in writing of the date of that event to the MIB or relevant insurer. The events are:

• the filing of a defence in the proceedings;

• any amendment made to the Particulars of Claim or amendment or addition to any schedule or other document required to be served with the Particulars of Claim;

• the setting down of the case for trial;

• the date when the court gave notice to the claimant of any trial date (but not it would seem the trial date itself).

The claimant is further required to supply the MIB or relevant insurer with a copy of any such defence, amended Particulars of Claim, schedule or other document.

This clause is yet another multiple strike out provision increasing the likelihood of default.

Where the MIB is joined in the proceedings from the outset as a second defendant the Amended Guidance Note 5.3 states that clause 11 does not apply at all.

So the only safe route now is to join the MIB from the start.

In circumstances where the MIB have not been joined as a second defendant at the outset the MIB have conceded that they will accept notice of the relevant clause 11 matters within 14 days rather than the 7 required in the 1999 Agreement. In order to take advantage of the concession it is necessary for the claimant to prove to the MIB the date upon which each notice was received. In circumstances where the MIB are later joined as a party by consent claimants should approach the MIB asking them to agree to waive the relevant parts of clause 11 eg the requirement to give notice of the setting down of the case for trial and of the trial date when decided by the court.

### 26.2.26   Providing other information (clause 11(2))

Clause 9(2)(g) of the 1999 Agreement empowered the MIB to require information from the claimant to keep them informed as the case went along.

The list of information and/or documentation is large. Claimant solicitors should not agree to 7 day time limits on any further information.

Clause 11(2) contains a catch-all provision insofar as the MIB can avoid liability if the claimant fails, within a reasonable time after the request, to provide them or the relevant insurer or solicitor with such other further information and documentation in support of the claimant's claim as the MIB reasonably requires to enable it to assess its liability under the agreement.

The wide wording of this clause is open to abuse by the MIB and may lead to default by the claimant's lawyers.

However in circumstances where the MIB are joined as a party at the outset, the MIB have agreed that clause 11 will not apply at all (see clause 5.3 of the Guidance Notes). No distinction has been drawn between sub-clause (1) and (2). It would seem that the MIB are thus unable to make any requests for information and documentation. Instead they are in the same position as other defendants and bound by the court timetable as to when and the circumstances in which the further information (such as witness statements) should be given.

## 26.2.27   Notice of intention to apply for judgment (clause 12)

The MIB can avoid its obligations under the agreement if the claimant fails to give notice in writing to the MIB or relevant insurer or solicitor of his intention to apply for judgment in the proceedings.

So as not to fall foul of this provision the claimant must give written notice not less than 35 days before making the application for judgment. There is no requirement for such notice to be given by any other claimant in any proceedings under the CPR.

The Amended Guidance Notes contain a complete waiver of this clause.

## 26.2.28   Complying with section 154 of the RTA 1988 (clause 13)

By clause 13, the MIB can avoid its obligations under the agreement if the claimant fails, as soon as is reasonably practicable:

- to demand the information and particulars specified in s 154(1) of the RTA 1988; and

- in the event of the requested person failing to comply, to make a formal complaint to a police officer; and

- to use all reasonable endeavours to obtain the name and address of the registered keeper of the vehicle; or

- where the MIB requires that the claimant authorise the MIB to take such steps on its behalf, the claimant fails to so authorise.

Section 154 requires the driver of a vehicle involved in a road traffic accident that has caused personal injury to provide the other party with his insurance details. It is a criminal offence for a driver to give false details or to unreasonably refuse to supply this information.

The claimant's obligations arising from clause 13 are numerous. The claimant must exchange details of names, addresses and insurance particulars at the scene of the accident, enter into correspondence with the owner of the vehicle or the driver or their representatives and, in situations where the registration number only is known, make enquiries of the DVLA.

Although the MIB have made an apparent concession in relation to this clause at 4.1 of the Amended Guidance Notes, in effect this is an empty one. The Guidance Notes state that provided the claimant properly completes and signs the MIB's application form then the claimant will be taken to have complied with clause 13.

Consideration of the MIB's application form shows that in order for the form to be properly completed the information required pursuant to s 154 is needed in any event. In other words the 'concession' still requires the claimant to comply with the requirements of s 154 of the RTA.

### 26.2.29 Suing other potential defendants (clause 14)

The MIB will incur no liability if the claimant fails to take all reasonable steps to obtain judgment against every person who may be liable in respect of the injury or damage claimed for. The claimant must have been required to take such steps by the MIB and the MIB must have granted the claimant a full indemnity as to costs on making such a request.

In *Norman v Ali and MIB*[36] the claimant was found to be in default of her obligation to take all reasonable steps to obtain judgment against all the persons liable in respect of her injury pursuant to clause 5(1)(d) of the 1988 Agreement. She had failed to join the owner of the car as a defendant until after the expiry of the 3-year limitation period. The MIB were not obliged to indemnify. It was suggested by the court that if the claimant wished to dispute the reasonableness of the MIB's requirement to join the owner of the vehicle as a defendant, she should have referred the matter to the Secretary of State.

### 26.2.30 Consenting to the MIB's application to join the action (clause 14)

Clause 14 also provides for the avoidance of liability by the MIB in circumstances where the claimant refuses to consent to the MIB being joined as a party to the proceedings after having been requested so to do by the MIB.

### 26.2.31 Assignment of judgment and undertakings

To ensure the MIB is liable, the claimant must:

- assign to the MIB or its nominee, the unsatisfied judgment and any order for costs. This must be done even if the judgment includes an amount in respect of a liability other than a relevant liability; and

- undertake to pay back to the MIB any sum paid to the claimant by the MIB in discharge of the MIB's obligation if the judgment is later set aside as a whole, or in respect of the relevant liability to which that sum relates; or by any other person, by way of compensation or benefit for injury or damage to which the proceedings relate. This includes a sum which would have been deductible pursuant to clause 17 if the sum had been received before the MIB satisfied the

---

[36]  [2000] RTR 107.

judgment. Clause 17 enables the MIB to take such sums received into account when calculating the amount of judgment it is required to satisfy.

The 'release form' which the MIB requires claimants to sign is objectionable. It requires the claimant to agree to pay back the sums received in certain circumstances which are not realistic. Lawyers advising on the form should read it carefully and advise accordingly.

### 26.2.32   Limitations on the MIB's liability for property damage (clause 16)

Clause 16 provides that where a claim under the agreement includes a claim in respect of damage to property and any losses arising therefrom ('property damage compensation') the MIB shall incur no liability where the compensation does not exceed the specified excess of £300. This is a breach of the Fifth Motor Insurance Directive which bans such deductions.

The MIB will only incur liability up to the sum of £250,000 (minus the excess) for any one accident. This limit has not been increased 20 years and should have been raised by the inflation rate over that period to at least £500,000. After the passing of the Fifth European Directive this limit was raised to £1,000,000 under the RTA 1988 by the Motor Vehicles (Compulsory Insurance) Regulations 2007.[37] However, government and the MIB have wholly failed to alter the sum in the Uninsured Drivers' Agreement 1999. This is a further breach of European Law.

### 26.2.33   Deduction of sums received from Policyholders Protection Board (clause 17)

If the claimant has received compensation from the Policyholders Protection Board under the Policyholders Protection Act 1975 (where the insurer has gone into liquidation before satisfying judgment) or from an insurer under an insurance agreement or arrangement or from any other source, in respect of the proceedings against the tortfeasor defendant and/or the MIB (if joined), the MIB are entitled to deduct from the relevant judgment sum (in addition to any deductions made under clause 16, see below) an amount equal to that compensation. It is not known whether the MIB can deduct CICA awards.

### 26.2.34   Reasoned replies and notifications of decisions by the MIB (clause 18)

The MIB must give a reasoned reply to any request made by the claimant relating to the payment of compensation in pursuance of the MIB's

---

[37]   SI 2007/1426.

obligations. Claimants are largely unaware of this provision. It is suggested it would be wise for claimants' lawyers to use it more often. The MIB must, as soon as is reasonably practicable, notify the claimant in writing of its decision with regard to the payment of the relevant sum and give reasons for that decision.

This obligation arises provided that the claimant has made an application pursuant to clause 7 above and has given proper notice of the relevant proceedings in accordance with clause 9(1) and (2).

It does not therefore appear to apply prior to proceedings being issued, which is rather odd.

### 26.2.35 Reference of disputes to the Secretary of State (clause 19)

Where the claimant disputes the reasonableness of a requirement made by the MIB for the supply of information or documentation or for the taking of any step by the claimant, the dispute may be referred by either the claimant or the MIB to the Secretary of State. The decision of the Secretary of State is final.

Different procedures exist depending upon whether the referral is made by the claimant or the MIB.

Where the MIB makes the referral it must supply the Secretary of State and the claimant with written notice of the disputed requirement, together with reasons for that requirement and such further information as the MIB considers relevant.

The claimant is only required to supply the Secretary of State and the MIB with written notice of the grounds on which he disputes the reasonableness of the requirement.

This appeal procedure has rarely if ever been used and should be abolished in favour of one operated by independent barristers experienced in PI law.

### 26.2.36 Recovery (clause 20)

The Agreement does not preclude an insurer from providing in a policy of insurance that all sums paid by the insurer or by the MIB by virtue of the 1999 Agreement, in or towards the discharge of the liability of the insured, shall be recoverable by them or by the MIB from the insured or from any other person. The principle here is that if the policyholder has breached the terms of the policy he should be made to indemnify the insurer for liability incurred to a third party victim.

## 26.2.37    Apportionment of damages (clause 21)

This follows on from the assignment provision at clause 15.

Once the unsatisfied judgment has been assigned to the MIB or its nominee and if that judgment includes an amount in respect of a non-relevant liability, the MIB shall:

*   apportion any sum that it receives in satisfaction (partial or otherwise) of the judgment according to the proportion which the 'relevant liability' damages bear to the 'non-relevant' damages awarded; and

*   account to the claimant in respect of monies received properly apportionable to the other liability.

This principle of apportionment also applies where the sum received includes an amount in respect of interest on the judgment sum and/or an amount awarded under an order for costs.

## 26.3    UNTRACED DRIVERS' AGREEMENT 2003

This agreement covers damages for victims of drivers who have never truly been identified. Please see the *Guide to MIB Claims* (Jordans), for an analysis of the law relating to these claims.

# INDEX

References are to paragraph numbers.